PROFITS AND SUSTAINABILITY

PROFITS AND SUSTAINABILITY
A History of Green Entrepreneurship

GEOFFREY JONES

OXFORD

UNIVERSITY PRESS

OXFORD
UNIVERSITY PRESS

Great Clarendon Street, Oxford, OX2 6DP,
United Kingdom

Oxford University Press is a department of the University of Oxford.
It furthers the University's objective of excellence in research, scholarship,
and education by publishing worldwide. Oxford is a registered trade mark of
Oxford University Press in the UK and in certain other countries

First Edition published in 2017

Impression: 3

Published in the United States of America by Oxford University Press
198 Madison Avenue, New York, NY 10016, United States of America

British Library Cataloguing in Publication Data

Data available

Library of Congress Control Number: 2016954971

ISBN 978–0–19–870697–7

Printed and bound by CPI Group (UK) Ltd, Croydon, CR0 4YY

Preface

This book is a global history of entrepreneurs who imagined that business could make the world more environmentally sustainable rather than less. It is unconventional in every sense. For a start, most people consider that such green businesses are a recent phenomenon, yet this book goes back to the nineteenth century. It is focused on individuals rather than large firms. Many of those people were unusual. More attention is given to the philosophical and religious beliefs that drove them than to the workings of their businesses. While most people associate green business with high-tech start-ups, this book looks instead at a set of people who worked in architecture, finance, organic food, natural beauty, tourism, waste management, and wind and solar energy. Many of their businesses were small, unprofitable, and transient. Most of their names are long forgotten, as are their contributions to sustainability. The book contains much original research, including from many interviews, but it is not the kind of business history based on deep research in corporate archives. In most cases, archives did not exist, and more unconventional sources needed to be used. The novelty of the book lies in its scope and point of view, and the reinterpretation of people and events explored in other literatures, but not as examples of entrepreneurship. It shows how individuals judged by their contemporaries as absurd or even crazy can, with enormous difficulty, help to change the world.

In researching this book, I have relied on the dedication of research associates. Oona Ceder and Loubna Bouamane did foundational research and conducted interviews in several languages. Their willingness to devote time and energy to this project, above and beyond the call of duty, was crucial. Andrew Spadafora, an outstanding historian of intellectual thought and accomplished linguist, traveled far and wide, from Costa Rica to Denmark, conducting research and making interviews, as well as critiquing in detail every draft of the text.

The assistance of the Global Research Centers of the Harvard Business School was also crucial. In Istanbul, the Executive Director Esel Cekin arranged with enormous efficiency a set of interviews in Turkey. I am also grateful to Cigdem Celik and Zeynep Maggonul for their help with these interviews. In São Paulo, I am very grateful for the assistance and hospitality of Ricardo Reisen de Pinho. In Tokyo, the Executive Director Nobuo Sato was unfailingly helpful. I benefited enormously from working with Mayuka Yamazaki, the Assistant Director, in the Tokyo office. She introduced me over the years to dozens of green entrepreneurs throughout Japan, and accompanied me to interview them. Our research visits in Nagasaki, Sapporo, and Tokyo were transformational. My understanding of both green business and Japan were fundamentally shaped by our research and discussions.

The research for writing this book rested on dozens of interviews with entrepreneurs and managers based in Asia, Europe, Latin America, and the United States. A full list is given at the end of the book. The willingness of so many practitioners to give their time and share their insights was crucial. Many others, including academics, students, and librarians have contributed to the book. I should especially like to thank Seema Amble, Hartmut Berghoff, Carlos Davila, Patrick Fridenson, Ben Gettinger, Per Hansen, Matt Hopkins, Bart van Hoof, Thilo Jungkind, Masato Kimura, Zhengyang Koh, Bill Lazonick, Laura Linard, Christina Lubinski, Chris Marquis, Ellen Mølgaard, Simon Mowatt, Manuel Rodriguez-Becerra, Keetie Sluyterman, Erik Stam, and Kazuhiro Tanaka. I very much appreciated feedback from participants in seminars in Auckland, Geneva, Ottawa, Tokyo, Umeå, Utrecht, and Washington, DC. Special thanks are due to the Auckland University of Technology in Auckland, New Zealand and the Universidad de Los Andes, in Bogotá, Colombia for hosting my visits.

I would like to give a special note of thanks to Ann-Kristin Bergquist, a pioneering historian of green business, and David Merrett, a formidable economic and business historian who has patiently critiqued early versions of my last five books. In 2015 they both read an early draft of this manuscript, and made extensive and lengthy suggestions how to restructure it, along with providing detailed chapter by chapter comments. They bear no responsibility for this final version, which neither has seen, but their intervention rescued the whole project. This manuscript has been rigorously and insightfully edited by Jeff Strabone, who has a remarkable ability to liberate text from obscurity. I am grateful for the patience and guidance of my editors at Oxford University Press, Clare Kennedy and David Musson.

The research for this book was generously funded by the Division of Research and Faculty Development at the Harvard Business School, to whom I am extremely grateful.

Finally, I owe a lot of thanks for their patience to Dylan Jones and Rattana Promrak.

Geoffrey Jones

Harvard Business School

Contents

List of Figures and Table

Figures

Table

Introduction

The Business of Sustainability

The degradation of the natural environment presents the greatest challenge faced by humanity. It is not the only or even the most immediate challenge: inequality and poverty, terrorism, rogue states, and regional conflicts plague billions of individuals all over the world. Nevertheless, in a worst-case scenario and absent a miraculous advance in interstellar travel, a massive deterioration in the natural environment here on planet Earth has the potential to wipe out our own species along with many others.

The progressive deterioration of conditions on Earth's surface has been documented by peer-reviewed and increasingly alarmist scientific reports. In 2013 and 2014 the International Panel on Climate Change published strong evidence of man-made global warming, rising sea levels, and many other signs of deterioration. It appears that man-made greenhouse gas emissions have raised average global temperatures by 1°C since the Industrial Revolution beginning in the eighteenth century. The most-discussed culprit is carbon dioxide released by the burning of fossil fuels, but important research has also identified the serious impact of methane gas emissions caused by livestock rearing, rice paddies, biomass burning, and hydraulic fracturing (or fracking) of rocks to capture oil and gas. Temperatures began rising at a much faster rate after 1980 than in any other decade since 1850.[1] Without significant action, some have predicted a rise of 6°C by 2100, threatening catastrophic global impact.[2]

By the 2000s satellites were also showing that Arctic ice was thinning, melting, and rupturing. The huge Ward Hunt Ice Shelf started cracking in 2000. In 2005, the United Nations Millennium Ecosystem Assessment documented deterioration of fifteen of the twenty-four ecosystems examined, including fresh water systems, coral reefs, wetlands, and forests.[3] Extreme weather events, such as heat waves, droughts, and wildfires, have been linked to climate change.[4] Growing populations face scarcities of the remaining fresh water, one-third of which lies in groundwater deposits which are rapidly being depleted in areas such as northwestern India and California's Central Valley. The Global Ocean Commission in 2016 reported that the 97 percent of the world's water that resides in the oceans was in a perilous condition because of pollution, over-fishing, and deep-sea oil and mineral mining.[5]

Meanwhile, the inhabitants of large cities in Africa, Asia, and Latin America, including Casablanca and Johannesburg in Africa, Beijing and Shanghai in China, New Delhi and Karachi in South Asia, and Rio de Janeiro and Santiago in Latin America, live under a haze of smog and pollution, for some or all of each year. Some scientists believe that a sixth mass extinction of life in Earth's history is underway, with more than 400 vertebrate species disappearing over the course of the twentieth century.[6]

As this book will show, warnings about the decimation of the natural environment are not new, but for a very long time they had no impact on mainstream policy-makers, firms, or consumers. However, beginning in the 1960s, and increasingly since the 1980s, an unprecedented amount of societal and governmental attention has been focused on environmental issues, especially deforestation, loss of biodiversity, water shortages, and climate change. By the first decades of the twenty-first century, the scientific evidence began to compel some world leaders to call for systematic action. They ranged from a former US Vice-President, Al Gore, whose documentary *An Inconvenient Truth* (2006), directed by Davis Guggenheim, is credited by some with greatly raising awareness about global warming,[7] to the head of the Catholic Church, Pope Francis, who issued the first encyclical in the Church's history to address the natural environment, in 2015. The Pope described global action on climate change and environmental degradation as a moral imperative for all human beings.[8]

Despite the evidence and rising chorus of alarm, entrenched interests and information voids have stifled large-scale action on a global scale. One academic study reported that 40 percent of adults worldwide in 2015 had no concept of global warning. Although adult awareness in the United States, Europe, and Japan hovered around 90 percent, it was far lower in many developing countries, including India and China.[9] Few governments have prioritized environmental sustainability over other concerns. Between 1997 and 2014 the Kyoto Protocol was the only credible attempt to forge an international binding treaty on global emissions cuts. By 2009 over 180 countries had ratified the Kyoto Protocol, but that number did not include the United States.[10] In 2015 the representatives of 195 nations attending a United Nations climate change conference in Paris did reach an agreement, designed to come into force in 2020, which aims to reduce carbon emissions sufficiently to keep global warming "to well below 2°C."[11] It remains to be seen whether this agreement is a breakthrough in achieving international consensus on policy, or a case of too little, too late, with unclear enforcement mechanisms.

This book focuses on the historical role of business in our environmental crisis—not on causing it, but on trying to mitigate it. In some ways, this is an unusual book of business history. Most business histories focus broadly on the vicissitudes of entrepreneurs and firms trying to succeed at making profits.

One thing that makes this business history distinctive is that it tells a different story about a different class of actors: people whose main motivation was to change the behavior of people and that of the world at large. Even to call the first green thinkers and activists "entrepreneurs" can feel wrong and anachronistic: most of them did not see themselves that way at all. And yet, the history of green business begins with these nineteenth- and early twentieth-century oddball characters—hippies a century too soon—such as Sylvester Graham, Bernarr Macfadden, and Benedict Lust.

Business histories sometimes allude to cultural changes at large in the world but often in a sideways anecdotal glance for embellishment or color. In this study, the cultural changes—Romanticism, vegetarianism, conservation, tree-hugging—are the intellectual foundation of today's wind energy, organic foods, natural beauty, and the expensive lengths corporations will go in order to rebrand themselves as "green." To trace the origins of these billion-dollar industries, this is where we must turn.

The book tells the unknown story of a cohort of entrepreneurs who believed business could help create a more sustainable world. It challenges the received point of view that green business begins in the 1960s,[12] and that green entrepreneurship, also variously described as sustainable, environmental, or eco, started even later, in the 1990s, when the first studies of the phenomenon began.[13] Its roots lie much further back, in the convictions of people committed to unusual lifestyles, in the zeal of radicals, and in the sometimes hapless efforts of visionaries to bring a new world into being long before the world was ready for it. For over a hundred years, entrepreneurs who never achieved scale, who left little trace, and some who never made a buck pioneered green entrepreneurship.

We need to revise our histories of green entrepreneurship to take the long view of a movement that took a long time to crest but is here just in the nick of time. This book is an attempt to start that revision and reconsideration.

Creating the Anthropecene Age

In 2000, Nobel Laureate Paul Crutzen and Eugene F. Stoermer proposed that humanity had driven the world into a new geological epoch, which they called "the Anthropocene," in which many geologically significant conditions and processes had been fundamentally altered by human activities.[14] Mounting scientific evidence corroborates this designation.[15]

Humans have always impacted the natural environment. Nature is violent and capricious, and as the nineteenth-century biologist Herbert Spencer famously observed, only the fittest survive. The evolution of humanity over the very long term has been intimately correlated with the progressive taming of this natural environment and its submission to man's purposes. The development of settled agriculture and the domestication of animals for use as food and clothing were milestones in this process. The building of shelters and cities, and the development of methods to trade and exchange over distances were further milestones. Even just locally, the draining of a pond or a bog can reduce mosquito-borne viruses and transform a village into the makings of a town.

By the eighteenth century, human intervention had radically changed the natural landscape across much of the habitable globe. Yet even in the most economically advanced regions, such the North Sea region of Europe and the cities of China and India, the autonomy of the natural world remained strong. Human lives were short and often unpleasant, even for wealthy elites. Infectious diseases like smallpox killed and blinded millions of people over the ages. Famines and pestilences were regular occurrences. Humans lived and died close to where they were born; even the elite of these societies could only travel as fast as a horse or a boat driven by sail.

This situation began to change with the Industrial Revolution beginning in eighteenth-century Britain. Crutzen and Stoermer date the start of the Anthropecene Age to 1820 because the Industrial Revolution resulted in such an enormous extension of humanity's ability to control, and damage, the natural environment. Subsequent research by geologists has indicated that, technically, the new geological age might be better dated from the middle of the twentieth century,[16] but there remains a consensus that the foundations of the process began with the shift to the use of coal instead of firewood and charcoal—a change that began with the Industrial Revolution—and the use of metals on a scale never seen before. The bio-based economy of the past was progressively replaced by a geo-based economy of coal, iron, and steel. In the early eighteenth century the provision of heat, power, and light still depended on animals and their fat, water, wind, and forests. In 1700 an estimated two-thirds of energy consumed in Britain came from animals.[17] As Britain became the first industrial nation, this changed. By 1850 steam power already provided 30 percent of Britain's power.[18]

Fossil fuels and the rise of modern science enabled massive increases in productivity through the spread of factory production and economies of scale and scope. This in turn drove global commerce. As steam-driven railroads spread from the 1830s, accompanied later by steam-driven ships, the constraints posed by geographical distance began to fall. This meant the opening of new markets and the possibility of exploiting natural resources in distant lands. Worldwide transportation infrastructures made possible large farms of cattle and sheep, which could be transported on an industrial scale to slaughterhouses to be killed for meat and skins. Crops were moved around the world to expand production. Plants and crops were moved between continents and their production vastly expanded.[19] Biodiversity was greatly reduced. Forests were cut for lumber or to produce commodities.[20] Alarm that the fertility of soil was declining as the growing of crops intensified led, first, to a worldwide search for natural fertilizers, and then to the development of synthetic fertilizers.

The so-called Second Industrial Revolution, beginning in the last decades of the nineteenth century, saw an amplified environmental impact associated with the expansion of heavy industries such as steel, innovation in chemicals, the increased use of fossil fuels, and electrification. A new source of fossil fuels emerged with petroleum, which could be used alongside coal to create steam, and was also the fuel used to power the newly created internal combustion engine. The discovery of the principles of electricity, the invention of the battery and the dynamo as sources of power, and the creation of devices to transmit and distribute electricity further dramatically boosted demand for energy.

The productivity advances which began with the Industrial Revolution contributed to lifting millions of people out of poverty. This represented an extraordinary break from human history. Previously, periods of economic growth and population growth had always been brought to a halt by scarcities of food and resources, the so-called "Malthusian trap." Although the income gains generated by the productivity advances were distributed highly unequally around the world—a large gap opened up between the industrialized West and the rest of the world in the nineteenth century—the living standards, longevity, and health of the average human being were transformed.[21]

The twentieth century saw further spectacular growth. Despite two world wars and the Great Depression, world GDP grew from $1.98 trillion in 1900 to $28 trillion in 1992.[22] It reached $77 trillion in 2014. Modern economic growth diffused outward from the West over the course of the century to Japan, the Communist regimes in the Soviet Union and China, and developing countries such as India and Brazil. There were waves of new industries: automobiles, pharmaceuticals, and after 1945 computers and information technology. All of these innovations required huge increases in energy use: one estimate was that the world has used more energy after 1900 than in all of prior human history. The use of fossil fuels was key, but after 1945 natural gas and nuclear energy provided additional sources of energy.[23]

The Romantic reaction

The downside of the remarkable growth of productivity and wealth was articulated by the ecologist Garrett Hardin in an essay on "The Tragedy of the Commons" published in 1968. He identified a central dilemma: the self-interest of rational (and well-meaning) individuals can lead to the harm of the common good. "The rational man," Hardin wrote concerning the problem of pollution, "finds that his share of the costs of the wastes he discharges into the commons is less than the costs of purifying his wastes before releasing them. Since this is true for everyone, we are locked into a system of 'fouling our own nest.'"[24] Hardin had identified a central point: in the language of economists, there were a lot of negative externalities from the activities of individuals and firms, which were almost entirely unaccounted for and untaxed. Indeed, that they are called "externalities" reveals something important about how little responsibility has been taken for them: they are considered "external"—outside—to what really matters: profit-making pursuits are the "internal" matter of business.

The "fouling" of the natural environment was not a secret, and Hardin was far from the first to observe it. It attracted warnings and stimulated the creation of conservation movements. This first wave of environmentalism which began in the nineteenth century, the environmental historian Ramachandra Guha has observed, "proceeded step-by-step with the Industrial Revolution."[25]

The destructive impacts of modern economic growth have been felt disparately both locally and globally. Western imperialism has, for instance, mined rare minerals in places like the Congo and left destruction in their place. Meanwhile at home, factories and power plants were located among the poor and minority groups. The Great Famines of the nineteenth century occurred in British colonies—Ireland and India—while the British remained well-fed and uninterested in the social and ecological dislocations their actions caused.

The adverse impact of industrialization on the natural environment of Western countries themselves attracted more criticism. The rapid expansion of European settlement in the United States, which saw whole species of animals, like the American buffalo, hunted to virtual extinction over a short period, led to voices calling for the "conserving" of the natural environment. By mid-century calls were being made to conserve nature from the destructive impact of human activity.[26]

A variety of nature, health, and spiritually oriented movements on both sides of the Atlantic fed a nascent conservation movement. As environmental loss became a public concern, new forms of reverence for nature emerged in the Romantic and Transcendental movements on both sides of the Atlantic. William Wordsworth, Henry David Thoreau, John Muir, and others invented new, quasi-religious ways of imagining and articulating humanity's relationship to nature.[27] The Hudson River School of landscape painters in mid-nineteenth-century America romanticized the country's natural beauty and the coexistence of people and nature.[28]

Conservation became institutionalized as a movement during the second half of the nineteenth century. In the United States, conservation sentiments led to the creation of Yellowstone National Park, the world's first national park, in 1872.[29] In 1892 the Sierra Club was founded in San Francisco by the Scottish-born California wilderness explorer John Muir. It would become America's most influential conservation society.[30] In Europe, too, scientists documented environmental problems such as the loss of habitats and species. Ernst Häckel, a German zoologist, coined the term "ecology" in 1866.[31]

Voluntary groups were formed to protect wildlife and conserve nature. The protection of birds from hunting, and from the growing demand for feathers to be used in women's hats and other clothes, became an early focus of attention.[32]

Conservation societies across Europe shared a common distaste for modernization, but they often took different forms. In Britain, painters, writers, and landscape architects led, as in the United States, an idealization of the rural world, seen as under threat by modernization. This new concept was taken up by organized groups of middle-class citizens interested in making privately owned places of natural and cultural beauty accessible to everyone, and not just their (often aristocratic) owners. In Germany, a cultural nationalism developed which was critical of industrialization. Unlike Britain, and more so than the United States, in Germany it was the government, especially individual state governments such as Prussia, rather than grassroots organizing that drove conservation efforts.[33] Generally, conservation was primarily driven by social elites in Europe and the United States, but it was certainly established as an issue of great urgency by the new century. In 1913 Paul Sarasin, a Swiss zoologist, brought representatives of sixteen European countries and the United States together to establish a Commission for the International Protection of Nature.[34]

A second cost of industrialization which also immediately attracted critics, and some responses from governments, was industrial pollution. The smoke caused by the burning of coal became a huge pollution problem in newly industrialized cities. London became known as the "big smoke" during the Victorian period. Fogs featured prominently in the stories of writers like Arthur Conan Doyle. There was considerable environmental activism against such pollution, which some have compared to later environmental movements.[35] In Britain, legislation was passed in the 1830s and intensified in the 1860s to control pollution, especially black smoke and coal emissions, drawing on the common law of nuisances. The strength of the legislation reflected the continuing influence in Britain's upper house of Parliament, the House of Lords, of the aristocracy. Rural landowners were especially concerned about the environmental impact of chemical factories on their lands.[36] In contrast, although there were thousands of complaints concerning smoke pollution in Germany, there was much less civil activism. Smoke pollution controls remained more ad hoc compared to both Britain and the United States. The protection of nature overshadowed pollution control as a cause demanding action.[37]

In the United States, air pollution provoked citizen activism, with dozens of anti-smoke associations formed to lobby for controls on smoke pollution in cities such as Baltimore, Chicago, Cincinnati, Pittsburgh, and St. Louis. Women's groups were quite prominent in many of the associations, as they were in wider campaigns for cleanliness and hygiene in America's cities.[38] Business leaders and organizations often opposed regulation over pollution, but were sometimes found among the supporters of it.[39] The campaign against smoke had some noteworthy victories. Ordinances against excessive smoke were followed by the city of Chicago passing, in 1907, pioneering legislation on smoke inspection. Under the Chicago legislation, municipal engineers enforced smoke controls and provided advice to businesses to reduce their emissions. This system spread across America's industrial cities.[40]

Smoke controls, as well as national parks and other outcomes from conservation movements, provided niche fixes for some of the more visible unintended consequences from modern economic growth before 1914. However, for the following half-century, an era which spanned two world wars and the Great Depression, the environmental downsides of modernization and industrialization intensified as these processes diffused and deepened. There were more warnings and proposed alternative paths, but environmental concerns motivated activists more than they did policy-makers.

By the 1920s, some warnings were also being sounded beyond Europe and the United States, though largely with equal lack of effect. Miguel Angel de Quevedo, a hydraulic engineer, campaigned to protect Mexico's depleting forests and founded the Mexican Forestry Society in 1922. Yet in 1939 he lamented that the country's forests continued to be "impoverished and ruined by greed."[41] In India in the same era, Mohandas K. Gandhi campaigned not only against British colonial rule but also against the impact of modern industrialization and the use of chemicals in agriculture, making the case for self-sufficiency of communities rather than global trade.[42] When India won its independence in 1947, however, the ecological concerns of Gandhi were swept away as the country opted for heavy investment in industrialization and the building of large dams.[43]

The problem of soil erosion arising from industrialized agriculture followed a similar outcome of activist energy foiled by governments' preference for development.[44] In 1939 two British soil scientists, Graham Jacks and Robert Whyte, employed by the Imperial Bureau of Soil Science, a government agency, published the evocatively named book *The Rape of the Earth* (renamed *Vanishing Lands* for the more squeamish American market).[45] This 300-page historical and worldwide review of the problems of soil erosion, which explored the political and social consequences of environmental degradation, discussed the trade-off between economic success and environmental cost. "Movements of capital," Jacks and Whyte wrote, "have been one of the mainsprings of progress, but capitalism has never seriously concerned itself with its repercussions on the humus content and structure of soils. Nevertheless, the repercussions have been shattering in their effect and can no longer be ignored."[46] The repercussions were not entirely ignored—scientists and activists continued to mark their effects—but governments and industry pursued other priorities.

The tradition of ignoring warnings in the halls of government continued after the end of World War II. William Vogt's book *Road to Survival*, published in 1948, presented a stark picture of rising populations and diminishing resources. The author had served as Associate Director of the Division of Science and Education of the Office of the Coordinator in Inter-American Affairs, a US federal agency, and the book included extensive discussions of environmental stresses in Latin America, as well as Africa, Asia, and the United States. Vogt documented serious problems of soil erosion, declining fertility, water shortages, and the depletion of non-renewable resources such as oil and minerals manifested by the "waster's psychology," which he considered most visible in the United States.[47] The trade-off between industry and the environment was again a prominent theme. "Man assumes that what has been good for industry must necessarily be good for the land," Vogt observed. "This may prove to be one of the most expensive mistakes in history."[48] Vogt's book sold well, but there was no discernible impact on policies or strategies.[49] As the environmental historian John McNeill has written, before 1970 "environmental thinking appealed only to a very narrow slice of society."[50]

If the voices warning of environmental damage struggled to get heard, an equally large problem was that some major environmental impacts were not understood. In particular, there was almost no understanding of the impact of the burning of fossil fuels, as well as methane emissions, on the climate. In 1896 Svante Arrhenius, a Swedish scientist, observed the potential of carbon dioxide to raise the global temperature, but this was not central to his work, and he predicted that any impact would occur over the very long term. During the 1930s an American geologist, T. C. Chamberlin, raised the issue more forcefully, after observing a warming of the North Atlantic region, but he was not taken seriously by the scientific community, which remained skeptical of a major climate change effect.[51]

In fact, it was not until the 1960s that even the possibility that human activity could impact the climate began to be more broadly discussed, and then within the context of an apparent cooling of the planet. In 1970 a month-long meeting held at the Massachusetts Institute of Technology concerning adverse environmental impacts of human activity, pointed to apparently rising CO_2, but participants lacked the tools to calculate its impact.[52] This initial conference led directly to a further conference in 1971 in Stockholm in which experts from fourteen countries met for the first-ever conference to focus on the Study of Man's Impact on Climate. The concluding report, entitled *Inadvertent Climate Modification*, discussed in detail emissions of pollutants and greenhouse gases, although there was no consensus on what was happening, let alone on the solutions.[53] Another lengthy period passed before the problem of climate change attracted extensive attention beyond the scientific community.

There was, thus, an unprecedented creation of wealth from the nineteenth century onwards, but there were costs which would, in time, accumulate sufficiently to initiate a new, distinct geological era. The realities of pollution, deforestation, soil erosion, and other environmental damage were known to a few, but the voices calling for action struggled to be heard. The gains from modern economic growth were so great that radically challenging the process proved not to be a serious proposition. The Romantic nature movements which drove many of the initial conservation efforts have traditionally been studied by scholars in the humanities, including in the recent field of ecocriticism. This book recasts the initial criticism of industrialization and its impact on nature in the nineteenth century as the first episode in a history of green businesses. These movements were not just poetry and the Hudson River School of painters. They spawned the first green businesses.

Business and the natural environment

Business enterprises were the central actors in the twin stories of wealth creation and environmental degradation. The Industrial Revolution was launched by many inventors and small entrepreneurial firms.[54] The spread of globalization in the nineteenth century was also driven by hundreds of European and US businesses. Many of these companies invested outside the West in search of raw materials and food for their industrializing and urbanizing home economies. They employed new powerful technologies to extract minerals. They supplied the copper needed to enable the spread of electricity by creating giant open-pit mines which destroyed whole mountains, and by building smelters which released toxic substances such as arsenic and sulfur.[55]

The second half of the nineteenth century saw the growth of big business in the United States and Western Europe. Transportation improvements coincided with the development of new technologies which permitted much greater reduction in cost per unit of output as volume increased. The first industries to secure these economies of scale included oil refining, metallurgy, and food processing, where continuous flow processes were applied. In time, they established internal research and development departments, which drove waves of innovation in industries such as chemicals and electricals. Electrical and utility firms created new communications technologies, such as the telegraph and later, telephones. Large diversified firms developed organizational structures, especially the multi-divisional structure, which permitted them to grow across products and geographies.[56] Managerial decision-makers became further and further removed from the local environmental consequences of their corporations' actions.

Modern corporations were, and remain, heterogeneous organizations. Although capitalism's objective will always be profit, there are at least two available models of corporate priorities and values: the shareholder model and the stakeholder model. While the former simply pursues profits, the latter allows judgments to be affected by a range of concerns besides profits. Historically there were always business leaders who took this broader view of the role of business in society. Firms, frequently family-owned, which pursued paternalistic policies towards employees and communities, could be found in the United States and Europe in the nineteenth century, and indeed much later. However, such strategies tended to become rarer as firms became public, and rarer still as the shareholder value model of capitalism spread around the world from the 1980s.[57] From a sustainability perspective, the problem with the shareholder model is that it allows no interest whatsoever in sustainability, except insofar as sustainability is fully aligned with maximizing shareholder value.

The green entrepreneurs discussed in this book represent a subset of the stakeholder model. They were focused on providing market-based responses to the environmental consequences of the huge success of business enterprises in raising productivity and driving growth. It is not a story of dirty firms trying to clean up their acts, but of new firms being created specifically to facilitate sustainability. The book considers a wide cross-section of industries: food, beauty, energy, waste, architecture, tourism, and finance. There is no claim to being comprehensive, however. This selection of industries is not meant to disparage the important stories of green business to be found in apparel, vehicles, and other industries.

The entrepreneurs seen here created for-profit ventures that sought to address perceived sustainability challenges by offering alternative value propositions to their consumers, often involving higher prices in return for lighter environmental footprints. The first cohort of such entrepreneurs can be found in the nineteenth century, but for a long time they remained niche actors in capitalist systems, as their value propositions had little appeal to consumers or policy-makers. They even had little appeal to most environmentalists, who perceived profit-motivated business in general as the primary cause of damage to the natural environment.

The history of green entrepreneurship has been partly obscured by the fact that the central areas of environmental concern, and the language used to describe such challenges, have changed greatly over time. No one called themselves a green entrepreneur until the 1990s, or even later. For this reason, this book employs a broad definition of green entrepreneurship which involves the establishment of for-profit businesses motivated by a desire to achieve environmental sustainability.

It is readily acknowledged, following studies of contemporary green entrepreneurship, that the category is heterogeneous with regard, for instance, to the strength and nature of a firm's ecological commitment. Robert Isaak, for example, has distinguished between "green-green" entrepreneurs, strictly founded on the principles of sustainability, and entrepreneurs who acquired ecological concerns over time, or who had several motivations, including ecological.[58] Liz Walley and David Taylor have identified four types of green entrepreneur. "Visionary champions," closest to Isaak's green-green entrepreneurs, want to make societies and economies more sustainable in a radical fashion. A second category, "ethical mavericks," were also values-driven, but their ideas emerged from their networks of friends and their lifestyle rather than their overriding visions of changing the world. Two other categories were profits-driven rather than values-driven. "Innovative opportunists" found ecological concerns to be a profitable niche, while "ad hoc" green entrepreneurs stumbled on ecological businesses through social or other networks.[59]

In this book, greenness is also defined by motivation. The green entrepreneurs here most closely match the categories of "green-green," "visionary champion," and "ethical maverick." However, historically and even today, ecological concerns often overlap with social and ethical concerns. Indeed, the historical story told in this book is, in part, one of social and health issues laying the basis for early green entrepreneurship. Entrepreneurs motivated by such broad sustainability concerns are included regardless of whether their business ventures had an impact on either real or perceived sustainability concerns. The green entrepreneurs considered here form a heterogeneous category spanning different industries. In addition, institutional entrepreneurs are considered. They all faced powerful incumbent competitors who pursued conventional, entirely profit-oriented business models.

A second set of entrepreneurs featured in this book were conventional in that their primary motivation was profit rather than sustainability concerns. They would align most closely with the categories of "innovative opportunist" and "ad hoc" just mentioned. They were found particularly in industries such as tourism and waste which contained some incentives for potentially sustainable actions regardless of intent. A number of green entrepreneurs were also found in these industries, while some conventional entrepreneurs developed sufficiently ecological views to challenge a simplistic binary distinction between green and conventional business. Waste and tourism as a whole are instructive because, in recent decades, incentives have shifted in other industries also to encourage conventionally motivated business to pursue more sustainable strategies or market niches.

This book asks three main questions. First, what was the motivation of green entrepreneurs and of conventional entrepreneurs who pursued ecological investments? The following chapters will explore their characteristics and motives, and how these varied over time and across industries and geographies. There will be a particular concern to identify how exogenous conditions—such as changes in culture, technology, regulation and law, industry structure, and shifts in demand for products or services—affected entrepreneurs' own motivations and their perceptions of business opportunities amid environmental problems. This line of inquiry raises a set of issues broadly similar to those found in the management literature on the creation of new ventures and categories. Both individual cognitive processes and the location of entrepreneurs within specific institutional contexts will be explored to address the question of why individuals "imagined" a different world than the one they lived in, and why they believed for-profit businesses were the means to achieve that world.[60]

Second, how did these entrepreneurs execute their strategies? The following chapters will explore how entrepreneurs acted disruptively by creating new markets and products in the course of building businesses. Like almost every entrepreneurial start-up, they faced limited or no access to finance or to existing distribution and/or retail channels. Compounding the problem, historically green entrepreneurs faced far higher skepticism from potential suppliers of finance—as well as from consumers—as to why a product or service being offered mattered. Entrepreneurs needed to challenge and modify existing consumer preferences and spending patterns. Crucially, they needed to find ways to establish their credibility and legitimacy. This involved institutional entrepreneurship, lobbying governments, and working with other environmental interest groups. The following chapters show just how difficult these challenges proved.

Finally, what were the financial and sustainability outcomes? This question will require considering whether and when being a green entrepreneur was profitable, or, in the words of the title of one academic study, "Does it pay to be green?"[61] More broadly, did the green businesses seen in this book contribute positively or otherwise to environmental sustainability? Does the historical evidence presented here suggest that profits and sustainability have been, or can be, compatible?

These questions are explored both over time and comparatively. In Part I, "Green Intentions," the foundation of green capitalism from the nineteenth century to 1980 is examined. This is a story of heroic, even eccentric, individuals who sought to build green businesses, typically against very difficult odds. The chapters consider in detail individual motivations, examine strategies employed, and explore outcomes. In Part II, "Green Business," the book turns to the period after 1980, when environmental concerns began to rise rapidly up the agendas of consumers and policy-makers. This section begins by considering the sudden scaling of many green businesses, and then turns to exploring key themes, including building institutions, green finance, and relations with governments. The final chapter of Part II deals with the rise and meaning of corporate environmentalism, or the sudden apparent greening of large corporations, despite the growth of shareholder capitalism. Finally, the book's conclusion offers a broad general overview of the lessons of the history of green entrepreneurship.

Notes

1. Intergovernmental Panel on Climate Change, Working Group 1, *Climate Change 2013: The Physical Science Basis* (2013).

2. Joseph B. Lassiter, Sid Misra, and Stephanie Fuzio, "Climate Change: An Unfolding Story," Harvard Business School Case No. 9-815-079 (rev. January 14, 2015); Pitila Clark, "Washington and Brussels Put Beijing and Tokyo in Shade on Emissions Cuts," *Financial Times*, October 23, 2015.

3. <http://www.millenniumassessment.org/en/Condition.html#download>, accessed October 22, 2016.

4. <http://www.wri.org/publication/fact-sheet-connection-between-climate-change-and-recent-extreme-weather-events>, accessed March 2, 2016.

5. <http://www.some.ox.ac.uk/wp-content/uploads/2016/03/GOC_2016_Report_FINAL_7_3.low_1.pdf>, accessed October 10, 2016.

6. Stuart L. Pimm, et al., "The Biodiversity of Species and Their Rates of Extinction, Distribution, and Protection," *Science* 344, no. 6187, May 30, 2014.

7. "An Inconvenient Truth," <http://www.imdb.com/title/tt0497116>, accessed February 3, 2016.

8. "Encyclical Letter Laudito Si of the Holy Father Francis on Care for Our Common Home," <http://w2.vatican.va/content/francesco/en/encyclicals/documents/papa-francesco_20150524_enciclica-laudato-si.html>, accessed January 1, 2016.

9. Tien Ming Lee, Ezra M. Markowitz, Peter D. Howe, Chia-Ying Ko, and Anthony A. Leiserowitz, "Predictors of Public Climate Change Awareness and Risk Perception around the World," *Nature Climate Change* 5 (2015), pp.1014–20.

10. Forest Reinhardt, Gunnar Trumbull, Mikell Hyman, Patia McGrath, and Nazli Z. Uludere Aragon, "The Political Economy of Carbon Trading," Harvard Business School Case No. 9-710-056 (rev. April 27, 2011).

11. United Nations Conference on Climate Change, <http://www.cop21.gouv.fr/en>, accessed January 2, 2016.

12. Pratima Bansal and Andrew J. Hoffman, "Retrospective, Perspective, and Prospective," in Hoffman and Bansal (eds.), *The Oxford Handbook of Business and the Natural Environment* (Oxford: Oxford University Press, 2012), pp.4–8.

13. Robert Isaak, "Globalization and Green Entrepreneurship," *Greener Management International* 18 (1997), pp.80–90; Michael Lenox and Jeffrey G. York, "Environmental Entrepreneurship," in Bansal and Hoffman (eds.), *Oxford Handbook of Business and the Natural Environment*, pp.70–82; Michael Schaper (ed.), *Making Ecopreneurs: Developing Sustainable Entrepreneurship* (Aldershot: Ashgate, 2005).

14. Paul Crutzen and Eugene F. Stoermer, "The Anthropocene," *Global Change Newsletter*, May 2000 <http://www.igbp.net/download/18.316f18321323470177580001401/1376383088452/NL41.pdf>, accessed October 22, 2016.

15. Colin N. Waters, et al., "The Anthropocene is Functionally and Stratigraphically Distinct from the Holocene," *Science* 351, no. 6269 (January 2016).

16. Ibid.

17. Roger Fouquet, *Heat, Power and Light* (Cheltenham: Edward Elgar, 2008).

18. Ibid., p.125.

19. Alfred W. Crosby, *Ecological Imperialism: Biological Expansion of Europe, 900–1900* (Cambridge: Cambridge University Press, 2004).

20. Richard P. Tucker, *Insatiable Appetite: The United States and the Ecological Degradation of the Tropical World* (Berkeley: University of California Press, 2000).

21. William Fogel, *The Escape from Hunger and Premature Death, 1700–2100: Europe, America, and the Third World* (New York: Cambridge University Press, 2004); Leandro Prados de la Escosura, "Capitalism and Human Welfare," in Larry Neal and Jeffrey G. Williamson (eds.), *The Cambridge History of Capitalism*, vol. 2 (Cambridge: Cambridge University Press, 2014), pp.501–29; Kenneth Pomeranz, *The Great Divergence: China, Europe, and the Making of the Modern World Economy* (Princeton, NJ: Princeton University Press, 2000).

22. J. R. McNeil, *Something New Under the Sun: An Environmental History of the Twentieth-Century World* (New York: Norton, 2000), p.6.

23. McNeil, *Something New*, pp.14–15.

24. Garrett Hardin, "The Tragedy of the Commons," *Science*, n.s., 162, no. 3859 (December 13, 1968), pp.1243–8.

25. Ramachandra Guha, *Environmentalism: A Global History* (New York; Longman, 2000), p.4.

26. George Perkins March, *The Earth as Modified by Human Action* (New York: Scribner, Armstrong & Co, 1874), p.vii; Roderick F. Nash, *Wilderness and the American Mind* (New Haven, CT: Yale University Press, 2001).

27. Stephen Hussey and Paul Thompson, "Introduction: The Roots of Environmental Consciousness," in Hussey and Thompson (eds.), *Environmental Consciousness* (New Brunswick, NJ: Transaction Publishers, 2004), pp.1–18.

28. Linda S. Ferber, *The Hudson River School: Nature and the American Vision* (New York: New York Historical Society, 2009).

29. Paul Schullery and Lee H. Whittlesey, *Myth and History in the Creation of Yellowstone National Park* (Lincoln: University of Nebraska Press, 2003).

30. Guha, *Environmentalism*, pp.49–54; Stephen Fox, *The American Conservation Movement: John Muir and His Legacy* (Madison: University of Wisconsin Press, 1985); Donald Worster, *A Passion for Nature: The Life of John Muir* (Oxford: Oxford University Press, 2008).

31. Robert J. Richards, *The Tragic Sense of Life: Ernst Haeckel and the Struggle over Evolutionary Thought* (Chicago, IL: University of Chicago Press, 2008).

32. Patrick Matagne, "The Politics of Conservation in France in the 19th Century," *Environment and History* 4 (1998), pp.362–3.

33. Karl Ditt and Jane Rafferty, "Nature Conservation in England and Germany 1900–70: Forerunner of Environmental Protection," *Contemporary European History* 5, no. 1 (1996), pp.1–28; William Rollins, *A Greener Vision of Home: Cultural Politics and Environmental Reform in the German Heimatschutz Movement, 1904–1918* (Ann Arbor: University of Michigan Press, 1997); Hans-Werner Frohn and Friedemann Schmoll, *Natur und Staat: staatlicher Naturschutz in Deutschland, 1906–2006* (Bonn-Bad Godesberg: Bundesamt für Naturschutz, 2006).

34. Fred Van Dyke, *Conservation Biology: Foundations, Concepts, Applications* (New York: Praeger, 2008), p.19.

35. Brian W. Clapp, *An Environmental History of Britain Since the Industrial Revolution* (London: Longman, 1994).

36. Ben Pontin, "Integrated Pollution Control in Victorian Britain: Rethinking Progress within the History of Environmental Law," *Journal of Environmental Law* 19, no. 2 (2007), pp.173–99.

37. Frank Uekötter, *The Greenest Nation? A New History of German Environmentalism* (Cambridge, MA: MIT Press, 2014), pp.43–66; Frank Uekötter, *The Age of Smoke* (Pittsburgh, PA: University of Pittsburgh Press, 2009), pp.28–44.

38. Suellen Hoy, *Chasing Dirt* (Oxford: Oxford University Press, 1995), chapter 3.

39. Christine Meisner Rosen, "Business Leadership in the Movement to Regulate Industrial Air Pollution in Late Nineteenth- and Early Twentieth-Century America," in Hartmut Berghoff and Adam Rome (eds.), *Green Capitalism? Business and the Environment in the Twentieth Century* (Philadelphia: University of Pennsylvania Press, 2017), pp.53–76.

40. Uekötter, *Age of Smoke*, pp.20–42; Christine Meisner Rosen, "Businessmen against Pollution in Late Nineteenth Century Chicago," *Business History Review* 69, no. 3 (1995), pp.351–97.

41. Guha, *Environmentalism*, pp.36–8.

42. Ibid., pp.19–24, 128–9.

43. Mahesh Rangarajan, "Of Nature and Nationalism: Rethinking India's Nehru," in John R. McNeill, José Augusto Pádua, and Mahesh Rangarajan (eds.), *Environmental History as if Nature Existed* (New Delhi: Oxford University Press, 2010), pp.111–29.

44. Randal S. Beeman and James A. Pritchard, *A Green and Permanent Land: Ecology and Agriculture in the Twentieth Century* (Lawrence: University of Kansas Press, 2001), chapters 1 and 2.

45. Stephen Mosley, *The Environment in World History* (London: Routledge, 2010), p.76.

46. Graham Vernon Jacks and Robert Orr Whyte, *The Rape of the Earth: A World Survey of Soil Erosion* (London: Faber and Faber, 1939), p.210.

47. William Vogt, *Road to Survival* (New York: William Sloane Associates, 1948), p.67.

48. Vogt, *Road to Survival*, pp.34–7.

49. Pierre Desrochers and Christine Hoffbauer, "The Post War Intellectual Roots of the Population Bomb: Fairfield Osborn's 'Our Plundered Planet' and William Vogt's 'Road to Survival' in Retrospect," *Electronic Journal of Sustainable Development* 1, no. 3 (2009).

50. McNeill, *Something New*, p.337.

51. Spencer R. Weart, *The Discovery of Global Warming* (Cambridge, MA: Harvard University Press, 2008).

52. Weart, *Discovery of Global Warming*, p.70.

53. Ibid., p.71; Carroll L. Wilson and William H. Matthews (eds.), *Inadvertent Climate Modification* (Cambridge, MA: MIT Press, 1971).

54. Robert C. Allen, *The British Industrial Revolution in Global Perspective* (Cambridge: Cambridge University Press, 2009), chapter 7.

55. Timothy J. LeCain, *Mass Destruction: The Men and Giant Mines that Wired America and Scarred the Planet* (New Brunswick, NJ; Rutgers University Press, 2009); Duncan Maysilles, *Ducktown Smoke: The Fight over One of the South's Greatest Environmental Disasters* (Chapel Hill: University of North Carolina Press, 2011).

56. Alfred D. Chandler, *Strategy and Structure: Chapters in the History of the American Industrial Enterprise* (Cambridge, MA: MIT Press, 1962); Chandler, *The Visible Hand: The Managerial Revolution in American Business* (Cambridge, MA: Harvard University Press, 1977); Chandler, *Scale and Scope: The Dynamics of Industrial Capitalism* (Cambridge, MA: Harvard University Press, 1990).

57. Geoffrey Jones, "Debating the Responsibility of Capitalism in Historical and Global Perspective," *Harvard Business School Working Paper*, No. 14-004, July 2013.

58. Robert Isaak, *Green Logic: Ecopreneurship, Theory and Ethics* (Sheffield: Greenleaf, 1998).

59. Liz Walley and David W. Taylor, "Opportunists, Champions, Mavericks . . .? A Typology of Green Entrepreneurs," in Schaper (ed.), *Making Ecopreneurs*, pp.27–42.

60. Joep P. Cornelissen and Jean P. Clarke, "Imagining and Rationalizing Opportunities: Inductive Reasoning and the Creation and Justification of New Ventures," *Academy of Management Review* 35, no. 4 (2010), pp.539–57.

61. Stefan Ambec and Paul Lanoie, "Does It Pay to be Green? A Systematic Overview," *Academy of Management Perspectives* 22, no. 4 (2008), pp.45–62.

Part 1

Green Intentions

1

Pioneering in Food and Energy

The pioneering green businesses in the nineteenth and early twentieth centuries emerged in food and energy. Both industries were transformed by the era of modern economic growth. As populations grew and moved away from farms and into cities, entrepreneurs built transportation networks for supplying agricultural commodities to feed the world's cities. A beehive of firms—from the farmers and ranchers who raise the food, to the commodity traders and shipping companies who move it, to the manufacturers and retailers who package and sell it—lay behind the branded consumer products that drove the growth of the food industry. Meanwhile, coal mining companies and oil companies created the huge expansion in energy production which enabled the stunning productivity increases of the era. These fossil fuels generated the energy which drove the industrial machinery which made and moved the food. Without each cog in this vast network, the urbanized world of the twentieth and twenty-first centuries would quickly starve. This is how we sustain urban populations. But is the system which sustains an urbanized world sustainable on a global scale?

It was against the background of these apparent huge success stories that some disparate individuals imagined an alternative world. They were not romantics for the pre-industrial age, campaigners against smoke pollution, or conservationists seeking to save forests and wildlife. Rather they sought to create for-profit businesses which were focused more on building a more sustainable future than on preserving the past. Many of them saw profits as a means to the end of remediating the ecological externalities of the conventional system. They are identifiable as precursors of contemporary green entrepreneurs, but their focus and mental framing reflected their own age, rather than ours. Eating healthily and the sustainability of communities without access to electricity were their concerns. In a broader sense, they can be seen as concerned with remediating the ecological externalities of the conventional capitalist system.

The businesses created during the first wave of environmentalism were mostly tiny, financially unsuccessful, endeavors. It is a story of eccentric, even outlandish, individuals, some of whom are well known, though not known as entrepreneurs. Their stories may seem anecdotal, but are important as representing the first cohort of entrepreneurs. Their experiences showed, vividly, how difficult it would be to create viable alternatives to conventional capitalism. Remarkably these apparently marginal endeavors laid a basis for technologies, techniques, and ideologies which would create the foundation for a greener entrepreneurial future.

The business of healthy food

With the rise of modern economic growth, there was a sudden and dramatic surge of population which posed unprecedented challenges to the existing supply of food. World population grew from 900 million in 1800 to 1.6 billion in 1900. Much of that growth was in the industrializing West: Europe's population expanded from 187 million to 400 million, and that of the United States from 5 million to 76 million. This was accompanied by urbanization. By 1850 more than half the British population lived in towns of more than 2,000 inhabitants, and fifty years later the proportion was three-quarters.[1] Food had been commercialized and traded since the first human cities had been built, but the population surge of the nineteenth century necessitated a vast scaling of both production and trade.

This scaling was achieved in several ways. There was a vast expansion of acreage under cultivation as lands were forcibly cleared of indigenous peoples in the United States and elsewhere, and as empty spaces elsewhere were colonized. There were major investments in raising agricultural productivity with new practices of cultivation which reduced rest periods for soil fertility, expanded the use of machines, and applied new chemical products, especially fertilizers.[2] Initially organic fertilizers—primarily guano and natural nitrates— were shipped from Peru and Chile for use in North American and European agriculture. The first chemical fertilizers were already in use in the nineteenth century, and there was a huge expansion in their use in the West after the Haber-Bosch process for capturing atmospheric nitrogen was invented in 1909. The use of nitrogen-based fertilizers in place of traditional animal or plant manures spread globally after the middle of the twentieth century. The production growth they enabled was the single most important factor in the quadrupling of world population over the course of the century.[3]

International trade in agricultural products grew faster than total output as countries and regions specialized in particular food commodities.[4] Technological advances such as refrigeration facilitated such specialization, enabling, for instance, Argentina to supply beef to world markets. Colonization helped British companies turn India into a giant tea plantation to supply British consumers with their favorite (non-native) beverage. Vertically integrated multinationals such as the United Fruit Company turned Central American countries into banana plantations, introduced Americans to eating the fruit, and through transport and marketing innovation ensured they could have as many as the desired.[5]

Food became more plentiful and diverse in the Western world during the nineteenth century, despite occasional famines elsewhere. Food in the more urbanized West also became more industrialized as specialized food processors and manufacturers emerged. Cheap sugar or chemical preservatives became regular additives in foodstuffs to extend shelf lives. The consumption of sugar soared, as did dental disease.[6] The brands of packaged food companies, like Heinz and Campbell's canned vegetables and soups, spread across international markets. Mass retailing institutions such as chain stores and cooperatives emerged, selling long-lasting food at lower prices by purchasing in high volumes.[7]

The adulteration of food was a long and widespread phenomenon, but urbanization, long supply chains, and the growing use of preservatives provided new opportunities for fraud in a climate of minimal regulation. During the second half of the nineteenth century there were repeated scandals of food adulteration in Germany, Britain, and the rest of Europe, especially in products for poor urban workers, including substantial numbers of deaths from food poisoning.[8] On both sides of the Atlantic, so-called "patent medicines" (many of which were sold as food or drink) offered cures for ailments, indigestion, and everything else, with no labeling of contents and no regulation over the inaccurate claims often made in selling products.[9] Historians have documented the growing alarm and campaigns against abuses, which eventually led to the growth of regulation. In Britain, for example, legislation was passed in 1875 which began to pursue greater enforcement of safety standards, although plenty of cases of the adulteration of milk and other products continued.[10] The problem of adulteration was at least as acute in the United States, which had limited local regulation over food adulteration. Campaigners finally secured federal legislation in 1906: the first Food and Drugs Act. This outlawed some harmful ingredients and misleading claims, and was enforced by the small Bureau of Chemistry.[11]

The story of the regulatory response to food adulteration and dangerous patent medicines has overshadowed the efforts of the disparate group of unconventional individuals who were the pioneers of green entrepreneurship. Although some of their views would not be unfamiliar to a twenty-first-century environmentalist, their core focus was more the health of human beings than the natural environment. They sought not to secure more regulation, but to create businesses which could both educate consumers about the increasing health risk they faced, and provide healthy food solutions.

The first such businesses often grew out of social and religious movements. In the United States, a social movement known as health reform provided a context and intellectual agenda for the first businesses. It emerged in early nineteenth-century Boston and was associated with Sylvester Graham. In 1829 this Presbyterian minister made the antecedent of what Americans know as the Graham cracker, made of whole-wheat and high-fiber flour, as an alternative to the increasingly popular white bread which employed chemical additives.[12] Graham believed the chemicals in white bread were unwholesome as they increased people's sex drive, and in particular their proclivity to masturbation, which he regarded as immoral and leading to declining intelligence. Instead he extolled the virtues of a healthy and bland diet with no meat or alcohol, accompanied by lots of exercise, which he saw as beneficial to individuals and to society as a whole.[13] Graham took part in the foundation of the American Vegetarian Society in New York City in 1850. In the United States and Europe vegetarianism became a frequently employed solution to the perceived failings of diet and lifestyle arising from modernity.[14]

Graham's ideas became the basis for entrepreneurial start-ups, though not by him personally. These included "Graham boardinghouses" and small stores. Dr. James Caleb Jackson combined Graham's views with a theory of water treatment for illness, founding a health spa and inventing, in 1863, the first cold cereal breakfast food called Granula, a baked flour bar consumed with milk. Jackson launched the Our Home Granula Company to manufacture the bar along with a so-called health coffee.[15]

Both Graham and Jackson influenced the founders of the Seventh-Day Adventist sect, for whom health reform became a central concern. The sect had been established at Battle Creek, Michigan in 1863, and three years later a convalescent home was established there. In 1876 Dr. John Harvey Kellogg, a passionate vegetarian and consumer of Graham crackers, became medical director of the sanatorium. Kellogg specialized in making vegetable-based foods that were healthy, discouraged masturbation, and were low in cost. In 1897 he and his brother Will Keith set up a company to develop his products. Concerned about the digestive qualities of bread, and in pursuit of bland foods which allegedly facilitated sexual abstinence, Kellogg asked his brother to experiment with a wheat paste, which had dried out after being accidently left out to stand all night. He ran the product through a set of rollers and ended up with a flaked wheat which became the basis for what would become the iconic breakfast cereal Kellogg's Cornflakes. In an early example of compromising values in order to create a broader market, Will Keith took the opportunity of his stricter brother being away in Europe to add sugar to the toasted cornflakes to make them more palatable. The resulting rift with John Harvey, who strongly opposed the consumption of sugar, resulted in Will Keith forming his own company in 1906, which achieved $1 million in sales within four years through good marketing and advertising. A decade-long legal battle over the use of the Kellogg name was won by Will Keith, who from 1922 drove the growth of Kellogg Cereal Company into a large, multinational consumer products firm, albeit one selling low-fiber sugary cereal.[16]

The American health reformers were in frequent contact with counterparts in Britain, which also saw small businesses making health food products for sale in spas and sanatoriums. One of the world's first health food stores opened in the industrial metropolis of Birmingham in 1898, when a group of vegetarian businessmen established a vegetarian restaurant, store, and hotel. It was managed by John Henry Cook, who coined the term "health food store" after a customer asked him what foods she should be eating for health. Cook, a Seventh-Day Adventist and vegetarian, acquired the store in 1901, stocking it with fresh fruits and vegetables, and packaged breakfast foods imported from Kellogg's. By 1908 Cook had established a factory making health foods, and he became a supplier to other stores. By 1925 his catalogue was being mailed to 500 health food stores and he shared his expertise six years later by publishing a book entitled *How to Run a Health Food Store Successfully by the Founder of the First.*[17]

Both in Britain and the United States the number of health food stores—most of which were small, and family-owned and managed—grew in the interwar years.[18] They catered to a niche market of people interested in healthier eating and lifestyles. Other entrepreneurs soon followed. These included Bernarr Macfadden, born as Bernard Adolphus McFadden in Missouri in 1868. After his mother died of tuberculosis when he was four, and he appeared to develop it when he was twelve, he sought to join a gym, but could not afford the membership. In time he established his own gym with bars and dumbbells, recovered from illness, and evolved the idea that his mission in life was to teach the "gospel of health." Moving to New York, in 1899 he founded a magazine called *Physical Culture*, and published the five-volume, 2,969-page *Encyclopedia of Physical Culture* (first issued in 1911 and periodically revised). He also opened a chain of one-cent Physical Culture restaurants, and established spas which he called "healthatoriums." Even amongst pioneers of healthy foods and lifestyles, McFadden was an eccentric. Following his theory of voice development, he would periodically, and without warning, break into loud mooing or braying. If Macfadden was sometimes absurd, he was able to build a viable business. The readership of *Physical Culture* reached half a million by 1918. In 1935 the combined circulation of his magazines was over 7 million.[19]

In Germany, which had started industrializing later than Britain but subsequently grew rapidly, especially after its unification as a nation-state in 1871, social movements concerning food and health also emerged.[20] These social movements sometimes overlapped with Romantic, nature-worshipping ideologies. There was a long-standing literary and philosophical tradition in Germany about the importance of trees and woods, with a particular veneration of old trees which has continued until the present day. Industrialization caused particular alarm as it seemed to encroach on the trees.[21] The Life Reform movement became the official name of a network of participating groups including naturopaths, nature healers, nudists, as well as vegetarians, who urged people to eat simple healthy food and take care of their bodies.[22] Young, unmarried, Protestant middle-class men were particular supporters of these ideas, eating in restaurants which served their favorite foods. These restaurants became the basis for small specialty retail shops which sold food and personal care products which enabled the customers to consume products representing the movement's ideals.[23]

The first such Reform House shop was opened in Berlin in 1887 by Carl Braun, a naturopath, who noticed that it was hard to buy the wraps and toweling he recommended. Within three years he had begun selling cocoa and chocolate, then seen as healthy foods, and later expanded more widely into food and health products.[24] In the early days, direct-mail merchandising was quite important because stores were found only in large cities, but gradually more shops were opened. They provided advice about products to customers and were especially active in popularizing consumption of fruit and margarine, then thought to be a healthy alternative to butter.[25]

There were about eighty Reform Houses by 1914, distributed across Germany but sparsest in the south of the country.[26] It was mostly, although not entirely, a matter of small-scale entrepreneurship, but a number of businesses grew larger. One of the most successful was the Berlin Gesundheits-Zentrale, founded by a merchant named Carl Mann. He had at least seven stores in the city by 1911, and annual revenues of around 1 million marks ($250,000). From 1911 onward Mann devoted all profits to an endowment for charitable purposes.[27] Although World War I caused many difficulties, the Reform Houses survived and became an established feature of the German business sector. By 1925 there were an estimated 200 Reform Houses in Germany, and over 1,000 by 1932, with close links developing between retail stores and the many small manufacturers of Reform products.[28]

Life Reform concepts concerning healthy food and natural healing had a significant global impact as Germans emigrated elsewhere, especially to the United States. Benedict Lust, born in 1872 and raised in the Black Forest region of Germany, was important in transferring these concepts. He first traveled to the United States in 1891 to work but contracted tuberculosis and returned to Germany for treatment from a naturopath, Father Sebastian Kneipp. When he recovered, he made Father Kneipp's teachings about natural medicine his own, and immigrated to the United States in 1896 as Kneipp's American representative. To become established, he enrolled and graduated from the New York Homeopathic Medical College in 1901.[29] That year he founded the American School of Naturopathy in New York City, the first naturopathic medical school in the world. He also founded the Naturopathic Society of America, renamed the American Naturopathic Association in 1919, the first national professional organization of naturopathic physicians in the United States.[30]

Lust founded his own spa sanatorium, Yungborn, in New Jersey.[31] In 1913, he founded a second Yungborn spa in Florida. He introduced to the United States the major naturist movements in Europe, including hydrotherapy, herbal remedies, air and light baths, and vegetarian diets, and translated a number of the natural health classics written in German.[32] He also founded magazines which, among other things, introduced the United States to the Indian concepts of Ayurveda and yoga. The Indian healer Paramahansa Yogananda was one of several Indians who wrote articles for his journal *Nature's Path* in the 1920s.[33] None of this was easy. Lust found himself harassed both by the authorities and by medical associations for his unconventional approach to healing, as it involved massage and nude sunbathing at his health resorts.[34]

Lust, like many of the early food and health enthusiasts, was a vegetarian, but other concepts of what constituted healthy food changed over time. As the Life Reform movement took shape in the 1870s, Eduard Baltzer, one of the movement's pioneers, criticized German agriculture for being too focused on animals and not growing enough plants to feed people sufficiently. He made the case for vegetarianism, but he also embraced the use of chemical fertilizers to grow more food because for him the key sustainability issue was hunger. The following four decades, however, saw the movement shift to making the case for using natural fertilizers.[35] Although the Life Reform movement was primarily urban, some members began to work as farmers or gardeners, experimenting with composting, green manuring, and mulching. In 1928, these farmers formed their own organization, the Arbeitsgemeinschaft Natürlicher Landbau und Siedlung (Working Group for Natural Agriculture and Settlement), or ANLS. It focused on fruit and vegetable production without artificial fertilizers.[36]

Among the Life Reform's agricultural suppliers was a venture called Eden. This fruit-growing cooperative was established as part of a back-to-the-land settling movement in 1893 by a group of vegetarians in Oranienburg near Berlin. Eden's initial land quality was poor, with sandy soil, but the settlers engaged in building it up through the use of mineral fertilizers, alongside Berlin street sweepings and sewage sludge. Within a few years, the use of natural fertilizers produced internally by the community was the norm. Although the original settlement did not envision producing Reform products for sale as opposed to communal use, they soon did so. The production of fruit, initially strawberries, as a for-profit business within the settlement began in 1898. Fruit and fruit juices were promoted as alternatives to alcohol, and as free from chemical preservatives. Natural honey, vegetarian meat-substitutes, and margarine were added over the following two decades.[37]

By the 1920s, a number of agricultural, retail, spa, and publishing businesses had been founded in Britain, Germany, and the United States which focused on natural foods, avoidance of chemical fertilizers, and healthy lifestyles. The figures behind these endeavors were heterogeneous, but revealed some characteristics which would reappear going forward. They were often motivated through connections with wider social movements, which also provided a customer base. Personal motivations were shaped by distinctive religious and spiritual concerns, as well as by countercultural beliefs, in this period including nudism and natural healing. Macfadden's and Lust's experience of ill health would also feature regularly among the motivations of later green entrepreneurs. Although the businesses created were not mainstream, some found sufficient niche markets to achieve scale, including some Reform House stores in Germany, Cook's health food business in Britain, and Macfadden's magazine business in the United States. It tells us something important about the readiness of consumers at large to embrace health foods that Kellogg's Cornflakes, the biggest success story of the lot, only broke into the mass market with the addition of Will Keith's sugar.

The founders of these businesses were fundamentally motivated by concerns that the industrialization of food and unhealthy urban lifestyles were ruining people's health, and posed a threat to society. The specifics of why eating a natural or vegetarian diet was good for people, that for example it reduced the propensity to masturbate, were distinctly odd even at the time. However, these arguments can be seen as the start of a broad trend in which the health arguments for eating natural or organic food were more asserted than proven. A century later the health benefits of eating organic food remained contested. A recent major study by medical researchers could not identify nutritional advantages of eating organic food as compared to conventional food, although it did identify some safety benefits, including avoiding eating pesticide residues.[38]

Rudolf Steiner, anthroposophy, and green business

Rudolf Steiner, a philosopher and founder of an esoteric spiritual movement, would appear at first blush to be an even more unlikely candidate to appear in a book on green entrepreneurship than Macfadden and Lust. Yet Steiner's philosophy, which was in a state of constant evolution, was destined to become a source of motivation for a cohort of green entrepreneurs right up until the present day. Steiner himself had a brief entrepreneurial career, and among other achievements laid the basis for the modern organic food industry.

Born in present-day Croatia, then part of the Austro-Hungarian Empire, Steiner claimed he was already communicating with the spiritual world when he was eight years old. He studied mathematics and physics in Vienna, and obtained a doctorate in philosophy from Rostock University in Germany. Steiner was heavily influenced by German Idealism, especially the work of Johann Wolfgang von Goethe, but upon moving to Berlin in 1897, he became involved with Theosophy, an occult movement influenced by Hinduism and Buddhism. Steiner disagreed with the movement's leaders, however, in maintaining the importance of scientific investigation, as well as asserting the unique importance of Jesus Christ. Steiner's own religious views, which included a belief in reincarnation, bore little resemblance to conventional Christianity. In 1913 Steiner broke away to found his own school of anthroposophy, a "science of the spirit," which essentially sought to occupy the middle ground between science and religion. Steiner believed that humans had lost awareness of their ancient understanding that they had bodies, souls, and spirits, with nineteenth-century materialism as the last straw. He saw human beings living both on earth and in the spiritual world, and asserted that they needed to operate competently in both. This was partly because they were constantly reincarnated, changing genders and cultures as they evolved over time.[39]

Steiner's ideas were regarded by most of his contemporaries as odd or even outlandish, and they have remained far beyond the mainstream.[40] Their relevance for sustainability lay in two particular aspects of his work. First, they offered profoundly holistic diagnoses, and solutions. Steiner's belief that a gap had opened up between the material and the spiritual worlds which needed to be healed laid a basis for a holistic view of environmental challenges and their solutions. In the chaotic political and economic situation at the end of World War I, Steiner also developed the concept of "social threefolding," which would be influential in later entrepreneurial ventures. He perceived three domains of human society—economic, legal, and cultural—which needed to remain autonomous, but should negotiate to achieve consensus, as the three domains were interdependent.[41] Second, Steiner's insights were accompanied by an emphasis, which grew over time, on working with others to find practical applications of his spiritual-scientific research. This resulted in the creation by Steiner and his followers of a raft of new institutions and techniques in medicine, agriculture, childhood education, and architecture, and a new form of capitalist enterprise.

It was concerns about health and medicine that would, eventually, lead Steiner into business. Like Kellogg, Lust, and many others concerned with healthy diets at this time, Steiner advocated a primarily vegetarian diet, stressing the importance for health of eating plants.[42] His ideas evolved through interaction with a number of key individuals. In 1907 Steiner was approached by Oskar Schmiedel, a chemist who was interested in Steiner's ideas and worried about his own health. They began researching together the healing power of ingredients derived from plants. Steiner had earlier met the young Ita Wegman, who had been born in the Dutch East Indies of a colonial family, and had earned her degree as a medical doctor at the University of Zurich in 1911. Wegman joined Schmiedel in working with Steiner on natural medicines developed using anthroposophical concepts about healing and pharmaceuticals.[43]

From 1913 Steiner, an extraordinary polymath with deep interests in the arts, began constructing the Goetheanum, a sculpted, double-domed wooden building, in Dornach, Switzerland, as a school for "spiritual science." It was finished seven years later after years of construction carried out by volunteers from seventeen different countries.[44] Although he never had any formal training in the profession, Steiner considered architecture as central to healing the gap between the material and the spiritual. "Every building," he noted, "deprives a portion of the earth of sun, wind and rain and probably plant and animal life as well. It must redeem this sacrifice by the healing quality of its architecture."[45] The Goetheanum was based on the concept of organic design in which each element, form, and color bears an inner relation to the whole and the whole flows organically into its single elements in a process of metamorphosis.[46] Steiner believed that people visiting his buildings would innately understand this spiritual message. This proved much too optimistic, but his attempt to introduce his spiritual philosophy into the practice of architecture was a radical idea and created an institutional framework for a future generation of architects.[47]

Meanwhile Steiner's school included departments run by pharmacists and chemists to develop the products of anthroposophical medicine, which was always envisaged as a complement rather than alternative to conventional medicine. In anthroposophical medicine, drugs derived from plants and minerals were combined with massage, exercise, and counseling. During World War I Wegman developed a cancer treatment using an extract of mistletoe following advice from Steiner. This became, and has remained, a widely-used alternative medicine for treatment of cancer, prescribed by some doctors in German-speaking Europe, but whose benefits remain to be demonstrated convincingly.[48]

Steiner's emergence as an entrepreneur began during World War I and its aftermath. In October 1919 Steiner gave a speech to anthroposophists at Dornach calling for an international movement of renewal based on his views of threefolding. Also speaking that day was Emil Molt, a German entrepreneur who owned the Waldorf-Astoria Cigarette Company and who was in the process of co-founding with Steiner the first Waldorf school in Stuttgart to serve the children of employees of the factory. Steiner's ideas on education had been developed earlier, but now moved to a practical application in actual schools.[49] Molt also suggested that businesses could be established to provide the financial means for supporting the diffusion of Steiner's views. After initial hesitation, Steiner came up with the idea of creating a "bank-like institution" to support businesses which would promote anthroposophical values. The bank itself was not to aim at profit-maximization, but rather to assist other companies with financial and managerial support. The vision was to create businesses which would be profitable and sustainable, with the aim of creating a new business culture.[50] In terms of threefolding, Steiner saw capital as created by entrepreneurship in the cultural sphere, used as loans in the legal sphere, deployed in the economic sphere, and then yielding profits to repay loans and support educational and cultural institutions, enabling the cycle to begin again.[51]

The first years of these business enterprises proved challenging. The proposed bank, known as Der kommende Tag A.G. ("the Coming Day"), or Komtag for short, was launched in 1920. Steiner was its chairman.[52] Komtag bought a consumer goods factory in the town of Schwäbisch Gmünd, where Steiner intended to construct an experimental laboratory for pharmaceutical products, in conjunction with the establishment of two new medical-therapeutic clinics in nearby Stuttgart and in Arlesheim, Switzerland.[53] Steiner worked with Schmiedel on the technical side of product development, both for medicaments and for a shaving soap and hair tonic. By 1922, 295 "preparations" had been suggested for production, over 100 by Steiner himself.[54] Steiner also designed packaging for his products, in both English and German.[55] In Switzerland, a similar model was used to establish a firm called Futurum A.G. in Arlesheim, which also aimed to combine production of pharmaceuticals with a medical clinic, which Wegman had opened.[56]

In a turbulent political and economic context, Steiner and his views attracted growing hostility. The Goetheanum was burnt down by arson in 1923; the construction of a second, this time built with reinforced concrete rather than wood, had just started when Steiner died in 1925, and was finally completed three years later. The design, materials, use of color and space, and harmony with the natural geography of the second Goetheanum represented a striking and unique architectural statement, which conventional architects largely ignored or abhorred.[57]

The new business ventures founded by Steiner also experienced challenging times. They experienced liquidity challenges. In 1922 the laboratories and Wegman's therapeutic institute were separated from Futurum to form a new Swiss joint stock company known as ILAG (formally renamed Weleda in 1927). Steiner declined to be on the board because of a desire to devote himself to spiritual tasks. Nevertheless he, Schmiedel, and Wegman are still featured even today on the company's website as the co-founders.[58] The company acquired the rump of Futurum, whose efforts at manufacturing had not gone well, and they formally merged in 1924.[59] Further reorganization led to the Anthroposophical Society becoming the formal owner of nearly one-fifth of the future Weleda's stock.[60] In 1924 the residual German assets were also placed under the control of the Swiss company, a step probably driven by Steiner's concerns about the future of German politics after an attempted coup by Adolf Hitler in Munich the year before. Steiner described his business as an "economic-spiritual enterprise" and remained committed to the view that it needed to be a sustainable and not a subsidized venture, even if the great majority of its shareholders were anthroposophists.[61]

By then Steiner had also begun developing ideas about how plants should be grown using anthroposophist principles. Steiner's involvement in agriculture came through the initiative of several German farmers, including Erhard Bartsch, who had become interested in anthroposophy after attending a Steiner lecture in 1913. Following military service in World War I, Bartsch studied agriculture and also benefited from a year's practicum at the

Koberwitz estate of Count Carl von Keyserlingk, another supporter. Alongside colleagues including Ernst Stegemann, Bartsch attempted to gauge the interest of German farmers in learning about the possible connections between anthroposophy and agriculture by sending out a survey. They worked out a set of questions and issues on which they hoped Steiner could elaborate his views and their relevance to farming. This helped prepare the ground for a course of lectures on agriculture by Steiner which took place on Keyserlingk's estate in 1924. Steiner incorporated many concepts already in circulation, including seeing farms as organisms, but he also added new components, including the value of mixed farming and the use of animals, the avoidance of chemical fertilizers, the use of cosmic forces to enrich the soil, and the control of pests and weeds without pesticides. The health of the soil, plants, and animals depended, he argued, on their connection with cosmic creative forces.[62]

Steiner saw his lectures as works in progress, as they established the principles of biodynamic agriculture, a term which originated with Bartsch and Stegemann rather than Steiner himself.[63] The principles featured the use of nine so-called "preparations" designed for soil health, and to stimulate plant growth alongside crop rotation, manuring, and the integration of crops with livestock. The preparations were a mixture of mineral plants and animal manure, which were fermented and applied to composts, soil, and plants. In addition, the method emphasized that plants come under astrological influences, and that planting and harvesting needed to coincide with movements of the moon and the planets.[64]

Steiner himself became ill, and during his last months he was cared for by Ita Wegman as they jointly wrote his last book, which provided a theoretical basis to the new medicine they were developing.[65] The company which became Weleda survived Steiner's death. Josef van Leer, who served as president of the management board, envisioned a role for the company that supplemented on a commercial and material level what the medical and clinical research section run by Wegman was doing on a scientific-spiritual level.[66] Its product line by the mid-1920s included remedies against a wide variety of illnesses and well-selling dietary supplements and digestive teas. Hair tonic and shaving soap were made from ingredients grown on biodynamic principles, making the venture the founder of the modern natural beauty industry.[67] Small Weleda subsidiaries were opened in Britain and the Netherlands in 1924, and in the United States and Czechoslovakia two years later.[68]

Steiner's legacy was fragile, but enduring. There were immediate challenges as the anthroposophical movement fragmented, especially internal divisions concerning the role of Wegman.[69] However, new Waldorf schools opened in Britain and the United States during the 1920s: sixty years later there were nearly 600 such schools worldwide.[70] Weleda also survived, even though its first dividend came only in 1929, and it was not to issue another one until after the end of World War II.[71] The biodynamic connection between health and cosmetics continued to be explored in the work of Dr. Rudolf Hauschka, an Austrian chemist influenced by Steiner, who worked with Wegman to create a water-based extract of rose petals in 1929, which became the basis for medicines, and enabled him to create the WALA laboratory in Germany in 1935. Three decades later he and Elisabeth Sigmund would launch an anthroposophically based skin care line.[72]

The principles of biodynamic agriculture were to become one of the key foundations for organic agriculture. Its supporters prioritized building institutions and establishing rules. Bartsch, von Keyserlingk, and Stegemann established the first formal anthroposophical-agricultural organization, the Experimental Circle (Versuchsring) of the Anthroposophical Society in 1924.[73] A second organization, Demeter, was founded in 1927, and the membership of this second organization was extended beyond the existing members of the Experimental Circle to other interested farmers, although the executive board was to have two-thirds of its membership derived from the former.[74] The Experimental Circle functioned as a research and standards body, and was the only manufacturer of special anthroposophical preparations which were kept from the non-anthroposophical members of Demeter. Demeter was concerned with execution, advising farmers interested in trying out Steiner's approach, and engaging in the marketing of biodynamic products. The Demeter trademark was used from 1928 onward to assist in marketing biodynamic produce.[75] For half a century, Demeter remained the only certification scheme for organic products.

Individuals spread biodynamic ideas elsewhere in Europe and across the Atlantic. During the late 1920s Ehrenfried Pfeiffer, a German chemist who had worked with Steiner, converted a farm owned by the wealthy daughter of a former prime minister at Loverendale in Walcheren in the Netherlands to the principles of biodynamic farming, and this became the largest biodynamic venture in interwar Europe.[76] Steiner's ideas reached the United States through American students who had studied with him. In 1926 members of New York City's Threefold Group bought a farm in rural Rockland County, northwest of New York City, which became the first piece of land farmed using biodynamic methods in North America. In 1933 they held their first summer school at Threefold Farm, and one of the invited speakers was Pfeiffer. He settled permanently in the United States in 1938, where he created a model biodynamic farm at Kimberton, Pennsylvania which played an influential role in the embryonic organic food market after the end of World War II.[77]

Rudolf Steiner was many things, and entrepreneurship was just one dimension of a truly multi-faceted man. How, and if, biodynamic preparations work, if mistletoe has any functionality to fight cancer, and the validity of many other claims by Steiner and his followers, remain unresolved issues to the present day, let alone the grander narratives about human beings and their worlds. Yet Steiner should also be seen as offering a radical holistic vision of sustainability, built partly around the concept of threefolding. He proposed practical ways to execute that vision through economic-spiritual enterprises, and specific methods in agriculture, as well as education and architecture. It is striking that Steiner's ideas, which were so at odds with modernity, came to resonate across both time and geography, and inspire new generations of green entrepreneurs.

Energy from the wind and sun

A second set of green entrepreneurs which emerged in the late nineteenth century were concerned with energy rather than food and health. They were the pioneers of today's wind and solar industries. While the food and health entrepreneurs were typically motivated by spiritual or social concerns, the alternative energy pioneers were more mixed in their motivations. There were strong religious and social motivations present, but there were also individuals who saw gaps in energy supplies in rural locations and far-flung European colonies which could be profitable to fill.

Whatever their motivations, the early wind and solar entrepreneurs faced, like their food counterparts, a hugely successful incumbent industry based on fossil fuels. The growth of fossil fuel production drove the growth of manufacturing industries and the productivity increases in the West. Over the course of the century the consumption of energy in Europe expanded over twenty times in absolute terms, and sevenfold in per capita terms. Coal accounted for 90 percent of the total increase in energy consumption between 1820 and 1910, and provided more than four-fifths of Western Europe's energy supply. Despite the growth of consumption, prices fell sharply.[78]

Coal power was a triumph of capitalist enterprise. In Britain, Europe's largest coal producer, landowners and, increasingly, specialist colliery companies pioneered the deep-shaft mining techniques which enabled massive amounts of coal to be mined. By the 1870s, a huge industry had developed which employed half a million workers and exported four-fifths of its output around the world. The German industry was the second largest in Europe by the 1900s. The United States had become the largest in the world by then, exploiting new technologies and the creation of a national market by the railroads. The American industry, favored by federal laws which enabled them to keep all they mined on public lands, featured both huge companies and thousands of small ventures with one or two employees.[79]

A second fossil fuel, petroleum, was initially much less important than coal. It accounted for less than 1 percent of Europe's energy consumption even in 1910.[80] However, after the first modern oil well was dug in Pennsylvania in 1859, entrepreneurs began a search for new supplies, first in the United States, and later elsewhere. Large vertically integrated firms like J. D. Rockefeller's Standard Oil and Royal Dutch Shell developed which spanned the production, refining, and distribution of petroleum. During the 1920s the leading Western powers engaged in constant diplomatic rivalries to secure access to the suspected oilfields of the Middle East.[81]

Fossil fuels, primarily coal, enabled the generation of electricity which progressively lit up the world with light bulbs and street lights, and allowed communication over distances with the new technologies of the telegraph, the telephone, and cinema. In 1882 the inventor Thomas Edison opened the first central power plant in the United States in Lower Manhattan in New York City. This venture evolved into the giant electrical company General Electric. In the following decade Samuel Insull began working for a utility known as Chicago Edison, consolidating small generators into larger units, using high-voltage transmission lines. Everywhere, cities were first electrified, and then with the development of steam turbines and transmission technologies, networks were formed and suburban and eventually rural areas were connected. Hydro-electricity, which began to expand especially in the United States and

Canada after plants were installed at Grand Rapids, Ottawa, and Niagara Falls in the early 1880s, stimulated developments in transmission, because although such plants were expensive, marginal costs thereafter were very small. By 1914 there were fifty-five transmission lines of between 70,000 and 150,000 volts in the world, ranging in length from 19 to 245 miles. The following two decades saw a massive rise in per capita electricity consumption.[82] As consumption grew, costs fell. The average price for electric energy fell 400 percent in the United States between 1902 and 1930. The provision of electricity came to be perceived as a public utility. In the United States and many European countries, municipalities created regulatory regimes for power stations, which they sometimes owned directly themselves, and in the interwar years national governments oversaw or planned national grid systems.[83]

These developments in fossil fuels and electricity provided a dynamic energy system. At its heart was the creation of transport systems which carried fossil fuels and transmitted electricity across geographies.[84] Governments supported the system. As noted in the introduction, there was zero understanding of the potential negative outcomes in terms of climate change. There was, as a result, no incentive or opportunity from that perspective to develop wind or solar energy technologies as non-polluting alternatives. There was considerable discussion of the finite nature of fossil fuels. The early conservation movement saw the depletion of natural resource endowments as a problem. As early as 1865 the leading British economist William Stanley Jevons warned that coal supplies were threatened. In his book *The Coal Question* he identified the "Jevons Paradox" by which increases in the efficiency of energy production led to more not less consumption.[85] Nevertheless, concerns about the finite nature of fossil fuels only rarely seem to have motivated the early entrepreneurial efforts to develop wind and solar businesses.

There was nothing new about seeing wind and the sun as sources of energy. Human beings had used windmills for at least two thousand years, but it was wholly uncompetitive as a power source compared to coal-generated steam. Instead, some windmills continued to be used for traditional purposes like grinding grain.[86] However, as mechanization became increasingly important, new opportunities arose in places where access to fossil fuels and electricity was difficult or expensive.

The vast open spaces of the interior of the United States prompted endeavors to develop businesses using wind technologies for mechanical water pumping using small systems with rotor diameters of one to several meters. The motivation was primarily to make money. These systems appeared first with the Halladay windmill in the 1850s, developed by a Connecticut mechanic for use in the Great Plains. The market was the transcontinental railroads, which needed to draw water for their steam loco-motives and faced high costs to transport coal for this purpose. The original windmills were steadily improved, especially with the development of steel blades in 1870. These low-cost American water-pumping windmills were made in large numbers, installed throughout the American heartland, and exported widely.[87]

Wind energy became in part the preserve of the curious inventor. There was experimentation using multi-blade windmill design to generate electri-city. The first use of a large windmill to generate electricity was a system built in Cleveland, Ohio, by the serial inventor Charles F. Brush, who had already made a considerable fortune inventing an arc-light system. In 1888 he built a sixty-foot tower in his backyard, and became the first person in the world to use wind to generate electricity. To store power, he installed batteries in his basement. It worked for twenty years but could only produce 12 kilowatts from a wind rotor which was 56 feet in diameter, with 144 wooden blades.[88]

During the 1920s wind generator electrical systems inspired by the design of airplane propellers and, later, monoplane wings found widespread use in the rural areas of the Great Plains, initially to provide lighting for farms and to charge batteries used to power crystal radio sets, and later to power refriger-ators, freezers, washing machines, and power tools.

The Jacobs Wind Energy Company was among the most important wind energy businesses of this era. This was the creation of Marcellus and Joe Jacobs, whose parents had relocated them in rural eastern Montana. The family wanted electricity yet needed to get gasoline from the nearest small town, which was forty miles away. The brothers first tried to build a wind plant from a water-pumping windmill. Both brothers were working full-time on the farm. Joe never received a formal education, whilst Marcellus only attended one year of high school where he picked up the basics of electricity, which was fundamental for people living on farms. Marcellus came back from school to the ranch and with his brother Joe they built their first turbine in 1922. After three years they concluded that the multi-bladed wheel turned too slowly to produce enough electricity. As Marcellus had learned to fly, he had the intuition that an airplane propeller might solve the problem. World War I left behind a tremendous amount of surplus, including plane propellers and engines. This equipment was available for purchase at low prices and could be used to develop wind turbine technology.[89]

Marcellus invented the three-bladed turbine which later became his trademark product in 1927, and officially started a business in 1929, supported by funds from neighboring farmers. The fact that the Jacobs farm was the only one lit up at night provided a powerful demonstration effect for their machinery. People would see lights from several miles away and would drive to the Jacobs' ranch to find out how they could get connected as well. In 1931 they relocated the business to Minneapolis, providing electricity to rural areas where power lines were not installed.[90]

It was in Denmark, the second pioneer of the modern wind energy industry alongside the United States, that wider sustainability issues became integrated into the development of windmills. Denmark was an unusual country in that it had experienced an eco-catastrophe in the middle of the eighteenth century due to over-population and over-exploitation of forests, and faced the likely prospect of being covered with sand. This prompted a major environmental response including planting lyme grass, enhanced drainage, and increased use of clover in crop rotation.[91] Arguably, this heritage resulted in an enhanced environmental sensibility in the country, which will feature as important in several green industries discussed later in this book.

Denmark had a long tradition of using windmills to mill grain for flour, but Poul la Cour took the technology to a new level. Growing up on a farm, and graduating from the University of Copenhagen in the new science of meteorology, la Cour became influenced by the ideas of nineteenth-century Lutheran pastor and philosopher N. F. S. Grundtvig, a formative figure in Danish national consciousness, who stressed the virtues of freedom and creativity, and has sometimes been compared to Ralph Waldo Emerson in the United States. In 1891 la Cour, who had become a teacher at the Folk High School in Askov in the south of the country, began experimenting with how wind turbines could generate electricity. He was the first person in the world to carry out systematic experiments with artificial air currents in a wind tunnel. He was motivated by his dislike for what he regarded as the poor social conditions in towns as they industrialized, and sought a way to improve rural life so people would not leave for such towns. He considered access to electricity as the key, but as power plants were only built as yet to serve the Danish cities, he wanted to find a way to generate electricity in rural areas. Drawing on the research of contemporary Danish engineers and scientists who had helped formulate the theory of aerodynamic lift and drag, la Cour built a windmill which initially powered a dynamo which generated electricity to provide lighting for the high school, as well as the houses of the nearby village.[92] La Cour patented a series of inventions, but making money was far from his focus. He sought to share his technology. To facilitate this process, he created a Society of Wind Electricians.[93]

Wind power boomed in Denmark during World War I, as scarcity of imported coal created an energy shortage. Unlike neighboring Sweden, the country had no forests, no hydro power, and no coal mines, so wind was the most plausible option if coal was in short supply. By 1918, 250 electricity-producing wind turbines had been built in Denmark, 120 of which were connected to power stations. Against this background, la Cour and one of his students launched a company called Lykkegaard to manufacture wind turbines. It was joined by a second venture organized by the cement group F. L. Smidth & Co., which, in cooperation with the aircraft company Kramme & Zeuthen, developed a new type of turbine with aerodynamic wings and a tower of concrete which had an output of 40–70 kW. Smidth became a leader in linking turbine manufacturing with the field of aerodynamics.[94]

The construction of national electricity grids supplied from coal-burning power stations during the interwar years blighted the wind energy industry, in Denmark and elsewhere in Europe. Lykkegaard and Smidth continued to manufacture turbines, but the number of power stations in Denmark using wind turbines dropped from 75 to 25 between 1920 and 1940, when the outbreak of World War II and resulting fuel shortages again provided a temporary opportunity.[95] Elsewhere in Europe there was significant experimentation, but little implementation. In 1927 the French engineer George Darrieus, who worked for an electrical machinery manufacturer, patented the first vertical axis wind turbine, which enabled a turbine to accept wind from any direction rather than being reoriented as the wind changes direction, but this invention remained unused until the late 1960s.[96]

In the United States, too, wind energy was challenged by ongoing modernization. Jacobs Wind faced the challenge of the federal government's strategies, through the Rural Electrification Association (REA), to stimulate the severely depressed agricultural economies by extending the electrical grid. REA became a competitor to Jacobs, because it had excess capacity and saw wind energy as a danger. However, some rural areas continued not to be connected to the grid, and although Jacobs machines were expensive pieces of equipment, they were sometimes the only option to get reliable electricity. Jacobs Wind reached its peak in terms of sales from 1946 to 1950. By the 1950s the company had built 50,000 wind plants, and a network of dealerships across the world sold machines to mostly affluent farmers with large tracts of land that needed power. As growth tapered off with the further spread of electricity supplied by the coal-powered grid, the company filed for bankruptcy at the end of the decade.[97]

There were many parallels between developments in the wind and solar energy industries. It was never a secret that the sun, like wind, was an energy source. Passive solar energy, or the use of the sun's energy for lighting and heating living spaces, had always been used, but no technology existed to store solar heat or even to capture it. There were new technical advances in the nineteenth century. The French mathematician Augustin Mouchot, motivated by a conviction that fossil fuels would eventually run out, created the first solar steam-powered plant using parabolic dish collectors. The production of steam using parabolic troughs would remain the key technology for using solar power until after World War II, when the conversion of sunlight directly into electricity using photovoltaic panels was developed. Mouchot developed a solar-powered steam engine, and supported by the French government to conduct experiments in the sun-soaked French colony of Algeria, he developed a solar generator which was a prize-winning attraction of the Universal Exposition in Paris in 1878, but there was no additional funding and it remained a curiosity which was not further developed.[98] Yet interest in the potential of solar energy endured. Between 1880 and 1914 one estimate is that there were almost fifty articles on solar energy published in *Scientific American*, the popular science magazine.[99]

As with wind, entrepreneurs saw profitable opportunities where coal was costly and the sun shone. During the 1890s several solar water heater companies were started in California, which had a lot of sun and no coal.[100] Aubrey Eneas, who had emigrated from Britain to Boston, launched a successful solar business in California. Eneas drew inspiration from a Swedish-born engineer whose design for the ironclad steam-powered battleship *The Monitor* was widely publicized during the American Civil War. Eneas founded the Solar Motor Company of Boston in 1892. He perceived an opportunity in the arid deserts of the American Southwest, where a growing need for steam-powered irrigation and lack of easily accessible coal presented a great opportunity for solar power. After unsuccessful experiments, Eneas adopted Mouchot's conical reflector design to heat the boiler more evenly and efficiently, producing a greater volume of steam. In 1903 Eneas relocated the Solar Motor Company to Los Angeles and began aggressively marketing his machine throughout the region.[101] He developed large solar collectors to power steam engines and pumps for agricultural irrigation water, and started selling all around California and Arizona. However, the construction methods of these large cone collectors could not withstand the unpredictable local weather of hail and strong winds. Eneas eventually withdrew from solar energy believing the costs were too high to make a profit.[102]

Eneas was not alone in exiting the solar business in the United States. During the 1920s the California solar heater business was damaged by the growing supply of cheap natural gas in California. There was new business in Florida, which was undergoing a real estate boom, and where natural gas was not cheap. The Solar Water Heater Company was launched in Miami, and it successfully fitted many houses in Miami with the technology. In 1926 the company failed following a massive hurricane and the end of Florida's building boom. There was a second short-lived solar boom in Florida after 1935, when Federal Housing Administration mortgage programs facilitated a housing boom in which solar heaters were widely installed. Rising copper prices after the outbreak of the Pacific War brought this boom to an end.[103]

It was in the hot and sunny countries in the developing world where solar energy seemed to have better prospects. The most important example was in the British protectorate of Egypt, where the American entrepreneur Frank Shuman established a solar business. Shuman was a Philadelphia inventor who had become rich through inventing a shatter-proof glass used for skylights, car windshields, goggles, and machine tool guards. He began experimenting with solar motors in 1906. Aware of Eneas's failures, Shuman worked on a less expensive design for a solar engine. In 1907 Shuman built a small-scale demonstration plant in his backyard. To promote his solar motor and trigger interest among potential investors, Shuman circulated advertisements throughout the city inviting the public to attend a demonstration of his sun machine. By 1910, in order to test his design, Shuman built a plant roughly ten times the size of the original installation. The total sun collection area was more than 10,000 square feet. It produced around 600 pounds of steam per hour, and generated 25 horsepower—enough to pump 3,000 gallons of water per minute to a height of 33 feet. In order to compete with coal, Shuman thought a solar plant would need to be much larger. He was soon envisaging 10,000 horsepower steam engines run by sun collectors covering 60 acres.[104]

Shuman, like Mouchot, was concerned about the finite supply of fossil fuels. In September 1911 he wrote in *Scientific American* that "the future development of solar power has no limit . . . and in the far distant future, natural fuels having been exhausted, it will remain as the only means of existence of the human race."[105] He wrote at a moment when there was much public debate about imminent shortages of coal and petroleum, yet he still struggled to attract investor interest. He turned to the vast and globally oriented London capital market, where his colleague and consultant, the engineer A. S. E. Ackermann, had contacts, as well as links to scientific circles. In 1911 Shuman and his partners were able to float a new company, Sun Power Company (Eastern Hemisphere) and persuaded a sufficient number of investors to buy its shares to launch a solar energy venture in Egypt.[106]

British-administered Egypt seemed ideal for Shuman. It had a lot of sun and no coal, while mechanized irrigation was increasing as the lands adjacent to the Nile River were arable only with proper irrigation. Shuman leased land in the farming village of Maadi, located a few miles from Cairo, and arranged for parts for an experimental plant to be shipped from Philadelphia to Egypt. The support of the British colonial government was essential, and Shuman soon learned it involved complications. The government's engineers sought costly improvements. To save on costs Shuman decided to build the plant from scratch in Maadi, using local materials instead of building parts in Philadelphia and having them shipped to Egypt. The first commercial-scale solar plant was successfully launched.[107]

The local government, thrilled at having found a cost-effective way to upgrade Egypt's irrigation system and increase the country's lucrative cotton crop, offered Shuman a 30,000-acre cotton plantation in British Sudan on which to build a larger version of the solar plant. Because of the rivalry between Germany, Britain, and France over the Middle East and Africa, the

German government took notice of the potential of solar and awarded Shuman $200,000 to design and construct a solar-powered irrigation system in East Africa. This success led the inventor to envision even larger solar power plants, including a 20,000 square mile plant in the Sahara desert to generate 270 million horsepower—an amount, he noted, equal to all the fuel burned around the world in 1909.[108]

Shuman's ambitious solar plans were brought to an end by the outbreak of World War I. Engineers working at the Maadi plant, including Shuman, returned to their home countries and within several months the plant itself was dismantled for parts and scrap metal. Shuman died of a heart attack in 1918. After the war, the momentum for further experimentation was lost, as the prices of fossil fuels fell sharply during the postwar recession.[109]

By the interwar years, entrepreneurial businesses had been created to make wind turbines and to heat water, and a solar thermal power station had been built in Egypt. There were mixed motives behind these endeavors: la Cour's religious beliefs and motivation to sustain rural societies by providing them with access to electricity provided a parallel with contemporary food and health entrepreneurs; Shuman's identification of solar power as a solution to the depletion of finite resources might also qualify him as a green entrepreneur interested in sustainability avant la lettre; and Jacobs and Eneas were conventional entrepreneurs who saw opportunities to profit from gaps in the emerging energy system based on fossil fuels. The challenge was that those gaps progressively declined with falling fossil fuel prices and the spread of national grids. The experience of Shuman in Egypt was an early indication that, absent a technological breakthrough which enabled solar and wind energy to become sufficiently cheap that it could compete with fossil fuels, it was only likely to progress if governments provided material support.

Conclusion

During the nineteenth century elite conservationists focused on preventing the wasteful depletion of the world's resources, whether pristine forests or colorful birds, by profit-hungry capitalists. A parallel development, virtually unnoticed by mainstream contemporaries let alone future historians, was the creation of for-profit businesses which offered alternatives to the dominant model. These proto-green businesses shared a perception that the industrialization of agriculture and of food might be polluting people's bodies with ingredients which damaged their health, and that communities lacking access to electricity were unsustainable. These early motives, including health and social improvement, would serve as foundations for later, more explicit, concerns for the natural environment. In food and health especially, but not exclusively, entrepreneurial motivation reflected engagement with wider social movements, distinctive religious and spiritual agendas, and countercultural beliefs. In solar and wind energy, similar types of entrepreneurs coexisted with conventional entrepreneurs who saw voids which could be profitable to fill.

In the big picture of the making of the industrial West, the entrepreneurs and firms examined here may appear marginal, even irrelevant. It was conventional firms in search of profits which pulled off the enormous task of feeding rapidly expanding populations and providing them with energy. In contrast, at best a niche market for healthy food and lifestyles was created in some industrialized countries. Wind energy helped provide electricity in rural Denmark and the United States, as did solar in Egypt, but they proved to be transient moments.

Yet in a longer-term perspective, many foundations of future green business had been laid. In food, health stores and Reform Houses proved durable creations. The insistence by Graham, Kellogg, and Cook onwards that processed food and food grown with chemicals was bad for human health became a fundamental assumption of the natural and organic food business. Poul la Cour, Frank Shuman, and others had identified the importance of access to energy for the sustainability of societies, and perceived that wind and the sun could provide that energy. Rudolf Steiner had offered a radical vision of sustainability, and outlined practical paths to achieve that vision through economic-spiritual enterprises, biodynamic agriculture, education, and architecture. These ideas, outlandish as they seemed to almost everyone, would drive future innovations across multiple industries. The practical achievements of these decades included the formation of foundational principles of organic agriculture, and the first parabolic solar troughs. These innovations would return decades later in greater force and motivated by new needs, not least of which was saving the planet from catastrophic climate change.

Notes

1. Rondo Cameron, *A Concise Economic History of the World* (Oxford: Oxford University Press, 1989), pp.189–93.

2. Giovanni Federico, "Growth, Specialization, and Organization of World Agriculture," in Larry Neal and Jeffrey G. Williamson (eds.), *The Cambridge History of Capitalism*, vol. 2 (Cambridge: Cambridge University Press, 2014), pp.52–60.

3. Stephen Mosley, *The Environment in World History* (London: Routledge, 2010), pp.73–5.

4. Federico, "Growth," p.49.

5. Geoffrey Jones, *Multinationals and Global Capitalism* (Oxford: Oxford University Press, 2005), pp.50–2.

6. Derek J. Oddy, *From Plain Fare to Fusion Food* (Woodbridge: Boydell Press, 2003), chapters 1–3.

7. Alfred D. Chandler, *Scale and Scope* (Cambridge, MA: Harvard University Press, 1990), pp.149–61.

8. Peter J. Atkins, Peter Lummel, and Derek J. Oddy (eds.), *Food and the City in Europe since 1800* (Aldershot: Ashgate, 2007), chapters 7–10.

9. Thomas Richards, *The Commodity Culture of Victorian England* (Stanford, CA: Stanford University Press, 1990), pp.168–204.

10. Oddy, *From Plain Fare to Fusion Food*, pp.30–2.

11. James Harvey Young, *Pure Food: Securing the Federal Food and Drugs Act of 1906* (Princeton, NJ: Princeton University Press, 1989).

12. In 1931 the Graham cracker was launched in its present sugary form. Adee Braun, "Looking to Quell Sexual Urges? Consider the Graham Cracker," *The Atlantic*, January 15, 2014.

13. Gerald Carson, *Cornflake Crusade* (New York: Rinehart & Co, 1957), pp.52–3; Samuel Fromartz, *Organic, Inc.* (New York: Harcourt, 2006), pp.148–9.

14. Peter J. Atkins and Derek J. Oddy, "Food and the City," in Atkins, Lummel, and Oddy (eds.), *Food and the City*, p.8.

15. Carson, *Cornflake Crusade*, chapter 5; Fromartz, *Organic, Inc.*, p.151.

16. Carson, *Cornflake Crusade*, chapters 8–10; Frank Murray and Jon Tarr, *More than One Slingshot: How the Health Food Industry is Changing America* (Richmond, VA: Marlborough House, 1984), pp.13–14; Fromartz, *Organic, Inc.*, pp.153–5.

17. Ray Hill, *The Health Food Store: A Nostalgic Look at the First—Its Origins, Philosophy and Development* (Stroud: Nuhelth Books, 1998), pp.5–10; William Shurtleff and Akiko Aoyagi, *History of Seventh-Day Adventist Work with Soyfoods, Vegetarianism, Meat Alternatives, Wheat Gluten, Dietary Fiber and Peanut Butter (1863–2013)* (Lafayette, CA: Soyinfo Center, 2014), p.248.

18. Murray and Tarr, *More than One Slingshot*, chapter 1.

19. Ben Yagoda, "The True Story of Bernarr Macfadden," *American Heritage* 33, no. 1 (1981).

20. Alain Drouard, "Reforming Diet at the End of the Nineteenth Century in Europe," in Atkins, Lummel, and Oddy (eds.), *Food and the City*, pp.220–1.

21. Christof Mauch, "Introduction," in Christof Mauch (ed.), *Nature in German History* (New York: Berghahn Books, 2004), pp.2–4.

22. Judith Baumgartner, *Ernährungsreform: Antwort auf Industrialisierung und Ernährungswandel* (Frankfurt: Peter Lang, 1992); Eva Barlösius, *Naturgemässe Lebensführung: zur Geschichte der Lebensreform um die Jahrhundertwende* (Frankfurt: Campus, 1997); Florentine Fritzen, *Gesünder leben: die Lebensreformbewegung im 20. Jahrhundert* (Stuttgart: Steiner, 2006).

23. Barlösius, *Naturgemässe Lebensführung*, pp.23, 103, 106–12, 129, 183: Baumgartner, *Ernährungsreform*, pp.115–16.

24. Fritzen, *Gesünder leben*, p.44.

25. Baumgartner, *Ernährungsreform*, p.109.

26. Fritzen, *Gesünder leben*, pp.46, 48.

27. Baumgartner, *Ernährungsreform*, p.116.

28. Fritzen, *Gesünder leben*, p.51.

29. Gordon Kennedy and Kody Ryan, "Hippie Roots & the Perennial Subculture," <http://www.hippy.com/php/article-243.html>, accessed August 20, 2009.

30. Gordon Kennedy, *Children of the Sun: A Pictorial Anthology, from Germany to California 1883–1949* (Ojai, CA: Nivaria Press, 1998), pp.125–6.

31. Kennedy and Ryan, "Hippie Roots."

32. Kennedy, *Children of the Sun*, pp.125–6.

33. Kennedy and Ryan, "Hippie Roots"; Benedict Lust, *Yungborn: The Life and Times of Dr. Benedict Lust and Pilgrimages to the Great Masters* (East Wenatchee, WA: Healing Mountain Publishing, 2006 edition); Friedhelm Kirchfield and Wade Boyle, *Nature Doctors: Pioneers in Naturopathic Medicine* (Portland, OR: Medicina Biologica, 1994).

34. Kennedy and Ryan, "Hippie Roots"; Lust, *Yungborn*; Kirchfield and Boyle, *Nature Doctors*.

35. Corinna Treitel, "Artificial or Biological? Nature, Fertilizer, and the German Origins of Organic Agriculture," in Denise Phillips and Sharon Kingsland (eds.), *New Perspectives on the History of Life Sciences and Agriculture* (Cham: Springer, 2015).

36. Holger Kirchmann et al., "Fundamentals of Organic Agriculture," in Holger Kirchmann and Lars Bergström (eds.), *Organic Crop Production: Ambitions and Limitations* (Dordrecht: Springer, 2008), pp.13–38; Gunter Vogt, "The Origins of Organic Farming," in William Lockeretz (ed.), *Organic Farming: An International History* (Trowbridge: Cromwell Press, 2007), pp.14–16; Gunter Vogt, *Entstehung und Entwicklung des ökologischen Landbaus im deutschsprachigen Raum* (Bad Dürkheim: Stiftung Ökologie & Landbau, 2000), chapter 3.

37. Baumgartner, *Ernährungsreform*, pp.125–33, 159–60, 191–2, 179.

38. Crystal Smith-Spangler et al., "Are Organic Foods Safer or Healthier Than Conventional Alternatives? A Systematic Review," *Annals of Internal Medicine* 157, no. 5 (2012), pp.348–66.

39. The best general introduction to Steiner is Gary Lachman, *Rudolf Steiner: An Introduction to His Life and Work* (New York: Penguin, 2007).

40. Peter Selg, *Rudof Steiner: Life and Work*, vol. 1 (Great Barrington, MA: Steiner Books, 2014), p.xv.

41. Uwe Werner, *Das Unternehmen Weleda, 1921–1945: Entstehung und Pionierzeit eines menschengemässen und nachhaltig ökologischen Unternehmens* (Berlin: BWV, 2014), pp.21–2; Rudolf Steiner, *The Threefold State: The True Aspect of the Social Question* (London: Allen & Unwin, 1920).

42. Drouard, "Reforming Diet," p.221.

43. Peter Selg, *Dr. Oskar Schmiedel, 1887–1959: Der erste anthroposophische Pharmazeut und Weleda-Direktor. Eine Dokumentation* (Arlesheim: Ita Wegman Institut, 2010), pp.52, 66–73; Werner, *Das Unternehmen Weleda*, pp.13–16.

44. Selg, *Steiner*, p.xix.

45. Cited in <http://architecturesteiner.com>, accessed October 22, 2016.

46. Kenneth Bayes, *Living Architecture: Rudolf Steiner's Ideas in Practice* (Edinburgh: Floris Books, 1994).

47. Fiona Gray, "Between Theory and Practice: Rudolf Steiner Philosopher and Architect," *Association of Architecture Schools of Australasia (AASA) Proceedings*, Deakin University, 2011; Carole M. Cusack, "'And the Building Becomes Man': Meaning and Aesthetics in Rudolf Steiner's Goetheanum," in Carole M. Cusack and Alex Norman (eds.), *Handbook of New Religions and Cultural Production* (Leiden: Brill, 2012), pp.173–91.

48. <http://cancure.org/12-links-page/45-iscador-mistletoe>, accessed January 4, 2016.

49. Liselotte Frisk, "The Anthroposophical Movement and the Waldorf Educational System," in Cusack and Norman (eds.), *Handbook*, pp.193–211.

50. Christoph Lindenberg, *Rudolf Steiner: Eine Biographie, Vol. 2: 1915–1925* (Stuttgart: Verlag Freies Geistesleben, 1997), pp.698–701.

51. Frederick Amrine, "Discovering a Genius: Rudolf Steiner at 150," <http://www.anthroposophy.org/fileadmin/vision-in-action/being-human-2011-01-Amrine-Discovering.pdf>, accessed July 18, 2016.

52. Werner, *Das Unternehmen Weleda*, pp.24–5.

53. Ibid., pp.28–9, 31.

54. Ibid., p.63.

55. Ibid., p.36.

56. Ibid., pp.35–6.

57. Fiona Gray, "Rudolf Steiner: Occult Crank or Architectural Mastermind," *Architectural Theory Review* 15, no. 1 (2010), pp.43–60; <https://www.goetheanum. org/The-Goetheanum-Building.133.0.html?&L=1>, accessed August 2, 2016.

58. Werner, *Das Unternehmen Weleda*, p.43. The initials IIAG stood for Internationale Laboratorien und Klinisch-Therapeutisches Institut Arlesheim A.G.

59. Werner, *Das Unternehmen Weleda*, p.48.

60. Ibid., pp.50–1.

61. Selg, *Schmiedel*, pp.10, 100–1; Werner, *Das Unternehmen Weleda*, pp.54–6.

62. Vogt, *Entstehung*, pp.98, 116, 126; Herbert H. Koepf, "Bartsch, Erhard," in Bodo von Plato (ed.), *Anthroposophie im 20. Jahrhundert: Ein Kulturimpuls in biografischen Porträts* (Dornach: Verlag am Goetheanum, 2003), p.53.

63. Uwe Werner, *Anthroposophen in der Zeit des Nationalsozialismus, 1933–1945* (Munich: Oldenbourg, 1999), p.82.

64. Alex Norman, "Cosmic Flavour, Spiritual Nutrition: The Biodynamic Agricultural Method and the Legacy of Rudolf Steiner's Anthroposophy in Viticulture," in Cusack and Norman (eds.), *Handbook*, pp.214–18.

65. Rudolf Steiner and Ita Wegman, *Fundamentals of Therapy* (Whitefish, MT: Kessinger Publishing, 2010 edition).

66. Werner, *Das Unternehmen Weleda*, pp.61–2.

67. Selg, *Schmiedel*, pp.101–2.

68. Werner, *Das Unternehmen Weleda*, pp.83, 87, 103.

69. Selg, *Schmiedel*, pp.120–54.

70. Heiner Ullrich, "Rudolf Steiner (1861–1925)," *Prospects: The Quarterly Review of Comparative Education* 24, no. 3–4 (1994), pp.555–72, reprinted at <http://www. ibe.unesco.org/publications/ThinkersPdf/steinere.pdf>.

71. Werner, *Das Unternehmen Weleda*, p.106.

72. <http://www.drhauschka.com/about-dr-hauschka-skin-care/our-history>, accessed January 31, 2016.

73. Koepf, "Bartsch, Erhard," p.53.

74. Herbert H. Koepf and Bodo von Plato, *Die biologisch-dynamische Wirtschaftsweise im 20. Jahrhundert: Die Entwicklungsgeschichte der biologisch-dynamischen Landwirtschaft* (Dornach: Verlag am Goetheanum, 2001), pp.73–5.

75. Gunter Vogt, "The Origins of Organic Farming," in William Lockeretz (ed.), *Organic Farming: An International History* (Trowbridge: Cromwell Press, 2007), pp.19–22.

76. Arie Hollander, "'Tegen Beter Weten In': De Geschiedenis van de Biologische Landbouw en Voeding in Nederland (1880–2001)," Utrecht University Ph.D., 2012. I am grateful to Dick Hollander for sharing his work.

77. Bill Day, "Ehrenfried Pfeiffer, the Threefold Community, and the Birth of Biodynamics in America," <https://www.biodynamics.com/threefold-day>, accessed February 3, 2016.

78. Astrid Kander, Paulo Malanima, and Paul Warde, *Power to the People: Energy in Europe over the Last Five Centuries* (Princeton: Princeton University Press, 2013), pp.131–8, 157.

79. Sean Patrick Adams, "The US Coal Industry in the Nineteenth Century," <http://eh.net/encyclopedia/?article=adams.industry.coal.us>, accessed January 8, 2016.

80. Kander, Malanima, and Warde, *Power*, p.131.

81. Geoffrey Jones, *Multinationals and Global Capitalism* (Oxford: Oxford University Press, 2005).

82. Kander, Malanima, and Warde, *Power*, p.267.

83. William J. Hausman, Peter Hertner, and Mira Wilkins, *Global Electrification* (Cambridge: Cambridge University Press, 2008), chapter 1; IER, "History of Electricity," August 29, 2014, <http://instituteforenergyresearch.org/history-electricity>, accessed June 13, 2016.

84. Christopher F. Jones, *Routes of Power: Energy and Modern America* (Cambridge, MA: Harvard University Press, 2014).

85. William Stanley Jevons, *The Coal Question: An Enquiry Concerning the Progress of the Nation, and the Probable Exhaustion of Our Coal-Mines* (London: Macmillan, 1865).

86. Kander, Malanima, and Warde, *Power*, p.155.

87. Robert W. Righter, *Wind Energy in America: A History* (Norman, OK: University of Oklahoma Press, 1996), pp.24–5.

88. Ibid., pp.42–54.

89. Interview with Paul Jacobs, December 1, 2010, Minnetonka, Minnesota.

90. Righter, *Wind Energy*, pp.90–104.

91. Thorkild Kjærgaard, *The Danish Revolution 1500–1800: An Ecohistorical Interpretation* (New York: Cambridge University Press, 1994).

92. Flemming Tranaes, *Danish Wind Energy*, <http://www.spok.dk/consult/reports/danish_wind_energy.pdf>, accessed July 2, 2016; Righter, *Wind Energy*, p.61.

93. Per Dannemand Andersen, "Review of Historical and Modern Utilization of Wind Power," <https://www.scribd.com/document/294233554/Review-HIstorical-rrghfgyhgvcModern-Utilization-Wind-Power>, accessed October 22, 2016.

94. Jens Vestergaard, Lotte Brandstrup, and Robert D. Goddard, "A Brief History of the Wind Turbine Industries in Denmark and the United States," *Academy of International Business (Southeast USA Chapter) Conference Proceedings*, November 2004, pp.322–7.

95. Ibid.; Paul Gipe, *Wind Energy Comes of Age* (New York: John Wiley, 1995), pp.53–4.

96. Robert Y. Redlinger, Per Dannemand Andersen, and Poul Erik Morthorst, *Wind Energy in the 21st Century* (Basingstoke: Palgrave Macmillan, 2002), p.44: Gipe, *Wind Energy*, pp.171–4.

97. Interview with Paul Jacobs; Marcellus L. Jacobs, "Experience with Jacobs Wind Driven Electric Generating Plant 1931–1957," *Proceedings of the United Nations Conference on New Sources of Energy*, 1961.

98. Jennifer Puddicombe, "Solar Thermal Electric Power," *Science Creative Quarterly* 6 (2011), <http://www.bioteach.ubc.ca/solar-thermal-electric-power/>, accessed February 2, 2016.

99. Frank T. Kryza, *The Power of Light: The Epic Story of Man's Quest to Harness the Sun* (New York: McGraw-Hill, 2003), p.28.

100. Alexis Madrigal, *Powering the Dream: The History and Promise of Green Technology* (Cambridge MA: Da Capo, 2011), pp.84–6.

101. <http://renewablebook.com/2010/08/03/chapter-excerpt-aubrey-eneas-and-the-birth-of-solar-steam-power/>, accessed August 22, 2011.

102. Travis Bradford, *Solar Revolution: The Economic Transformation of the Global Energy Industry* (Cambridge, MA: MIT Press, 2006).

103. Daniel M. Berman and John O'Connor, *Who Owns the Sun? People, Politics, and the Struggle for a Solar Economy* (White River Junction, VT: Chelsea Green Publishing, 1996), p.15.

104. Ibid., chapter 1.

105. Frank Shuman, "Power from Sunshine: A Pioneer Solar Power Plant," *Scientific American*, September 30, 1911, p.291.

106. Kryza, *Power of Light*, pp.81–9.

107. Anonymous, "An Egyptian Solar Power Plant, Putting the Sun to Work," *Scientific American*, January 25, 1913, p.88.

108. <http://renewablebook.com/chapter-excerpts/350-2/>, accessed August 22, 2011.

109. Kryza, *Power of Light*, p.257; L. C. Spencer, "A Comprehensive Review of Small Solar-Powered Heat Engines: Part 1. A History of Solar-Powered Devices Up to 1950," *Solar Energy* 43, no. 2 (1989), pp.191–6.

2

Poisoned Earth: Green Businesses, 1930s–1950s

From the 1930s through the 1950s, environmental advocates struggled to appeal to wider constituencies across the world, as the momentum of the earliest environmental efforts began to dissipate or fizzle. By mid-century, green-inclined businesses faced an uphill battle to win over consumers and influence policy.

There are several metrics of declining environmentalism. Fewer new environmental associations were created than previously. Social campaigns against coal smoke pollution foundered, and in Germany the antismoke campaign almost entirely wilted after World War I.[1] The globalization of environmental concerns which appeared to be underway before World War I also dissipated. Paul Sarasin's Commission for the International Protection of Nature was rendered moribund by the outbreak of the war, and his efforts to revive it before his death in 1929 were unsuccessful. International conferences on protecting wild fauna and flora were held in 1923 and 1928 but yielded no notable outcomes.[2]

The momentum behind conservation slowed down also, although not entirely. In the United States, President Franklin Roosevelt was an ardent conservationist who established, among other things, twenty-nine national parks and monuments, and oversaw the planting of two billion trees—while simultaneously building dozens of hydroelectric dams which destroyed habitats.[3] There were also some connections between government and ecology in Nazi Germany after 1933. Adolf Hitler, a vegetarian, passed a major animal protection law soon after getting into power. Although Nazi environmentalist policies were as incoherent as most of their other policies—party factions took quite different positions— concrete policies were enacted, including the Reich Nature Protection Law in 1935, which extended some environmental protections.[4]

Beyond the concerns of right-wing ideologues, the attention of much of the world was preoccupied by other crises. The Wall Street Crash of 1929 ushered in the Great Depression, an era of high unemployment and falling incomes. Attention shifted to socioeconomic sustainability, not environmental sustainability, with the introduction of Social Security in the United States in 1935 and the development of the welfare state in much of Western Europe after World War II. The war itself wrought unprecedented environmental destruction, but it also drove technological innovation, in weapons, computers, and medical vaccines. The victory of the Western democracies was widely interpreted as a triumph of superior technology. The result was a new era of confident belief that technology was a force for good, as well as an essential tool in winning the subsequent Cold War between the West and the Soviet Union.[5] By then industrial production had spread beyond the Atlantic economy. During the 1930s the Soviet Union launched a planned economy based on heavy industrialization. After the war, the newly independent countries of Asia and Africa turned to state planning and heavy industry to try to build modern economies, and to counter the poverty seen across all of them.[6]

In the industrialized world, recovery from wartime devastation and renewed growth were the top priorities. As the 1950s got underway, the era of the economic miracle began in Europe and Japan, greatly assisted by expanding oil production and falling energy prices. There were new goods and new patterns of distribution, and new ways of advertising thanks to television. Multinational firms led the renewal of global capitalism after the era of war and depression. They diffused innovations made in corporate research laboratories in the United States, which had become the primary driver of industrial innovation. They proved remarkably successful at diffusing the spread of desirable consumer goods, such as automobiles and refrigerators, blissfully ignorant of the resulting growth of emissions of lead and CO_2 from automobiles and fluorocarbons from refrigerators.[7]

Conventional capitalism was equally creative and triumphant in meeting the appetites of Western consumers. During the 1950s, US beef producers turned to the Central American rain forests for the lean beef needed for hamburgers. Coffee companies sought new sources of supply for the surging instant coffee market. There were massive social and ecological consequences, mostly negative, including the destruction of large amounts of forest.[8] The environmental historian Christian Pfister has popularized the phrase "the 1950s syndrome" to describe the era's unprecedented wasteful consumption of resources and energy.[9]

The darkening ecological clouds did not pass unnoticed. Many in the scientific community expressed grave concerns. The botanist Roger Heim, the director of the French National Museum of Natural History, published a book called *Destruction et protection de la nature* in 1952 which laid out in a broad fashion the global environmental challenges, but it struggled to make an impact outside the scientific community.[10] An initiative by a small group of American scientists led to a new nonprofit organization called The Nature Conservancy in 1951, but this had no full-time staff for another decade.[11] There were also local social movements objecting to environmental degradation. In the United States, left-wing anti-nuclear movements campaigned against the environmental damage of nuclear testing.[12] In West Germany, there were also local protests against deforestation and industrial pollution, but there was no relevant legislation before the 1960s.[13] Nevertheless, for most governments, voters, and consumers, the occasional pollution incident was a price worth paying for affluence, especially at a time when science and technology were assumed to have enormous capability to solve the world's problems.[14]

Consequently, the decades immediately before and after the war were an era when environmental concerns were largely muted, even as environmental problems intensified. The entrepreneurs who sought to build ecological concerns into their business models faced an uphill struggle to consumers who shared their concerns. One such case is the American publisher and organic food publicist Jerome Rodale, who, beginning in the 1930s, campaigned in favor of organic food and warned of environmental threats. As we will see later in the chapter, his message was heard by only a few, even three decades later when he published *Our Poisoned Earth and Sky* in 1964.[15] His and other stories of mid-century green businesses—across food, health, solar and wind energy, the beauty industry, and architecture—are the subject of this chapter. As we will see, green entrepreneurs, across a disparate range of industries, faced similar challenges at a time when environmental awareness was in decline.

The slow growth of the organic food business
We saw in Chapter 1 that by the 1920s a number of businesses had been founded in Germany, Britain, and the United States, with a focus on the

importance of eating food grown without chemicals and not processed with them. The huge declines in incomes ushered in by the Great Depression and the destruction caused by World War II left little room for businesses and movements organized around food quality. The postwar decades were no less challenging as large corporations delivered increasing amounts of processed and frozen food at cheap prices supported by skillful marketing and advertising campaigns. The world agricultural system continued to be remarkably successful: between 1938 and 2010, production per capita grew 60 percent. There remained much hunger and malnourishment in the world, but this was primarily the result of waste and inequality.[16] Growth in food production was largely driven by enhanced technology. The application of chemical fertilizers spread from the West to Asia and Latin America, whose agricultural systems had remained "natural," as they had previously lacked the money to pay for such innovations. This trend intensified from the 1960s.[17] Entrepreneurs who offered alternatives to the mainstream food industry faced multiple barriers. Consequently, green entrepreneurs in food simmered below most consumers' awareness as a small, geographically fragmented business.

It was in German-speaking Europe, with the Reform Houses and the biodynamic movement that the cause of natural food found its largest support, but even there turbulence was the norm rather than the exception. The Demeter organization went into liquidation in 1930. It was rebuilt by Erhard Bartsch who expanded activities to more products than just grains, and developed closer ties with the Reform Houses in Germany.[18] He also developed clearer criteria that farmers needed to follow to be certified, including that seeds had to come from plants which had been grown for three generations of the plant without use of chemical fertilizers, and that the land should not have had any chemical fertilizers used during the previous three years. A new Demeter organization was launched in 1932.[19] Demeter formally trademarked its logo with the Munich patent office in 1932, limiting it carefully to products deriving solely from biodynamic methods. The Experimental Circle continued to conduct certification, and checked the practices of farms using the Demeter trademark. By the early 1930s, Demeter connected around fifty completely biodynamic farms and some 400 that engaged in partially biodynamic agriculture. Biodynamic agriculture was especially taken up by large estates in the eastern parts of Germany, but could also be found in farms in Switzerland and Austria, as well as the Netherlands, Britain, Sweden, and Norway.[20]

The advent of the Nazi regime in Germany in 1933 impacted both the bio-dynamic movement and Reform Houses. Elements of the Nazi Party were supportive of organic agriculture. This fitted a broader pattern, also seen in Britain and elsewhere, in which extreme right-wing groups supported organic farming and other natural lifestyles which they contrasted with the modern decadence they perceived all around them.[21] In Germany, some parts of the biodynamic movement also cultivated and benefited from the Nazi government. The Demeter organization became attached to the Nazified Life Reform movement in 1935.[22] After 1939 the Nazi paramilitary SS even established a venture which opened agricultural plantations around concentration camps which were operated according to biodynamic principles, and which marketed Demeter products.

Yet the occult nature of biodynamism was strongly disliked by other elements in the Nazi regime. The Anthroposophical Society was banned in 1935. Waldorf schools were also banned for a period after 1938.[23] Weleda came under criticism, but survived by stressing its Swiss ownership.[24] Reform House retailers also faced political challenges. There were accusations of undermining the fertility of German soil through opposition to artificial fertilizers. Like many other German institutions, the Reform movement survived by compromising with Nazi ideology. An estimated 2,000 Reform Houses in Germany remained in business at the end of the 1930s.[25]

In retrospect, one of the most important developments of the era was the development of alternative models of organic farming in the English-speaking world which were largely unrelated to Rudolf Steiner's philosophy. Instead, traditional agricultural systems in East Asia provided the inspiration. The first steps in this direction had already been taken before World War I. Franklin H. King, an American agricultural professor, traveled through China, Korea, and Japan to observe local agricultural methods. Alarmed by the use of chemical fertilizers in the United States, he published a book in 1911 calling for a "world movement" for an alternative agriculture based on the natural principles he had seen in Asia.[26] Subsequently British scientists working in interwar British India took this insight further. Robert McCarrison, a doctor, studied Hunza tribesmen (in present-day Pakistan) and concluded that their apparent longevity rested on a nearly vegetarian diet of whole grains, vegetables, fruit, and milk products.[27]

Albert Howard, the most influential figure for the further development of organic agriculture, was also profoundly influenced by India. The son of a farmer, Howard was trained in agricultural chemistry and graduated from Cambridge University in natural sciences. He joined the British colonial service, and during the 1920s worked at an agricultural research institute in India. Charged with improving plant productivity, he studied the traditional agricultural methods practiced in the country, and read King's work on Chinese farming. He developed the "Indore method" of composting out of experiences in India.[28] Retiring to Britain in 1931, Howard continued his experimentation. He was aware of, but skeptical about, biodynamics, and had no interest in Steiner's esoteric theories. In 1940 he published the hugely influential *An Agricultural Testament*.[29] The book made the case against the use of chemical fertilizers, and instead advocated environmentally informed practices to enrich soil fertility. The book represented a milestone in the theory and practice of organic agriculture, and was highly influential in ecological thought on both sides of the Atlantic.[30]

Howard had no entrepreneurial interests. Nevertheless, his work had an important influence on postwar organic agriculture in both Britain and the United States In the former country, Howard, along with McCarrison, was a formative influence on Lady Eve Balfour, a British farmer who launched an experimental organic farm after studying their research. In 1943 she wrote *The Living Soil*, which had already gone into five editions by 1945. It drew on evidence on farming and diet throughout the world, to argue that the healthiest food was grown without chemicals. Balfour maintained that all living things were integrated in a holistic way and mutually dependent. "The false idols of comfort and money," she wrote in the postscript of the first edition, "must be dethroned, and the Christian God of service put in their place."[31] Balfour drove the creation of the organic advocacy group in Britain known as the Soil Association in 1946 which would, in time, become important in developing non-biodynamic organic standards. However, attempts to link the few organic farms in the country with consumers were largely unsuccessful. A journalist and farmer, Frank Newman Turner, established the Wholefood Society in 1948. It developed a certificate of authenticity, the Whole Food Mark, but these initiatives never achieved traction through lack of funding.[32] Donald Wilson, a founding member of the Soil Association, took a further step in this direction by establishing the Organic Food Society in 1959, which opened a retail shop in London called Wholefood. This was the sole retail outlet for organic food in Britain, and it took years just to break even.[33]

The challenges of developing an organic food business were not unique to Britain. There was a range of such challenges, from how and by whom to grow organic food, to persuading consumers to buy it. Even if supply and demand could be created, there remained the challenge of how to penetrate existing conventional distribution and retail channels in order to meet the hoped-for demand.

In the context of affluent, consumerist postwar America, these challenges were as much, or even greater, than in Britain, and it took persistence and patience to begin to tackle the issues. These virtues were symbolized by Paul Keene. A math teacher at a New Jersey college, he encountered the work of Howard while living in India on a two-year teaching contract. In 1939, he also met and was deeply impressed by the Indian spiritual guru Mohandas K. Gandhi. "My experience in India inspired me to change my life completely," Keene later recalled. "After my contacts with Indian life I was no longer content with formal teaching. I had to get closer to the basics of life. I had to become more directly dependent on the soil."[34]

While in India, Paul Keene met his wife Betty, an American born to missionary parents. After the couple returned to the United States, they began teaching at the Threefold Farm, where they met Ehrenfried Pfeiffer, still working at the Kimberton farm in Pennsylvania. Exposed to the ideas of both Howard and Steiner, in 1946 the Keene's bought a 100-acre farm called Walnut Acres in central Pennsylvania and began organic farming: their first harvest came from six old apple trees on the farm. The Keene's slowly developed a business selling the products of the farm using mail order: a clever solution to reaching consumers when conventional channels had no interest in organic foods. By the 1960s, Walnut Acres had sufficient sales that it began buying natural foods produced elsewhere for its mail order business. The business became the pioneer of a commercial market for organic food, and served as a role model for a new generation of organic farmers in the United States.[35]

Another entrepreneur would also have a major formative impact on the embryonic organic food market in the United States, although this was not obvious from his initial career. The son of a New York grocer and one of eight children, Jerome I. Rodale was physically weak as a child. In 1914, the death of his father, at the age of 50, when he himself was only 15, heightened Rodale's personal health concerns. Changing his surname from Cohen to Rodale in 1921 because of fears that anti-Semitism was retarding his career, he worked as an accountant, including for the Internal Revenue Service, until 1923, when he and his brother Joe established a small electrical manufacturing business called Rodale Manufacturing in New York. In 1930, after falling sales due to the Great Depression, the company moved to cheaper premises in Pennsylvania. It was at this stage that Rodale began to pursue an interest in publishing as a small and unprofitable part of their larger and profitable electrical manufacturing business.[36]

Rodale's preoccupation with health drove his publishing activities. In 1939 he published a book called *Sleep and Rheumatism*, which recommended people with the disease should sleep in bigger beds with ergonomic mattresses.[37] In his new rural location, he planted his own vegetables in the small yard behind his house. However, it was an encounter with the work of Albert Howard which transformed Rodale. He bought a farm near Emmaus, Pennsylvania on which to experiment with Howard's methods of enriching the fertility of the soil. The farm lost money, but Rodale observed that his health improved as he worked on the farm and ate an organic diet. In 1942 he started a magazine called *Organic Farming and Gardening* to chronicle his experiments on the farm. The first issue featured an article by Howard. Rodale printed 14,000 free copies of the first issue, and sent them to farmers. The twelve paid subscriptions the magazine received in return indicated the low level of interest in the farming community, but interest emerged among home gardeners. The journal was soon renamed *Organic Gardening*.[38]

It was in publishing rather than farming that Rodale made his greatest impact. At a time when there was minimal interest in ecology, let alone organic farming, he strove tirelessly to emphasize the importance of the subject. *Organic Gardening* and the many books published under the imprint of the publishing house he founded, Rodale Press, were important in getting the term "organic" into more widespread use in the United States.[39] In 1947 he launched the Rodale Diet, which listed foods appropriate to an organic diet. In the same year he launched a nonprofit foundation—the US Soil Association, later known as the Rodale Institute—to encourage research in organic farming. It was financed by his conventional manufacturing business, which was as profitable as Rodale Press was unprofitable. His foundation supported Pfeiffer's research which appeared to show that mice fed on an organic diet were less irritable and less likely to die of stomach disorders than mice that ate food employing chemical fertilizers.[40]

Rodale focused much of his critical attention on the United Stated Department of Agriculture (USDA), the long-established US federal agency for agriculture, which he blamed for being unwilling to consider the claims of organic agriculture as legitimate. He also disliked the medical profession for prescribing pharmaceuticals to patients instead of a healthy organic diet.[41] After the death of his brother Joe, and the consequent need to buy out his widow's 50 percent share in the manufacturing company having put Rodale Press under great financial pressure, the business was restructured. It began to seek more advertising revenues. By 1958 the press's sales reached $2 million, and it finally became commercially viable. In 1960 Rodale started a new publication, *Compost Science, The Journal of Waste Recycling*, sold to large firms and city governments concerned with waste disposal.[42]

Rodale had an increasingly broad vision of the environmental challenges faced by the world. The 700-page *Our Poisoned Earth and Sky*, published in 1964, discussed in detail the environmental and health challenges in food production, drugs and cosmetics, water and air, and ended with the dangers of nuclear power. It was a deeply holistic analysis, based on the view that humans had a "common interest shared by every living thing in the welfare of the whole biological community."[43] The book was full of vivid examples of environmental degradation, including London's smog, the polluted air of Los Angeles, and the "black rain" of oily soot which rained on South Boston on May 13, 1960.[44] However, the book was more earnest than influential, being hardly noticed compared to Rachel Carson's *Silent Spring*, published two years earlier, which will be discussed in Chapter 3.[45]

There were no real European equivalents of Keene and Rodale, but the Reform and biodynamic traditions kept the organic food market alive in German-speaking countries even as postwar consumerism got into full swing. In Germany, the Reform Movement survived the embarrassments of collaboration with the Nazi regime, and the postwar division of the country into West and East Germany. By 1956 there were still up to 190 Reform Houses operating in Communist East Germany, but they were tightly controlled and were not part of the trade association of the Reform Houses in West Germany.[46] In West Germany there was renewed growth both in the number of Reform House shops and their revenues, despite ideological tensions between new entrants and older firms concerning whether products were being made in accordance with the ideals of the movement.[47] There were new supply challenges too because of the loss of supplies from the large estates now in located in East Germany. It was more challenging to conduct the farming in the smaller family-run farms in West Germany, where many farmers' Christian beliefs were hostile to anthroposophical ideology, and where there was competition from farmers whose yields increased with chemical use. Consequently, there were fewer than 100 biodynamic farms in West Germany at the end of the 1950s.[48]

The Eden cooperative, discussed in Chapter 1, also survived the Nazi era, but the original settlement was located in East Germany. The Communist regime allowed it to continue operating without direct state control until the early 1970s, but it had little impact on the Reform products business in the West. However, a cooperative member and Eden employee named Kurt Grossmann set up a new West German subsidiary in 1949, which became the new center of the business. The old cooperative owned half the shares. Grossmann was at first the only employee, renting space in a fruit juice production plant; the firm subsequently rented the full plant in 1958 and bought its own facility in 1963, by which time the firm had over 100 employees. The new company took up the old Eden principles for production once again, but added greater emphasis on avoiding harmful substances and on using produce from organic-biological farming as much as possible. Fruit juices, canned goods, and honey were the major products, sold only through Reform House retailers.[49]

In neighboring Switzerland, a different organic tradition emerged. The key figure was Dr. Hans Müller, the head of the Swiss Farmers' Movement for a Native Rural Culture, which sought from the 1930s to protect farmers' traditional way of life, including strong Christian beliefs, from the threats posed by the industrialization of agriculture. Müller sought to build on traditional farming methods to pursue organic farming without chemical pesticides and fertilizers, a method which he called "organic-biological."[50] After the war Müller founded an organic product distributor which undertook direct shipping of food packages to customers, and sold to Reform Houses. In the Zurich area, he even sold to Migros, the large conventional Swiss cooperative retailer. Migros did not identify Müller's produce in its stores as organic, yet the products sold well.[51]

Müller had an early awareness that consumers might be prepared to pay a premium for better food devoid of chemicals, if there could be legible standards. He thus introduced a certification system which included guidelines, a quality seal, and model contracts which ensured that a whole farm must be converted to organic methods. Müller specified the allowed fertilizers and even imposed fines for breaking the rules. He and his wife also ran an educational institution to help farmers with the shift to organic operations. His ideas were derived in part from Reform natural farming, but he also incorporated ideas from Albert Howard and other English-speaking authors.[52] It still remained a challenge to get farmers to convert, however, as pesticide-free yields typically went down and neighboring farmers often looked askance at them.[53]

Müller's farmers eventually found a market in the Hipp baby food business which spanned Switzerland and Germany. Founded in Bavaria by Georg Hipp in 1932, it ran into political problems because the strongly Catholic Hipp family were critical of the Nazi regime. The business survived the war, and in the late 1950s launched pre-cooked baby food, a product then only seen in the United States. By then Hipp had begun using organic ingredients.[54]

The involvement in organics arose by a circuitous route. The Hipp family had a strong Swiss connection, as Georg's wife was Swiss. When one of the firm's managing directors became sick in 1954, he visited a well-known doctor in Zurich, Dr. Max Bircher-Benner. The doctor had become a passionate advocate of natural foods after one of his patients had miraculously recovered after he had prescribed, on the recommendation of a vegetarian acquaintance, a diet of raw fruit and vegetables.[55] He had invented, decades previously, a special cereal he called "muesli," which consisted of freshly-ground grains soaked in water and mixed with grated apples. When he met Bircher-Benner, the doctor advised the Hipp manager to eat muesli for breakfast. Georg soon resolved to manufacture it commercially for the Swiss market, but it needed to be made from naturally grown grains that contained no chemical substances.[56]

Hipp found a solution when he met Hans Müller. The firm began buying the products of Swiss farmers influenced by Müller. It also bought an old farm near Pfaffenhofen in Bavaria to start growing products themselves. They began making muesli in Switzerland in 1954 and opened an Austrian factory in 1967 to produce baby food in glass bottles. However, it was Georg's eldest son Claus, who became head of the firm in 1967, who began to accelerate the conversion of products to organic, and even then the conversion to wholly organic took decades.[57]

Beyond Germany and Switzerland, there were solitary efforts to promote organic farming and consumption. In France, Henri-Charles Geffroy founded

La Vie Claire, a magazine designed to disseminate information on natural food products, in 1946. Suffering from poor health since childhood, he found relief after encountering a treatment based on Reform House practices in Berlin which included avoiding processed foods and meat, and emphasized cereals, fruits, and vegetables usually eaten raw. In 1948 he created a cooperative with a group of friends which sold fruits, vegetables, and wheat bread grown without chemical fertilizers to subscribers of the magazine. In 1950 he developed a new recipe for pure wheat bread. In the following year he launched a company, L'Aliment Sain, which sold his bread along with other organically grown products, and publicized a diet with a strong emphasis on organic agriculture.[58]

In other European countries, there was virtually no organic movement. This was the case in the Netherlands, where government policy focused on raising production and productivity through large land reclamation projects and the vigorous use of chemical fertilizers. During the postwar decades, the Netherlands featured the highest use of pesticides and fertilizers per hectare in the world, a strategy supported by the government, and no farmers appear to have been interested in organic practices. A Dutch branch of the Soil Association was founded in 1950, but it remained marginal for another two decades.[59]

By the 1960s, then, there had only been very slow progress in spreading organic agriculture, creating distribution channels and building a customer base in Western markets. Motivated by personal experiences of bad health and/or religious convictions, a handful of individuals sought to make the case to farmers and consumers, and to create distribution channels to link the two parties. Jerome Rodale stands out as the most emblematic figure, less through the scale of commercial success than through his persistence, his use of his conventional business to fund his publishing efforts, and his holistic vision that it was the very nature of consumer society itself which was the root cause of environmental problems. Still, the German-speaking countries, thanks to the Reform Movement, had created the greatest number of retail outlets for natural and organic food.

Contesting unnatural beauty

If the natural and organic foods market was still tiny by the 1960s, it was relatively enormous compared to the emergent natural beauty business. This was an inherently challenging business for entrepreneurs who wanted to employ natural ingredients: the modern industry which had emerged during the nineteenth century was the antithesis of green for multiple reasons.

First, the industry grew on the basis of aspirational brands sold in stylish packaging, and typically advertised by using attractive celebrities and models who seemed capable of defeating the aging process. Cosmetics companies such as Max Factor were closely connected with Hollywood. The make-up they made for movie stars was then sold to the general market. Based on the argument that people, more particularly women, could take control of their appearances and make themselves more attractive, the whole point of the modern industry was to avoid looking natural. Skillfully exploiting fears of aging and unattractiveness, the industry grew rapidly, scarcely being touched by the Great Depression and the world wars. As it grew, the industry became profitable for department stores and other retailers, who invested in its further growth.[60]

A second challenge for entrepreneurs was that the pre-modern beauty industry, which stretched back thousands of years to the ancient Egyptians, had been based on natural ingredients, many of which, such as the white lead widely used in cosmetics and hair dyes, were hazardous. There was nothing safe about many natural ingredients. The creation of the modern industry had been based on the replacement of hazardous natural materials by the apparently safer, as well as more effective, ingredients produced by the science of chemistry.

Unlike the case of food, the use of chemicals in cosmetics was strongly associated with making things safer and more effective. Some leading companies, including the French hair care company L'Oréal and the American cosmetics company Helena Rubinstein, made much of the fact that they sold the products of modern science, and were safe as a result. When consumer safety legislation began to be passed, the beauty industry was excluded. It was not included, for example, in the Food and Drug Act passed in the United States in 1906. It was only after serious consumer campaigning which highlighted safety risks from some products that, in 1938, the regulation of the cosmetics industry was placed under the jurisdiction of the Food and Drug Administration (FDA). However, there was no requirement for manufacturers to submit information on cosmetic product ingredients, with the exception of the statement of warning that certain hair dye ingredients could cause injury.[61]

It was against this background that the entrepreneurs who sought to create a market for beauty products using only natural ingredients encountered, for decades, little interest. Natural beauty became the preserve of the eccentric and the marginal. Among the former was Emil Bronner, a scion of a soap-making factory going back five generations to mid-nineteenth-century Germany. Trained as a soap-maker, the 21-year-old Bronner immigrated to the United States in 1929 and moved to Milwaukee two years later. He had strong, thoroughly unconventional views. He was a Jew, his wife was Catholic, and his three children were baptized as Lutherans. A vocal campaigner for global peace, he became increasingly eccentric after his wife died in 1944, being temporarily committed to a lunatic asylum by his sister before moving to Los Angeles in 1947.

In Los Angeles, Bronner, in the midst of campaigning against both Communism and water fluoridation, started a health food and soap business. He had worked for a soap and perfume company in the 1930s, and had already developed an aversion to synthetic detergents. In his new start-up, he sold health foods, mainly mineral salts, to health food stores, and he also began to mix peppermint soap, which he initially gave away during his speeches about world peace and religious tolerance. In 1948 he began selling Dr. Bronner's Pure Castile Soap, made on a craft basis using natural ingredients, with no advertising. Bronner put his spiritual thoughts on product labels, including the moral ABC that "Absolute Cleanliness is Godliness."[62]

Bronner saw business in the same manner as Rudolf Steiner: as a means to support his social and ideological agenda. He spoke in Pershing Square in Los Angeles, a hot-bed of radical activism, about the need for world unity, for people to respect each other and the environment. He argued that planetariums were the temples of the future, where humanity could see how trivial their differences were in the context of the universe as a whole.[63] Although he always preferred natural ingredients, his ecological convictions grew after he met his fourth wife at a health food convention. In 1963 they moved to Escondido, a small town just outside San Diego. Bronner put his phone number and address on signs in front of his house, as well as on his soap bottles, so consumers could contact him directly. When people rang, conversation regularly turned to his religious and political ideas. The message and the products attracted a small niche market. By the late 1960s sales were $1 million per annum.[64]

In early postwar Europe, too, and especially France, there were efforts to develop natural cosmetic products, often by people with formal education in biology and medicine, with an interest in the health benefits of natural products, and sometimes with a social agenda. The latter included Yves Rocher. Concerned that his small village of La Gacilly in Brittany was losing its population as people moved to the towns, Yves Rocher started a company in 1959 to create jobs. The small venture made plant-based cosmetics distributed through mail order.[65]

By the 1960s none of the natural beauty businesses had reached the scale of even Walnut Acres. They faced a powerful incumbent industry, whose very rationale was that it was effective in changing natural appearances. Not surprisingly, the few entrepreneurs who tried to create alternative businesses were motivated by concerns other than getting rich. These individuals shared either a strong social agenda or a concern about health. Their ventures remained wholly marginal to the mainstream market.

Building for sustainability

During the nineteenth century industrialization had been accompanied by fast urbanization in the West. By 1910 over 40 percent of Americans and Western Europeans lived in towns, while only 18 percent of the world population did so. During the middle of the twentieth century urbanization intensified and spread. By 1970 around 70 percent of Americans and Western Europeans were urban dwellers, as was 37 percent of the (much increased) world population. This reflected fast urbanization in the Western world; while 7 percent of Latin Americans lived in towns in 1910, the urban share had risen to 57 percent in 1970.[66] Over time there was a huge increase in the size of cities also. In 1950 there were only two "mega cities" with populations of over 10 million: New York/Newark (12.3 million) and Tokyo (11.3 million). By 1975 there were three: Tokyo (26.6 million), New York/Newark (15.7 million), and Mexico City (10.7 million). By 2000 there were eight such cities.[67]

The unprecedented scale of urbanization involved an enormous amount of new design and construction. The new homes that needed building were not simply functional; they became symbols of status and wealth. They were designed by architects who formed their own professional associations as urbanization took hold: the Royal Institute of British Architects was formed in 1834, and the American Institute of Architects in 1857. While the norm in pre-industrial societies was that large buildings were primarily the preserve of aristocratic elites and religious faiths, this was no longer the case in the new industrial era. Industrial magnates built mansions in towns and estates in the countryside both to enjoy and as signs of conspicuous consumption.

The building of houses, towns, and factories involved millions of builders and contractors. Over the course of the nineteenth century architects and builders also increasingly worked with urban planners.[68] The expansion of the built environment by private and public actors was a logistical triumph, but posed a massive challenge for the natural environment. The wholly new challenges of collecting and disposing of urban waste are discussed in Chapter 4. Industrial cities consumed resources on an unprecedented scale, increasingly globally.[69] They burned and consumed energy on a massive scale. The coal smoke that blanketed Victorian cities drove early environmental activism. When regulations began to control pollution, the height of industrial chimneys was raised to limit the human health consequences of toxic emissions. Sulphur dioxide emissions when mixed with moisture form acid rain, which by the 1960s caused lakes and rivers to acidify.

As cities expanded geographically, their inhabitants used automobiles to travel, resulting in massive generation of greenhouse gases such as carbon dioxide. They also lived in high-rise buildings, or skyscrapers, which first appeared in late nineteenth-century Chicago and New York, made possible by the invention of elevators, steel beams, and big pieces of glazing. They consumed large amounts of energy and emitted large amounts of greenhouse gases as they were continuously heated in the winter, and continuously cooled with air conditioning systems in the summer. Skyscrapers that were constructed with a mainly glass façade, which proliferated from the 1950s, consumed particularly huge amounts of energy because of heat loss and gain.[70]

Buildings and cities, then, were at the center of many of the world's ecological problems. Architects became an important source of ideas about how the built environment should contribute to a more sustainable world. They were inherently engaged in broader lifestyle issues and the ways societies were organized. Although not trained as an architect, Rudolf Steiner's Goetheanum buildings had been an early statement of the case that the design of buildings exercised a profound influence on people. However, like the growers and retailers of organic food, architects needed consumers. While Steiner and his supporters paid for their own building, the architectural profession needed to persuade clients to commit money to turn ecological ideas into buildings. If the cost of construction and operation of a proposed building was too high compared to a conventional building, typically it would not be commissioned. Over the next century, the more ecologically minded architects typically had to struggle to find commissions beyond wealthy individuals and, occasionally, public institutions, even as they developed important visions of how the built environment of the industrial age could become more sustainable.

Wealthy individuals formed the bedrock of commissions in the lengthy career of the American architect Frank Lloyd Wright. Wright coined the term "organic agriculture" to describe an architectural philosophy which sought to achieve harmony between buildings and the natural environment. During the 1900s Wright developed his Prairie House style outside of Chicago, drawing on Japanese traditions adapted to the specific environmental conditions of the Midwestern prairie. The houses were open plan with long windows facilitating the connection between the interior and the outside. His style evolved through several stages over the following decades, and his many contributions included a "solar hemicycle house" in 1943 which established him among the pioneers of using engineered passive solar design. In 1936 he also founded and designed a utopian community in Wisconsin, where he lived, called Taliesin. After contracting pneumonia in 1936, he moved to Arizona and began building Taliesin West, the first of a series of architectural utopias built in that state.[71]

A visionary on an even grander scale was Buckminster Fuller, who never formally qualified as an architect, and did not even have a license until he was awarded an honorary one in the late 1960s. Born in 1895 to a wealthy family in Massachusetts, he was a rebel who got expelled from Harvard before patenting, with his father-in-law, a new process for producing reinforced concrete buildings. He developed a business around the idea of creating an inexpensive, mass-produced building that could be airlifted to its location, but the venture went bankrupt in 1927. This episode appears to have ended Fuller's hope of a successful entrepreneurial career, and he began reinventing himself as a visionary expert on how science and technology could save the planet, especially by developing low-cost, mass-produced housing.[72]

This was the purpose of the Dymaxion House, planned in the 1920s and revised in 1945, which was a circular aluminum house that included an interior space which was completely flexible, and which could be mass-produced and erected in two days. In 1947 Fuller developed the geodesic dome. Lightweight, cost-effective, and easy to assemble, the dome could enclose more space without intrusive supporting columns than any other structure. Unlike many of Fuller's ideas, which were either never turned into reality or were self-financed, the dome found clients. In 1953 he designed his first commercial dome for the Ford Motor Company headquarters in Dearborn, Michigan, and created a 250-foot dome for the United States Pavilion at the World's Fair in Montreal in 1967. The US military became a big client also, using lightweight domes to cover radar stations at installations around the Arctic Circle.[73]

Fuller was a polymath. He was an inveterate publisher and inventor, and taught at multiple universities. His Dymaxion Map, patented in 1946, was a flat world map designed to make people think differently and holistically about the Earth.[74] He was an early user of the term "spaceship Earth." In 1969, three years after the economist Barbara Ward had published a book entitled *Spaceship Earth*, he published a wide-ranging book called *Operating Manual for Spaceship Earth* which, among other things, warned of the fateful consequences of running out of fossil fuels.[75]

While Wright and Fuller might be seen as embracing some ecological elements rather than being entirely green—Fuller's use of aluminum would later be seen as environmentally damaging—a more clearly environmentalist approach emerged in the concept of bio-climatic architecture. This was developed during the 1950s by Victor and Aldar Olgyay, twin brothers who had opened an architecture practice in Budapest, Hungary in 1938, and moved to the United States ten years later. They asserted that each climatic region demanded different architectural forms, in contrast to the homogenization that seemed to be spreading with industrial architecture. They were especially important in encouraging the use of passive solar energy. The brothers were prolific authors, held university posts, and unlike many ecological architects were able to secure some commissions: Victor designed around twenty buildings, mainly between 1957 and 1963. Although the concept of climate responsiveness was accepted, cost and other considerations limited its application.[76]

It was beyond the West that the concepts of climate-responsive design and the avoidance of excessive energy and resource consumption were taken up in radical ways. The use of passive solar, outdoor living spaces and local and recycled materials were central tenets of the school of tropical architecture associated with Otto Koenigsberger.[77] The use of traditional building techniques was the major theme of the work of the Egyptian architect Hassan Fathy, the most clearly ecological figure working in the profession at the time. He grew up in a prosperous Egyptian landowning family, but he never visited the land as his father considered the countryside dirty. His mother had a more romantic view of the countryside, which Fathy followed. After being refused admission to the School of Agriculture in Cairo, he graduated in architecture at what became Cairo University in 1926. He was sent to supervise the construction of a school at a small town on Talkha and was horrified by the squalor. "Neither capitalists nor the state seem willing to undertake the provision of peasant houses, which return no rent to the capitalists and too little glory to the politicians," he later wrote. "Abandoned by God and man, they dragged out their short, diseased, and ugly lives in the dirt and discomfort to which they had been born."[78]

Fathy began to explore how cheaper houses could be built for the poor, and started to turn away from the modern styles which were, by then, dominant in Egypt. He turned instead towards rediscovering vernacular traditions. He designed his first mud brick buildings in the late 1930s. Sun-dried earth block is a poor conductor of heat, keeping houses cool in the day. He used ancient design methods and materials, as well as knowledge of the rural Egyptian economy and a wide array of ancient architectural and town design techniques. He trained local inhabitants to make their own materials and build their own buildings. While seeking to serve the poor, he also worked for rich clients who wanted their houses built in traditional styles. In 1946 he was commissioned by Egypt's Antiquities department to build New Gourna Village for 3,000 families who were raiding the ruins at Luxor. He launched a visionary project which sought to rediscover local tradition. His purpose, he wrote, "was always to restore to the Gournis their heritage of vigorous locally-inspired building tradition, involving the active cooperation of informed clients and skilled craftsmen."[79] A vital part of the project, Fathy wrote, was "to extend the resources of the Gournis by giving them trades that would earn them money." These included traditional building skills, which, once learned, villagers could sell to adjacent villages.[80]

The Gourna project received international acclaim, but Fathy's career did not flourish. In 1957, frustrated with bureaucracy, he moved to Athens to collaborate with international planners evolving the principles of ekistical design under the direction of Constantinos Doxiadis. He returned to Egypt in 1962, and began a second major town-planning project at New Baris, but found himself widely dismissed as a romantic dreamer. Both at Gournis and New Baris he found the residents were not enthusiastic about building their own homes. This idea worked even less well when he was invited, shortly before his death in 1989, to design a new community for Muslims called Dar-al Islam near Abiquiu in New Mexico. Cost overruns finally resulted in Saudi Arabia pulling out its financing of the project. While Fathy's book *Architecture for the Poor*, published in English in 1973, turned him into an international figure, he was not able to achieve his radical social ideas in practice, and he spent the last years of his career testing his ideas on commissions from wealthy clients for rest houses.[81]

As industrialization and urbanization intensified, the built environment became highly problematic for the natural world. Cities and their buildings consumed natural resources on an unprecedented scale, and emitted greenhouse gases on an equally impressive scale. A number of architects explored ways to consume fewer resources in buildings, and to make them relevant to the natural environment rather than in opposition to it. Their journeys down this route were sometimes triggered by physical encounters, such as Fathy's with rural poverty in Egypt. Although a disparate cohort of individuals and views, a number of these figures such as Buckminster Fuller attracted much more attention than their counterparts in organic food, natural beauty, and wind and solar energy. As innovative and skillful architects, many of them had wealthy clients for their designs. Unfortunately, their radical visions, whether Fuller's Dymaxion House or Fathy's broader social vision, could not be executed. The achievements might be best summarized as laying intellectual foundations rather than transforming their profession.

Alternative energy: who cares?

The middle decades of the twentieth century were challenging for wind and solar businesses. As we saw in Chapter 1, many of the early ventures in the late nineteenth century had been driven by conventional entrepreneurs motivated by the opportunities of filling voids in the supply of energy. By the middle decades of the twentieth century, such opportunities had largely disappeared.

The fundamental challenge was the cheap cost and government support of fossil fuels. In the early 1950s coal still provided over three-quarters of Western Europe's energy use and half of that of the United States. Despite widespread government protection for their giant coal industries—in Britain and some other European countries the industry was nationalized and turned into giant state corporations—this dominance was increasingly challenged by oil as large corporations expanded supplies from the large and favorable concessions they held across the Middle East, Africa, and Latin America. Between 1958 and 1970, world oil prices were near stable at $3.00 per barrel, but adjusted for inflation and expressed in 2010 dollars, the price of crude oil declined from $19 to $14 per barrel over the period.[82] By 1972 coal accounted for one-fifth of US energy and petroleum just under one-half by that date.[83] Carbon emissions soared in this period.[84]

Across the world electricity production soared and was closely controlled by governments. Britain and other European countries nationalized their electricity supply industries after World War II. In the United States, the Public Utilities Holding Company Act of 1935 created a system of closely regulated regional monopolies.[85] By the 1960s electrical utilities provided power to 90 percent of American households from central power plants.[86] In Germany, electricity was supplied by thousands of municipal monopolies, which were closely controlled and coordinated through the Deutsche Verbandgesellschaft, founded in 1948 on the initiative of RWE, the largest electricity and gas utility company, which ran the national grid.[87] Beyond the West, electricity expansion soared, with national governments increasingly taking control of the foreign-owned utilities which had frequently created the electricity systems of Asia, Africa, and Latin America as they sought cheap electricity supplies to drive economic growth.[88]

The combination of closely regulated or government-owned electricity industries, state-owned or protected coal companies, and an oligopolistic petroleum industry producing cheap oil supplies resulted in almost no market opportunity for the wind and solar industries. There were occasional moments when supply concerns made policy-makers consider that it might be strategic to invest in renewable energy capabilities. In 1952 a report to the US President suggested that fossil fuels might be in declining supply. The report devoted a whole chapter to solar energy, which it identified as a major future energy source of what it termed "comfort heating," including hot-water heating and the use of solar energy to power heating and air conditioning systems. It even talked briefly of the possibilities of developing wind energy.[89] Yet this report led to no new policies, in part because of the apparent promise of nuclear energy. The Atomic Energy Commission, created in 1946, raised expectations that a cheap and safe primary source of power was about to come on stream.[90] The US government, like those of Britain and France, was highly invested in the development of civilian nuclear energy because of the overlap with their production of nuclear weaponry. The world's first nuclear power plant for commercial electricity generation, Calder Hall in Sellafield in Britain, opened in 1956, producing both electricity and plutonium for defense purposes.

Solar and wind experiments at this time yielded little commercial success. In wind energy, some individuals explored the potential for scaling up wind machines from Jacobs-style individual wind electric systems. Palmer Putnam, the owner of a large publishing house, became an enthusiastic inventor of wind machines. He secured $1 million in funding to build a pilot large plant from a manufacturer of hydraulic turbines, seeking diversification opportunities. Palmer built his large turbines on Grandpa's Knob in the Green Mountains in Vermont, and in October 1941 made history by delivering power into the electric utility's system. Between 1941 and 1945 the machine, which was connected into the Central Vermont Public Service Corporation's network, accumulated about 1,100 hours of operation. In 1945 one of the blades broke off, and the costs of repair were so great that it never operated again.[91]

There was further technical experimentation in the American industry building on the technical results of the Putnam wind turbine, but the government was now seen as the best hope for funding. Percy H. Thomas, an engineer with the Federal Power Commission, designed two large wind turbines, which he believed could be used in conjunction with hydro-electric power, especially in the American West, where wind could be used when there was a water shortage, and water stored in reservoirs could be used when the winds were not strong. In 1951 Thomas lobbied the US Congress for $2 million to fund a prototype of his wind turbines. The plan envisaged development by a private contractor, but with the electric power integrated into the grid. The draft bill contained several visionary notions that wind power might facilitate the conservation of non-renewables and even have strategic benefits, including reducing dependency on foreign supplies. It found no political support.[92]

In Denmark, too, there was more experimentation. Johannes Juul, the chief engineer at a power utility in Falster, in the south of the country, who had known Paul la Cour, built and put into operation a large wind turbine in 1959. At 78 feet high, it was less complex than the Putnam design, and contained a major innovation—emergency aerodynamic tip breaks—which became a permanent feature of the industry. The turbine operated in regular service for a decade, being the largest turbine in the world, but it was not repaired when a bearing failed in 1967.[93]

It was evident that, absent a major shift in the relative price of fossil fuel versus renewable energy, the wind industry made no economic sense. It was in solar, rather than wind, that a new technology offered the prospect of a breakthrough. The innovation was the development of the photovoltaic cell (hereafter PV) which converted solar radiation directly into electricity, offering an alternative way to generate energy other than by parabolic troughs. There was nothing ecological about this invention, as the research took place at Bell Laboratories, the research facility of the US telecommunications giant AT&T. The physicist Russell Ohl's invention of the silicon solar battery in 1946 was a key breakthrough. In 1954 other Bell Laboratory scientists, including Daryl Chaplin, invented the first PV cell which could produce significant electric power. Their public demonstration of the cell inspired a *New York Times* article to predict that solar cells would eventually lead "to the realization of one of mankind's most cherished dreams—the harnessing of the almost limitless energy of the sun."[94]

The challenge was to execute the dream. The technology was complex, and far too expensive to compete with fossil fuels. The only potential market was one for which cost was not a consideration: the US space program. The program needed a power source for the satellites it was planning. As a result, the US government became the major market for the new industry which developed around Los Angeles, the home of two key institutions developing the space program, Caltech and the Jet Propulsion Laboratory. They were to design the first successful US satellite, Explorer 1, launched in 1958.[95]

The commercialization of the PV solar industry was led by small firms based in the Los Angeles area attracted by the potential of the new satellite market. Leslie Hoffman was a pioneer. He had founded Hoffman Electronics in Los Angeles in 1946 to manufacture small tube radios, then moved into making televisions, and later semiconductors. In 1956, Hoffman acquired National Fabricated Products, which owned the original patent license of the PV Bell Labs technology, and he became increasingly interested in the commercial opportunities of the new technology. He tried to market its value to the US Forest Service to provide batteries for unattended relay stations and envisaged solar cells being used to run emergency call boxes on freeways in southern California.[96] He finally found a market in the US space program. Hoffman's solar cells were used in satellites, beginning with the Vanguard I, the second US satellite which was partially powered by PV cells. This satellite used a small solar array, less than one watt, to power its radios.[97]

A second venture in solar cells was led by Alfred Mann. He had studied physics at UCLA, graduating with bachelor's degrees in 1949 and 1951. His interest in studying light led to a first job with Technicolor, a Los Angeles firm whose color film processes dominated the Hollywood film industry. The Army approached Technicolor for help with light filtering for a missile guidance system but, when Technicolor did not want the work, Mann pursued the $11,200 Army contract by leaving the company and forming a small company called Spectrolab in 1956. Two years later Mann was approached by someone from the Air Force who said they wanted to build a spacecraft powered by solar cells, but there was a problem: solar cells lost efficiency when they got hot.[98] Mann placed the production of solar cells in another company he had founded, Heliotech, which made semiconductors. In 1960 Mann sold the Spectrolab and Heliotech subsidiaries for the (then) substantial sum of $10 million to a fast-growing conglomerate Textron, which was building a presence in military procurement. Former Spectrolab employees would lead a new wave of entre-preneurship in solar. Mann himself became a highly successful serial entrepre-neur over the following six decades, inventing a series of medical products including heart pacemakers, but he never returned to solar.[99]

Hoffman and Mann competed for a very small market for solar PVs, estimated at between $5 and $10 million per year, and almost entirely dependent on the US space program. This had the advantage of restricting interest in the category from larger electronics companies such as Texas Instru-ments, which entered the market only to leave shortly after. The disadvantage, however, was that demand was small and unpredictable; one estimate was that production capacity exceeded demand through the 1960s.[100] Beyond the United States, absent a space program, there was limited investment in solar energy. European electrical companies such as Philips and Siemens conducted some experimental research, but there was no commercial production.[101]

These decades thus saw limited progress in wind and solar energy. Fossil fuels were too cheap for businesses in wind and solar to compete against them, and if governments were interested in a new power source, it was nuclear energy. There were significant technical achievements in wind energy by Palmer Putnam and Johannes Juul in particular, but the costs were too high given the existing technologies. PV solar technology was a breakthrough, but the technology was complex and in need of copious investment to reduce the costs. Leslie Hoffman and Alfred Mann found a small niche market in the US space program, but solar otherwise remained an aspiration rather than a reality as a viable energy supply.

Conclusion

During the decades of the 1930s through the 1950s, most policy-makers, voters, and consumers paid limited attention to the challenges faced by the natural environment, even as ecological costs mounted thanks to urbanization and the burning of fossil fuels. The problem was not ignorance—William Vogt was one of many who identified the mounting environmental challenges—but, rather, the succession of other challenges, from the Great Depression to World War II to the Cold War, and the promise of new technologies, including nuclear energy, to provide a happy ending. With the exception of the niche market for the new technology of PV cells in the US space program, there were no incentives for conventional entrepreneurs to commit to solar or wind as industries. Meanwhile, the barriers for green entrepreneurs were high. Absent major technology advances, wind and solar were wholly unable to compete with conventional fuels. The same challenges stymied the greening of other industries. Most consumers had little interest in organic food or cosmetic products using plants rather than chemical ingredients. The figures considered here all worked on the margins of the business world—some were downright eccentric—and they achieved little towards legitimizing their alternative views in the eyes of consumers and others.

Still, in the face of these obstacles, it is the achievements of the green entrepreneurs rather than their failure to carve out large markets which is so striking. In diverse ways, they stood apart from the prevailing consensus of their time by pursuing, ahead of their time, a model of sustainability. Jerome Rodale, Hassan Fathy, and others stood up to make the case that the conventional world was not heading in a sustainable direction. Motivated by personal experiences of bad health and/or religious convictions, a handful of individuals such as Hans Müller, Claus Hipp, Paul and Betty Keene, and Henri-Charles Geffroy sought to make the case for organic food to farmers and consumers, and to create distribution channels to link the two parties. Emil Bonner and Yves Rocher made beauty products from plants and begun to figure out how to distribute them. There were foundational technological advances in wind energy by Palmer Putnam and Johannes Juul. Architects like Frank Lloyd Wright and Buckminster Fuller proposed radical new ways of thinking about the relationship between architecture and the natural environment. These achievements were dwarfed by the successes of conventional business at the time, but in retrospect they were laying foundations for the future.

Notes

1. Frank Uekötter, *The Age of Smoke* (Pittsburgh, PA: University of Pittsburgh Press, 2009), pp.69–74, 87–103.

2. Fred Van Dyke, *Conservation Biology: Foundations, Concepts, Applications* (New York: Praeger, 2008), p.19.

3. Douglas Brinkley, *Rightful Heritage: Franklin D. Roosevelt and the Land of America* (New York: HarperCollins, 2016).

4. Frank Uekötter, *The Green and the Brown: A History of Conservation in Nazi Germany* (Cambridge: Cambridge University Press, 2006); Uekötter, *Age of Smoke*, pp.103–12; Gesine Gerhard, "Breeding Pigs and People for the Third Reich," in Franz-Josef Brüggemeier, Mark Cioc, and Thomas Zeller (eds.), *How Green Were the Nazis?* (Athens, OH: Ohio University Press, 2005); Karl Ditt and Jane Rafferty, "Nature Conservation in England and Germany 1900–70: Forerunner of Environmental Protection?" *Contemporary European History* 5, no. 1 (1996), pp.16–19.

5. Ramachandra Guha, *Environmentalism: A Global History*x (New York: Longman, 2000), pp.63–8.

6. Ibid., pp.63–6.

7. Stephen Broadberry and Kevin O'Rourke (eds.), *The Cambridge Economic History of Modern Europe*, vol. 2 (Cambridge: Cambridge University Press, 2010), esp. chapters 12 and 15; Victoria De Grazia, *Irresistible Empire: America's Advance through Twentieth-Century Europe* (Cambridge, MA: Belknap Press of Harvard University Press, 2005); Geoffrey Jones, *Multinationals and Global Capitalism* (Oxford: Oxford University Press, 2005), pp.92–101.

8. Richard P. Tucker, *Insatiable Appetite: The United States and the Ecological Degradation of the Tropical World* (Berkeley, CA: University of California Press, 2000), esp. chapters 4 and 6.

9. Christian Pfister, "The '1950s Syndrome' and the Transition from a Slow-Going to a Rapid Loss of Global Sustainability," in Frank Uekötter (ed.), *The Turning Points of Environmental History* (Pittsburg, PA: University of Pittsburgh Press, 2010), pp.90–118.

10. Michael Bess, *The Light-Green Society: Ecology and Technological Modernity in France, 1960–2000* (Chicago, IL: University of Chicago Press, 2003), pp.71–2.

11. <http://www.nature.org/about-us/vision-mission/history/index.htm>, accessed June 1, 2013.

12. Thomas Jundt, *Greening the Red, White, and Blue: The Bomb, Big Business, and Consumer Resistance in Postwar America* (Oxford: Oxford University Press, 2014).

13. Frank Uekötter, *The Greenest Nation? A New History of German Environmentalism* (Cambridge, MA: MIT Press, 2014), pp.60–5.

14. Andrew J. Hoffman, *From Heresy to Dogma* (Stanford, CA: Stanford Business Books, 2001).

15. Jerome I. Rodale, *Our Poisoned Earth and Sky* (Emmaus, PA: Rodale Books, 1964).

16. Giovanni Federico, "Growth, Specialization, and Organization of World Agriculture," in Larry Neal and Jeffrey G. Williamson (eds.), *The Cambridge History of Capitalism*, vol. 2 (Cambridge: Cambridge University Press, 2014), p.49.

17. Stephen Mosley, *The Environment in World History* (London: Routledge, 2010), p.74.

18. Koepf and von Plato, *Die biologisch-dynamische*, pp.121–2.

19. Ibid., pp.122–3.

20. Werner, *Anthroposophen*, p.82; Schmidt, "Landwirtschaft," p.1022.

21. Philip Conford, *The Origins of the Organic Movement* (Edinburgh: Floris Books, 2001), chapter 9; Anna Bramwell, *Ecology in the 20th Century: A History* (New Haven, CT: Yale University Press, 1989), pp.136, 140–8.

22. Gunter Vogt, *Entstehung und Entwicklung des ökologischen Landbaus im deutschsprachigen Raum* (Bad Dürkheim: Stiftung Ökologie & Landbau, 2000), pp.133–51.

23. Uwe Werner, *Das Unternehmen Weleda, 1921–1945: Entstehung und Pionierzeit eines menschengemässen und nachhaltig ökologischen Unternehmens* (Berlin: BWV, 2014), p.149; Peter Staudenmaier, "Organic Farming in Nazi Germany: The Politics of Biodynamic Agriculture, 1933–1945," *Environmental History* 18 (April 2013), pp.383–411.

24. Werner, *Das Unternehmen Weleda*, pp.146, 183, 188.

25. Florentine Fritzen, *Gesünder leben: die Lebensreformbewegung im 20. Jahrhundert* (Stuttgart: Steiner, 2006), pp.78–97.

26. John Paull, "From France to the World: The International Federation of Organic Agriculture Movements (IFOAM)," *Journal of Social Research & Policy* 2 (December 2010), p.94.

27. Vogt, "Origins," p.25.

28. Philip Conford, "Howard, Sir Albert (1873–1947)," *Oxford Dictionary of National Biography*; Conford, *Origins*, pp.51–9.

29. Albert Howard, *An Agricultural Testament* (London and New York: Oxford University Press, 1940).

30. Randal S. Breeman and James A. Pritchard, *A Green and Permanent Land. Ecology and Agriculture in the Twentieth Century* (Lawrence: University Press of Kansas, 2001).

31. Eve Balfour, *The Living Soil* (London: Soil Association, 2006 edition), p.199.

32. Philip Conford, *The Development of the Organic Network* (Edinburgh: Floris Books, 2011), pp.35–6, 223–5.

33. Ibid., pp.226–7.

34. Paul Keene, *Fear Not to Sow Because of the Birds* (Chester, CT: Globe Pequot, 1988), p.vii.

35. Packaged Facts, *The Organic Food and Beverage Market 1996*, Pub ID LA-41900 (April 1996); George de Vault, "What Became of Walnut Acres?," *The Natural Farmer* (Spring 2006).

36. Daniel Gross, *Our Roots Grow Deep: The Story of Rodale* (Reading, PA: Rodale, 2008), pp.1–44.

37. Ibid., p.48.

38. Ibid., pp.55–63.

39. Packaged Facts, *Organic Food*.

40. Gross, *Our Roots*, pp.70–4.

41. Maria McGrath, "Food for Dissent: A History of Natural Foods and Dietary Health Politics and Culture since the 1960s," Lehigh University, Ph.D., 2005.

42. Gross, *Our Roots*, pp.96–100, 106.

43. Rodale, *Poisoned*, p.9.

44. Ibid., pp.488–9.

45. Warren J. Belasco, *Appetite for Change* (Ithaca, NY: Cornell University Press, 1993), p.71.

46. Fritzen, *Gesünder leben*, pp.107, 122–4.

47. Ibid., pp.115.

48. Vogt, *Entstehung*, pp.128–9, 160–79.

49. Judith Baumgartner, *Ernährungsreform: Antwort auf Industrialisierung und Ernährungswandel* (Frankfurt: Peter Lang, 1992), pp.239–51.

50. Vogt, *Entstehung*, pp.197–9.

51. Ibid., p.256.

52. Ibid., pp.202–5.

53. Ibid., pp.222–3.

54. Claus Hipp, with Eva Eleonore Demmerle, *Die Freiheit, es anders zu machen* (Munich: Pattloch, 2008); Claus Hipp, *Das Hipp Prinzip: Wie wir können, was wir wollen* (Freiburg: Herder, 2012); interview with Claus Hipp, February 25, 2013.

55. Albert Wirz, *Die Moral auf dem Teller* (Zurich: Chronos, 1993).

56. Interview with Claus Hipp.

57. See Chapter 6.

58. "Association les Guides de la Nature de la Vie et de la Santé, Biographie d'Henri-Charles Geffroy précurseur en écologie: Pourquoi 'L'Alimentation Saine'?" <http://agnvswebmestre.free.fr/biographie_nadh.html>, accessed August 4, 2011.

59. Arie Hollander, "'Tegen Beter Weten In'. De Geschiedenis van de Biologische Landbouw en Voeding in Nederland (1880–2001)," Utrecht University Ph.D. thesis, 2012.

60. Geoffrey Jones, *Beauty Imagined: A History of the Global Beauty Industry* (Oxford: Oxford University Press, 2010).

61. Norman F. Estrin (ed.), *The Cosmetic Industry: Scientific and Regulatory Foundations* (New York: Marcel Dekker, 1984), pp.164–9.

62. Christina Lubinski, "Emanuel Bronner," in R. Daniel Wadhwani (ed.), *Immigrant Entrepreneurship: German-American Business Biographies, 1720 to the Present*, vol. 5 (German Historical Institute, October 25 2013), <http://immigrantentrepreneurship.org/entry.php?rec=134>, accessed October 22, 2016.

63. <https://www.drbronner.com/our-story/timeline>, accessed October 22, 2016.

64. Lubinski, "Emanuel Bronner."

65. Jones, *Beauty Imagined*, pp.280–1.

66. John McNeil, *Something New under the Sun* (London: Penguin, 2000), pp.281–3.

67. <http://www.un.org/esa/population/publications/WUP2005/2005WUP_FS7.pdf>, accessed December 14, 2015.

68. Anthony Sutcliffe (ed.), *The Rise of Modern Urban Planning, 1800–1914* (New York: St. Martin's Press, 1980); Greg Hise, *Magnetic Los Angeles: Planning the Twentieth-Century Metropolis* (Baltimore, MD: Johns Hopkins University Press, 1993).

69. William Cronin, *Nature's Metropolis: Chicago and the Great West* (New York: W. W. Norton, 1991).

70. McNeil, *Something New*, pp.100–8, 281–95; Mosley, *Environment*, pp.100–10.

71. James Steele, *Ecological Architecture: A Critical History* (London: Thames & Hudson, 2005), pp.71–6.

72. Loretta Lorance, *Becoming Bucky Fuller* (Cambridge, MA: MIT Press, 2009).

73. Steele, *Ecological Architecture*, pp.143–7; "About Fuller," <http://www.bfi.or g/about-fuller/biography>, accessed January 2016.

74. <https://bfi.org/about-fuller/big-ideas/dymaxion-world/dymaxion-map>, accessed July 23, 2016.

75. Buckminster Fuller, *Operating Manual for Spaceship Earth* (New York: Pocket Books, 1970), p.79.

76. Victor and Aladar Olgyay, *Design with Climate: An Approach to Bioclimatic Regionalism* (Princeton, NJ: Princeton University Press, 1963); Vandana Baweja, "A Pre-History of Green Architecture: Otto Koenigsberger and Tropical Architecture, from Princely Mysore to Post-Colonial London," University of Michigan Ph.D., 2008, pp.134–5.

77. Baweja, "Pre-History."

78. Hassan Fathy, *Architecture for the Poor* (Chicago, IL: University of Chicago Press, 1973), p.3.

79. Ibid., p.43.

80. Ibid., p.61.

81. Steele, *Ecological Architecture*, pp.85–93; James Steele, *Hassan Fathy* (New York: St. Martin's Press, 1988).

82. WTRG Economics, "Oil Price History and Analysis," <http://www.wtrg.com/ prices.htm>, accessed January 14, 2016.

83. Martin Chick, *Electricity and Energy Policy in Britain, France and the United States since 1945* (Cheltenham: Edward Elgar, 2007), p.7.

84. Astrid Kander, Paulo Malanima, and Paul Warde, *Power to the People: Energy in Europe over the Last Five Centuries* (Princeton: Princeton University Press, 2013), p.277.

85. Chick, *Electricity*, p.1.

86. Adam Harris Serchuk, "Federal Giants and Wind Energy Entrepreneurs: Utility-Scale Wind Power in America, 1970–1990," Virginia Polytechnic Institute Ph.D., 1995, p.10. In 1963 gas supplied 21%, hydro 19%, and nuclear 0.3% of the electrical utility industry.

87. Luz Mez, "The Germany Electricity Reform Attempts: Reforming Co-optive Networks," in Atle Midttunn (ed.), *European Electricity Networks in Transition* (Oxford: Elsevier, 1997), pp.232–5, 241–3; Robert Milward, *Private and Public Enterprise in Europe: Energy, Telecommunications and Transport, 1830–1990* (Cambridge: Cambridge University Press, 2005).

88. William J. Hausman, Peter Hertner, and Mira Wilkins, *Global Electrification* (Cambridge: Cambridge University Press, 2008), chapter 6.

89. United States, President's Materials Policy Commission, *Resources for Freedom; A Report to the President* (Washington, DC: U.S. Government Printing Office, 1952), vol. 4, chapter 15.

90. Robert W. Righter, *Wind Energy in America: A History* (Norman, OK: University of Oklahoma Press, 1996), p.144.

91. Ibid., pp.126–36.

92. Ibid., pp.136–43.

93. Soren Krohn, "Danish Wind Turbines: An Industrial Success Story" (2002), <http://www.ingdemurtas.it/wp-content/uploads/page/eolico/normativa-danimarca/Danish_Wind_Turbine_Industry-an_industrial_succes_story.pdf>, accessed October 22, 2016; Flemming Tranaes, *Danish Wind Energy*, <http://www.spok.dk/consult/reports/danish_wind_energy.pdf>, accessed July 2, 2016, p.2; Righter, *Wind Energy*, p.150.

94. "Vast Power of the Sun Is Tapped by Battery Using Sand Ingredient; New Battery Taps Sun's Vast Power," *The New York Times*, April 26, 1954, p.1.

95. Phech Colatat, Georgeta Vidican, and Richard Lester, "Innovation Systems in the Solar Photovoltaic Industry: The Role of Public Research Institutions," *Working Paper MIT-IPC-09-008*, Industrial Performance Center Massachusetts Institute of Technology, June 2009.

96. John Perlin, *From Space to Earth* (Ann Arbor: Aatec, 1999), pp.37–8, 164.

97. D. J. Flood, "Space Photovoltaics—History, Progress and Promise," *Modern Physics Letters B* 15.17/18/19 (2001), p.561.

98. Interview with Alfred Mann, August 5, 2002, <http://www.audiologyonline.com/interviews/interview-with-alfred-mann-founder-1745>, accessed October 22, 2016.

99. "Textron Unit Plans to Buy Spectrolab, Inc.," *Wall Street Journal*, June 26, 1961; Stuart Pfeifer, "At 88, Billionaire Inventor Alfred Mann's Motivated by More than Money," *Los Angeles Times*, September 14, 2014, accessed February 7, 2016.

100. Colatat, Vidican, and Lester, "Innovation Systems."

101. Geoffrey Jones and Loubna Bouamane, "'Power from Sunshine': A Business History of Solar Energy," *Harvard Business School Working Paper*, No. 12-105, May 2012.

3

Earthrise and the Rise of Green Business

A sudden emergence of environmentalism as a popular movement during the 1960s and 1970s took many people who had been campaigners for environmental causes by surprise. "Those of us who had been active in the conservation movement for many years, and formerly regarded as eccentrics," William Siri, an American biophysicist and environmentalist who served as President of the Sierra Club, observed, "all of a sudden found ourselves respectable, and no longer called conservationists, but 'environmentalists.'"[1] Paradoxically, green businesses struggled to take advantage of the broader environmental revival of the era.

There are several potential explanations for this second wave of environmentalism, as this shift has often been termed by environmental historians.[2] First, there were serious and very visible water pollution episodes. The synthetic detergents industry's use of non-biodegradable surfactants resulted in foam covering lakes and rivers across Europe and the United States, provoking new regulations over the industry.[3] In June 1969, chemical waste caused the Cuyahoga River in Cleveland, Ohio to catch fire and burn for about twenty minutes. It had happened before, but this time the episode caused a major outcry about water pollution.[4] A few months earlier a disastrous Santa Barbara oil well blowout had spilled 200,000 gallons of oil onto the Californian coastline for eleven days. This event directly led to the National Environmental Policy Act in 1969, a landmark piece of legislation in the United States that required federal agencies to prepare environmental assessments and environmental impact statements.[5]

Second, although environmental disasters were not new, a new generation of articulate writers reached a wider audience about them than had, say, Jerome Rodale. Rachel Carson's *Silent Spring*, published in 1962, is sometimes credited for single-handedly starting the second wave of environmentalism.[6]

Her particular focus was a new set of chemicals patented during and after World War II, especially the pesticide DDT, which she described as poisoning wildlife, fish, and birds. She also implied that DDT was a human carcinogen.[7] The book spent thirty-one weeks on the *New York Times* bestseller list, and sold half a million copies in hard copy, an achievement much assisted by the furious response of the American pesticides industry association, which raised its profile.[8]

There were probably several reasons behind the success of the book, many of whose scientific arguments have not been fully demonstrated. The underlying theme of the interconnectedness of life was effective at reaching a broad spectrum of people extending from bird-watchers to people concerned about their personal health. Carson was also a skilled writer, who had already published a bestseller, which enabled her to give up her job as a zoologist with the US Fish and Wildlife Service. She was also deeply invested in threats to human health after her own diagnosis with breast cancer in 1960, a disease from which she died four years later. Most importantly, she was savvy: she drew heavily on materials on the impact of pesticides collected by two female biodynamic farmers in New York, including a pamphlet by Ehrenfried Pfeiffer, the biodynamic pioneer discussed in Chapter 1, warning of the dangers of DDT. Carson avoided mentioning their contribution out of concerns that a link with organic farming might be used to discredit her arguments.[9]

Carson's book was the first in a series of influential publications warning of environmental dangers by American and European authors, often biologists, during the decade. A year after Carson's death in 1964, Raymond Dasmann warned of the destruction of the natural beauty of California. Jean Dorst and Paul Ehrlich extended the idea of environmental threats to include issues such as over-population.[10] Meanwhile, the economist Barbara Ward, who exercised considerable influence on policy-makers both in her home country of Britain and the United States, joined her long-term concerns for development and social justice with debates concerning environmental sustainability in *Spaceship Earth*, published in 1966.[11]

A third influence on the emergence of the second wave of environmentalism were new social movements which fundamentally questioned existing social and political frameworks. In the United States, anti-Vietnam War protests, women's liberation, and the civil rights movement were the most influential of these movements during the 1960s. During 1968 European capitals, Paris most famously, were swept up in radical student protests. Environmental concerns were only one small dimension of an emergent counterculture, which embraced hippies and political dissent, but these wider social movements facilitated wider citizen participation in environmental protests. Charles Reich's *The Greening of America*, published in 1970, explicitly sought to integrate the need for environmental protection into a broader set of issues including feminism, gay rights, racial equality, and an end to military conflict, excessive consumerism, and corporate power.[12] Social movements sometimes encouraged nascent entrepreneurial activity in green industries such as wind energy, disrupting existing institutional arrangements and values in markets.[13] Yet the very same countercultural energies which drove interest in alternative lifestyles, foods, and energy sources were sometimes, or even often, at odds with the profit motive and capitalism.

The space race unwittingly contributed an iconic image which the nascent environmental movement adopted as a rallying point. On December 24, 1968 American astronaut William Andrews photographed the Earth rising over the lunar horizon on Apollo 8, the first spaceship to orbit the moon. The stunning visual image of the small blue and white planet set against the darkness of space captured imaginations. Named "Earthrise," the photograph was immediately and widely adopted by the environmental movement.[14]

As images of the Earth from space became pervasive, the environmental movement developed powerful institutions within the space of three years. New environmental NGOs were created.[15] The Friends of the Earth was founded in San Francisco in 1969 by naturalist David Brower, the former executive director of the Sierra Club. When the Sierra Club refused to oppose the development of nuclear power in the United States, Brower resigned and started his own group, which became central to the movement. In 1971 Friends of the Earth went international after a meeting in Sweden of environmentalists from Sweden, France, Britain, and the United States.[16] Greenpeace was created in Victoria, Canada in 1971 to oppose US atomic testing in Alaska.[17] On April 22, 1970 the first Earth Day was held in the United States as 20 million Americans took to the streets to demonstrate the need for a healthier environment. The idea originated with Gaylord Nelson, then a Democrat Senator from Wisconsin, after witnessing the oil spill in Santa Barbara. He persuaded Pete McCloskey, a conservation-minded Republican Congressman, to serve as his co-chair.[18]

In 1972 came the first ever United Nations conference on international environmental issues. The initial idea for such a conference arose four years earlier, from the Swedish delegation at the United Nations, which wanted to present an alternative to planned conferences on the peaceful use of nuclear energy. The Swedish Ambassador to the United Nations reached out through a mutual friend to Maurice Strong, a former oil entrepreneur in Canada who had been recruited into the Canadian International Development Agency, and he was appointed the Secretary-General of the conference in Stockholm.[19] Strong was an articulate and passionate leader, heavily influenced by the writings of authors such as Rachel Carson and Barbara Ward.[20] He was particularly successful in figuring out how to overcome some of the skepticism in developing countries towards the environmental worries of the rich West by linking their concerns about development with industrialized countries' concerns about pollution.[21]

Strong secured the attendance of representatives of 113 countries at the conference, although not the Soviet bloc because of an argument about the ability of East Germany, not a UN member, to attend the conference. Strong was determined to make the conference a broad-based event. He commissioned a one-hour film called *Survival of Spaceship Earth* ahead of the event, which appropriately began with the images of the Earth from space.[22] He also encouraged, for the first time, the engagement of NGOs in the event; they were prominent actors in the numerous parallel conferences involving thousands of (mostly younger) people, who were concerned about the environment. Considerable attention was paid to symbolic details, with a mass riding of bicycles by attendees at the start of the conference.[23]

Strong also commissioned an NGO, the International Institute for Environmental Affairs, to prepare a background report for the conference.[24] Written by Barbara Ward and the microbiologist René Dubos, the study was published as *Only One Earth*, with an image of Earth from space on the cover.[25] The book, like the subsequent conference, ranged over multiple issues, including food contamination, agricultural degradation caused by soil erosion and pesticides, waste, and the need to secure clean water.[26] There was even a brief mention in the book of the "so-called greenhouse effect" and the risk that if developing countries used increasing amounts of fossil fuels as they developed, emissions "might set in motion the long-term warming up of the plant."[27] The conference itself led to a new agency, the United Nations

Environment Programme (UNEP), but it lacked the resources and capabilities to achieve much.[28] Indeed, although the Stockholm meeting may have been behind the increase in the number of government bodies worldwide with responsibility for the environment from ten to 100 over the following decade, governmental coordination on environmental policies was to prove challenging.[29]

The new era of increased concern about the natural environment also did not immediately result in a sudden surge of support for green business models. The perceived role of business at the Stockholm conference was decidedly unglamorous. The widespread assumption was that markets were unable to address the environmental externalities which were so damaging on their own, and that "producers"—their terminology for firms—were polluters. Business was not perceived as part of a solution, but rather as central to the problem, something which incidents such as the pesticide industry's attacks on Rachel Carson only confirmed. Ward and Dubos argued that international governmental coordination was the solution, which they argued "required the adoption of a planetary approach by the leaders of nations."[30]

The emphasis on governments reflected dominant beliefs in many countries at the time. In many European countries state ownership of industries was prevalent, while in most of the developing world import-substitution and state planning were in vogue. Within this context, some of the most influential environmental thinkers of the era thought replacing free markets and conventional capitalism was the way to save the planet. It was seen as the most effective means of dealing with the externalities issue. In 1971 the American biologist Barry Commoner, in a bestselling book called *The Closing Circle*, argued that the American economy needed to be restructured to conform to the unbending laws of ecology. He wanted polluting products like detergents to be replaced with natural products like soap.[31] In *The Poverty of Power*, published five years later, Commoner argued that the only effective solution to environmental challenges was to abolish capitalism entirely.[32] A different but equally radical critique of society arose in 1973 when the British economist Ernst F. Schumacher published *Small Is Beautiful*. The book argued that the contemporary focus on size, output, and technology was fundamentally flawed. Instead it championed small, appropriate technologies that empowered people. Schumacher warned of the enormous consumption of finite resources in the postwar era of steady growth. The book described the private ownership of big firms as a "fiction for the purpose of enabling functionless owners to live parasitically on the labour of others," and called for half of the equity of such firms to be socialized.[33]

Ironically, a handful of business leaders, including Maurice Strong himself, were at the forefront of expressing environmental concerns during these two pivotal decades. For example, Robert O. Anderson, who had created a large oil company called ARCO, was prominent in environmental education and campaigning through the Aspen Institute in Colorado.[34] He helped Martin Brower establish Friends of the Earth, and used funds from his personal trust to establish the IIEA to support Strong's Stockholm conference.[35] In Europe the Club of Rome—founded in 1968 by Italian industrialist Aurelio Peccei, a long-time executive of the automobile company Fiat and subsequently the President of the electrical company Olivetti, and the British chemist Alexander King—became an important patron of environmental thinking. In 1972 it commissioned a report from a team at the Massachusetts Institute of Technology to model the consequences of rapid population growth under conditions of limited natural resources. The report, entitled *The Limits to Growth*, predicted that, by the middle of the twenty-first century, the Earth's ecosystem would collapse unless economic growth was curbed.[36]

Yet the relationship between such environmentally conscious business leaders and environmentalists of the era was distinctly uncomfortable. Strong remarked that his business associates often saw him as "flaky," while environmentalists saw his business life "as somehow irreconcilable with the ideologies which drive them."[37] It was not hard to see why this should be the case. Strong returned to Canada in 1976 as head of the newly created state-owned oil company Petro-Canada. Two decades later he took over Ontario Hydro, a huge utility and generator of nuclear energy. Anderson's ARCO discovered the largest pool of usable crude oil in North America at Prudhoe Bay on Alaska's North Slope in 1967, and the pipelines it built through Alaska attracted continued environmentalist protests.[38] Contemporary critics alleged that even the Swedish government's motivation to host the Stockholm conference included showcasing the products of the country's pollution-control technology industry. Swedish engineering companies advertised at the conference, while the automobile manufacturer Volvo hosted a tour of its plant.[39]

It was, as a result, not surprising that the initial outcome of the new environmentalism was to increase regulations over firms. From the 1960s the United States took the lead in the West in introducing new consumer safety and environmental regulations, often serving as a regulatory model for other countries.[40] In 1970 the federal government formed the Environmental Protection Agency, which moved assertively to enforce new environmental regulations over the chemical and other industries, motivated especially by concerns for human health.[41] In 1972 the United States banned the pesticide DDT, two years after Sweden, but over a decade before some European countries such as Britain. After the Stockholm Conference, the United States also took a leading role in new international treaties, such as the London Convention on Dumping at Sea in 1972 and the Convention on International Trade in Endangered Species and Fauna in 1973.[42] In Western Europe, there was also a spate of new environmental legislation, including consumer-related laws on food and drug safety, but the region's laws and regulations were typically behind those of the United States.[43] The impact on environmental regulation in developing countries was less dramatic, as governments there remained focused on development, although there were some cases such as Colombia, which passed its first laws on the environment as a result of the Stockholm conference.[44]

These two decades, then, represent a remarkable break from the subdued environmental concerns for the middle decades of the twentieth century. This was an era of bestselling environmentalist books, mass social movements, United Nations conferences, and new regulatory agencies. Business was now seen, even more than in the past, as the problem, and not the opportunity. There would be no free ride for green business in the second wave of environmentalism.

Prophets in the wilderness

The continued marginalization of green businesses was evident in the case of organic food. Rachel Carson's careful avoidance of a public association with organic agriculture was indicative of this marginalization. Jerome Rodale applauded *Silent Spring* as a "masterpiece" in his journal *Organic Gardening and Farming*, the subscribers to which increased from 300,000 to 750,000 between 1962 and 1972.[45] Carson's warnings of the dangers of pesticides on agriculture eventually resulted in the banning of DDT and others, but not the end of all chemical pesticide use, nor did it spark any growth the market for organic food.

The Rodale business itself struggled for much of the 1960s, entangled in a legal case with the US government over whether a Rodale publication called *Health Finder* had made deceptive claims in its advertising. Rodale focused on writing plays, which were often focused on health issues but were poorly received by critics, as his son Bob took on more responsibility for running the company.[46] It was not until the start of the new decade that things started to look brighter. In May 1970, weeks after the first Earth Day, Rodale convened the first-ever Organic Food Symposium in Allentown, Pennsylvania, which attracted 175 organic growers and owners of organic food stores. On June 6, 1971 Rodale was featured in the cover story of the *New York Times Magazine*. The cover showed him in a suit and tie, walking through a field on the farm, and described him as the "foremost prophet" of the organic movement.[47] Two days later Rodale died of a heart attack while appearing as a guest on *The Dick Cavett Show*.

In both the United States and Europe, organic food businesses and farms remained largely limited to religious, countercultural, or other niche groups. The conventional food industry was huge, and supported—especially in the United States—by government subsidies given to dairy and corn farmers, among others, which kept prices low for consumers. Canned, frozen, and processed products were ubiquitous, thanks to sophisticated advertising campaigns which pitched them as fresh and natural. Food was grown and served using predictable colors, achieved either by favoring genetic strains or else by adding chemicals.[48] Fast food restaurants, beginning with McDonald's in the mid-1950s, built extensive retail and supply chains which offered novel food products at very low prices. Although these innovations started chiefly in the United States, they spread in time to Europe alongside self-service supermarkets.[49]

Within the context of the industrialized food system, interesting farmers and consumers in organic food was an uphill task which only a few people ventured into. In 1960, Frank Ford, a graduate in agriculture, and his wife Marjorie bought a small venture with a stone mill and a storage bin in Hereford, Deaf Smith County, Texas. Ford began selling stone-ground flour to grocery stores against the dominant processed white flour. It took five years for Arrowhead Mills to become profitable, as he slowly built a packaged organic foods business. Even by 1970 their sales were only $100,000. Following an unsuccessful suicide attempt in 1973, Ford was born again as a Christian, and his company took on an increasingly religious dimension. By the follow-ing year Ford had reached thirty-two retailers by traveling around the country and meeting "people who had a little store, almost invariably young folks with a big dream and no financial backing."[50] Ford disliked the idea of scaling his business and wanted people to grow their own food, but by the late 1970s Arrowhead Mills was probably the largest distributor of organic foods in the United States, with 300 products and sales of $10 million.[51] By contrast, McDonald's fast food restaurants alone had annual sales of over $3 billion by then.

During the late 1960s a new generation of entrepreneurs, often coming out of counterculture movements, emerged in organic retailing. They were heavily concentrated in cities with large numbers of students and countercultural activists. A number belonged to supporters of the macrobiotic movement, which emphasized the health benefits of the traditional Japanese diet based on unrefined foods with very little or no milk or red meat, and the avoidance of refined salt and sugar. Healthy food, in turn, was regarded as key to societal health and peace. Macrobiotics came to the United States via Japanese teachers of this philosophy, especially George Ohsawa and his wife Lima. During the 1950s several of Ohsawa's students, especially Michio Kushi and Herman Aihara, settled in the United States. They eventually established tiny restaur-ants and small food stores selling imported miso (fermented soybeans) and natural shoyu.[52]

In 1966 Kushi and his wife Aveline opened a small, below-street-level macrobiotic and natural foods store called Erewhon, named for a utopian novel by the British writer Samuel Butler, in Boston. Kushi had studied political science and law at Tokyo University, and had gone to the United States to do further research at Columbia University, though with his poor spoken English he ended up doing numerous odd jobs. He had arrived with a passionate belief that politics was the way to secure world peace, but over a number of years became disillusioned and more interested in the ideas of Ohsawa. Kushi and Aveline, another Ohsawa student, moved to Massachu-setts, initially teaching shiatsu and aikido, and later macrobiotics. Erewhon initially sold several soyfoods, mainly imported miso and shoyu, purchased from suppliers in New York. Although initially the sales were tiny, the business had a number of distinctive features which set it apart. Like bio-dynamic agriculture, macrobiotics was not simply confined to eating healthier foods without unpleasant additives. Kushi, harking back to nineteenth-century discourses on the societal importance of healthy eating, stressed that healthier eating was part of a lifestyle change which would bring peace to the world. An employee for Kushi noted that they "were intent on changing the world, nothing less."[53] While wholly utopian for a tiny retail shop, it can also be seen as a renewed attempt to position diet beyond the specific concerns of individual health and, instead, to draw attention to its wider role in making societies more sustainable.

However visionary or utopian they were, the Kushis also had a practical side to their plans. Their store tried to educate every potential customer who came through the door, even if there were few of them. There was an early understanding that it was hard to access most products they recommended and that they needed to build a supply-and-distribution chain. In order to achieve this, they hired talented and visionary people.[54]

In 1967 the 21-year-old Paul Hawken was given the management of the store. Hawken, who would in time become a high-profile environmental author, had grown up in Berkeley in California. Berkeley was a veritable epicenter of countercultural ideas at that time. The University of California campus at Berkeley, where his father worked and which he attended without graduating, was a hotbed of political activism. Berkeley was also associated with radical environmental ideas: in 1967 a new radical society there known as Ecology Action began campaigns for recycling and against consumer culture in general.[55] Hawken himself had worked with Martin Luther King's civil rights movement, and in 1965 had been briefly kidnapped by the Ku Klux Klan in Mississippi.[56]

Hawken came into contact with Frank Ford and other natural foods proponents such as Fred Rohe, a leader of San Francisco's hippie community. They traveled together speaking to small groups and, as Ford later wrote, "sitting up to the wee hours of the morning plotting the natural-foods revolution."[57]

Hawken pioneered the concept of contracting with farmers to produce organic crops, which proved a critical step to expand organic agricultural production. In 1968 he established an agreement with Erewhon's first supplier of organically grown grains, a wheat farmer in Montana. Within five years Erewhon had contracts with fifty-seven farms in thirty-five states to provide the company directly with organically grown foods. Erewhon also developed a wholesale distribution business which helped drive overall sales to over $3 million by 1973. This established a standard model which other start-ups followed, sometimes with help from the Kushis and Hawken.[58] However, there was continued fragility in a sector full of small-scale ventures started by countercultural visionaries, and quite divided between macrobiotic and non-macrobiotic views. In 1969 Hawken himself left for Japan, visiting suppliers, and he left Erewhon entirely four years later. In 1981 Erewhon, whose sales had reached $10 million, went bankrupt after accumulating large legal bills after being sued by retailers who complained that it was undercutting them by selling at wholesale prices.[59]

Entrepreneurial ventures in health food did better when they were clustered in areas where the countercultural scene was strong—strong enough to provide a potentially viable market. California was the heart of both the countercultural scene in the United States and significant developments in organic farming. In 1967 the recently created University of California at Santa Cruz hired Alan Chadwick to create a Student Garden Project. The son of affluent parents, Chadwick had studied as a young man with Rudolf Steiner at Dornach and developed a career as a gardener in Britain, South Africa, and the Bahamas, where he transformed a steep hillside into a prolific garden working only with hand tools and biodynamic methods. Chadwick stayed at Santa Cruz for six years, and the Garden Project became a major formative influence on a new generation of Californian organic farmers.[60]

It was also first in California that the pervading dull image of organic food began to be challenged. The San Francisco Bay Area, the center of political activism and countercultural movements, also saw the beginning of a new cuisine which employed organic foods. The key actor was Alice Waters, a graduate of the University of California, Berkeley where she joined the Free Speech Movement and worked in the congressional campaign of an anti-Vietnam War politician. In 1971 Waters opened a small café in Berkeley called Chez Panisse, dedicated to using fresh, local, and seasonal ingredients. She was thus the first restaurant owner to put the word "organic" on her menu. Her invention of "California cuisine" started a revolution in American food tastes, which included a new interest in organic food.[61] By 1980, however, there had hardly been an organic revolution in California. The number of organic farms remained tiny, and hostility from conventional farmers remained high.[62]

Colorado, especially the city of Boulder, also developed a cluster of natural foods businesses. Like parts of California, the state included areas of great striking beauty, which were a draw for hiking and mountain sports enthusiasts who were potential customers and entrepreneurs. From the late 1950s the Boulder city government was active in protecting the environment by not supporting development on the surrounding mountains, purchasing green space around the city, and limiting new housing builds to 2 percent a year.[63] The faculty of the University of Colorado at Boulder included from 1967 the British-born economist Kenneth Boulding, whose warnings about resource scarcity in the "coming spaceship earth" had made him a public figure at environmentalist events before and after the first Earth Day.[64] In 1973 the state introduced the first organic labeling law in the United States. Boulder was also replete with countercultural movements. It was a major center for Buddhism. In the town of Trinidad, about two hundred miles from Boulder, a rural commune known as "Drop City" was established in the late 1960s. Known for its hippie art and Buckminster Fuller-inspired geodesic dome buildings, it was profiled in *Time* and *Life* magazines.[65]

Boulder's entrepreneurial cluster began with a number of small ventures. In 1955 Margaret and Philip Isely began selling vitamins and wholegrain foods, and in 1963 opened a small store in Lakewood while campaigning for a world government. Forty years later, their company Natural Grocers was a half-billion-dollar business still headquartered in Lakewood.[66] The herbal tea company Celestial Seasonings was created in Boulder by Mo Siegel in 1970. Plagued by asthma as a child, he attended a monastery and college preparatory school as a boarder, and was introduced to the mystical *Urantia Book* by a girlfriend. The book, he later observed, "made me examine my values and commit myself to doing something worthwhile with my life . . . I immediately turned to the health food industry."[67] Collecting wild herbs that grew around Boulder, he began experimenting with making herbal tea, launched Mo's 36 Herb Tea, found a steady buyer when a health foods store opened, and by 1974 had sales of $1 million.[68] In 1984 the company was sold to Kraft for nearly $40 million.[69]

Celestial Seasonings served as a successful entrepreneurial role model for other Colorado-based firms, as well as an important employer in the region and source of expertise. By 1980, a business culture grew which saw countercultural figures transition into natural foods retailers and brand-building entrepreneurs. In the former category, Mark Retzloff and S. M. "Hass" Hassan opened Pearl Street Market in Boulder in 1979. Retzloff, an environmental activist at college, and Hassan were followers of an Indian spiritual guru whose Divine Light Mission was then headquartered in Denver. Retzloff went on to found Alfalfa's Market in 1983, which became one of the first retailers to include multiple categories of organic products in a supermarket format, including not only food but vitamins, supplements, and other products.[70]

In Europe, there were fewer examples of distribution companies like Arrowhead Mills or organic brands such as Celestial Seasonings. Instead, multiple small retail outlets and farms reflecting older traditions, including the Reform Movement and biodynamics, coexisted and sometimes conflicted with new start-ups inspired by the countercultural movements and macrobiotics.

In German-speaking countries, the Reform movement continued to provide a retail outlet for natural food products, even though the emergence of supermarkets and self-service stores disrupted their traditional model of offering advice along with products in shops. Reform retailers in Germany had annual revenues of over $64 million in the mid-1960s. There was even some interest in Reform products from conventional retailers, which were required to take classes and pay fees to ensure products bearing the Reform label were not being adulterated.[71]

A new generation of small organic retailers also emerged out of countercultural movements, competing to some extent with the Reform Houses.[72] This was the origin of Rapunzel, which would much later become one of Germany's leading organic food producers, which began when the young married couple Joseph Wilhelm and Jennifer Vermeulen started a self-sufficiency commune on a farm with a small natural health food store in the city of Augsburg in Bavaria, near the farm where Wilhelm had grown up. They had been inspired by friends serving them organic food and visiting an organic retailer in Belgium, Vermeulen's home country. The small shop sold muesli, nut butter, and fruit bars. In 1979 they bought a new farm which operated as a commune in the Allgäu region of southern Germany, a center for people living alternative lifestyles, as well as a long-established location for natural beauty and health tourism.[73]

German organic farming as a whole changed as the techniques developed by Hans Müller in Switzerland spread to the country through the influence of a German doctor named Hans Peter Rusch. Rusch argued that nature consisted of "living particles." He developed a soil fertility test method called "Test Rusch," which was sold to farmers. The scientific basis of these ideas was widely perceived as fragile even at the time, provoking a rift with biodynamic farmers who were more interested in scientifically informed research, even if they also believed in astrological influences and magic preparations.[74]

As in the United States, the macrobiotic movement became an important inspiration for some new start-ups. The most important example in Britain was the expatriate serial green entrepreneur Craig Sams. As so often, an experience of illness during his childhood started an interest in health and food. Born on a farm in Nebraska, his marine father became ill after serving in the Pacific during World War II but staged a full recovery after adopting a diet recommended by a Japanese doctor in Hollywood which included brown rice and whole wheat bread. The family moved to Britain in the 1950s as his father worked for the US Army. Sams, already a vegetarian, got a scholarship to attend Wharton School of Business, where he encountered macrobiotics for the first time and, as he later wrote, "saw organic agriculture and food as the essential foundation on which social justice, environmental integrity and human health could be built."[75]

Sams returned to London and in 1967 he and his brother opened a small macrobiotic restaurant in London, inspired by a restaurant he had seen in New York's East Village. It failed, but a second one called Seed became a center for counterculture artists, with regulars including the Beatles' John Lennon and his wife Yoko Ono, who had followed a macrobiotic diet in Japan. Sams developed a mail-order business, a grain store, and a bakery which made its own peanut butter. Suspecting that the product could find a market beyond people on a macrobiotic diet and countercultural hippies, Sams launched the peanut butter under the Harmony brand in 1972. Within four years, it had sales of $5 million and was sold in conventional food stores.[76] In 1977 he also created a pioneering fruit-juice-sweetened jam which created a whole "no sugar added" category of jam. Because it was not strictly macrobiotic, Sims used another brand name: Whole Earth.[77] Sams was, like Hipp in Switzerland, one of the few European-based natural foods businesses which had built commercially successful brands by the end of the 1970s.

Elsewhere, the combination of for-profit business and organic values created tensions. In France an emergent organic movement split during the 1960s over the difficulties in reconciling the two. The commercialization of a natural fertilizer from calcified seaweed, based on the concepts of Hans Peter Rusch provoked a hostile reaction from supporters of biodynamic agriculture, who founded a new organization called Nature et Progrès (N & P) in 1964. N & P wanted to educate consumers about organic food but struggled to create a business like that of Sims. In 1966 a venture called Solsain, meaning 'healthy soil', was planned in Paris by Roland Chevriot and Claude Aubert, who were associated with the founders of N & P. Chevriot was an engineer with no agricultural training, who became a philosophical adviser to the founders, whilst Aubert was an agronomist who provided technical training for farmers. The original goal was to transport natural foods from rural areas to Paris, and to educate the urban population about the difference between organic and traditionally grown products.[78] However, they had little interest in building such a business. "We were militants," Aubert later explained. "We really were not interested in a business venture, and the profit making part of it did not appeal to us. We ended up selling organic vegetables and fruits here and there, but it never really took off as a fully-fledged business. We had neither the funds nor the will to launch a business venture...we wanted to stay in the non-profit world."[79] As Chapter 6 will show, N & P was indeed more successful at building institutions for organic food than at selling vegetables.

By 1980 the market for organic food remained very small in both the United States and Europe. There had been minor victories: Rodale had been hailed as a prophet days before his death; some viable retail and distribution business had been created; and brands such as Celestial Seasoning and Harmony had broken out of niche markets. Green entrepreneurs such as Frank Ford, Mo Siegel, and Craig Sims, motivated by religious, health, and other non-financial concerns, had brought new ideas and methods to the natural foods business. The most significant developments were not measured in the number of organic vegetables sold, but in the further progress made, by the macrobiotic and other entrepreneurs, in associating the purchase of more natural foods with broader issues of sustainability and the environment. Despite these outcomes, it remained challenging to progress in the context of the vast conventional food industry of branded food producers and supermarket chains, let alone huge government subsidies for conventional farming. Differences within the organic movements themselves, and reluctance or aversion to commercialization and growing, added to the problem of making any impact beyond subcultures.

Beauty and counterculture

If the second environmental wave and related social movements were fairly irrelevant to the organic foods business, it was actually detrimental to the further development of the tiny natural beauty industry. A resurgent feminist movement included a stream of thought that decoration of any sort was oppressive and a symbol of patriarchy. Many radical and educated young women, some of whom no doubt enjoyed organic food, expressed their resistance by no longer wearing make-up or shaving their body hair during the late 1960s and 1970s.[80]

Nor were prominent environmentalists fans of the beauty industry. In *Silent Spring*, Carson wrote of the cancer-inducing chemicals, especially synthetic estrogen, widely used in the industry.[81] Indeed, the people who had strong ecological sentiments typically disliked the whole idea of the industry, regardless of the ingredients of the products. Rodale, for example, devoted an entire chapter of *Our Poisoned Earth and Sky* to criticizing what he described as "synthetic beauty." He complained of health risks of the chemicals in make-up and skin preparations, noted the potential carcinogenic risks posed by some hair dyes, and complained of the absurdities of the advertising. "Cosmetics are really one thing a health-conscious person can and should avoid," Rodale noted.[82]

If the beauty industry was treated as a problem rather than an opportunity by environmentalists and others, a further problem was that quasi-greenness was seen as an opportunity by the marketing-driven conventional industry. As environmental concerns spread and hippies celebrated flower power, the conventional industry moved quite rapidly to use the word "natural" in advertising. This was easily done as plant ingredients had always been used in the industry, but combined with chemicals to act as preservatives. There was a proliferation of mainstream brands which emphasized their natural ingredients and which were advertised using models walking through the countryside and other symbols of the environment.[83] It was not until the mid-1970s that mounting scientific evidence about potentially carcinogenic ingredients used in hair dyes began to direct more attention to actual ingredients, with some prominent brands needing to be reformulated.[84]

During most of these two decades, then, there were only a few new start-ups, primarily in health-related personal care by entrepreneurs with quite similar profiles to those in organic food. Tom's of Maine in the United States originated when the 23-year-old Tom Chappell and his wife Kate left Philadelphia, where he worked for an insurance company, and moved to rural Kennebunk, Maine with the desire to simplify their lives. They did their own organic gardening and ate unprocessed foods. Unable to find natural personal care options for themselves and their children, the Chappells decided in 1970 to create and sell their own in the belief that "environmental protection and profit could be merged."[85]

The Chappells began by making a phosphate-free laundry detergent and then launched the first natural toothpaste in 1975. Shortly afterwards their daughter was born, and they developed the first natural baby shampoo. Natural deodorants, mouthwash, and shaving cream soon followed, all sold through health food stores. Tom Chappell was always a devout Christian, although it was only subsequently that Chappell went to Harvard Divinity School, and the business incorporated a more Christian evangelical set of values. By 1981 the firm had sales of $1.5 million.[86]

Despite the Chappells' success, it was two other businesses, founded on either side of the Atlantic during the second half of the 1970s, that were to mark a step change in scaling the natural beauty industry. The first was called The Body Shop, which began when the 34-year-old Anita Roddick opened a store selling skin and hair care products in the town of Brighton, England. Roddick, the daughter of Italian Jewish immigrants, had been involved previously in women's rights issues in developing countries while working for an international agency in Geneva, and had later traveled throughout Africa and the South Pacific. The decision to open a beauty shop came as a consequence of her husband's desire to spend two years riding on horseback from Buenos Aires to New York City, which required them to sell their existing small hotel business.[87]

Roddick wanted to use natural ingredients, an idea inspired by seeing the traditional beauty practices of women in Tahiti and elsewhere during her travels. After approaching cosmetics manufacturers to make products for her, and being told that the ingredients she proposed were "ridiculous," she reached out to a radical young local herbalist and frustrated make-up artist, Mark Constantine, who would found another natural personal products company called Lush. Roddick prepared product batches in her own kitchen, and packaged them in the cheapest containers she could find—urine-sample bottles. Roddick's breakthrough insight was that much of the dissatisfaction with the conventional beauty industry was not about the ingredients, but about the treatment of women in advertising and the industry's exaggerated claims about its products. She resolved to sell cosmetics in different sizes, rather than big bottles, and to use cheap containers, believing that many women felt, as she did, "conned" that much of the cost of cosmetics was due to "fancy packaging."[88]

The first store did well enough, and when her husband returned in 1977 after his horse died crossing the Andes, the couple began to expand the business. Roddick's emphasis on cheap packaging and environmentally friendly ingredients proved a powerful marketing success, as did her explicit denunciation of the industry for exploiting women. The brand found a market especially among young women who broadly supported environmental issues, and who liked the firm's emphasis on recycling, avoiding animal testing, and supporting social causes. The company used soy inks to print catalogues on recycled paper, for example, and promised it would plant two trees for every tree used to make the paper for its catalogues.[89] Roddick was at the forefront of a trend of cooperation between small entrepreneurial firms and NGOs: in the mid-1980s she was active in supporting Greenpeace's "Save the Whales" campaign.[90] Meanwhile the firm's fast growth was enabled by the creation of its own marketing channel by using a franchising strategy. This turned out to be very effective in presenting the values of the brand directly to potential customers. By 1984 The Body Shop had sales of almost $7 million, with forty-five outlets in Britain and eighty-three elsewhere, and was able to go public.[91]

Roddick's achievement was not so much to grow a successful franchising business but, rather, to build the connection between using plant-based cosmetics and environmental sustainability. The implication was that such products were good for the planet more broadly, in a way which Rodale, for example, could never have imagined. From quite a different basis, this was also the achievement of a start-up founded by Horst Rechelbacher. His father a shoemaker and his mother a herbalist, Rechelbacher was born in Austria in 1941. Forced by poverty to end his schooling early, he apprenticed as a hairdresser. From the age of 17, he worked in Rome and London in hair salons for five years and then moved to New York. He opened his own salon in Minneapolis in 1965, after being hit by a drunk driver whilst attending a hair show, which left him hospitalized for six months and owing huge medical bills. Rechelbacher built a successful salon business, but the task left him exhausted. After hearing the Swami Rama, then a prominent Indian guru, speak at the University of Minnesota on the ancient practice of Ayurvedic medicine, Rechelbacher followed him to India in 1970, where he stayed for six months and studied the use of herbs and plants to promote health and longevity.[92]

When Rechelbacher returned to the United States, he began developing products for his salons using essential oils derived from plants, introducing consumers to Ayurvedic philosophy and aromatherapy. He made batches of his first product, a clove shampoo, in his kitchen sink in Minneapolis. Aveda was founded in 1978. The first products were hair care products initially manufactured to be used exclusively at Rechelbacher's chain of hair salons in Minnesota. As in the case of The Body Shop, the salons were key to building a market for the brand. Subsequently, he popularized the concept of aroma-therapy, which linked the sense of smell to health and well-being, and steadily expanded the product range to a full range of beauty products, while becoming an ever-more vocal supporter of environmental and social causes.[93] Aveda aimed, Horst Rechelbacher wrote later in 1999, "to create products that make intelligent use of the planet's resources; we support the rights of indigenous peoples; we do not conduct animal testing. In our view, these policies make good sense financially, environmentally, and morally."[94] A decade later, he hailed the power of "eco-preneurship" to be the "innovative servant and healer of our wounded planet."[95]

The key breakthroughs for the natural beauty industry occurred right at the end of the 1970s and into the 1980s when Anita Roddick and Horst Rechel-bacher broke out of the tiny niche in which the industry had formerly existed. They succeeded at reframing plant-based cosmetics in much broader envir-onmental and societal contexts than previously. Both of them solved the problem of accessing conventional marketing and retail channels by having their own retail outlets, which was important for carrying their messages to consumers. Even so, it is important to keep these achievements in perspective. The Body Shop's sales of $7 million made it the world's biggest natural beauty company in the mid-1980s. The world's largest cosmetic companies at that time, led by L'Oréal, Shiseido, Avon, and Estée Lauder, had annual sales of several billion dollars each. In the big picture, natural beauty remained an inconsequential component of the industry.

Earthships, compost toilets, and the renewal of ecological architecture

As in the case of the natural beauty industry, the second wave of environmentalism during the 1960s appeared to make a limited impact on dominant styles of architecture and construction. This was a decade when municipalities, universities, and other public bodies commissioned numerous giant, exposed concrete buildings at the high point of brutalist architecture. Enormous brutalist buildings, such as the J. Edgar Hoover Building in Washington, DC, City Hall in Boston, or the Bull Ring Centre in Birmingham, England, became much-hated symbols of this era. Across the Western world, sprawling suburbs spread alongside the use of the automobile. Cities across the United States and Europe were often redesigned for ease of access by automobiles, isolating pedestrians and neighborhoods, and sending greenhouse gas emissions soaring.

It was not until the following decade that a new awareness of the importance of buildings for the natural environment could be discerned in conventional architecture. Four years after the Stockholm conference in 1972, the United Nations held the first conference on Human Settlements in Vancouver, Canada. The event, known as Habitat 1, drew attention to the "social, economic, ecological and environmental deterioration" caused by, among other things, excessive urbanization.[96] The sharp spike in oil prices in 1973, as we will see shortly, was partly responsible for these new concerns about the impact of the built environment. The American Institute of Architects (AIA) began to discuss energy conservation much more seriously than in the past, with a particular focus on achieving greater efficiency in energy use with better insulation.[97] In most other Western countries there were shifting architectural norms, sometimes encouraged by policy-makers, towards smaller windows and more insulation. There was also a revival of interest in passive solar energy. Edward Mazria in *The Passive Solar Energy Book*, published in 1979 and written in non-technical language, championed the potential of passive solar to enable people to live off-grid. It proved to be especially influential in the years to come.[98]

Against this background, a number of architects emerged as ecological champions, whose work and thought are worthy of attention, even if their impact on the built environment in general was mostly marginal. These included Malcolm Wells who, after serving in the US Marines and studying engineering, initially worked as a draftsman for the large consumer products company RCA. Qualifying as an architect in 1953, he had successful commissions, designing the RCA pavilion at the 1964 World's Fair in New York City. However, the realization that his pavilion would be torn down within two years, along with the unexpected deaths in the previous year of his father, President Kennedy, and the Pope, served as an epiphany. As he reevaluated his work, he reflected on how his other buildings had destroyed whatever had lived there before them. He began to develop theories of "gentle architecture," influenced by the environmental movement and by the work of a contemporary French architect, Jacque Couëlle, who was designing free-form houses. Wells became a vegetarian and started walking rather than driving to work.[99]

Writing in the professional magazine *Architectural Digest* in 1971, Wells set forth major goals that he thought new buildings should meet, including the ability to use and store solar energy, to consume their own waste, to provide wildlife habitat and human habitat, and to be beautiful.[100] He dedicated his own practice to underground architecture. A suggestion to RCA that they move their factories underground resulted in the firm ending its business relationship with Wells. Nevertheless, Wells persisted. After the oil price rises in 1973, he finally began to receive commissions. In 1975 the local government of Moorestown, New Jersey, commissioned Wells to build an administrative complex underground. This was followed by other public commissions, including a building in the New York Botanical Gardens. It proved harder to get commissions for private houses, but Wells had financial success in 1977 when he self-published *Underground Designs*, a handwritten, stapled book of plans which sold more than 100,000 copies due to the interest in superefficient homes. The profits from the book enabled Wells to move to Cape Cod in Massachusetts, where he designed a house illustrating his principles.[101]

Michael Reynolds was younger than Wells, and also more radical. By the time he graduated in architecture from the University of Cincinnati, he had concluded that "architecture as it stood then was worthless. It had nothing to do with the planet."[102] In 1972 he built his first house in New Mexico from recycled materials, which became the basis for his new profession of "biotecture," which he defined as "the profession of designing buildings and environments with consideration for their sustainability."[103] This "Thumb House" used recycled beer cans wired together into "bricks." Reynolds's highly experimental houses, which came to be called Earthships, were designed to be fully self-sustainable, incorporating their own wind and solar power, as well as greenhouses. They secured few commissions. In the neighboring state of Arizona, the Italian architect Paolo Soleri built an entire settlement based on a philosophy he developed called "arcology," which combined architecture with ecology. Soleri's settlement was designed to house 5,000 people, but it never grew larger than to accommodate a few hundred. By the early 1970s it had received thousands of visitors, however, and it has continued as a permanent feature of the tourist landscape as well as an educational center.[104]

Two other architects had a significant impact beyond their profession. Ian McHarg grew up in the highly industrialized Scottish city of Glasgow, but already by the age of 10 had begun taking long hikes into the countryside.[105] After service in World War II, McHarg went to the United States to study joint degrees in landscape architecture and city planning at Harvard. This was a radical departure, as the two fields had become very separate, with landscape architecture focused on park and garden design rather than city planning. McHarg built a career trying to reintegrate them.[106]

McHarg contracted tuberculosis at Harvard, which, combined with his heavy smoking, resulted in chronic health problems. After a depressing six months in a Scottish hospital, McHarg secured a transfer to a Swiss sanatorium in the Alps in his capacity as a former soldier, which encouraged exercise and fresh air rather than confinement. The experiment, he later wrote, "hardened my recognition of the importance of health, dignity and freedom, of the power of nature to heal. It directed my life's work."[107] The disease meant that his initial career plans to become a planner in Scotland were thwarted, as he was denied permanent civil servant status. Instead, he took up an invitation to build a new graduate program in landscape architecture at the University of Pennsylvania, which became a major training ground for a new generation of architects. A book published in 1969 called *Design with Nature*, commissioned by the Conservation Foundation, became a landmark publication about the need to incorporate ecology into planning. It sold more than 250,000 copies.[108] During the first Earth Day in 1970, McHarg was a prominent figure. He appeared on NBC's *Today* show which focused on environmental issues for the week of April 20–24, making the point in a roundtable discussion that the root cause of environmental degradation was "the attitudes of Western man to nature."[109]

In 1963 McHarg also co-founded an architectural practice. The firm worked on multiple planning projects for cities and regions in the United States, mostly related to managing growth of suburbs, including the impact of the expansion of the federal highway program, and by the mid-1970s, received many commissions from public agencies needing to respond to new federal environmental quality regulations. However, the ambitious McHarg was seldom hired for design rather than planning, and sensing an opportunity, during the mid-1970s he accepted a commission to design a huge environmental theme park for the Shah of Iran. The firm opened an office in Tehran in 1977. The project proved complex and, worse still, was fundamentally environmentally damaging, as it required huge amounts of irrigation and air-conditioning. The project was cancelled following the Islamic Revolution, leaving his firm with huge debts and forcing him to resign from the practice.[110] McHarg's talents lay more in education and serving as a public intellectual than in building a business around his ideas.

Sim Van der Ryn was another major figure in sustainable architecture whose impact reached beyond the profession. Born in the Netherlands, his Jewish family had fled to London the day before the outbreak of World War II, and finally settled in the borough of Queens in New York. Van der Ryn believed this traumatic experience gave him an early and lasting concern for both social justice and ecology. "When you escape one holocaust," he observed, "you don't want to be part of creating another."[111] The very small pieces of nature he saw growing up in Queens also inspired a specific interest in the natural environment. "My connection to nature started there," he noted later.[112]

Discouraged by his parents from pursuing an interest in art, he studied architecture at the University of Michigan—with little enthusiasm until Buckminster Fuller came to speak. Fuller, Van der Ryn later noted, "really provided a larger vision that was far more than just designing a building. And that for me was the kind of Satori moment—learning from him that the issue was much larger than the building. He was thinking in 'whole systems' terms and I have been ever since."[113] On graduating, Van der Ryn joined the faculty of the University of California, Berkeley.

In 1969 Van der Ryn took a leave of absence from Berkeley when campus unrest led to a new round of violence between students and the police. He moved to a five-acre rustic compound, which included a chicken coop, and began to teach there, and engaged in architectural experiments.[114] These included taking part in the building of the Green Gulch Farm Zen Center, a

Soto Zen Soto community founded in 1972 and located seventeen miles outside of San Francisco. Alan Chadwick had started a garden there after leaving Santa Cruz.[115] Two years later Van der Ryn built the first of a number of composting toilets for the community, a cause he spent this period promoting. "The soil, now compressed and lifeless dirt," he wrote in a book on toilets "will be restored to life with our composted wastes and greywater."[116] The toilets, however, violated the local building code, and Van der Ryn found himself charged with multiple offenses.[117] In the same period he created the Farallones Institute for researching and teaching self-sustaining living patterns, including appropriate technologies, energy efficiency, organic agriculture, and composting toilets.[118]

It was at this stage that Governor Jerry Brown, who had been elected governor of California in 1975 aged only 36, approached Van der Ryn about rebuilding state government buildings in the capital, Sacramento. Brown became associated with multiple environmental policies, beginning with repealing an oil depletion allowance which had provided a tax break for California's oil companies. He also placed a moratorium on the building of new nuclear reactors in the state. Brown's initial interest in Van der Ryn arose from his concern about the potential of an earthquake to damage buildings. Van der Ryn was not convinced that there was significant seismic risk, but he was convinced that there was a growing environmental risk, to the state and to the world. He recommended that Brown read Schumacher's *Small is Beautiful*. In subsequent conversations, Van der Ryn advised Brown to invest in renewable energy and promote ecologically appropriate technology on the lines suggested by Schumacher.[119]

Brown appointed Van der Ryn as the State Architect, with a large budget and staff. Laws were passed mandating 40 percent reductions in energy consumption in new buildings, and the state began building new energy-efficient public buildings designed by Van der Ryn. The Bateson Building in Sacramento opened in 1977 with an 80 percent reduction in energy consumption. It became a "personal landmark" for Van der Ryn.[120]

Brown also followed Van der Ryn's recommendation to appoint him to head a new Office of Appropriate Technology. The agency began by launching many small initiatives. Van der Ryn, influenced by what we had seen in Amsterdam, bought fifty bicycles and instructed employees to use them rather than cabs on journeys of less than two miles in Sacramento.[121] Much more significantly, he was given a $200 million renewable energy and conservation program which was to have transformational consequences for the wind energy industry globally, as we will see in Chapter 8. Van der Ryn himself returned to Berkeley after four years, the longest leave of absence permitted by the university, having proven himself as an unusually effective administrator and line manager.[122]

In most respects, these were disappointing decades for green architects. Ecological architecture remained far from mainstream. The most visionary architects engaged in projects which either failed to generate a market or were just unsuccessful, including underground buildings, Earthships, compost toilets, and theme parks for the Shah of Iran. Soleri's Arcosanti community had a physical and ongoing presence, but his philosophy of arcology did not become mainstream. In another sense, however, it was striking how, especially during the 1970s, architects like Wells, McHarg, and Van der Ryn broke out of the world of professional architecture through widely selling books, television appearances, and, in the most notable case, serving in state government. Although these architects did not receive many commissions for their designs, they were more effective at making the case for why ecology mattered for architecture.

Revisiting wind and solar power

The countercultural and environmental awakening of the 1960s had little initial impact on the small number of wind and solar energy firms in existence at the time. In an era when the concept of human-induced climate change was barely discussed, green activism focused more on the overuse of chemicals and industrial pollution, not the energy economy and carbon emissions. Rachel Carson did not mention energy in *Silent Spring*. Rodale made no mention of wind or solar energy in *Our Poisoned Earth and Sky*. Wind and solar had no popular appeal in the age of cheap oil. In Denmark, the price per kilowatt produced by the Gedster wind turbine, closed in 1967, was double that of the power produced by a power station using oil, which by then was responsible for almost all of Denmark's electricity generation.[123]

Wind energy in particular seemed like a relic from the past. In the United States, after the bankruptcy of Jacobs Wind in the late 1950s, Marcellus Jacobs and his sons started a new business in Florida, where they built what were then called "environmental subdivisions" involving environmentally friendly construction and waste management. After a few years, however, they went back north to relaunch Jacobs Wind Electrics. But there was no return to the glory days; at the end of the 1960s many of the wind chargers built by Jacobs and other small firms sat rusting in junk piles on farms.[124]

In solar energy, the high cost of photovoltaic cells (PVs) made serving niche markets, like the American satellite market, the only viable business strategy. Even then the challenges were so great that only businesses concerned with matters other than making a lot of money, and which were well-capitalized, became involved. This seems to be the explanation for the entry into PV manufacturing of Sharp, a large Japanese electronics company, which made radios and televisions, followed by calculators in the 1960s. "I believe the biggest issue of the future is the accumulation and storage of solar heat and light," the company's founder Tokuji Hayakawa wrote in an autobiography in 1970. "[W]hile all living things enjoy the blessings of the sun, we have to rely on electricity from power stations. With magnificent heat and light streaming down on us, we must think of ways of using those blessings."[125] Hayakawa found a market in navigation aids. Between 1961 and 1972 Sharp solarized 256 lighthouses along the Japanese coast.[126]

By then a significant shift in the intellectual and policy milieu was underway. The conference on Man's Impact on Climate in Stockholm in 1971 had raised the profile of the possibilities of climate change. Within two years the era of cheap oil dramatically ended in October 1973 when, in the wake of the Six-Day War between Israel and its Arab neighbors, the Organization of Arab Petroleum Exporting Countries reduced their production and proclaimed an embargo on oil shipments to the United States and some European countries which had supported Israel. Within three months the price of oil rose from $3 per barrel to $12, and it stayed high after the embargo was lifted in March 1974. The upshot was a major reexamination of energy policies in the United States and Western Europe.

In 1974 the Ford Foundation produced a major report entitled *A Time to Choose: America's Energy Future*. The report took a long-term view of energy supplies from all sources, including the prospects for making fossil fuels such as coal less climatically damaging. It talked of a "greenhouse" effect at length. The potential of nuclear energy was stressed, but the risks and the unsolved waste problems were also identified. Wind energy, however, was only briefly mentioned in the 500-page report. The prospects for solar energy, especially rooftop collectors on houses, becoming a significant source of energy received a bit more attention, largely with the proviso that solar could only scale if the United States government chose to provide as much seed money as it had earlier for nuclear energy.[127]

The following years saw many new energy policies, including conservation and efficiency measures. There was a real shift away from the voracious consumption of what appeared to be limitless supplies of cheap oil. In the United States new legislation included the Energy Policy and Conservation Act of 1975 and the creation of the Department of Energy in 1977. New energy conservation measures included a nationwide 55-mile-per-hour speed limit and mandatory fuel economy standards. There was also a search for new sources of energy. Between 1973 and 1979 federal research funds for energy rose by a factor of seven. This included large spending on nuclear energy.[128]

The same enthusiasm for nuclear energy was seen elsewhere. Between 1960 and the late 1970s, the world's nuclear capacity grew from barely 1 GW to over 100 GW, with much of that growth happening during the 1970s. Although some environmental activists, such as Rodale in *Our Poisoned Earth and Sky*, warned of the risks of radiation leaks and the unsolved problem of disposing of nuclear waste,[129] others saw the possibilities of nuclear as a source of limitless and sustainable energy. In *Only One World*, for example, Ward and Dubois dismissed the prospects of wind and solar energy ever amounting to much, while arguing that nuclear energy could provide a serious alternative in the face of finite supplies of fossil fuels.[130]

Nuclear energy was generally thought to be the key to securing a stable supply of energy, one which could not be disrupted by hostile geopolitical events. In France, where the state-owned electricity monopoly EDF was also very supportive of nuclear energy, by the 1980s nearly fifty nuclear plants supplied 70 percent of the country's electricity.[131] In Germany, where the first commercial nuclear power plant began operating in 1969, there was also a great expansion. Sweden, although an early mover in environmental legislation, was also a strong investor in nuclear power. The country lacked coal let alone oil supplies of its own, while Swedish governments sought to promote economic growth and a competitive export industry to fund their welfare state. Swedish policy-makers also linked their country's prized neutrality in the Cold War to self-sufficiency in energy. As a result, the state-owned Vattenfall, which held a monopoly over electrical supplies and controlled the country's vast hydro-electric facilities, commissioned its first two nuclear reactors in the mid-1970s. After 1975 there was also government investment in research on the potential of bio-energy.[132]

Nor was the enthusiasm for nuclear energy limited to Europe. In Japan, which had commissioned its first nuclear reactor in 1966, the government's reaction to the energy crisis of the early 1970s was also to accelerate the development of nuclear power, while working towards securing stable oil supplies, and to encourage energy conservation. The country's ten electric companies, led by the Tokyo Electric Power Company, monopolized the energy market and had no interest in wind and solar energy, even as oil prices rose.[133]

The outcome was that, despite the changed policy context after the first oil price crisis, governments and even some environmentalists considered wind and solar power as a nice idea whose time had not come, and probably never would. Over the next few years the limited public funds allocated to research in them were, typically, poorly allocated. In the United States, federal funding for research in renewable energy was allocated through the space agency NASA and its Jet Propulsion Laboratory (JPL). This resulted in a focus on the design and building of large wind turbines by leading aerospace and technology firms, including Boeing, General Electric, and Westinghouse. The result was a massive technological dead-end, as the large turbines which were built experienced multiple technical failures over the following decade.[134] Nor was the United States alone. In Sweden, when some government R&D in wind energy began in 1975, it was almost entirely focused on giant turbines, with a similar negative outcome.[135] As a result, especially but not only in wind energy, the important foundations for the future of renewable energy which were laid in the 1970s were primarily despite, rather than because of, governments.

This was clearly demonstrated in the case of Denmark, which would emerge during the following decade as the global technological leader in wind energy. Despite the country's tradition of small-scale experimentation in wind reaching back to la Cour in the late 1890s, the Danish government responded to the oil price rises by launching a program in 1976 designed to transition the country's energy source from oil to coal and nuclear energy, with six new nuclear plants to be built by the end of the century.

However, there also continued to be experimentation with windmills to meet entirely local needs. Christian Riisager, a carpenter in Jutland, installed a waterwheel in the stream in his backyard to produce electricity for his garden. As the stream was weak in the summer, in 1975 he began building a wind turbine using Juul's Gedster design with materials such as wood and truck gears. He created a prototype 7 kW turbine, and took the radical step of connecting it to the grid, for which he subsequently secured permission from the local electricity distribution company. The turbine attracted the attention of journalists, and Riisager began making turbines for other people. In 1979 he helped form a small new company for this purpose.[136]

This tradition of local experimentation might well have remained on a modest scale if it had not converged with emergent radical environmentalist activists. These included Mogens Amdi Petersen, a Maoist teacher who had founded a collective in Western Jutland called Tvind. The group spent three years building a turbine which opened in 1978, and which attracted considerable attention and raised the profile of wind energy in the country. Petersen himself disappeared in the following year, becoming a shadowy force behind the creation of a complex set of institutions including an international relief organization and the Humana People-to-People NGO which, by the 2000s, had become the subject of allegations and court cases concerning massive financial fraud.[137]

A less controversial figure was Erik Grove-Nielsen, an engineer who combined an interest in flying planes with concerns about sustainable lifestyles, acquired whilst in college in the early 1970s.[138] He campaigned against the government's plans for nuclear energy and joined a new grassroots activist group, the Organization for Renewable Energy (OVE) formed in 1976, which promoted alternatives to nuclear, including wind and solar. The campaign against nuclear energy formed part of a wider transnational wave of anti-nuclear energy which gathered pace in the 1970s.[139] In Denmark, after first dabbling with solar energy, Grove-Nielsen shifted his attention to wind and began work on blade reliability. He founded a bootstrap company, Økær Vind Energi, in 1977, which built a business selling blades to self-builders. The endeavor was unprofitable and only survived with the help of donations from OVE, but it achieved significant improvements in blade design.[140]

Grove-Nielson's story typified how the wind industry was molded in Denmark. Reflecting the country's overall business system, which was characterized by numerous small and medium-sized firms and a tradition of collaborative learning networks, blades were slowly made more efficient by clusters of small, geographically concentrated firms advancing by incremental innovation. They relied on skilled workers, technicians, and a few practical engineers.[141] The small size of the country enabled manufacturers to directly service their turbines. This model provided further learning opportunities, as well as a demonstration effect for potential buyers who could see turbines working nearby.[142]

During the late 1970s turbine engineering and environmental activism increasingly overlapped, creating a virtuous circle through learning and institutionalization. The Danish Wind Turbine Owners Association was formed in 1978 to both oppose nuclear power and to promote solar and wind alternatives. It lobbied electricity boards, diffused engineering information, and facilitated design features to enhance the safety of turbines. In the same year the Danish Wind Turbine Test Station was founded by four engineers. When the government required wind turbines to be certified before owner-users could gain access to subsidies, this institution established testing criteria for gaining such subsidies.[143]

The challenge of finding organizational competences and money remained. A solution came in the wake of the second surge of oil price rises in 1978 and 1979 following the Islamic Revolution in Iran. Three agricultural equipment manufacturers, Vestas, Nordtank, and Bonus, diversified into wind turbines. They were conventional firms motivated by a search for new profitable opportunities because of stagnating agricultural markets rather than environmental activism. The largest of them employed only 120 workers but knew how to build heavy machinery for a rural market. These competences were augmented by collaboration with activist entrepreneurs. Vestas, Nordtank, and Bonus bought blades from Økær Vind Energi. When another young activist, Henrik Stiesdal, who built an improved turbine, wanted to leave to study at university, he licensed it to Vestas, providing the basis for the firm to build a turbine business which would find a big new market in California in the next decade.[144] It was only at this late stage, as shown in Chapter 8, that the government and utilities became supportive of the wind industry.

In the United States too, a renewal of wind energy began in the 1970s initially with no public support. Marcellus Jacobs re-entered the turbine business, designing a new 7.5 kW turbine. However, being both politically conservative and independent-minded, he disliked embryonic attempts to build institutions for the industry. He opposed the American Wind Energy

Association, a small group formed in 1974 primarily to lobby for government funds, and within a few years sold his small business to the computer company Control Data Corporation.[145] The Association was the brainchild of Allen O'Shea, a Detroit-based salesman for wind and solar equipment, and he represented the Association at the first World Energy Congress, held in Detroit. A modest affair, the meeting took place in the basement of a police station, which offered a free space across from the store where O'Shea worked.[146]

The Association sought to bring together the new wave of entrepreneurial start-ups which emerged, often but not only, in the rural areas of the country. The entrepreneurs included Paul Gipe, a major in environmental science, who began searching for junked wind chargers in Montana in the mid-1970s, having concluded that finding renewable energy sources was vital for society. After initially planning to reconstruct a Jacobs machine and sell it to a commune in Pennsylvania to provide energy self-sufficiency, he developed a business wholesaling junk wind machines, providing training, and advocating wind energy through publishing.[147]

In Massachusetts, Russell Wolfe and Stanley Charren launched a start-up called U.S. Windpower in 1974. Wolfe, an engineer, became interested in wind energy through his daughter, who had been taught by the University of Massachusetts engineer William Heronemus, a former navy captain and one-time proponent of nuclear energy, who in the late 1960s had predicted a coming energy crisis. Heronemus advocated the use of "Grand Scale Renewables" to gradually replace fossil fuel and nuclear energy. In the early 1970s he had constructed a 25 kW wind turbine on campus.[148] Wolfe turned to the serial entrepreneur Stanley Charren, who had earlier helped him fund a start-up through a small-business-incubating venture he had established. Charren, sensing a profitable opportunity, tried to engage Heronemus in the idea of a company. When Heronemus declined, Charren hired some of his students to develop a business in which intermediate-sized turbines could be grouped and their power sold to a utility. They raised over $1 million from private investors, and in 1978 Wolfe and Charren erected twenty windmills on New Hampshire's Crotched Mountain, which became America's—and the world's—first wind farm. However, initial attempts to raise further funds failed.[149] As we will see in Chapter 8, as in Denmark, public policy suddenly became more supportive to ventures like Wolfe and Charren's at the end of decade.

A final, and unlikely, center of experimentation in wind energy was Japan. The epicenter was a skunkworks inside the giant Nagasaki plant of Mitsubishi Heavy Industries, a diversified manufacturer of power machinery, steel, and shipbuilding. The initiative emerged out of the concern of one executive, Kentaro Aikawa, to develop a clean energy business, following his experience in manufacturing boilers for thermal power plants, which burnt oil and coal. He built a geo-thermal plant, and then ordered a team to work on the development of a wind turbine in 1978. The team was only given a limited budget and could only spend some of their time on the project, so they had to improvise. They used a tower they had found at the shipyards and blades from a helicopter at nearby Nagasaki airport which was about to be scrapped. In 1980 they completed a 40 kW wind turbine in Nagasaki Shipyard. It produced only a small amount of energy and was used for internal purposes in the shipyard, such as boiling water for tea. In 1982 they sold a commercial 300 kW wind turbine to an electrical utility, which installed it on an island near Okinawa. However, both the Japanese government and the country's electrical utilities were unsupportive of wind energy, which also faced other obstacles in the domestic market. The country had only a limited amount of flat area, which was usually heavily populated, so any windmill needed to be installed on mountains, which was more costly. Seasonal typhoon winds increased risks of machinery fatigue. Although Mitsubishi would start building an international business in California, the domestic market was doomed to remain tiny.[150]

The solar industry, like wind, only attracted a limited boost from the first oil price rises, despite a flurry of reports about its potential by consultants and foundations.[151] US government investment and research in solar remained primarily focused on its use in defense and the space program. Federal legislation in 1974 set up the Solar Energy Research Institute which opened in Golden, Colorado three years later. Critics identified the same syndrome as in US government spending on wind. During Congressional hearings in 1978, Jim Harding of Friends of the Earth, and the co-author of a large study on the benefits of solar energy, unfavorably compared US spending with the advances in solar-heated home technology seen in Germany, Denmark, and Canada. Harding noted the program was "ill-funded" but also that "much of the money has been misused...our U.S. solar program is an international embarrassment. It is an embarrassment because it stresses overbuilt, over-designed, far too expensive technologies that will never be solutions."[152]

By then, however, two American start-ups in 1973 had set the PV cell industry on a new course through their vision of expanding the market beyond niche and expensive uses, primarily in space programs. The first start-up was launched by an American industrial chemist named Elliot Berman who took PV cell technology to a new level through both innovation and innovative financing. Berman worked for the Itek Corporation, a large US defense contractor which made cameras for spy satellites, but which shared the period's fashion for business diversification. Berman successfully enabled the firm to enter photographic materials, and in 1968 he was asked to consider new businesses. Berman, feeling a desire to develop products which had a positive social impact, identified a correlation between "energy availability and quality of life," and became interested in exploring ways to provide electrical power for the rural poor in developing countries. He found the solution in the promise of solar energy. In view of the high cost of PV cells, he suggested that his company needed to invest in a new type of solar cell, made from the photographic film on which he had worked. Finding no support for his idea, he left the company.[153]

After eighteen months fruitlessly attempting to interest venture capitalists in backing him, a chance conversation led Berman to Exxon, the world's largest oil company. It had just begun looking at alternative energies in the expectation that conventional energy prices would rise substantially over time. After persuading Exxon to make an investment, in April 1973 Berman launched Solar Power Corporation as a wholly owned Exxon affiliate. This became the first company to specifically manufacture terrestrial PV cells in the United States. Critically, Berman did not use the expensive pure semiconductor-grade crystalline silicon employed in the space industry, but instead opted for the cheaper silicon wafers rejected by the semiconductor industry, and he packaged the cells with cheaper materials. Berman's solar cells had the eventual result of reducing the price of electricity per watt from $100 to $20.[154]

But Berman still needed a market. He initially looked to the US Coast Guard, but the agency, noting the diversity of geographical conditions it faced, declined to commit. Instead, Berman started manufacturing PV cells to be used on Exxon's offshore platforms in the Gulf of Mexico, where there was a need for something other than the large and expensive lead-acid batteries then in use. In 1978, the Environmental Protection Agency outlawed

disposing of such batteries in the ocean, a move which added to the attractiveness of solar batteries. By the end of the 1970s solar-powered navigation
systems had been installed across production platforms in the Gulf of
Mexico.[155]

Exxon was not the only oil company drawn into PV cells. Government
contracts encouraged Boston-based Tyco, which made semiconductors initially for defense and other markets, to experiment with using ribbon silicon in
order to produce lighter-weight PV cells. In 1974 the giant oil company Mobil
formed a joint venture with Tyco to pursue this strategy, which was to prove
very technologically challenging.[156]

However, a second start-up in 1973 joined Berman in pioneering the
terrestrial market for PV cells: Solarex was the creation of Joseph Lindmeyer
and Peter Varadi, two Hungarian-born engineers who had fled the country
after the unsuccessful uprising against the Communist government in 1956.
After being employed working on solar cells by the government-sponsored but
privately owned satellite company COMSAT, which launched the first commercial communications satellite Early Bird in 1965, they set up their own
company, called Solarex, in 1973. Lindmeyer and Varadi believed that they
had accumulated enough knowledge to expand solar into the terrestrial
market, and that this would be profitable. They differed from the consensus
that a huge program of research would make solar cells cheaper and capable of
providing energy for central grid systems. Instead, they saw PV cells as a
decentralized electric energy source, and one that could, as Sharp had
demonstrated in Japan, be sold to a terrestrial market.[157] Unlike Berman,
Lindmeyer and Varadi had no significant sustainability motivations but,
rather, saw the potential of a profitable niche. Asked about his motives in a
subsequent interview, Varadi responded: "Money. We all have to make a living
right? So the main concern was to make money... to buy some food. That's
what everybody wants, to make money to survive, right?"[158] As we have
repeatedly seen, this was in fact *not* the typical motivation of alternative energy
pioneers.

After experiencing the familiar problems of finding funding, Lindmeyer and
Varadi raised $250,000 from friends and family and opened a small facility
making PV cells in Rockville, Maryland.[159] Within eight months, Solarex
became profitable, greatly assisted by the fortuitous timing of the first oil crisis
when they suddenly received, as Varadi noted, "a lot of publicity from the

media."[160] However, the start-up did not enjoy smooth sailing. In 1974 COMSAT sued the company and its two founders for taking proprietary information, a suit which was eventually abandoned but which caused great disruption.[161] It also proved hard for the company to get beyond the market for watches and calculators until the second oil crisis, when the potential of solar, and more government funding, suddenly became more attractive. In 1979 Solarex got new equity funding from two European electrical companies, interested in licensing its technology in Europe, and a more substantial $7 million investment from the oil company Amoco. Solarex invested in a new "breeder" plant powered by PV cells to produce PV cells. In 1983 Amoco purchased the whole company.[162]

A final formative figure in the American solar industry had started his career with Spectrolab in Los Angeles: John "Bill" Yerkes, a mechanical engineer, had worked at Boeing on solar arrays for the space program before becoming president of Spectrolab, then owned by Textron, where he was responsible for developing the solar technology which was left behind on the moon by Apollo 11. A Spectrolab product became the first PV panel on the moon. Yerkes and his wife had strong environmentalist convictions and lived an alternative, environmentally friendly lifestyle for nearly two years in a 24-foot house trailer in which all appliances, including an electric composting toilet, were powered solely by PV cells, despite the presence of adjacent power lines.[163]

When Textron sold Spectrolab in 1975, Yerkes lost his job and resolved to build his own solar company. Using his own money and support from his family and friends as seed capital, he founded Solar Technology International (STI) in a 4,000-square-foot facility in Chatsworth, California, and set about the task of trying to reduce the cost of terrestrial solar cells and modules. By getting rid of silicon as the top cover and replacing it by tempered glass, a more resistant and easily available material, he solved serious maintenance problems, and he also restructured cell production methods by screen-printing contacts onto the cells. The materials and methods he introduced in the late 1970s became standards for the industry.[164] In 1976, STI got its first significant order from a motor home company which Yerkes convinced to install small panels on its motor homes to keep batteries charged during storage. The JPL placed an important order, but as spending mounted he struggled to raise more funds. In 1977, Yerkes sold his company to Atlantic Richfield Oil

Company (ARCO), forming ARCO Solar which he headed.[165] The company reached industry milestones, beginning with the first 1 MG (megawatt) of annual production in 1980.[166]

The United States was the center of the world PV industry at this stage. In 1978, Solarex accounted for 45 percent of the world market (measured by kW peak power), Solar Power Corporation for 17 percent, and ARCO Solar for 12 percent. The US semiconductor manufacturer Motorola, which was about to divest from the industry, accounted for a further 7 percent of the market. The French affiliate of the Dutch-owned Philips electronics company was the largest non-US PV manufacturer, with 5 percent of the market. Sharp, the largest Japanese producer, had 1 percent.[167]

The Japanese industry, although small, was in the midst of welcoming a new entrant. As in the United States, public policy initiatives in Japan were a mixed blessing. The Japanese government funded Project Sunshine in 1974 to explore the prospects of solar energy. This turned out to be ineffective given that the focus was on solar thermal energy and Japan experienced frequently cloudy skies, while an ocean thermal energy conversion technology developed by the project exacerbated stratospheric ozone depletion.[168]

However, an especially innovative electronics entrepreneur was drawn to the industry. The Kyocera Corporation, which made ceramic components for electronic and structural applications, was founded in 1959 by Kazuo Inamori. As his own firm grew rapidly, Inamori became increasingly aware of the country's environmental degradation arising from rapid industrialization. During the late 1960s, seeing that the water from his own factories polluted rivers and killed fish, he began investing in water purification technology, even though it drove up the costs of his still medium-sized company. These environmental concerns led him to consider the potential of solar power, which he deemed "a most ideal alternative energy source. Japan had no energy sources and had to import everything including coal, oil and natural gas, and I thought it was a weak point of the nation." Coming into contact with Tyco just as the first oil price rises happened, he learned that the firm had developed a new crystallization technology for sapphires with potential to transform PV manufacture.[169]

Inamori's willingness to invest in solar technology rested on religious and philosophical beliefs about the responsibilities of business. His early views on business were primarily shaped by his study of Confucian thought; much later, in 1997, he became a Zen Buddhist priest. In his book *A Compass to Fulfillment*, Inamori stressed the "will of the universe," which he called a "cosmic force that seeks to cultivate all things, that encourages development and evolution."[170] If a leader was to attain the Confucian supreme virtue of "ren," he or she needed to attain the will of the universe by encouraging the growth and development of others. Confucian thought also led Inamori to discount narrow concepts of profit maximization. In the long run, he observed, "actions based on a solid philosophy never result in a loss. Despite the fact that they appear disadvantageous, in the end such genuine actions will profit you."[171]

Although Inamori was excited at the prospects of making PV cells at a cheaper cost, he was not excited about Project Sunshine and refused to be involved, following his basic assumption "that what the government offers is usually not good."[172] Instead, he contacted the heads of Sharp and Matsushita, another leading Japanese electronics company, and the three companies established a joint venture, the Japan Solar Energy Corporation. Inamori mobilized his own engineers to work on the development of solar cells. Over the following years it proved difficult to develop the Tyco process and to develop a market. Inamori personally came up with several new products, including solar-powered batteries for portable radios and road signs, and in 1979 the joint venture received its first large order: for panels to power a microwave telecom relay station located in the Peruvian Andres.[173]

However, as costs stubbornly refused to come down, the solar joint venture stumbled, and Kyocera was left as the sole owner. Inamori again found a foreign technology which could help. Wacker, the German electronics company, had developed a multi-crystal silicon wafer. Inamori scrapped all of his firm's existing production facilities and shifted to a multi-crystal approach which produced silicon ingot by molding, which would in time become a major production method for solar cells. By 1982, the firm's Shiga Yohkaichi factory was mass-producing multi-crystalline silicon solar cells.[174] Within a decade Kyocera and other Japanese electronics companies would make Japan the world's largest manufacturer of PV cells.

The decades from 1960 to 1980, then, can be seen as both disappointing and foundational for solar and wind energy. On the disappointing side, the two industries initially gained little from the second wave of environmentalism. It took the sudden spikes in oil prices in the 1970s to raise their profiles, and the willingness of policy-makers to provide support. However, the costs of these alternative energy sources kept them non-competitive with fossil fuels and nuclear energy, both still heavily subsidized by many governments. There were significant technological advances in both industries during the 1970s, but they did not come easily and they did not provide a disruptive technological shift.

By 1980 both solar and wind energy capacity remained tiny worldwide. The world production of PV cells that year was 7 MG and mostly US-based. Cumulative installed wind capacity was 8 MG in the United States, 5 MG in Denmark, and little elsewhere.[175] Wind contributed 0.04 percent of Denmark's electricity generation, which was the highest percentage for either wind or solar anywhere in the world. The share of combustible fuels (coal, oil, and natural gas) in electricity generation was 85 percent for Britain, 83 percent for Germany, 76 percent for the United States, and 69 percent for Japan, although only 48 percent for France, where nuclear and hydro contributed a sizeable 23 percent and 28 percent respectively.[176]

A more positive interpretation was that foundations had been laid, mostly by small entrepreneurs in Denmark and the United States, primarily but not entirely motivated by sustainability concerns. In wind energy, incremental innovation in Denmark had increased the efficiency of blades, while the first wind farm had been developed in the United States. In solar, there had been innovation aimed to reduce the cost of PV cells, especially through the start-ups of Berman, Lindmeyer, and Varadi, to envisage a terrestrial market. There was also institutionalization in the form of the American Wind Energy Association and the Organization for Renewable Energy in Denmark. Large conventional firms, including electronics companies, oil companies, and agricultural machinery manufactures, had also begun to allocate capital for these industries.

Conclusion

The second wave of environmentalism beginning in the 1960s, and intensifying in the 1970s, ended the long-standing popular neglect of environmental damage caused by industrialization. There were mass social movements, a swarm of new environmental NGOs, United Nations conferences, and new environmental agencies and laws across the United States and Western Europe.

Green entrepreneurs struggled to take advantage of this changed context. Their businesses were largely disconnected from the central concerns of the new environmentalism. Rachel Carson and others stressed the health risks of pesticides and the pollution caused by chemical and oil companies. Connections between the counterculture and the green entrepreneurs were haphazard. Counterculture and entrepreneurialism sometimes worked at cross-purposes. Most environmentalists saw the solution to chemical-contaminated food in banning pesticides, not in buying organic food associated with hippies. Critics of wasteful use of fossil fuels and other energy abounded, but few made the connection to compost toilets and underground houses as solutions. Although the finite nature of fossil fuels emerged as an acknowledged problem, developing solar and wind energy was not widely seen as a solution. On a deeper level, some of the most influential green writers of the 1970s, including Commoner and Schumacher, argued that for-profit capitalist enterprise by definition could not solve the world's environmental challenges.

The motivations of many green entrepreneurs in this period look familiar. Many held religious views, whether Christian, Buddhist, or more unorthodox, including Frank Ford, Tom Chappell, Mo Siegel, Horst Rechelbacher, and Kazuo Inamori. The macrobiotic movement shaped the views of Michio Kushi and Craig Sims. There were further examples of ill-health apparently shaping ecological concerns, as in the cases of Siegel and Ian McHarg. A new development was the number of entrepreneurs associated with the counterculture and the new environmental and social movements, including Paul Hawken, Alice Waters, Joseph Wilhelm, Anita Roddick, Sim Van der Ryn, Bill Yerkes, and Erik Grove-Nielson.

Only in the PV industry did the prospects for significant financial returns attract conventional profit-seeking entrepreneurs, like Joseph Lindmeyer and Peter Varadi. This was because the challenges faced by green businesses remained considerable. Typically they had to be self-financed or raise funds from friends and family. In the case of a capital-intensive business such as solar PV, the main solution turned out to be to sell start-ups to cash-rich oil companies. In other cases, innovative ways were found to secure cash. Malcolm Wells was unable to attract enough commissions for his underground houses, but he wrote a popular book which funded his research. Anita Roddick expanded The Body Shop business employing a franchising strategy, which was cheaper than owning her own retail outlets and enabled faster growth. An important solution to shortage of finance, and customers, was to cluster in hubs of environmental and social activism, like Allgäu, Berkeley, Boulder, and rural areas of Denmark. These clusters enabled small firms to build skills and competences which could eventually be used to expand into more mainstream locations. The key challenge, however, was to build identities for these businesses as components of the solutions for broad environmental and sustainability issues, rather than niche products or services. This was one of the key achievements of The Body Shop and also of the Danish wind energy entrepreneurs, who by combining the development of viable turbine technologies with anti-nuclear social movements, positioned wind energy as the best solution to the generally acknowledged problem of the price and insecurity of oil supplies.

The outcomes of this period were more significant than they seemed at the time. In organic food, and later in natural beauty, commercially viable green businesses and brands had been built, and distribution channels created which enabled consumers beyond the manufacturers' immediate localities to buy their products. Among green architects, Ian McHarg became a public intellectual, while Sim Van der Ryn found a position in state government from which to execute his ecological ideas. As we will see, the competences in wind and solar developed in California in the 1980s provided a model for the entire world.

Notes

1. William E. Siri, "Reflections on the Sierra Club, the Environment and Mountaineering, 1950s–1970s," an interview conducted by Ann Lage, Co-chairman, Sierra Club History Committee, Regional Oral History Office, The Bancroft Library, UC Berkeley, California, April 1979.

2. Ramachandra Guha, *Environmentalism: A Global History* (New York: Longman, 2000), pp.2–4, 68.

3. Geoffrey Jones and Christina Lubinski, "Making 'Green Giants': Environment Sustainability in the German Chemical Industry, 1950s–1980s," *Business History* 56, no. 4 (2014), pp.623–49.

4. David Strading and Richard Strading, "Perceptions of the Burning River: Deindustrialization and Cleveland's Cuyahoga River," *Environmental History* 13, no. 3 (2008), pp.515–35.

5. Andrew J. Hoffman, *From Heresy to Dogma: An Institutional History of Corporate Environmentalism* (Stanford: Stanford Business Books, 2001), pp.53–6.

6. Guha, *Environmentalism*, chapter 5.

7. Rachel Carson, *Silent Spring* (Boston: Houghton Mifflin, 1962).

8. Paul Brooks, "Introduction," in Martha Freeman (ed.), *Always, Rachel: The Letters of Rachel Carson and Dorothy Freeman 1952–1964* (Boston: Beacon Press 1994), p.xxviii.

9. John Paull, "The Rachel Carson Letters and the Making of Silent Spring," *Sage Open* (July–September 2013), pp.1–12; Michael Ruse, "Rachel Carson and Rudolf Steiner: An Unknown Debt," <http://www.huffingtonpost.com/michael-ruse/rachel-carson-and-rudolf-_b_3639684.html>, accessed July 25, 2016.

10. Raymond Dasmann, *The Destruction of California* (New York: Macmillan, 1965); Jean Dorst, *Avant que nature meure* (Neuchâtel: Delachaux et Niestlé, 1965); Paul Ehrlich, *The Population Bomb* (New York: Ballantine Books, 1968).

11. Barbara Ward, *Spaceship Earth* (New York: Columbia University Press, 1966).

12. Charles Reich, *The Greening of America* (New York: Random House, 1970).

13. Wesley D. Sine and Brandon H. Lee, "Tilting at Windmills? The Environmental Movement and the Emergence of the U.S. Wind Energy Sector," *Administrative Science Quarterly* 54 (2009), pp.123–55.

14. "In the middle of the 20th century, we saw our planet from space for the first time." In *Our Common Future: World Commission on Environment and Development* (Oxford and New York: Oxford University Press, 1987), p.3; William Harold Bryant, "Whole System, Whole Earth: The Convergence of Technology and Ecology in Twentieth Century American Culture," University of Iowa Ph.D., 2006, pp.115–17.

15. The Environmental Defense Fund had already been co-founded in New York in 1967 by scientists and teachers Art Cooley, Charlie Wurster, and Dennis Puleston, concerned about the impact of DDT on birds. <https://www.edf.org/about/our-history>, accessed July 16, 2015.

16. Russell J. Dalton, "The Environmental Movement in Western Europe," in Sheldon Kamieniecki (ed.), *Environmental Politics in the International Arena: Movements, Parties, Organizations, and Policy* (Albany: SUNY Press, 1993), pp.52–3.

17. Rex Weyler, *Greenpeace* (Vancouver, BC: Raincoast Books, 2004), Book One.

18. <http://www.earthday.org/earth-day-history-movement>, accessed January 29, 2014; <http://www.aip.org/history/climate/aerosol.htm>, accessed January 30, 2014.

19. Maria Ivanova, "Moving Forward by Looking Back: Learning from UNEP's History," in Lydia Swart and Estelle Perry (eds.), *Global Environmental Governance: Perspectives on the Current Debate* (New York: Center for UN Reform Education, 2007), pp.26–47; Maurice Strong, *Where on Earth Are We Going?* (New York: Textere, 2001), pp.120–1.

20. Cited in <http://www.mauricestrong.net/index.php/strong-stockholm-leadership?showall=1&limitstart=>, accessed January 30, 2014; "A Tribute to Maurice

Strong (1929–2015)," <https://www.youtube.com/watch?v=C-hjSkorNCA>, accessed January 27, 2016.

21. Anne E. Egelston, *Sustainable Development: A History* (Dordrecht: Springer, 2013), pp.61–6; Strong, *Where on Earth*, chapter 6.

22. Survival of Spaceship Earth, <https://www.youtube.com/watch?v=W-Em9A_Alck>, accessed July 2016.

23. Egelston, *Sustainable Development*, pp.71–3; interview with Jan Martenson, February 24, 2010.

24. The name was changed in 1973 to the International Institute for Environment and Development.

25. Barbara Ward and René Dubos, *Only One Earth: The Care and Maintenance of a Small Planet* (New York: W. W. Norton, 1972).

26. United Nations Conference on the Human Environment, Educational, Informational, Social and Cultural Aspects of Environmental Problems: Provisional Agenda Item 13, December 21, 1971; United Nations Conference on the Human Environment, Environmental Aspects of Natural Resource Management: Provisional Agenda Item 11, January 26, 1972, Part 11, Box 13, Peter S. Thacher Environment Collection, 1960–1996, Environmental Science and Public Policy Archives, Harvard College (hereafter Thacher Archives).

27. Ward and Dubos, *Only One Earth*, p.193.

28. Felix Dodds and Michael Strauss with Maurice Strong, *Only One Earth: The Long Road via Rio to Sustainable Development* (London and New York: Routledge, 2012), pp.14–16.

29. Egelston, *Sustainable Development*, p.65.

30. Ward and Dubos, *Only One Earth*, p.217.

31. Barry Commoner, *The Closing Circle: Nature, Man, and Technology* (New York: Alfred Knopf, 1971).

32. Barry Commoner, *The Poverty of Power* (New York: Alfred Knopf, 1976).

33. E. F. Schumacher, *Small Is Beautiful: Economics as if People Mattered* (London: Blond and Briggs, 1973), pp.284, 304.

34. Kenneth Harris, *The Wildcatter: A Portrait of Robert of Anderson* (New York: Weidenfeld & Nicolson, 1987), pp.98–110.

35. Ibid., pp.126–31.

36. Donella H. Meadows, Dennis L. Meadows, Jørgen Randers, and William W. Behrens III, *The Limits to Growth: A Report for the Club of Rome's Project on the Predicament of Mankind* (New York: Universe Books, 1972); Egelston, *Sustainable Development*, pp.78–9.

37. Strong, *Where on Earth*, p.48.

38. Harris, *Wildcatter*, chapters 3–5.

39. Egelston, *Sustainable Development*, p.71.

40. David Vogel, *The Politics of Precaution* (Princeton: Princeton University Press, 2012), pp.1–3.

41. Ibid., pp.45–60; Andrew J. Hoffman, *From Heresy to Dogma* (Stanford, CA: Stanford Business Books, 2001), pp.64–86.

42. Vogel, *Politics*, p.6.

43. Russell J. Dalton, *The Green Rainbow: Environmental Groups in Western Europe* (New Haven: Yale University Press, 1994), pp.38–9.

44. Egelston, *Sustainable Development*, pp.63–5; Manuel Rodriguez-Becerra and Bart van Hoof, *Environmental Performance of the Colombian Oil Palm Industry* (Bogotá: Fedepalma, 2005), p.20.

45. Paull, "Rachel Carson."

46. Daniel Gross, *Our Roots Grow Deep: The Story of Rodale* (Reading, PA: Rodale, 2008), pp.110–17, 114–32.

47. Ibid., pp.137–9.

48. Warren Belasco, *Food* (London: Bloomsbury Academic, 2012), pp.21–2.

49. Peter Lummel, "Born-in-the-City: The Supermarket in Germany," in Peter J. Atkins, Peter Lummel, and Derek J. Oddy (eds.), *Food and the City in Europe since 1800* (Aldershot: Ashgate, 2007), pp.165–75.

50. Susan and Bruce Williamson, "Frank Ford: Founder of Arrowhead Mills," *Mother Earth News*, September–October 1974, <http://www.motherearthnews.com/nature-and-environment/frank-ford-arrowhead-mills-zmaz74sozraw>, accessed October 12, 2016.

51. John Bloom, "Doing What Comes Naturally...Made Frank Ford Healthy and Wealthy," *Texas Monthly*, June 1979, p.86.

52. William Shurtleff and Akiko Aoyagi, "George Ohsawa, the Macrobiotic Movement," <http://www.soyinfocenter.com/HSS/George_ohsawa_macrobiotics_soyfoods1>, accessed February 2, 2016.

53. Joe Dobrow, *Natural Prophets* (New York: Rodale, 2014), p.35.

54. Ibid., pp.36–8.

55. Adam Rome, *The Genius of Earth Day* (New York: Hill & Wang, 2013), pp.150–1.

56. <http://www.paulhawken.com/biography.html>, accessed August 9 2016.

57. Bloom, "Doing What Comes Naturally," pp.82–4.

58. Dobrow, *Natural Prophets*, pp.38–9.

59. William Shurtleff and Akiko Aoyagi, "History of Erewhon—Natural Foods Pioneer in the United States (1966–2011)," <http://www.soyinfocenter.com/pdf/Erewhon.pdf>, accessed February 3, 2014.

60. Stephen J. Crimi, "Entrée to Alan Chadwick's Garden," in Stephen J. Crimi (ed.), *Performance in the Garden* (Mars Hill, NC: Logosophia, 2007), pp.17–21; Julie Guthman, *Agrarian Dreams: The Paradox of Organic Farming in California* (Berkeley: University of California Press, 2004), p.16.

61. Thomas McNamee, *Alice Waters and Chez Panisse* (New York: Penguin, 2007).

62. Interview by Ellen Farmer with Jim Cochran, December 10, 2007, UC Santa Cruz Library, Oral History Collection, "Cultivating a Movement: An Oral History of Organic Farming and Sustainable Agriculture on California's Central Coast."

63. Burt Helm, "How Boulder Became America's Startup Capital: An Unlikely Story of Tree-Huggers, Commies, Eggheads, and Gold," December 2013/January 2014, <http://www.inc.com/magazine/201312/boulder-colorado-fast-growing-business.html>, accessed January 12, 2016.

64. Rome, *Genius*, pp.179–84.

65. <http://www.cpr.org/news/story/colorado-was-ground-zero-hippies-68>, accessed March 18, 2015; Amy Azzarito, "Libre, Colorado, and the Hand-Built Home," in Elissa Auther and Adam Lerner (eds.), *West of Center: Art and the Counterculture Experiment in America, 1965–1977* (Minneapolis: University of Minnesota Press, 2012), pp.95–110.

66. <https://www.naturalgrocers.com/about/the-natural-grocers-story>, accessed October 22, 2016; Ellen Sweets, "They're Good for You: With an Emphasis on Supplements and Organics, Family-Owned Vitamin Cottage is the Scrappy Little Guy in the Health-Food Ring," *Denver Post*, April 26, 2006.

67. Mo Siegel, "Colorado Country Boy Finds a Revelation," in Jack Canfield and Gay Hendricks, *You've GOT to Read This Book!: 55 People Tell the Story of the Book That Changed Their Life* (New York: HarperCollins, 2006).

68. Mike Taylor, "The Natural Wonder of Boulder: 'We're Going to Revolutionize the Way People Eat'," *ColoradoBiz*, March 2005, <http://findarticles.com/p/articles/mi_hb6416/is_3_32/ai_n29164723/>, accessed September 15, 2009.

69. <http://www.celestialseasonings.com/about/timeline.html>, accessed August 2, 2011.

70. Lauren Duncan, "The Return of Alfalfa's," *Boulder Weekly*, July 29, 2010. In 2004 Retzloff helped found a venture capital firm, Greenmont Capital Partners, to finance companies in the organic and health business.

71. Florentine Fritzen, *Gesünder leben: die Lebensreformbewegung im 20. Jahrhundert* (Stuttgart: Steiner, 2006), pp.115–17.

72. Judith Baumgartner, *Ernährungsreform: Antwort auf Industrialisierung und Ernährungswandel* (Frankfurt: Peter Lang, 1992), p.234.

73. Greta Tüllmann, "Bio aus Liebe zur Erde und zur Natur," interview with Jennifer Vermeulen (January 2005), <http://www.ab40.de/seiten/archiv_skizzen/05_1/05_1_4a.html accessed July 8 2015>: Eva Wonneberger, *Die Alternativebewegung im Allgäu: Landkommunen, Biohöfe und andere Initiativen* (Wangen: FIU Verlag, 2008), pp.34–5.

74. G. Vogt, "The Origins of Organic Farming," in William Lockeretz (ed.), *Organic Farming: An International History* (Wallingford: CAB International, 2007), pp.18–19; U. Niggli, "FiBL and Organic Research in Switzerland," in Lockeretz (ed.), *Organic Farming*, pp.246–7.

75. Craig Sams and Josephine Fairley, *The Story of Green & Blacks* (London: Random House, 2009), pp.13–14.

76. Craig Sams, "The Craig Sams Story," <http://www.macrobiotics.co.uk/thecraigsamsstory.htm>, accessed October 22, 2016; Philip Conford, "'Somewhere Quite Different': The Seventies Generation of Organic Activists and their Context," *Rural History* 2, no. 19 (2008), p.226.

77. Sams and Fairley, *Story of Green & Blacks*, pp.19–20.

78. "Commercialization au Salon de la Diététique," *Nature et Progrès Newsletter* 4, October–December 1966, p.23.

79. Interview with Claude Aubert, January 12, 2012.

80. Geoffrey Jones, *Beauty Imagined: A History of the Global Beauty Industry* (Oxford: Oxford University Press, 2010), pp.291–3.

81. Carson, *Silent Spring*, p.237.

82. Jerome I. Rodale, *Our Poisoned Earth and Sky* (Emmaus, PA: Rodale Books, 1964), pp.409–10.

83. Jones, *Beauty Imagined*, pp.281–2.

84. Ibid., pp.277–80.

85. Tom Chappell, *The Soul of a Business* (New York: Bantam, 1994), p.24.

86. Ibid., pp.8–10.

87. Anita Roddick, *Body and Soul: Profits with Principles—The Amazing Success Story of Anita Roddick & the Body Shop* (New York: Crown Publishers, 1991), p.67.

88. Ibid., pp.69–73.

89. Christopher A. Bartlett, Kenton W. Elderkin, and Krista McQuade, "The Body Shop International," Harvard Business School Case no. 9-392-032 (July 13, 1995).

90. Roddick, *Body and Soul*, p.111.

91. Bartlett, Elderkin, and McQuade, "Body Shop."

92. Jones, *Beauty Imagined*, p.285.

93. <http://www.fundinguniverse.com/company-histories/Aveda-Corporation-Company-History.html>, accessed February 7, 2016.

94. Horst Rechelbacher, *Aveda Rituals: A Daily Guide to Natural Health and Beauty* (New York: Henry Holt, 1999), p.ix.

95. Horst M. Rechelbacher, *Minding Your Business: Profits that Restore the Planet* (San Rafael, CA: EarthAware, 2008), p.xii.

96. <http://habitat.igc.org/vancouver/van-decl.htm>, accessed July 28, 2015.

97. Kira Gould, "AIA/COTE: A History Within a Movement," <http://www.aia. org/practicing/groups/kc/AIAS077347>, accessed June 13, 2015.

98. Edward Mazria, *The Passive Solar Energy Book: A Complete Guide to Passive Solar Home, Greenhouse, and Building Design* (Emmaus, AP: Rodale Press, 1979), p.1; Ralph M. Lebens, *Passive Solar Architecture in Europe: The Results of the First European Passive Solar Competition—1980* (London: Architectural Press, 1981).

99. Eve Kushner, "Rebels with a Cause" (December 2007), <http://www. evekushner.com/writing/rebels-with-a-cause-part-1>, accessed April 5, 2014.

100. Bruce Webber, "Malcolm Wells, Champion of 'Gentle Architecture,' Dies at 83," *New York Times*, December 5, 2009.

101. James Steele, *Ecological Architecture: A Critical History* (London: Thames & Hudson, 2005), pp.149–52; Eve Kushner, "Rebels," part 5, <http://www.evekushner. com/writing/the-vision-becomes-a-reality-part-5-in-the-outsiders-series>, accessed March 3, 2016.

102. "Garbage Warrior—Full Length Documentary," March 10, 2013, <https:// www.youtube.com/watch?v=4IxUQ5MXhmo>, accessed July 29, 2016.

103. Wendy Jewell, "Earthkeeper Hero: Michael Reynolds Garbage Warrior," <http://www.myhero.com/go/hero.asp?hero=Michael_Reynolds_2008>, accessed July 29, 2016.

104. Paolo Soleri, *Arcology: The City in the Image of Man* (Cambridge, MA: MIT Press, 1969); Steele, *Ecological Architecture*, pp.135–41.

105. Ian L. McHarg, *A Quest for Life: An Autobiography* (New York: John Wiley, 1996).

106. Anne Whiston Spirn, "Ian McHarg, Landscape Architecture, and Environmentalism: Ideas and Methods in Context," in Michel Conan (ed.), *Environmentalism in Landscape Architecture* (Dumbarton Oaks: Research Library and Collection, 2000), pp.99–100.

107. McHarg, *Quest for Life*, p.99.

108. Ian L. McHarg, *Design with Nature* (New York: American Museum of Natural History, 1969); Andrew C. Revkin, "Ian McHarg, Architect Who Valued a Site's Natural Features, Dies at 80," *New York Times*, March 12, 2001.

109. Rome, *Genius*, pp.162–3.

110. Spirn, "Ian McHarg," pp.105, 110–12.

111. <http://simvanderryn.com>, accessed October 22, 2016.

112. Interview with Sim van der Ryn, January 28, 2011.

113. Mathew Knight, "Sim Van der Ryn—Pioneer of Green Architecture," July 28, 2008, <http://www.cnn.com/2008/TECH/science/07/03/derryn.interview/index.html?_s=PM:TECH>, accessed July 24, 2016; Sim Van der Ryn, *Design for Life: The Architecture of Sim Van der Ryn* (Layton, UT: Gibbs Smith, 2005), pp.16–17.

114. Patricia Leigh Brown, "It Happened Here First" *New York Times*, November 17, 2005.

115. Crimi, "Entrée," p.23.

116. Sim Van der Ryn, *The Toilet Papers* (Santa Barbara: Capra Press, 1978), p.118.

117. Interview with Sim Van der Ryn, January 28, 2011.

118. Van der Ryn, *Design*, pp.52–4.

119. Interview with Van der Ryn.

120. Ibid.; Van der Ryn, *Design*, pp.60–1

121. Van der Ryn, *Design*, pp.67–8.

122. Ibid., p.69.

123. Soren Krohn, "Danish Wind Turbines: An Industrial Success Story" (2002), <http://www.ingdemurtas.it/wp-content/uploads/page/eolico/normativa-danimarca/Danish_Wind_Turbine_Industry-an_industrial_succes_story.pdf>, accessed October 22, 2016; Flemming Tranaes, *Danish Wind Energy*, <http://www.spok.dk/consult/reports/danish_wind_energy.pdf>, accessed July 2, 2016, p.2; Robert W. Righter, *Wind Energy in America: A History* (Norman: University of Oklahoma Press, 1996), p.150.

124. Interview with Paul Jacobs, December 1, 2010, Minnetonka, MN; Righter, *Wind Energy*, p.163.

125. Cited in Bob Johnstone, *Switching to Solar: What We Can Learn from Germany's Success in Harnessing Clean Energy* (Amherst, NY: Prometheus, 2010), pp.125–6.

126. John Perlin, *From Space to Earth* (Ann Arbor: Aatec, 1999), p.67, n. 7; Sharp Global, <http://sharp-world.com/corporate/info/his/h_company/1962/index.html>, accessed February 2, 2014.

127. Ford Foundation, *A Time to Choose: America's Energy Future* (Cambridge, MA: Ballinger), p.313–14.

128. Michael L. Ross, "How the 1973 Oil Embargo Saved the Planet," *Foreign Affairs* (October 15, 2013).

129. Rodale, *Poisoned*, pp.610–20.

130. Ward and Dubos, *Only One Earth*, p.137.

131. Martin Chick, *Electricity and Energy Policy in Britain, France and the United States since 1945* (Cheltenham: Edward Elgar, 2007), pp.28–30.

132. Ann-Kristin Bergquist and Kristina Söderholm, "Sustainable Energy Transition: The Case of the Swedish Pulp and Paper Industry 1973–1990," *Energy Efficiency* 9, no. 5 (2015), pp.1179–92.

133. <http://www.greentechmedia.com/articles/read/japans-wind-power-problem-828/>, accessed October 22, 2016.

134. Righter, *Wind Energy*, pp.172–5; Janet L. Sawin, "The Role of Government in the Development and Diffusion of Renewable Technologies: Wind Power in the United States, California, Denmark and Germany," Doctoral Dissertation, The Fletcher School of Law and Diplomacy, September 2001, p.102.

135. Paul Gipe, *Wind Energy Comes of Age* (New York: John Wiley, 1995), pp.109–10.

136. <http://www.windsofchange.dk>, accessed March 28, 2014.

137. Ben Blackwell, *Wind Power: The Struggle for Control of a New Global Industry* (London: Routledge, 2015), pp.8–10; Michael Durham, "Enigma of The Leader," *The Guardian*, June 8, 2003.

138. "A Personal Story in Photos, Told by Early Blade-Manufacturer Erik Grove-Nielson, Covering Years 1949–2000," <http://www.windsofchange.dk>, accessed March 28, 2014.

139. Astrid Mignon Kirchhof and Jan-Henrik Meyer, "Global Protest against Nuclear Power: Transfer and Transnational Exchange in the 1970s and 1980s," *Historical Social Research* 39 (2014), pp.177–9.

140. Ion Bogdan Vasi, *Winds of Change: The Environmental Movement and the Global Development of the Wind Energy Industry* (Oxford: Oxford University Press, 2011), pp.144–8.

141. Raghu Garud and Peter Karnoe, "Bricolage versus Breakthrough: Distributed and Embedded Agency in Technology Entrepreneurship," *Research Policy* 32 (2003).

142. Gipe, *Wind Energy*, 56.

143. Garud and Karnoe, "Bricolage," p.282.

144. Peter Karnoe, "When Low-Tech Becomes High-Tech: The Social Construction of Technological Learning Processes in the Danish and the American Wind Turbine Industry," in Peter Karnoe, Peer Hull Krisensen, and Poul Houman Andersen (eds.), *Mobilizing Resources and Generating Competencies* (Copenhagen: Copenhagen Business School Press, 1999), p.167; Gipe, *Wind Energy*, p.56; Vasi, *Winds of Change*, pp.150–2; Torben Pedersen, "Vestas Wind Systems A/S: Exploiting Global R&D Synergies," *SMG Working Paper* No. 5/2009 (July 14, 2009), <http://ssrn.com/abstract=1433811>, accessed May 19, 2015.

145. Righter, *Wind Energy*, pp.166–9; interview with Paul Jacobs.

146. American Wind Energy Association, <http://www.awea.org/About/content.aspx?ItemNumber=772>, accessed October 22, 2016.

147. Righter, *Wind Energy*, pp.163–5.

148. Forrest Stoddard, "The Life and Work of Bill Heronemus, Wind Engineering Pioneer," <http://www.umass.edu/windenergy/about.history.heronemus.php>, accessed May 28, 2016.

149. Peter Asmus, *Reaping the Wind: How Mechanical Wizards, Visionaries, and Profiteers Helped Shape Our Energy Future* (Washington, DC: Island Press, 2001), pp.57–62; Righter, *Wind Energy*, pp.213–14.

150. Interview with Yuji Matsunami, Mitsubishi Heavy Industries, Nagasaki, May 28, 2010; Thomas Ackermann and Lennart Söder, "An Overview of Wind Energy-Status 2002," *Renewable and Sustainable Energy Reviews* 6, nos. 1–2 (2002), pp.67–127.

151. Arthur D. Little, "Project Plan for a Program to Develop a Solar Climate Control Industry," April 1974; Arthur D. Little, "Solar Heating Market," Progress Bulletin 6 (circa 1980), Polaroid Archives, Baker Library, Harvard Business School, Box 61.

152. Statement of James Harding, Friends of the Earth, *Solar Energy: Hearings before a Subcommittee of the Committee on Government Operations, House of Representatives, May 12, June 12, 13 and 14, 1978* (Washington, DC: U.S. Government Printing Office, 1979).

153. Perlin, *From Space to Earth*, p.52.

154. Elliot Berman, interviewed by Bob Johnston and cited in Johnstone, *Switching to Solar*, p.49; B. McNelis, "The Photovoltaic Business: Manufacturers and Markets," in M. D. Archer and R. Hill (eds.), *Clean Electricity from Photovoltaics* (London: Imperial College Press, 2001), pp.713–40.

155. Perlin, *From Space to Earth*, pp.58–9; McNelis, "Photovoltaic Business."

156. Perlin, *From Space to Earth*, pp.168–71.

157. Peter F. Varadi, *Sun Above the Horizon: Meteoric Rise of the Solar Industry* (Singapore: Pan Stanford, 2014), pp.31–8.

158. Interview with Peter Varadi, September 7, 2011.

159. Varadi, *Sun*, pp.41–3.

160. Interview with Varadi, September 7, 2011.

161. Varadi, *Sun*, pp.49–66.

162. Neville Williams, *Chasing the Sun* (Gabriola Island, BC: New Society Publishers, 2005), pp.84–5; Varadi, *Sun*, p.250.

163. James Quinn, "Maverick Using New Technology: Arco Solar Official Left to Build Own Photovoltaic Cells," *Los Angeles Times*, April 2, 1985, <http://articles.latimes.com/1985-04-02/business/fi-19489_1_photovoltaic-cells>, accessed April 11, 2012.

164. Perlin, *From Space to Earth*, pp.117–18.

165. Quinn, "Maverick."

166. Stephen W. Hinch, "Solar Power," *High Technology*, August 1984, p.46, Polaroid, Box M60.

167. Varadi, *Sun*, p.130; Michael Starr and Wolfgang Palz, *Photovoltaic Power for Europe: An Assessment Study* (Dordrecht: D. Reidel, 1983), pp.131–2.

168. Johnstone, *Switching to Solar*, p.123; Miwao Matsumoto, "The Uncertain but Crucial Relationship between a 'New Energy' Technology and Global Environmental Problems: The Complex Case of the 'Sunshine' Project," *Social Studies of Science* 35 (2005).

169. Interview with Kazuo Inamori, Tokyo, May 27, 2010.

170. Kazuo Inamori, preface to *A Compass to Fulfillment: Passion and Spirituality in Life and Business* (New York: McGraw-Hill, 2009).

171. Ibid., p.32.

172. Interview with Inamori.

173. Johnstone, *Switching to Solar*, p.127.

174. Arnulf Jäger-Waldau, "PV Status Report, 2004," <http://iet.jrc.ec.europa.eu/remea/pv-status-report-2004>, accessed January 14, 2016.

175. Earth Policy Institute, <http://www.earth-policy.org/data_center/C23>, April 15, 2015, accessed February 19, 2016.

176. OECD, *World Energy Outlook, 1999* (Paris: OECD).

4

Accidental Sustainability:
Waste and Tourism as Green Businesses

The previous chapters focused on the growth of green business between the nineteenth century and the late 1970s. Profit was typically not the primary motivation for the early entrepreneurs whose values and beliefs drove them to reduce the negative environmental impacts of their businesses. It proved difficult to compete against powerful conventional incumbents who had successively fed, clothed, and provided energy for the world. Building alternative businesses required a huge investment in educating consumers, suppliers and policy-makers. In the cases of solar and wind energy, it involved developing new technologies in a milieu where competing established energy sources were highly privileged by governments and utilities.

The two industries—waste and tourism—covered in this chapter are different. They are conventional industries led by conventional entrepreneurs, and, in the case of waste, often operated by public agencies. Despite all that is traditional and mainstream about these two industries, the pursuit of profits in waste and tourism has sometimes remarkably aligned with positive environmental impacts. Although we may think of waste and tourism as wildly different industries, they share a common orientation in the roles they played in the business history of sustainability: they created businesses which did environmental good without having a foundation in environmentalist belief. In a few instances, though, recognizably green entrepreneurs emerged where they might otherwise least be expected.

Waste and tourism illustrate the twin forces of industrialization and urbanization which have hastened the Anthropocene Age. They resulted in the creation of rising, unprecedented amounts of waste, some of it toxic; simultaneously, pre-industrial traditions of reuse and recycling waste were overwhelmed and steadily marginalized. Waste became the first major environmental problem of the nineteenth century, and it proved intractable. Although some risks, including the damage to human health and soil and water pollution were well understood two centuries ago, other negative impacts were only recognized once evidence of climate change began to emerge in the 1980s. Scientists discovered that the methane released by the organic materials in the modern waste stream was a substantive contributor to heat-trapping greenhouse gases. Landfills thus joined cattle-grazing as a major source of methane gas. Waste reached epidemic levels over time. In 2013 it was estimated that one-third of all the food grown for human consumption was wasted in a world where nearly 1 billion people were hungry. Over half of the wastage occurred in developing countries which lacked adequate storage, transport, and refrigeration. In the developed world, waste was pervasive from retail chains to restaurants to consumer habits. The United States wasted up to 40 percent of its food annually, including an estimated six billion pounds of fruits and vegetables which were either not harvested or not sold as they looked less than perfect in shape.[1]

Meanwhile, the global tourist industry, whose size had reached $7 trillion by the twenty-first century, was indicative of the economic success of the industrial age. The transport revolution and rising incomes beginning in the nineteenth century provided more and more people with the leisure and money to travel. From the middle of the twentieth century, tourism grew exponentially, as did the adverse environmental impact as pristine nature was converted to tourist resorts, historic sites were overwhelmed by unprecedented visitors, and greenhouses gases were generated in moving people around, and cooling and heating them in hotels.

We will see in this chapter how waste and tourism—more profit-driven than the Romantics and hippies discussed so far—could have green benefits more by the nature of their activities than by the ecological zeal of their entrepreneurs. In the matter of waste, reduce/reuse/recycle was a business model before it became a green mantra. Prodded by municipal concerns for public health, early waste companies developed environmentally friendly practices which remain in use today. Likewise, entrepreneurs in tourism were motivated more by profit than by ecological commitments, but by monetizing the appreciation of nature, they created profit-driven incentives to preserve it. In both industries, the results were mixed: environmental benefits went hand in hand with environmental damage. If Chapters 1 through 3 were about unusual people becoming unlikely entrepreneurs, this chapter addresses businesses which contributed to sustainability almost by accident.

The waste industry
An abundance of garbage

As industrial capitalism created growing wealth in the nineteenth century, it also created abundant waste or as it was mainly known before the 1960s, rubbish, refuse, or garbage.[2] There was nothing new about waste, but the amount began to grow exponentially as Western populations, increasingly urban, soared. In pre-industrial societies, the amount of waste, certainly in rural areas, was limited. Low incomes meant that there was every incentive to reuse old textiles and metals, while organic kitchen waste and animal carcasses were used for fodder or glue, and bodily wastes as fertilizer. While in the past most goods were made from simple materials which were biodegradable, this was increasingly not true in the industrial age, especially as glass and metal packaging increased.[3] There was also rapid growth in industrial waste, like spent coals, from new manufacturing processes.

Over time, materials and food became literally "wasted" because rising incomes enabled people to buy new products even when they did not need them, and to buy more food than they needed to survive. The growth of consumerism resulted in what one American cultural historian called a "throwaway society," based on the rejection of older habits of care for or "stewardship" of objects.[4] By the new century Americans were already producing far more waste per capita than Europeans: in 1905, for instance, the US per capita rate (across fourteen cities) was about 860 pounds annually; meanwhile across seventy-seven German cities, the rate was 319 pounds.[5] Across Europe, consumers retained habits of thrift and reuse much longer than their American counterparts.[6]

By the twentieth century waste became endemic. It was driven by affluence, increasingly quick fashion cycles, and technological advances which made products redundant after a few years. The amount of waste horrified environmentalist writers. In *Road to Survival*, published in 1948, William Vogt lamented the "waster's psychology."[7] The problem was not merely that scarce resources were being consumed with no sense of stewardship for the planet. A greater problem still was what happened to the waste. Household waste was typically dumped in open pits. Sometimes it was dumped in the oceans.

Industrial and chemical waste was dumped into rivers. Although for many decades accepted as the cost of progress and inevitable externalities, as noted in the last chapter, by the 1960s rivers were foaming and catching fire, and protests spread beyond ecological activists.

The traditional practices for dealing with waste were in some respects highly sustainable. As waste mounted in the nineteenth century, thousands of scavengers collected and recycled waste throughout Europe and the United States. They were known by different names in different countries—rag pickers in Britain, chiffonniers in France—and were not green entrepreneurs in intent: they were typically impoverished, and often immigrants, who saw trash as the best way to earn income. Yet they often had a positive environmental impact. They went through garbage and open dumps looking for items to recycle, and sometimes they functioned as refuse collectors, working in teams to collect garbage in big industrial cities like Boston and Chicago. Many wastes were recycled. Rags were used to make paper until wood pulp, made using sulfurous acid, replaced it in the late nineteenth century. Dead animals, including many of the horses that died in city streets, were cooked or "reduced" to produce grease which was used in making soap, candles, and perfume.[8] Rags and, later, scrap metal were collected on a large scale by small firms established by Jewish and Italian immigrants to the United States, with some larger companies and more extended trade networks emerging over time.[9]

While traditional practices might have been environmentally sustainable, they were not always healthy. As traditional small waste collection and disposal businesses struggled to respond to urban expansion, they also contributed to public health problems and epidemics, including cholera.[10] The upshot was that, throughout Europe and the United States, municipal governments began to intervene in waste collection and disposal. This followed earlier efforts by cities to build water supply systems and write regulations for fire safety.

From the 1880s public health infrastructures of major Western cities were transformed. In New York City, under the direction of Sanitation Commissioner George Waring, white-uniformed street sweepers began to clean every street, and neighborhoods received regular waste collection.[11] Waste management became a civil service profession run by municipal departments.[12] By 1914 many of the bigger cities in the United States and Europe municipalized refuse collection and disposal or awarded exclusive contracts to private companies.[13] Private firms which contracted with municipalities had little autonomy and needed to respond to idiosyncratic local regulations. For example, in 1895, Berlin, one of the fastest growing cities in Europe, enacted an ordinance requiring all waste removal firms to adopt "dust-free" collection practices using closed containers which the firms were obligated to provide, a provision which put many smaller firms out of business.[14]

Across the cities of the industrialized world, the main aims of either municipal agencies or private contractors were to insure public health, provide efficient service, and limit costs to residents.[15] Garbage disposal contracts could be lucrative, but there was limited regard for environmental impact. The Philadelphia-based New York Sanitary Utilization Company, for example, held contracts for the garbage of New York City between 1895 and 1917. The business had multiple subsidiaries which also held monopoly contracts in Washington, Wilmington, Newark, Atlantic City, and elsewhere. The venture's main capabilities rested on the support of powerful politicians and bankers in Philadelphia. Its New York operation discharged large amounts of polluted effluent into Long Island's Jamaica Bay. The company did not just dispose of waste: it also ran what were called "reduction" plants which manufactured grease, soap, glycerin, and fertilizer from household waste, as well as glue and fertilizer from dead animals, dumping the boiled up bones into the water.[16]

There were many municipal experiments with recycling household waste. In 1896, for example, a mandatory separation of household wastes in New York City was instituted by Colonel George Waring.[17] Subsequently, the wealthy German city of Charlottenburg (today part of Berlin) contracted with a firm called Charlottenburger Abfuhrgesellschaft (CAG) to introduce a three-way separation system for the recycling of household wastes. Citizens were obliged by city ordinance to separate their waste into the three categories of ashes, organic waste, and other bulky items, while CAG provided residents with tripartite bins for their homes or in apartment house courtyards. The firm owned its own piggery, for which it boiled the organic matter, and it resold useful scrap materials. The main entrepreneur behind CAG, Carl von der Linde, conducted extensive public relations work through brochures and newspaper articles aimed at persuading residents to sort their trash, and providing instruction in schools. Von der Linde wrote two books emphasizing the need to husband scarce resources, showing an early awareness of the dangers of groundwater contamination from dumping, and praising CAG's own system as "natural" compared to the ways of modern cities.[18] Von der Linde's belief in the moral value of preserving useful materials was replicated elsewhere in Central Europe.[19] The costs of running three separate collection wagons made the service the most expensive in Germany and, thus, dependent on subsidies. The withdrawal of most of its man- and horsepower during World War I caused the company to close its doors in 1917.[20]

It proved difficult to scale recycling businesses without subsidies, in part because of the mismatch between collection, which was typically continual, and demand, which was often cyclical. A for-profit waste-sorting facility owned by Lajos Cséry opened in Hungary in 1895 on the basis of a contract with the city of Budapest. Although the city's waste collection was municipalized, much of what was gathered found its way by horse-drawn carts to Cséry's privately owned sorting facility originally on the outskirts. The plant sold kitchen scraps as fertilizer, generated its own energy from incinerating some of the fibrous material, and fired the locomotives used to transport the recovered items for resale using recovered coals. The Budapest firm contracted with a firm in Munich, Germany to introduce its system.[21] The latter facility opened in 1898. There, more so than in Budapest, recovered materials were treated and disinfected before being resold. Kitchen garbage was boiled and used as fodder for the firm's own piggery. The city of Munich renewed the contract with the firm several times, but the firm remained dependent on the payment of a subsidy from the city.[22]

Public health concerns drove technological innovation in the management of waste. A commission by a local sanitary inspector in Britain led to the development of incineration as an alternative waste disposal method. In 1874, Albert Fryer, an engineer, invented the first "destructor" in the city of Nottingham. Fryer formed a partnership with a local company to build and distribute the technology. Fryer's business model rested not simply on using incineration to remove waste but on generating electricity for sale from the steam produced in the process. By 1914 there were 338 such destructors operating in Britain, with 77 of them generating electricity.[23] In Germany, municipal governments in seven cities built and operated incinerators by 1914, selling the electricity generated, as well as slag for constructing roads.[24] Merely incinerating waste can be regarded as the opposite of sustainable—it is a cause of urban air pollution. The benefits of waste-to-energy incineration remain contested; one much-cited study argued that recycling most materials from municipal solid waste saved on average three to five times more energy than did burning them for electricity.[25]

Still, a number of entrepreneurs were, at the time, quite explicit in seeking to recover as many materials as possible from incineration. In 1925 Kurt Gerson, an engineer, founded the publicly traded company Müllverwertung AG to take over Berlin's failed incineration plant. He sought to produce what he called "garbage-wool" made from cellulose and animal fibers from the refuse gathered for the plant, which could be resold for use in papermaking and construction, while the dust and ash produced in the process were to be employed in synthetic fertilizers. The prospectus for his company was explicit on both the environmental and commercial benefits. "The Gerson procedure," it explained, brought a "new economical solution to bear on the whole municipal waste and sewage problem. River courses and groundwater tables are cleaned, garbage dumps disappear, and for small cities the usage of all municipal wastes offers the possibility of profitable industry." Gerson lost control of his plant after the Nazis came to power in 1933. The plant continued operating through the 1930s, while Gerson himself moved to Britain and continued his career as an inventor, filing a series of US patents for breathing equipment.[26]

The Berlin region also saw private efforts to recycle waste for soil enrichment on a larger scale. A farmer named Arthur Schurig, known as a restless innovator, began purchasing organic kitchen wastes from Von der Linde's Charlottenburg sorting facility as the sole fertilizer for his estate in Etzin, to the west of the capital. Schurig's farms came to use 20–25 tons of composted and uncomposted Berlin household refuse daily by the 1920s. He eventually owned or leased five agricultural estates, often including formerly unproductive sandy soil or moorland. As he expanded, he also used Berlin garbage to create a loamy surface on moorland and sandy soil for later planting. Schurig bucked the trend towards animal-based farming in the area and became the largest vegetable producer in Germany, and a supplier for much of Berlin.[27]

There were innovative ventures in making machinery to facilitate composting. The Dano Engineering Company, formed in 1912 in Denmark by Kai Petersen and Christoffer Müller, became a major innovator in composting from the 1920s. The company originally specialized in the manufacture of mechanical under-carriage stokers for industrial furnaces, which were highly efficient. Their very efficiency aroused Petersen's concerns, for he concluded that mechanization was problematic in both reducing employment and separating man from nature. During the late 1920s he invested in a gardening school established by Folke Jacobsen, including buying a large mansion house outside Copenhagen where students could spend weekends on small allotments. He also responded positively when George Müller, his partner's deeply religious brother, approached him with a composting scheme. George had failed to persuade the City of Copenhagen to abolish sewers and collect the waste of citizens for compost, but he did persuade Petersen to adopt such a scheme at his factory. After the stench proved overwhelming, Petersen studied the work of Sir Albert Howard and figured out that air needed to circulate through the mass of wastes. In 1933 Petersen patented the Dano drum, a large rotating cylinder which became a key technology for many composting plants, and a number of Danish municipalities subsequently adopted the machine.[28] The company articulated a clear environmentalist viewpoint, criticizing the impact of artificial fertilizer on microbial life in the soil, and advocating an ecological cycle in which wastes were put back to use.[29]

Between the second half of the nineteenth century and the 1920s, the growth of household waste from rising populations and urbanization generated extensive governmental regulation and even ownership of companies. The streets of cities were literally cleaned up. The stated purpose was public health and not sustainability per se. Recycling by scavengers was replaced by more organized systems of systematic dumping in pits and in oceans and by incineration. Within this broad context, a handful of entrepreneurs, often engineers, developed technologies or systems which sought to profit from waste through a business enterprise. They developed clear ecological arguments. In Central and Northern Europe, there was the initiation of many of the processes for sorting and recycling waste materials still used today. These included source separation with special containers and separate collection: sorting plants employing magnets to separate metals; fans, sieves, and rolling drums to separate lighter-weight and fine particles from other wastes; and conveyor belts for hand-sorting of the remainders. Most ventures struggled to achieve profitability without public funds, however.

Municipal dominance

Between the 1920s and the 1950s the scope for for-profit businesses in waste and recycling further diminished. Governments and municipalities set the rules, performed many of the tasks, and owned many of the disposal facilities. Early policies were driven by public health needs, which were often directly at odds with environmental concerns. Indeed, in this early period few, if any, efforts were made to balance the sanitary needs of the cities with the waste problems they sent out of cities.

Public health drove a new innovation called sanitary landfills to replace open pit dumping. These involved a system in which waste was buried either underground or in large piles. These landfills ensured that the wastes were compacted and each layer covered over daily with dirt to prevent odors, vermin, and wind-scattered litter. The concept had already been developed in Britain before 1914, where it was called "controlled tipping," and by 1939 it accounted for 60 percent of that country's municipal waste disposal. Germany, and other European countries, followed suit over time.[30] In 1935, the city of Fresno in California introduced the first sanitary landfill in the United States, after which they quickly spread over the country.[31]

Although these sanitary landfills resolved certain public health issues in the cities, their environmental impact was felt elsewhere. As the accumulated waste broke down, methane gas was released. Besides air pollution, sanitary landfills also posed a threat to water systems. The environmental hazards from leachate were not taken seriously before the 1960s at the earliest.[32] It was only from the 1970s that the practice spread of siting sanitary landfills far more carefully with regard to groundwater, engineering appropriately for drainage, and lining them to prevent leachate from entering the surrounding water or land.

The second concern of policy-makers was the recovery of scarce resources. In both world wars governments encouraged recovery.[33] During the 1930s the Nazi regime in Germany implemented some of the most interventionist recovery policies designed to achieve domestic reuse of waste materials to promote national autarky and to prepare for war. There was a high level of inefficiency, with the expropriation of scrap firms owned by Jews causing a shortage of skilled capabilities.[34]

Government and municipal regulation left the private sector with limited autonomy, though entrepreneurs with ecological commitments continued to emerge. In 1930 a composting company called the Edaphon-Müllverwertung Commanditgesellschaft was launched in Austria on the basis of a patent held by Professor Raoul HeinrichFrancé, a prominent biologist and philosopher, whose extensive writings on micro-organisms in the soil would (retrospectively) earn him a reputation as a pioneering figure in organic agriculture and ecology. His process recycled municipal solid waste, street sweepings, and sewage to provide a nitrogen-enriching natural fertilizer for use in organic agriculture. Francé's factory plants were subsequently adopted in other European cities including Salzburg, Munich, and Milan. Francé's pitch emphasized the moral imperative of using waste rather than dumping or incinerating it. "There is value in this garbage which one throws away," he maintained in a 1936 presentation to city officials in Salzburg, "instead of reusing it and returning it to the economic cycle."[35]

Francé's wife, Annie Francé-Harrar, also a biologist and a prolific writer, carried on his work after his death in 1943.[36] Her writings reached a wider audience than her husband's did. Her 1950 book, entitled (in English) *The Last Chance: For a Future without Want*, focused on the importance of micro-organisms in generating the humus needed for soil fertility.[37] Although few municipal or national governments listened, Francé-Harrar carried on their shared work and spread the science and knowledge of humus and compost as an economy.

After the end of World War II, the West's accelerated economic growth and abundance of cheap energy generated not just more waste but different kinds of waste. In the United States, daily rates of waste generation, already high compared with the rest of the world in 1940 at an average of two pounds per person, rose to four pounds per person in 1968.[38] The spread of self-serve supermarkets across Europe promoted the use of packaging as a means of ensuring freshness, hygiene, and the prevention of theft, among other things.[39] There were further shifts in the composition of waste which vexed the environment: new synthetic materials, led by plastic, started to be used on a wide scale; there was also a vast expansion of disposable convenience goods, thanks in part to planned obsolescence models in consumer durables. The waste stream changed by weight as well thanks to heavy consumer goods like automobiles.[40] Products increasingly contained composite parts formed from various materials, and these new or newly complex materials created significant obstacles to environmentally friendly waste management.[41]

Landfilling remained the preferred municipal postwar option. It kept tax-payers mollified while permitting high labor costs and sometimes low productivity when waste department jobs were used for patronage.[42] In 1960, 94 percent of American municipal waste went to landfills. In Germany the percentage may have been even higher.[43] This landfilling was dramatically more environmentally damaging than at any earlier period because of the presence of materials which, on a chemical compound level, had never been produced in the history of the planet. Organic waste decomposes because the planet's bacteria have evolved to eat it. But Earth has never had bacteria that eat plastics. Consequently, plastics do not decompose in the way organic material does: they take decades, even centuries in some cases, to decompose. They are also difficult to combust in incineration plants: not only do they generate noxious odors, but (as later became apparent) they also spread dangerous toxic substances such as dioxins into the atmosphere.[44]

American law at this time did not specifically address waste. There were US laws governing pollution, including the Federal Water Pollution Control Act of 1948 and the Air Pollution Control Act of 1955, but these were, until replaced by the Clean Water Act of 1972 and the Clean Air Act of 1963, advisory and oriented towards experimental funding and research. The few state laws on the books at the time were similarly ineffective.[45] In many European countries, the first legislation concerning groundwater pollution only came in the mid-1950s, such as the Swiss federal water protection law in 1955 and the West German federal water reservoir laws passed in 1957 and 1960. These statutes aimed to regulate waste dumping by requiring the strict separation of waste burial sites from water flows and aquifers; as in the United States, enforcement was typically lax.[46]

The most active proponents of recycling were not private or municipal waste companies, but conventional companies which had a commercial interest in recycled materials. The Chicago-based Container Corporation of America, a large manufacturer of recycled paperboard, was a major example in the United States. In 1940, the chief executive Walter Paepcke launched an official reforestation program. He went on to develop Aspen, a former silver mining town in Colorado, as an elite resort, and base for a think tank known as the Aspen Institute.[47] Subsequently, the Corporation invested resources to encourage the Boy Scouts and other civic groups to organize and sponsor recycling projects.[48] This promotion of recycling took place years before the environmental activist groups in the late 1960s, such as Ecology Action in California, began their campaigns. Container Corporation disseminated the language of recycling in multiple ways: in the early 1970s, for example, it sold ecology-themed coasters illustrating the importance of preserving natural resources through recycling.[49] Most significantly, in 1970 it sponsored a contest for art and design students to develop designs that symbolized the recycling process. The winner was a senior at UCLA who developed a symbol with a three-chasing-arrows Möbius loop. The company licensed the design to the three principal paper industry groups, after which it fell into the public domain. This became, and remains, the global symbol of recycling.[50]

During the middle decades of the twentieth century, then, the primary obstacle to more environmentally friendly waste management was not powerful incumbent conventional firms, as in the food industry, but public policies which prioritized health over ecology. As in energy, governments were the problem and not the opportunity for sustainability.

Waste and Earthrise

It was only from the 1960s that environmental considerations began to impact governmental and municipal policies towards waste management. In the United States, the Clean Air Act of 1963 and the Air Quality Act of 1967 began to ramp up federal control of interstate air pollution. But apart from sharply reducing incineration activities, these laws had only a minor impact on solid waste, an area neglected in federal legislation.[51] In 1965, however, the Solid Waste Disposal Act, the first federal statute designed to address solid waste pollution, was passed, although it concentrated on promoting research rather than implementing federal regulation and controls.[52] The Office of Solid Waste was formed out of the US Public Health Service under the act. This agency at first cooperated closely with the industry, less so after it was folded into the Environmental Protection Agency (EPA) in 1970 and increasingly became an enforcer of legislation.[53]

Further legislation followed. In 1976 the Resource Conservation and Recovery Act made federal financial support contingent on the development of the state and local waste management plans, and not only actively regulated landfills for the first time, but also set standards whose enforcement required the closing of thousands of open dumps. Resource recovery explicitly included methods of incineration with energy production or "waste-to-energy." This federal legislation began to powerfully shape markets in waste management, as well as to provide companies with the funds to experiment with new recovery efforts.[54]

In Europe a new wave of more stringent national legislation crested in the 1970s, often explicitly following the American model. In Germany, the Waste Disposal Law of 1972 ended uncontrolled dumping and set environmental standards for landfilling activity. The great reduction in the number of dumps which followed ensured that landfill space would be at a premium, and practicable only on a larger scale.[55] The growth of legislation encouraged consolidation in the highly fragmented private sector of the industry. In the postwar United States, large numbers of small-scale, traditional hauling firms divided up commercial and industrial customers and some residences in large cities. There were at least ten thousand private waste-hauling companies during the postwar decades. They were typically ethnic-niche family businesses. In Chicago, for example, family-owned ethnic Dutch firms were pre-eminent.[56] Typically, they formed trade associations in their cities, which both set minimum technological standards in collection, and acted as a cartel to prevent new entry.[57]

In Chicago one of these small firms became an industry giant. The catalyst for change was Dean Buntrock, who had married Elizabeth Huizenga, whose family ran Ace Scavenger Service, one of the Dutch garbage-hauling firms. Buntrock moved to Chicago in 1956 to help run his wife's family's hauling business after his father-in-law died. He was a first mover in seeing the opportunity to roll up a fragmented industry whose many small firms were now faced by rising capital expenditure because of regulation. He invested in new technologies such as containerization. He also fostered the consolidation of the many small private associations into the National Solid Wastes Management Association (the name taken in 1968), with himself as president.[58] This Association became an active lobbyist, working especially to make sure that federal involvement in waste management would not lead to subsidization of the municipalities' programs.[59]

In 1971 Buntrock floated Waste Management Inc. on the New York Stock Exchange with an initial public offering (IPO) which raised $4 million. The name itself was interesting, both because Waste was left general and not limited by the adjective "Solid," and because Management was used rather than Scavenger. While Ace Scavenger Service advertised itself as removing garbage and rubbish, Buntrock conceived of himself as managing waste.[60] This was one of the first times that a waste company had accessed capital markets, and it was almost a decade before the first wind companies would experiment with them. Access to the markets was transformational, as it gave Buntrock the ability to buy small firms around the country. The annual revenues of Waste Management rose from $17 million in 1971 to $800 million in 1981, by which time it had secured 175 municipality-wide contracts. It also began to expand globally after securing a contract for the provision of waste management services in Riyadh, Saudi Arabia in 1975.[61]

Capital markets were also key to the growth of Browning-Ferris Industries (BFI), founded as American Refuse Systems in Houston by the 28-year-old Tom Fatjo, Jr., who had trained as an accountant. In 1967 Fatjo was the president of a community association dissatisfied with its local garbage collection service, and, convinced that he could do better, he bought a single truck with his cousin and began operating.[62] Two years later he acquired a controlling interest in the NYSE-listed firm of BFI, a long-established firm which manufactured heavy equipment, including for landfills. Subsequently Fatjo acquired small firms elsewhere, often paying using common stock of the public company, and implemented a strategy based on owning disposal capacity, primarily landfills, and using the acquisitions to build dense collection routes. By 1981 revenues were over $660 million, and the firm operated in thirty-six US states, as well as Canada, Spain, Kuwait, Saudi Arabia, and Australia.[63] Fatjo stepped down as chief executive in 1975, but remarkably founded three more waste companies over the following three decades, growing and selling two of them.[64]

Buntrock and Fatjo were for-profit entrepreneurs who identified profitable opportunities to build businesses on the basis of municipal contracts. They had no known environmentalist views, although interestingly theirs were among the first conventional companies to see value in aligning corporate images with environmentalist language, especially after the oil price rises and energy crisis of the early 1970s. BFI's annual report in 1973 noted that it provided "services which will enhance the environment."[65] The firm made early use of the phrase "printed on recycled paper" in its annual report for the following year.[66]

Both Buntrock and Fatjo also entered the waste paper/fiber recycling business in the early 1970s. In 1974 BFI acquired one of the country's largest paper recyclers, Consolidated Fibers Inc. (CFI), which both operated recovery facilities and had established secondary (recycled) paper markets in numerous US and Canadian cities. A collapse in prices in secondary markets during 1974-5, especially for waste paper, soon led both companies to divest themselves of large parts of their recycling divisions.[67] The economics of recycling waste rather than burying it remained unattractive. It involved a constant waste stream on the collection side and a seasonal and cyclical demand for recycled products on the disposal side. The economics of recycling of plastics, for example, was heavily influenced by fluctuations in energy prices, which affected both the cost of electricity and the cost of virgin plastic. Waste Management and BFI opted to refocus on the environmental benefits of their high-tech landfill systems, hazardous waste systems, and energy recovery plants.[68]

Europe saw a similar concentration in ownership. In postwar Germany, for example, there were still many small-scale family firms, which filled the gaps in services not provided by municipal departments, including services to residents of small towns and rural areas, and to businesses.[69] As the volume of garbage grew, the fragmented private sector began to create associations. Gustav Edelhoff and Norbert Rethmann were among the important figures in the consolidation of smaller firms into larger ones.

Edelhoff was the owner of a small family business in Iserlohn which had originated as sewage remover. He observed both the growing volume of waste and the need for more capital to invest in new technologies.[70] He also pushed for the creation of a trade association. In 1961 he gathered forty colleagues and competitors in the city of Offenbach and founded the Verband des privaten Städtereinigungsgewerbes (VPS, or Association of Private City Sanitation Trades).[71] Earlier than the American firms, Edelhoff also began to employ quasi-environmental language. His annual report for his trade association's 1962/1963 annual meeting asserted that the business distanced itself from "companies which are prepared to offer their services at cutthroat prices and thereby to proceed without consideration of what the national economy, national health, water- and landscape-protection require."[72] Edelhoff devoted increasing attention to water pollution and other environmental issues in the trade association's journal.[73]

Similar ecological language was used by Norbert Rethmann who had taken over the Rethmann family waste business following his father's retirement in

1969. A practicing Catholic with strong ethical values, Rethmann expanded his business throughout northwest Germany over the following decade, with revenues increasing forty-two times to reach $23 million. In 1977, concerned about the landfilling of plastic waste, Rethmann added the tenet that "Recycling comes before disposal for us" to the company guidelines.[74]

Insofar as recycling was practiced in Germany in the 1970s, it was done by the private sector. The companies sought municipal guarantees of minimum compensation because of the same problem of secondary-market volatility that drove the American companies out of the recycled paper business in the mid-1970s.[75] In both countries there was interest in the potential for recycling, both for commercial and ecological reasons, but it was tempered by the risk and difficulty of making the operation profitable: waste firms were reluctant to invest resources in the activity unless they could get a guarantee of some sort of return.

Between the 1920s and the 1950s, then, municipal governments in Europe and the United States bounded the roles that for-profit businesses could assume. It was only beginning in the 1960s that public policies turned to environmental issues rather than public health alone. The growth of legislation in the 1960s aiming at improved environmental performance provided the incentives for the merger of many smaller firms into larger groups. The opportunity was seized by the likes of Dean Buntrock, Tom Fatjo, Jr., and Gustav Edelhoff, who were conventional entrepreneurs who saw profitable opportunities in consolidating a fragmented industry. Their companies professionalized the waste industry, and disseminated new technologies and best practices, but they were reluctant to invest much capital or time into recycling, at least without municipal guarantees.

Nature-based tourism

Historically only the rich elites of the world had either the time or the money to travel for purposes of leisure and entertainment. This began to change in the late eighteenth century when a middle class arose with enough disposable income to emulate habits of travel and recreation previously reserved for the aristocracy. During the nineteenth century, as incomes continued to rise and mobility was transformed by the railroads beginning in the 1840s, a much wider democratization of tourism began, reaching first the middle class, and then by the end of the nineteenth century, blue-collar workers in industrialized economies. Britain was at the forefront in the development of seaside resorts, beginning with cities such as Brighton on the south coast, patronized first by the upper class and then by wider social groups. By the late nineteenth century there were vast blue-collar resorts in English seaside towns such as Blackpool and Southend, which had music-halls, zoos, opera houses, theatres, pleasure gardens, and exhibitions.[76] In the United States, the seaside resort of Atlantic City in New Jersey grew to become a giant resort in the late nineteenth century.[77]

Tourism transformed the natural environment into an attraction to be appreciated, even revered. Nevertheless, as nature became commodified for profit, tourism also carried substantial environmental and social dangers for the natural world. The early entrepreneurs interested in developing businesses based on people's desire to pay to see preserved landscapes and other natural phenomena were conventional, that is, motivated more by profit than by conservation for its own sake. In the case of tourism, despite its drawbacks, the pursuit of profits could significantly align with positive environmental impacts.

A prominent nineteenth-century example of the commodification of nature was the Swiss Alps. Britain's Thomas Cook, a pioneer tour operator who sought to democratize travel beyond the elites by taking advantage of newly built railroads, began taking groups of British tourists to see the Swiss Alps during the 1860s.[78] Entrepreneurs built hotels and other tourist facilities, generating strong clustering effects which grew the reputation of the Swiss Alps as a tourist destination. An association was established by the hoteliers to develop industry standards. From the 1860s entrepreneurs pitched the Alps as healthy places, enabling the development of a medical tourism business in the region.[79] The hotelier Johannes Badrutt, recognizing that he could much more easily cover his fixed costs and expand revenues by extending his season of operations into the winter months, previously seen as a cold, snowy, and highly undesirable time to be in the mountains, began promoting the health benefits of sunlight and lack of pollution of the winter days.[80] By the 1880s Switzerland was already attracting a million visitors per year, primarily to experience the natural environment.[81]

None of these entrepreneurial endeavors expressed explicit ecological or even conservationist sentiments. The most that can be said is that they promoted a favorable view of pollution-free air.[82] The same can be said of early nature tourism in the United States, which expanded from trips to mineral springs and spas to visiting natural sites such as New Hampshire's White Mountains and Niagara Falls. Landowners and hoteliers began building accommodation and offering guided tours.[83]

It was in the creation of the world's first national parks in the United States that an explicit connection emerged between the business of nature tourism and conservation. California's Yosemite Valley, first explored by white Americans in the 1830s, began to draw its tourism businesses soon after its natural beauty was first described in the national press in the 1850s. The potential for tourism was quickly identified. A Canadian-American gold prospector named Galen Clark built the first "hotel" in the valley in 1857, a twelve-by-sixteen-foot cabin known as Clark's Station or Clark's Crossing, in which tourist parties could stay by a bridge he built across the Merced River. Clark added an encampment of tents with a second log cabin for a restaurant across the river in 1859.[84] Clark and others pressed for protection of the area. In 1864, new federal legislation allowed California to set Yosemite aside as a state park.[85] In 1874 California restricted business development in the park to concession contracts, at which time there were at least four hotels, two general stores, and other service providers active in it.[86]

Business was also important in the creation of the first national park in Yellowstone in 1872. In this case it was the financier Jay Cooke, who controlled the Northern Pacific Railroad. Cooke and his manager, A. B. Nettleton, perceiving the opportunity for tourism, hired expeditions to map the area. In 1871 an expedition led by the geologist Ferdinand Hayden was joined by the artist Thomas Moran after Cooke and Nettleton requested that he be invited in order to produce images of the valley's wonders for promotional purposes. Nettleton, Cooke, and a Congressman associate of Cooke's—William Darrah Kelley, a Republican member of the House of Representatives from Pennsylvania—were the first to suggest the idea of making the "Great Geyser Basin" into a public park. Cooke saw the idea as a way of keeping small claimants out of the territory and ensuring both that the only private interest to negotiate with the government was the Northern Pacific and that commercialization did not ruin the natural features.

Cooke did not ultimately benefit from his efforts, as a financial crisis in 1873 brought down his firm and delayed the Northern Pacific's extension of its line to a point near the park borders until 1883. Nonetheless, the railroad invested significantly in the park's infrastructure thereafter. A subsidiary constructed a hotel at Yellowstone's Mammoth Hot Springs in 1883, and other large hotels near the park's major features followed. By 1910 hotel-building and other improvements had cost the railroad and its business partners about $1 million, but the facilities were profitable while the attraction—which the Northern Pacific emphasized in its advertising—had successfully generated additional passenger traffic.[87]

The Yellowstone experience of cooperation between railroads and conservationists was not unique. Each of the major US trunk lines attempted to promote the creation of protected national parks for tourism purposes along their transcontinental routes, particularly in the sparsely settled regions of the West.[88] Before the Grand Canyon was officially named a "national monument" in 1908, the head of the Atchison, Topeka & Santa Fe Railway had seen the advantage of replacing the local mining industry with tourism, and began developing a tourist infrastructure as soon as he could buy a local spur line to the canyon around 1900. He cooperated with the British expatriate entrepreneur Fred Harvey to extend his chain of restaurants and lodgings into the canyon. When the National Park Service was established in 1916 and came to take over ranger duties from the forestry service, large tourism enterprises like Harvey's were further entrenched.[89]

These for-profit hotels, restaurants, and guides played an important role in the development of the national parks alongside the government roads and rangers that helped maintain the parks against poachers. By the 1920s this private sector role in conservation had declined as the growing role of the National Park Service increased governmental management of the parks, while routinizing relations with concessionaires rather than providing incentives for entrepreneurial innovation. Simultaneously, the use of automobiles both expanded the tourist market and made the connection between the tourism business and conservation more tenuous, as it led to pollution and the spread of businesses selling souvenir merchandise alongside the parks in a way which would have been impossible during the era of railroad dominance.[90]

There were many other aspects of nature tourism which were straightforwardly negative in ecological terms. These included the growth of hunting for large game animals and birds. Professional hunting safaris reached their heyday in East Africa, especially Kenya, after 1900 as the region became

more populated under British colonial rule.[91] Over time there were unantici-
pated positive consequences for the region's ecology, if not its people, as the
scaling up of slaughter weighed on individuals.[92] Frederick Selous, a prominent British hunter in East Africa, transitioned from hunting for himself to
commercializing the activity, serving as a guide and organizer, including for a
massive safari for former US president Theodore Roosevelt in 1909. The scale
of the killing affected Selous, and he began proclaiming the need for conservation.[93] Other Victorian hunters who became tour guides and operators
pioneered what would become a basis for eco-tourism one hundred years
later: the photographic safari. Such was the case of Edward North Buxton, who
switched his activities from shooting guns to shooting photos around 1890,
and became a vocal supporter of wildlife conservation during the 1900s.[94]
By the 1920s there was a considerable business in photographic safaris in
East Africa.[95]

While the era of the Great Depression and World War II was not associated
with significant innovations in tourism, the subsequent decades saw a major
growth of the industry, rarely with positive environmental outcomes. In 1950,
there were about 25 million international tourism arrivals worldwide,
95 percent of which went to Europe and the United States. By 1960 international tourist arrivals had reached 69 million. By 1980 the number of
arrivals had reached 278 million. Two-thirds of those arrivals were in Europe,
but there had also been a significant geographical diffusion. Africa, for
example, had 7 million arrivals that year.[96]

These were decades when commercially driven tourism scaled up. A tourist
infrastructure developed with travel agents, tourist organizations, and hotel
chains proliferating. In France, for example, new tourist organizations
emerged like Club Méditerranée, founded in 1950, which sold all-inclusive
holidays. There were 2,000 travel agencies in the country by the 1970s, the
largest of which were owned by big corporate groups like the news agency
Havas and the state-owned airline Air France.[97] Ski resorts proliferated. There
was a huge development in the German and Swiss Alps during the 1950s, with
little concern at all for the environment.[98] In contrast, Walter Paepcke's
enormous postwar investment in turning the town of Aspen in Colorado
into a cultural retreat focused on the renewal of the inner spirit was aimed
at an elite market. Although he invested in skiing facilities, he rigorously
opposed mass skiing. Even then there was still substantial repurposing of the

mountains for leisure activities, the building of ski lifts, and other interventions designed to turn the location into a commercial enterprise.[99]

The democratization of tourism was driven by increased paid leisure time, the spread of automobile ownership, and the expansion of civilian aviation. In 1948 Pan American World Airways, the biggest US and world airline at the time, introduced "tourist class," signifying that air travel was no longer to be the preserve of a tiny elite. The process intensified with the advent of jet travel symbolized by the Boeing 707 jet aircraft launched in 1957.[100] Subsequently, the development of wide-bodied planes opened up travel from the West and Japan to destinations in the developing world. The resulting growth of mass tourism, which responded to prices rather than environmental concerns, resulted in the over-development of entire coastlines, such as those of Spain, through hotels and huge resorts, ecological damage to tropical islands such as Maui in Hawaii, the growth of sex tourism in Thailand and elsewhere, and multiple other negative environmental and social impacts. The emissions from air and road travel soared, becoming significant contributors to global warming.[101]

Unlike their role in waste, governments played little role in tourism. Initially, their intervention was primarily driven by conservation motives. The American national park system inspired other countries, including Australia (1879), Canada (1885), and New Zealand (1887), to create national parks. In 1909 Sweden became the first country in Europe to designate national parks. After World War II, European governments became proactive in encouraging tourism, which was seen as a development tool for creating jobs in under-performing regions.[102] During the late 1960s the World Bank began investing in tourism in developing countries, focused especially on supporting the expansion of luxury hotels. During the 1970s the Inter-American Development Bank provided large loans to encourage the development of large resorts in the Americas, such as Cancún in Mexico. The development of Cancún was instituted by the country's president as a development strategy. The government joined both ends of the island to the mainland with roads, established drainage and electricity systems, and provided incentives to foreign investors. The result was a major environmental shock which damaged the lagoon, obliterated sand dunes, led to the extinction of multiple species of animals and fish, and destroyed the rainforest which had once surrounded Cancún.[103]

Notwithstanding the huge growth of state-supported conventional tourism which paid little if any regard to environmental impact, a number of entrepreneurs beginning in the 1960s sought to develop businesses to appeal to affluent consumers who were becoming more interested in environmentally sensitive tourism. The most important entrepreneur in creating and shaping this niche was Lars-Eric Lindblad. The Swedish-born Lindblad parlayed an early fascination with polar exploration and world travel into work at the retail travel offices of Thomas Cook & Son in Stockholm and Zurich during the late 1940s. Emigrating to the United States in 1951, Lindblad worked first for American Express and then, between 1953 and 1958, for a Dutch wholesale tour company, Lissone-Lindeman. He became concerned that the visits of a growing number of Americans to historically and culturally significant sites in Europe caused damage to those sites, represented a minimal educational experience, and overlooked cultural and natural wonders outside the West. He thus developed a business taking wealthy Americans to visit India. Lindblad opened his own firm, Lindblad Travel, based in New York in 1958.[104]

Lindblad's new business focused on taking wealthy and prominent American individuals, families, and organizations to destinations around the world. It was a niche market, which initially required limited capital as he rented necessary facilities rather than owning them. He concentrated first on historical and archaeological attractions, but his organization of a world tour for the Garden Clubs of America in 1960, involving sixty travelers, set the pattern for Lindblad's subsequent tours by procuring a highly-credentialed lecturer to make the tour educational as well as comfortable for the guests.[105]

During the early 1960s Lindblad began offering safaris in East Africa. This became a profitable business, and it helped Lindblad's more radical ventures. Lindblad Travel as a whole grew quite rapidly, with gross revenues expanding from $1 million in 1964 to $4 million in 1972.[106]

In 1966 Lindblad launched his first voyage to Antarctica, chartering a transport ship from the Argentinean navy involving an upfront cost of $100,000 even before any reservations were made. The first cruise, involving fifty-six passengers for thirty-one days, was widely reported in the American press, and his subsequent trips were immediately booked.[107] The tickets were expensive: the cost was between $2,800 and $3,000 per person (between $20,000 and $22,000 in 2015 dollars).[108] Lindblad broadened the market for nature tourism by adding services beyond observing the natural environment.

He upgraded the educational component of his trips by hiring leading scientists to come on the voyage. Lindblad also specified that the food served on his vessels should be excellent, and over time it became legendary.[109] The Antarctic tour set the model, subsequently known as the "Lindblad pattern," for environmentally sensitive Antarctic tourism with his limitation of tour groups to small numbers of tourists who were given extensive ecology-education preparation onboard and allowed to walk on the continent in limited areas, while avoiding direct contact with wildlife and vulnerable natural features.[110]

Lindblad's contacts in South America allowed him to extend his reach to the then-inaccessible Easter Island. In 1967 Lindblad offered the first trip to the island, lasting two weeks and involving forty-eight clients.[111] Lindblad donated all the company's profits from operations there to efforts to preserve its archaeological heritage and gathered donations from some clients, raising $500,000. "My conviction," he later wrote, "is that intelligent tourism can preserve the past by this kind of restoration, so that instead of damaging a historical site, tourism can enrich it."[112] In 1967 Lindblad also applied his Antarctic model to Ecuador's Galápagos Islands, where he became the first tour operator.[113] Lindblad sought to make both conservation and minor scientific assistance a part of his operations in the islands. He paid for the first study on the impact of visitation to the islands that would help establish guidelines to avoid harm to the wildlife or ecosystems from tourists. He noted that such use of funds was justified even for business reasons, as "the preservation of nature is actually one of Lindblad Travel's most valuable assets."[114]

Conservation efforts continued as Lindblad's firm opened new destinations. In 1974 the government of Bhutan contracted the company to assist in opening the previously reclusive country to tourism. Lindblad was concerned about the danger of over-development that was taking place in Nepal at that time and worked with the Bhutanese government to settle on a high price ($160 per day) for the tourist entry visa, with the revenue going to the government for preserving cultural monuments and avoiding deforestation, rather than to tour operators like himself.[115]

Lindblad's advice to the Bhutanese government indicated his commitment to sustainability over profitability. His son, Sven-Olaf, who would found his own tourism business, subsequently observed that his father was a better explorer than businessman, whose exceptional talent for innovation was not always matched by attention to the profitability of trips.[116] An idealistic belief that travel would promote peace led Lindblad to develop tours taking people to the Communist regimes in Asia, in defiance of US government bans on doing business with Vietnam and Cambodia.[117] During the 1980s the firm had more than 40 percent of its business in China. In 1989 Lindblad Travel went bankrupt after being fined the small amount of $75,000 by the American government for violating trade embargoes, and then experiencing a sharp drop in bookings due to the Tiananmen Square massacre in China and major disturbances in Kenya.[118] Lindblad's son, who had been operating the "Special Expeditions" subsidiary of Lindblad Travel since 1979, went on to found his own successful travel company.[119]

Lindblad built the largest business in environmentally sensitive tourism in the 1960s, but certainly not the only one. During that decade, a cluster of expatriate-owned firms were created in regions of great natural beauty. In Kenya, the firm of Abercrombie & Kent was founded by Geoffrey Kent and his parents in 1962, who were British settlers, shortly before they lost their family farm at the time of Kenyan independence. The name Abercrombie was invented, and was chosen only because it would allow the firm to appear alphabetically at the top of the advertising pages.[120] When his parents retired from the business in the late 1960s, Kent began to expand beyond East Africa, including South Africa. Upon his marriage to Jorie Butler of Chicago, the company opened a sales office in Oak Brook, Illinois to assist with the rapidly expanding American market, later joined by comparable offices in Britain and Australia. The firm's safaris were noted for their luxury, and motivated by the slogan "shoot with a camera, not a gun."[121] The company expanded beyond Africa, employing 800 people with revenues of $27 million in the mid-1980s.[122] It grew as the world's largest luxury adventure company, which it combined with advocacy for new reserves to protect endangered species and the creation of its own philanthropic foundation to promote social and environmental projects in regions where it operated.[123]

The natural environment was thus commoditized by the modern tourist industry. Initially, the scale was small and the damage limited. As conventional customers wanted to see pristine nature, tour companies and railroad companies were almost compelled to limit damage. As a result, unlikely figures such as the US financier Jay Cooke became co-creators of the world's first national park system. In Africa, too, Frederick Selous and others discovered there was a market for photographing wild animals as well as killing them.

Nature tourism assisted conservation by promoting a love of nature and interest in conservation among tourists. This is not to deny that conservation, both in the nineteenth century and afterwards, took place in an imperialist political and economic setting.[124]

The democratization of tourism during the twentieth century, however, first with automobiles and then with jets, raised the scale of the environmental damage of the industry as a whole. There was decimation of coastlines, and surging emissions from travel. From the 1960s figures such as Lars-Eric Lindblad and Geoffrey Kent built businesses catering to, and driving, demand from affluent consumers for luxury nature tourism with a strong educational component which actively sought to be sustainable. They laid down many of the principles which would be formally identified as eco-tourism during the 1980s, as we will see in Chapter 5. Yet the numbers involved represented a tiny percentage of the 277 million international tourist arrivals in 1980. By then, the tourist industry had become part of the environmental problem, rather than the solution.

Conclusion

The waste and tourist industries were industries in which the profit motive of conventional business was preeminent. They were two sides of the same coin. The former dealt with the consequences of the industrial age and consumer society, while the latter was the result of the wholly unprecedented rise in incomes, increased leisure time, and travel mobility which was the result of the industrial age in the West. Both industries had positive outcomes. The waste industry saved urban populations from epidemics and other health issues, while tourism enriched the lives of many people. But there were negative environmental impacts. Many of the practices the waste industry undertook to process trash, such as landfilling, had negative consequences, though from the late nineteenth century, municipal governments defined what firms could do, or else did it themselves. They were motivated by concerns about hygiene and cost, and often—as in the case of landfills—that cost was not fully understood. In nature tourism, railroad companies and other conventional businesses sometimes played proactive roles in seeking to prevent environmental despoliation. The scaling of the industry resulted in growing environmental damage. Massive resorts despoiled pristine beaches and native species of flora and fauna, and put increasing strain on water supplies. The mass movement of people in automobiles and planes raised greenhouse emissions exponentially.

The environmental awakening of the 1960s had a markedly different impact on the two industries. In the waste industry, US and European governments introduced increasingly stringent environmental legislation. These laws reframed waste as an environmental issue. They encouraged the highly fragmented industry to consolidate, and reimagine itself as an environmental services provider, even if this apparent greening of a conventional industry often appeared more like public relations than reality at times. The opposite happened in the tourist industry, whose growth was strongly encouraged by governments as a development strategy. Governments became co-creators with business of huge environmental damage.

Green entrepreneurs were few and far between in both industries, although they were also not entirely absent. In the waste industry, Carl von der Linde was motivated by a clear vision of stewardship of scarce resources and introduced a pioneering recycling program. Kai Petersen and Raoul Heinrich and Annie Francé made significant technological innovations enabling waste to be used as compost. In nature tourism, Frederick Selous, through developing the photographic safari, provided a sustainable alternative to simply killing animals. Lars-Eric Lindblad built connections between the environment and education, and sought to use the income created by tourism to help local inhabitants. The market for all these endeavors was tiny compared to the conventional industry. It was largely wealthy elites who were willing to pay. Von der Linde's venture was based in the wealthy city of Charlottenburg, and eventually failed in World War I. Lindblad, like Geoffrey Kent, found a niche among wealthy clientele who were interested in distinctive luxury products, but by 1980 there had been no mainstreaming of greener strategies in tourism as a whole.

Notes

1. Food and Agriculture Organization, *Global Food Losses and Waste: Extent, Causes and Prevention* (2011), <http://www.fao.org/docrep/014/mb060e/mb060e00.pdf>, accessed July 8, 2016; Food and Agriculture Organization, *Food Wastage Footprint* (2013), <http://www.fao.org/docrep/018/i3347e/i3347e.pdf>, accessed July 8, 2016; Elizabeth Royle, "Eating Ugly," *National Geographic* (March 2016), pp.50–3.

2. In German, the most common traditional term was "Kehricht," which was eventually replaced by "Müll" in much the same way as in English "waste" came to be used. In France, the terms for waste were "ordures" and "déchets."

3. Susan Strasser, *Waste and Want: A Social History of Trash* (New York: Metropolitan, 1999), chapter 1.

4. Ibid.

5. Martin Melosi, *Garbage in the Cities: Refuse, Reform, and the Environment*, rev. edn. (Pittsburgh: University of Pittsburgh Press, 2005), p.20.

6. Ruth Oldenziel and Heike Weber, "Introduction: Reconsidering Recycling," *Contemporary European History* 22, no. 3 (2013), pp.347–70.

7. William Vogt, *Road to Survival* (New York: William Sloane Associates, 1948), p.67.

8. Martin Medina, *The World's Scavengers: Salvaging for Sustainable Consumption and Production* (Lanham, MD: AltaMira, 2007), chapter 2.

9. Carl A. Zimring, *Cash for Your Trash: Scrap Recycling in America* (New Brunswick, NJ: Rutgers University Press, 2005), chapters 1 and 2.

10. Richard Evans, *Death in Hamburg: Society and Politics in the Cholera Years, 1830–1910* (New York: Penguin, 2005); Hildegaard Frilling and Olaf Mischer, *Pütt und Pann'n: Geschichte der Hamburger Hausmüllbeseitigung* (Hamburg: Ergebnisse Verlag, 1994); Peter Münch, *Stadthygiene im 19. und 20. Jahrhundert* (Göttingen: Vandenhoeck & Ruprecht, 1993).

11. Daniel Burnstein, *Next to Godliness: Confronting Dirt and Despair in Progressive Era New York City* (Urbana: University of Illinois Press, 2006).

12. Raymond G. Stokes, Roman Köster, and Stephen C. Sambrook, *The Business of Waste: Great Britain and Germany, 1945 to the Present* (Cambridge: Cambridge University Press, 2014), p.26.

13. Melosi, *Garbage*, pp.23–5, 142–3; Münch, *Stadthygiene*, p.111; John Capie Wylie, *The Wastes of Civilization* (London: Faber and Faber, 1959), pp.70–1.

14. Maria Curter, *Berliner Gold: Die Geschichte der Müllbeseitigung in Berlin* (Berlin: Haude & Spener, 1996), pp.25–7; Annual Reports of the Wirtschafts-Genossenschaft Berliner Grundbesitzer e.G.m.b.H., 1903–4 and 1910–1918, Federal Environment Ministry, Dessau, Germany, Sammlung Erhard Collection, Sign. A 747–749, C V 10–17, Sign. A 279. "Berliner Müllabfuhr, A.-G.," n.d. (circa 1923).

15. Stokes et al., *Business of Waste*, p.7.

16. Benjamin Miller, *Fat of the Land: Garbage in New York—the Last Two Hundred Years* (New York: Four Walls Eight Windows, 2000), pp.84–9.

17. Melosi, *Garbage*, pp.57–60.

18. Carl von der Linde, *Die Müllfrage und ihre Lösung nach dem neuen Separations-System der Charlottenburger Abfuhrgesellschaft m.b.H.* (Charlottenburg: Adolf Gertz, 1902), Sammlung Erhard, Sign. A 716.

19. Heike Weber, "Müllströme, Müllrecycling und das 'Rohproduktengewerbe' als Wiederverwerter am Anfang des 20. Jahrhunderts," *Ferrum* 85 (2013), pp.5–14.

20. Sonja Windmüller, *Die Kehrseite der Dinge: Müll, Abfall, Wegwerfen als kulturwissenschaftliches Problem* (Münster: LIT, 2004), pp.167–71, 174; Carsten Jasner, "Frühe Alternative: Das Charlottenburger Dreiteilungsmodell," in Susanne Köstering and Renate Rüb (eds.), *Müll von gestern? Eine umweltgeschichtliche Erkundung in Berlin und Brandenburg* (Münster: Waxmann, 2003), pp.115–20.

21. Etienne de Fodor, *Elektrizität aus Kehricht* (Budapest: Julius Benko, 1911), pp.33–44; Bruno Röhrecke, *Müllabfuhr und Müllbeseitigung: Ein Beitrag zur Städtehygiene* (Berlin: Skrzeczek, 1901).

22. Fodor, *Elektrizität*, pp.7–10, 44–8; Windmüller, *Kehrseite*, p.165.

23. Martin V. Melosi, "Technology Diffusion and Refuse Disposal: The Case of the British Destructor," in Joel A. Tarr and Gabriel Dupuy (eds.), *Technology and the Rise of the Networked City in Europe and America* (Philadelphia: Temple University Press, 1988), pp.208–21.

24. Carmelita Lindemann, "Verbrennung oder Verwertung: Müll als Problem um die Wende vom 19. zum 20. Jahrhundert," *Technikgeschichte* 59, no. 2 (1992), p.97.

25. Jeffrey Morris, "Recycling versus Incineration: An Energy Conservation Analysis," *Journal of Hazardous Materials* 47 (1996), pp.277–93.

26. Windmüller, *Kehrseite*, pp.178–84; Müllverwertung Aktiengesellschaft, "Die Gersonschen Verfahren der Müllverwertung," Sammlung Erhard, Sign. C IV 113, p.3; US patents US 1593491 A (91926), US 2160542 A (1939).

27. Renate Rüb, "Grenzen eines tradierten Systems: Vier Jahrzehnte Mülldüngung bei Nauen," in Susanne Köstering and Renate Rüb (eds.), *Müll von gestern? Eine umweltgeschichtliche Erkundung in Berlin und Brandenburg* (Münster: Waxmann, 2003), pp.87–100; and Susanne Köstering, "'Der Müll muss doch heraus aus Berlin!,'" *Werkstatt Geschichte* 3 (1992), pp.23–4.

28. Wylie, *Wastes*, pp.137–40.

29. DANO Ingeniørforretning og Maskinfabrik, Untitled Brochure, n.p., n.d. (circa 1937–43), Sammlung Erhard, Sign. D II d., pp.2, 5. Petersen died in 1948, but the company continued and built plants in Europe and the United States in the postwar decade. See Wylie, *Wastes*, pp.140–1.

30. Stokes et al., *Business of Waste*, pp.74–81.

31. Strasser, *Waste and Want*, pp.271–2.

32. Stokes et al., *Business of Waste*, pp.78, 185.

33. Strasser, *Waste and Want*, pp.153–5, 231–8.

34. Friedrich Huchting, "Abfallwirtschaft im Dritten Reich," *Technikgeschichte* 48, no. 3 (1981), pp.254, 260–3.

35. Francé's 1936 talk is reprinted in Edaphon-Müllverwertung Commanditgesellschaft, "Über Müllverwertung und Edaphon-Humus-Düngung" (1947), Sammlung

Erhard, Sign. D II; see also the 1930 prospectus, "Edaphon Dünger. Februar 1930," typescript, Sammlung Erhard, Sign. C V 8.

36. "Edaphon Duenger. Februar 1930," Sammlung Erhard, Sign. C V 8; "Über Müllverwertung und Edaphon-Humus-Düngung," Sammlung Erhard, Sign. D II.

37. Annie Francé-Harrar, *Die Letzte Chance: für eine Zukunft ohne Not* (Munich: Bayerischer Landwirtschaftsverlag, 1950), pp.616–19; <http://www.france-harrar.de/index.php>, accessed March 12, 2015.

38. Martin Melosi, *The Sanitary City: Urban Infrastructure in America from Colonial Times to the Present* (Baltimore: Johns Hopkins University Press, 2000), p.339; Melosi, *Garbage*, pp.205–9. For critiques of the throwaway thesis, see Daniel Walsh, "Urban Residential Refuse Composition and Generation Rates for the 20th Century," *Environmental Science and Technology* 36 (Nov. 2002), pp.4936–42; Martin O'Brien, *A Crisis of Waste? Understanding the Rubbish Society* (London: Routledge, 2008).

39. Arne Andersen, *Der Traum vom guten Leben: Alltags- und Konsumgeschichte vom Wirtschaftswunder bis heute* (Frankfurt: Campus, 1997), pp.52–69; Sibylle Brändli, *Der Supermarkt im Kopf: Konsumkultur und Wohlstand in der Schweiz nach 1945* (Vienna: Böhlau, 2000), pp.87–90; Christian Pfister, "The '1950s Syndrome' and the Transition from a Slow-Going to a Rapid Loss of Global Sustainability," in Frank Uekötter (ed.), *Turning Points in Environmental History* (Pittsburgh: University of Pittsburgh Press, 2010), pp.90–117.

40. Louis Blumberg and Robert Gottlieb, *War on Waste: Can America Win Its Battle with Garbage?* (Washington, DC: Island Press, 1989), pp.11–14, and especially chapter 9 on plastic packaging.

41. Andrea Westermann, *Plastik und politische Kultur in Westdeutschland* (Zurich: Chronos, 2007), pp.123–6, 288–306; Stokes et al., *Business of Waste*, pp.139–45.

42. Lilo Fischer and Ulrich Petschow, "Municipal Waste Management in Germany," in Nicolas Buclet and Olivier Godard (eds.), *Municipal Waste Management in Europe: A Comparative Study in Building Regimes* (Dordrecht: Kluwer, 2000), p.8.

43. U.S. Environmental Protection Agency, Office of Resource Conservation and Recovery, "Municipal Solid Waste Generation, Recycling, and Disposal in the United States, Tables and Figures for 2012" (Washington: EPA, February 2014), Table 30; Verband privater Städtereinigungsbetriebe (Private Sector Waste Trade Association), *Rundschreiben* 4 (May 20, 1964), p.4. SASE Archive, Iserlohn, Germany.

44. Westermann, *Plastik*, pp.288–306; Manfred Grieger, "Going Round in Circles? The Disposal of PVC and Plastic at the Volkswagen Plant in Wolfsburg between Industrial Incineration and Landfilling, since 1955," *Jahrbuch für Wirtschaftsgeschichte* 50, no. 2 (2009), pp.81–98.

45. Frank J. Barry, "The Evolution of the Enforcement Provisions of the Federal Water Pollution Control Act: A Study of the Difficulty in Developing Effective Legislation," *Michigan Law Review* 68, no. 6 (May 1970), pp.1103–30.

46. Stokes et al., *Business of Waste.*

47. William Philpott, *Vacationland: Tourism and Environment in the Colorado High Country* (Seattle: University of Washington Press, 2013), chapter 1.

48. Container Corporation of America, *The First Fifty Years 1926–1976* (Chicago: the firm, 1976); Greg Ruth, "The Son of a Prussian Immigrant, Walter Paepcke was the President of the Container Corporation of America (CCA) and Founder of the Aspen Institute" (May 27, 2014), <http://www.immigrantentrepreneurship.org/entry.php?rec=67>, accessed June 6, 2015.

49. Container Corporation, *First Fifty Years.*

50. Penny Jones and Jerry Powell, "Gary Anderson Has Been Found!" *Resource Recycling* (May 1999).

51. Melosi, *Garbage*, pp.200–5.

52. Lanny Hickman, *American Alchemy: The History of Solid Waste Management in the United States* (Santa Barbara: Forester Press, 2003), pp.37–42.

53. Ibid., pp.56–8.

54. Ibid., pp.62–8, 70–6; Blumberg and Gottlieb, *War on Waste*, pp.63–7.

55. Nicole Pippke, *Öffentliche und private Abfallentsorgung: Die Privatisierung der Abfallwirtschaft nach dem Kreislaufwirtschafts- und Abfallgesetz* (Berlin: Duncker & Humblot, 1999), pp.33–59; Stokes et al., *Business of Waste* pp.183–5, 205–6.

56. For the Dutch-American firms in Chicago, see Timothy C. Jacobson, *Waste Management: An American Corporate Success Story* (Washington, DC: Gateway Business Books, 1993), chapter 2.

57. Ibid., pp.74–5; Harold Crooks, *Giants of Garbage: The Rise of the Global Waste Industry and the Politics of Pollution Control* (Toronto: James Lorimer, 1993), pp.41, 76–7.

58. Jacobson, *Waste Management*, pp.75, 102–10.

59. Hickman, *American Alchemy*, pp.55–6, 95–6; Thomas Metzger, "Golden Garbage," *Waste Age* (June 2012), p.56.

60. Jacobson, *Waste Management*, pp.103–4.

61. "Waste Management, Inc.," in James R. Grossman, Ann Durkin Keating, and Janice L. Reiff (eds.), *The Encyclopedia of Chicago* (Chicago: University of Chicago Press, 2004), p.950; Jacobson, *Waste Management*, pp.151–98; Crooks, *Giants*, pp.81–4, 92.

62. Hickman, *American Alchemy*, p.89.

63. Crooks, *Giants*, 40; Hickman, *American Alchemy*, p.89; Craig R. Waters, "The Gospel according to Fatjo," April 1, 1982, <http://www.inc.com/magazine/19820401/7476.html>, accessed June 8, 2016.

64. Tom Fatjo Jr., *Bloomberg Business*, March 25, 2015.

65. BFI Annual Report, 1973.

66. BFI Annual Reports 1973–5.

67. BFI and Waste Management Annual Reports, 1973–6.

68. Hickman, *American Alchemy*, p.90; Jacobson, *Waste Management*, pp.123–4, 140–2; BFI and Waste Management Annual Reports.

69. Bundesverband der deutschen Entsorgungswirtschaft E.V. (ed.), *1961–2001: 40 Jahre BDE. Von der Stadthygiene zur Kreislaufwirtschaft* (Cologne: BDE, 2001), pp.58–63.

70. Ibid.; Fischer and Petschow, "Municipal Waste Management in Germany," p.13.

71. BDE, *1961–2001: 40 Jahre BDE*, p.64.

72. VPS Rundschreiben, 1963, no. 5, p.2, SASE Archive, in Iserlohn, Germany.

73. VPS Rundschreiben, 1963–70.

74. Peter Mugay, Hermann Niehues, Reinhard Lohmann, and Claus Andreas, *"Verantwortung übernehmen und unternehmerisch handeln": Norbert Rethmann 60 Jahre* (Selm: Rethmann, 1999), pp.62–3.

75. Stokes et al., *Business of Waste*, pp.223–6.

76. John K. Walton, *The English Seaside Resort: A Social History, 1750–1914* (New York: St. Martin's Press, 1983).

77. Bryant Simon, *Boardwalk of Dreams: Atlantic City and the Fate of Urban America* (New York: Oxford University Press, 2004); Laurent Tissot (ed.), *Construction of a Tourism Industry in the 19th and 20th Century: International Perspectives* (Neuchâtel: Alphil, 2003); John K. Walton, "Prospects in Tourism History: Evolution, State of Play and Future Developments," *Tourism Management* 30 (2009), pp.783–93.

78. Edmund Swinglehurst, *Cook's Tours: The Story of Popular Travel* (Poole, Dorset: Blandford Press, 1982); James Buzard, *The Beaten Track: European Tourism, Literature, and the Ways to "Culture" 1800–1918* (Oxford: Oxford University Press, 1993), pp.51, 56, 62.

79. Theo Wyler, *Als die Echos noch gepachtet wurden: aus den Anfängen des Tourismus in der Schweiz* (Zurich: NZZ, 2000), pp.68–71; Susan Barton, *Healthy Living in the Alps: The Origins of Winter Tourism in Switzerland, 1860–1914* (Manchester: Manchester University Press, 2008), p.21.

80. Barton, *Healthy Living*, pp.39–41.

81. Jim Ring, *How the English Made the Alps* (London: John Murray, 2000), p.140.

82. Barton, *Healthy Living*, p.41.

83. Richard H. Gassan, *The Birth of American Tourism: New York, the Hudson Valley, and American Culture 1790–1830* (Amherst: University of Massachusetts Press, 2008).

84. Linda Greene, *Yosemite, the Park and Its Resources: A History of the Discovery, Management, and Physical Development of Yosemite National Park, California* (Washington, DC: U.S. National Park Service, 1987), vol. 1, pp.76–7.

85. Ibid., pp.78–9.

86. Ibid., p.115.

87. Alfred Runte, *Trains of Discovery: Railroads and the Legacy of Our National Parks*, 5th edn. (Lanham, MD: Roberts Rinehart, 2011), pp.24–32; Richard West Sellars, *Preserving Nature in the National Parks: A History* (New Haven, CT: Yale University Press, 1997), pp.8–12, 15, 19–20.

88. For the case of the Southern Pacific Railroad and John Muir, see Greene, *Yosemite*, pp.304, 308, and Richard J. Orsi, *Sunset Limited: The Southern Pacific Railroad and the Development of the American West, 1850–1930* (Berkeley: University of California Press, 2005), pp.360–7, 370–1.

89. Hal K. Rothman, *Devil's Bargains: Tourism in the Twentieth-Century American West* (Lawrence, KS: University Press of Kansas, 1998), chapter 3; Marta Weigle and Barbara Babcock (eds.), *The Great Southwest of the Fred Harvey Company and the Santa Fe Railway* (Phoenix, AZ: University of Arizona Press, 1996).

90. Rothman, *Devil's Bargains*, pp.162–4; Runte, *Trains of Discovery*.

91. Bartle Bull, *Safari: A Chronicle of Adventure* (London: Penguin, 1988); Kenneth M. Cameron, *Into Africa: The Story of the East African Safari* (London: Constable, 1990).

92. John M. MacKenzie, *The Empire of Nature: Hunting, Conservation, and British Imperialism* (Manchester: Manchester University Press, 1988), chapters 8–11.

93. Bull, *Safari*, chapter 3.

94. Ibid., pp.136–42.

95. Cameron, *Into Africa*, pp.89–91.

96. United Nations World Tourism Organization (UNWTO), *Tourism Market Trends 2006: World Overview & Tourism Topics* (Madrid: UNWTO, 2006), Annex: International Tourist Arrivals, 1950–2005.

97. Ellen Furlough, "Making Mass Vacations: Tourism and Consumer Culture in France, 1930s to 1970s," *Comparative Studies in Society and History* 40, no. 2 (1998), pp.274, 277–81.

98. Andrew Denning, *Skiing into Modernity: A Cultural and Environmental History* (Berkeley: University of California Press, 2015).

99. Philpott, *Vacationland*, pp.33–42.

100. Martha Honey, *Ecotourism and Sustainable Development* (Washington, DC: Island Press, 2008), p.9.

101. Walton, "Prospects," p.788; Mansel Blackford, *Fragile Paradise: The Impact of Tourism on Maui, 1959–2000* (Lawrence, KS: University Press of Kansas, 2001); John

Littlewood, *Sultry Climates: Travel and Sex since the Grand Tour* (London: John Murray, 2001); Ashley Mason, "Tourism and the Sex Trade Industry in Southeast Asia," *Totem: The University of Western Ontario Journal of Anthropology* 7, no. 1 (2011), <http://ir.lib.uwo.ca/cgi/viewcontent.cgi?article=1060&context=totem>, accessed June 19, 2015.

102. Furlough, "Making Mass Vacations," pp.260–1, 273.

103. Honey, *Ecotourism*, pp.17–18; Cancun Case, <http://www1.american.edu/TED/cancun.htm>, accessed June 20, 2015.

104. Lars-Eric Lindblad with John G. Fuller, *Passport to Anywhere: The Story of Lars-Eric Lindblad* (New York: Times Books, 1983), pp.26–34. The firm moved from New York to Westport, Connecticut in the 1970s.

105. Ibid., pp.36–7.

106. Ibid., pp.45–54, 168–9.

107. Ibid., pp.88, 94, 96, 128.

108. Beth J. Harpaz, "Lindblad Marks 50th Anniversary of Antarctica Trips," *Chicago Tribune*, January 26, 2016.

109. Nigel Stilwell, "Obituary: Lars-Eric Lindblad," *The Independent*, July 16, 1994.

110. Bernard Stonehouse and Kim Crosbie, "Tourism Impacts and Management in the Antarctic Peninsula," in Colin Hall and Margaret Johnson (eds.), *Polar Tourism: Tourism in the Arctic and Antarctic Regions* (Chichester: John Wiley, 1995), pp.221–2.

111. Lindblad, *Passport*, p.111.

112. Ibid., pp.111, 123, 126.

113. Ibid., p.131.

114. Ibid., pp.146–7.

115. Ibid., p.243.

116. David Carroll, "Lessons from a Father Fuel a Son's Success," *The Australian*, July 19, 2013.

117. Janet Piorko, "Lars-Eric Lindblad, 67, Pioneer of Tours to Exotic Destinations," *New York Times*, July 13, 1994.

118. Jill Arabas, "Bankruptcy Petition Marks End of Road for Lindblad Travel," *The Hour* (Norwalk, Connecticut), October 27, 1989.

119. <https://www.expeditions.com/why-us/expedition-heritage>, accessed February 18, 2015.

120. Interview with Geoffrey Kent, <http://www.youtube.com/watch?v=fQ1Ed1fVtuU>, accessed July 9, 2015.

121. Interview with Geoffrey Kent, *TravelAge West*, April 6, 2012, <http://www.travelagewest.com/News/Industry-Interviews/Abercrombie—Kent-Turns-50>, accessed August 2, 2015.

122. Frances X. Frei et al., "Abercrombie & Kent," Harvard Business School Case no. 9-603-002, September 3, 2002.

123. <http://www.akphilanthropy.org/history.cfm>, accessed January 3, 2016.

124. MacKenzie, *Empire of Nature*; Rothman, *Devil's Bargains*; Catherine Cocks, *Tropical Whites: The Rise of the Tourist South in the Americas* (Philadelphia: University of Pennsylvania Press, 2013); Bram Büscher, *Transforming the Frontier: Peace Parks and the Politics of Neoliberal Conservation in Southern Africa* (Durham, NC: Duke University Press, 2013).

Part 2

Green Business

5

Making Money by Saving the World

In the 1960s and 1970s the new wave of environmentalism did not translate into robust growth for most green entrepreneurs. Environmentalists had looked to regulation and to governments for solutions, not to capitalist enterprise. The subsequent decades saw a momentous shift. Awareness of environmental damage grew steadily as people watched ever-more powerful images of famines, dust storms, and melting ice caps on their television screens, and scientists produced ever more scientific evidence. So, too, grew an emerging idea that, faced with environmental calamity, business might save the world instead of destroying it.

This first chapter in Part II begins an examination of the scaling and diffusion of green entrepreneurship since the early 1980s. The growth of green businesses took place amid a major shift in attitudes towards the natural environment across the world. Environmental problems such as deforestation, threats to biodiversity, and pollution galvanized people around the world to become politically active. There has also been, especially in the twenty-first century, increasing action among environmentalist activists, scientists, and international agencies about climate change. Climate change both increased the sense of urgency felt about the environment, and globalized the issue since no city, region, or country alone could insulate itself from its effects. Climate change could be quantified, even if there were arguments about the data and their interpretation. The scale and frequency of extreme weather events convinced even people with little knowledge of science that human actions affected the natural environment.

Indeed, further environmental disasters heightened awareness of the fragility of the planet. The 1980s were replete with man-made disasters. These included a fatal gas leak at US chemical company Union Carbide's factory in Bhopal, India in 1984 which killed about 4,000 people and injured half a

million. An explosion at the nuclear plant in Chernobyl in the Soviet Union in
1986 spread radioactive contamination over much of Europe. There was a
massive leakage of 11 million gallons of crude oil from the *Exxon Valdez*
tanker into the pristine waters of Alaska's Prince William Sound three years
later. The oil spill damaged 1,300 miles of shoreline and decimated populations of killer whales, Pacific herrings, and pigeon guillemots.[1] In 1986 the
discovery of "mad cow disease" in Britain, and its subsequent spread to
humans who had consumed beef and which killed nearly two hundred people,
raised alarm about industrial farming practices.

These disasters spurred the development of a new environmentalist concept: sustainability, or sustainable development. The United Nations commissioned a report on environment and development by a group headed by the
former Norwegian prime minister, Gro Harlem Brundtland. The Brundtland
Commission's report on *Our Common Future* in 1987 framed poverty reduction, gender equity, wealth redistribution, and environmental conservation as
inseparable challenges of sustainability, which it defined as "meeting the needs
of the present without compromising the ability of future generations to meet
their own needs."[2] While the Commission's identification of three main pillars
of sustainable development—economic growth, environmental protection,
and social equality—might be seen now as contradictory, at best, its work
also broadened environmental debates by placing them in an economic and
social context and by engaging the non-Western world in discussing them.[3]

The Earth Summit in Rio de Janeiro in June 1992, organized by Maurice
Strong, was attended by over 20,000 participants from 9,000 NGOs working in
171 countries; over 1,000 meetings were held between NGO representatives in
a forum parallel to official intergovernmental discussions. Climate change
joined deforestation and loss of biodiversity as the most pressing global
problems. There were 108 heads of state or government in attendance, including President George H. W. Bush of the United States. It was, by some counts,
the largest international conference ever held.[4]

While the concern over the state of the natural environment had been led by
social movements and NGOs during the 1960s and 1970s, it now became more
of a mainstream political concern, although more so in some countries than in
others. In 1979 Switzerland became the first country in the world to have a
Green member in its parliament. In 1983 the Green Party won twenty-eight
seats in the West German parliament. According to one historian, it was

during the 1980s that the image of "green Germany" emerged.[5] In 1998 the Green Party entered a coalition government with the Social Democratic Party of Germany.[6] This was atypical, with organized Green parties remaining marginal in most of Europe. The same was true in the United States. The consumer activist Ralph Nader made little impact in attracting voters when he ran as the Green Party's nominee in the 1996 and 2000 presidential elections. Nonetheless, major-party politicians began to raise environmentalist issues. In 1992 Al Gore, then a US Senator, published the first of his books on the environmental challenges faced by the world.[7]

Across Europe and the United States, and to a lesser extent elsewhere, there were many new environmental laws and agencies.[8] This rise of environmental legislation, in the 1980s especially, made an interesting contrast with the overall agendas of the Reagan and the Thatcher governments in the United States and Britain to replace decades of state regulation and ownership with the liberalization of markets and deregulation. The same spirit of market liberalization swept through Asia, Africa, and Latin America beginning in the 1980s, but it took considerably longer for environmental legislation to be introduced in the developing world. With development/industrialization came smog, pollution, and carbon emissions with environmental protections not yet on the horizon.

There were a growing number of international treaties concerning the natural environment. In 1987 the Montreal Protocol on Substances that Deplete the Ozone Layer was designed to reduce the production and consumption of ozone-depleting substances in order to protect the Earth's fragile ozone layer. In 1988 an Intergovernmental Panel on Climate Change was created by the United Nations.[9] In the following year the Basel Convention on the Control of Transboundary Movements of Hazardous Wastes and their Disposal was adopted in response to the discovery that in Africa and other parts of the developing world, toxic waste had been imported from abroad for deposit.

In 1997 the Kyoto Protocol sought to create the first international binding treaty aimed at reducing global emissions. Most developed nations committed themselves to targets for cutting or slowing their greenhouse gas emissions. As noted in the Introduction, the Protocol was eventually not ratified by the United States, and the overall outcomes were mixed. Some countries, especially Russia and others in Eastern Europe, achieved large reductions, but the headline statistics were misleading as the Protocol enabled carbon emissions trading. Governments were required to establish an acceptable level of pollution, which was capped, and then issue pollution permits or allowances which matched it. If a participant exceeded its target for reduction, it got a credit which it could trade.[10] Overall, the sum of emissions from nations with Kyoto targets fell over the following years, but emissions in the rest of the world increased sharply, especially in China and other developing economies. It was not until 2015 that a second United Nations treaty signed in Paris resumed the quest for a binding policy to stop global warming—and included developing nations for the first time.

This chapter begins by describing how a set of writers and entrepreneurs worked to develop greater environmental legitimacy for business as a positive agent for sustainability. If business was to contribute to environmental solutions, these actors knew it would have to be regarded as something other than an ineluctable part of the problem. The chapter then turns to the experience of entrepreneurial firms in organic food, natural beauty, architecture, and eco-tourism. The proliferation of green businesses in these industries during these decades was striking. As we saw in Part I, it had not been possible for such ventures to achieve significant growth. However, these new successful outcomes also created a new set of tensions around questions of authenticity and legitimacy. Green entrepreneurs also began to experience new competition from conventional firms which had become convinced that there was now a viable consumer niche they could serve. Quite often, as we will see here and in Chapter 9, large conventional firms acquired successful green brands in order to secure access to the green consumer segment. The boundaries of greenness, always porous, became increasingly blurred. As the industries examined in this chapter show, green and conventional firms were often co-creators of expanding markets.

Making the case

During the 1970s influential environmentalist writers—Charles Reich, Barry Commoner, E. F. Schumacher, to name a few—were either downright hostile to capitalism or else called for a fundamental restructuring of it. Historical events later in the twentieth century would create a new optimism, even a triumphalism in some quarters, about capitalism. The fall of the Berlin Wall and the buoyant American stock market of the 1990s dot.com boom further stimulated a spirit of optimism, for a time, that a new world order had arrived. As the virtues of capitalism came back into fashion, business was once more seen as the driver of economic growth and market solutions were increasingly favored, even for environmental and social issues.

The linking of environmental concerns with the wider concept of sustainability eased the way for businesses to claim a role in forging potential solutions. It also had the potential to increase the interest of firms in environmental subjects: while politicians often had short time-horizons, firms had long-term stakes in their markets and supplies being sustainable. In the early 1990s, for example, "oilman-turned-environmentalist" Maurice Strong convinced Stephan Schmidheiny, a prominent Swiss business leader and billionaire who had inherited his father's construction and asbestos business Eternit, to establish the Business Council for Sustainable Development (BCSD) to bring together business leaders of the world's largest companies to address environmental issues. In 1992 this group published a report for the Earth Summit in Rio called *Changing Course*, which argued that the way to achieve sustainability was through the market, including the use of full-cost pricing and tradable permits.[11] Three years later BCSD merged with the International Chamber of Commerce's Business Charter for Sustainable Development, launched in 1991, to form the World Business Council for Sustainable Development. Many of the world's leading firms became associated with the Council, which developed the concept of "eco-efficiency," which offered a path that corporations could follow to combine profits and sustainability.[12]

Within this context, a number of individuals developed frameworks and concepts exploring how profits and sustainability could be made compatible, at least if goals and practices were honestly and appropriately aligned along ecological lines. They can be described as green entrepreneurs of thought, though for the perceived public good, rather than individual profit. Jerome Rodale and others could also be described in such terms, but the new generation of green entrepreneurs were more visible. They were better storytellers, but they also told their stories in a favorable context in which concerns about the environment and belief in the capabilities of private capitalism were on the rise.

John Elkington was one of the most important of these figures. His passion for the natural environment was triggered by a nighttime encounter with baby eels while walking in the dark in his home in Northern Ireland when he was five years old. By his teens in the early 1960s, Elkington was fund-raising for the World Wildlife Fund.[13] Elkington undertook graduate work in Environmental Studies, becoming influenced by the writings of Ian McHarg and Buckminster Fuller. During 1973 he also visited Paolo Soleri's Arcosanti project in Arizona. He later noted that "Soleri's thinking around archology had quite an impact" on him. The visit led to his first published article in the *Architectural Association Quarterly*.[14]

This proved to be the start of an extensive publishing career. In 1987 Elkington co-authored a book entitled *The Green Capitalists* which described the importance for sustainability of an emergent group of "environmental entrepreneurs."[15] A decade later Elkington launched the concept of a "triple bottom line" of profitability, environmental quality, and social justice (or people, planet, and profit) in a book called *Cannibals with Forks*.[16] As later chapters will show, this triad became a hugely influential concept shaping environmental corporate reporting.

Elkington was also an early mover in identifying the emergent phenomenon of the "green consumer." In 1988 he co-wrote, with Julia Hayes, a book called *The Green Consumer Guide*, which offered advice to eco-minded consumers as to which brands and products sold in Britain matched their values. The book contained a foreword by The Body Shop's Anita Roddick. It combined a globalized view of environmental issues with specific information about particular brands, companies, supermarkets, travel agents, and much more.[17] By providing such specific information, however, the book not only targeted the green consumer, but it explicitly sought to create such consumers by giving them information to guide their buying decisions. "Demand green products," the authors wrote, "and you help develop new market opportunities for manufacturers and retailers."[18]

The book, which went into many editions, would subsequently sell over a million copies worldwide over the following decades. If such sales are not a concrete measure of impact, they at least indicate the emergence of a consumer segment interesting in buying products deemed to be eco-friendly, which was substantially different from the smaller, alternative lifestyle type who had been the prime customers in the past. In the mid-1990s the entrepreneur Jirka Rysavy, based in Boulder, Colorado, had a similar insight when he developed the concept, initially for internal marketing purposes, of a consumer segment who enjoyed Lifestyles of Health and Sustainability, or

LOHAS. This became the basis for a publishing and consulting business which identified six market segments: personal health (including organic foods), natural lifestyle, green building, alternative transportation, eco-tourism, and alternative energy.[19] The growth of this customer base was key to the further growth of green capitalism, even if the desires and identities of consumers across these six segments were disparate.[20]

In 1987 Elkington and Hailes themselves co-founded a for-profit business consultancy and think tank called SustainAbility to advise firms how to become more sustainable. It seemed destined to have a short life after the burger company McDonald's, and other firms, threatened to sue the company over comments made in *The Green Consumer Guide*, although the case did not go to court.[21] Elkington's vision was that "if we wanted to try to change the world, working with the private sector" rather than with governments was key.[22] His firm was selective about clients, declining to work with McDonald's but working with large, conventional firms such as Shell and Toyota, as well as high-profile social-activist firms such as the ice cream company Ben & Jerry's. SustainAbility became an early mover in trying to develop data on environmental performance. Two years after its founding it began work on a report called "The Environmental Audit" with the World Wildlife Fund which raised awareness of the potential of corporate reporting and auditing. In 1994 SustainAbility and the United Nations Environmental Programme launched regular surveys of corporate environmental reporting called the Engaging Stakeholders Programme.[23] In 2008 the restless Elkington launched another consultancy called Volans Ventures Ltd. designed to promote "breakthrough capitalism" which would develop radical new technologies to facilitate sustainability. In a 2012 book, Elkington described his vision of the "Zeronauts" who were entrepreneurs and innovators who would tackle what he saw as the five key challenges faced by the world: population growth, pandemics, poverty, pollution, and the proliferation of weapons of mass destruction.[24]

A number of green entrepreneurs, mostly American, who had built businesses, emerged as high-profile advocates of green capitalism. Among the most influential was Paul Hawken, who would in due course be crowned by Elkington as a Zeronaut. After leaving the pioneering Boston organic food retailer Erewhon, Hawken moved to Findhorn, in the northeast of Scotland on the Moray Firth coast, where he wrote a study of the remote ecological and spiritual community.[25] He went on to co-found the Smith & Hawken garden tool supply company in 1979, which grew as a successful garden lifestyle brand and retailer.

It was with well-honed skills as a writer that Hawken set out his case in two major books on green capitalism. In 1993, after selling Smith & Hawken, he published *The Ecology of Commerce*. The preface of *Ecology* began with a sobering assessment: "If every company on the planet were to adopt the best environmental practices of the 'leading' companies—say Ben & Jerry's, Patagonia, or 3M—the world would still be moving towards sure degradation and collapse."[26] Hawken's solution was not to replace capitalism but to change "the dynamics of the market."[27] His vision of what he termed a "restorative economy" had a restructured capitalism at its heart.

Hawken's co-authored book *Natural Capitalism*, published in 1999, suggested a new business model. The book's core argument was that the environment had been decimated because capitalism's negative externalities on the environment were not accounted for properly. As a result, price signals did not work properly and markets were both imperfect and incomplete. Frequently distorted regulations aided and abetted these market failures.[28] The authors recommended a system of "natural capitalism" which pursued business profitability while protecting natural resources. They went into the specifics of designing production systems that eliminate waste, adopting technologies that extend natural resources' usefulness, and reinvesting in nature's capital by, for example, planting trees to offset power-plant carbon emissions. The market could benefit sustainability, the book argued, if only it accounted for and quantified environmental benefits and costs. Even the strongly free-market magazine *The Economist* reviewed the book favorably. "What makes this book worth reading," the review noted, "is the fact that the authors have taken as first principles for their Utopia the harsh truths of Darwinian capitalism: individuals and companies act in their self-interest, and markets guide that impulse through prices."[29]

Hawken was not a lone wolf. The owners of iconic green brands emerged as public ambassadors for sustainability. Many of the creators of successful brands wrote books about how the right kind of capitalism could facilitate sustainability. Gary Hirshberg, the co-founder of the successful organic yogurt brand Stonyfield, subtitled his book "How to Make Money and Save the World."[30] John Mackey, the co-founder of the organic retailer Whole Foods Market, wrote on the potential of *Conscious Capitalism*.[31] Yvon Chouinard, the founder of the Patagonia apparel line, opined on his evolving ecological views and the vision of his firm becoming "a model other businesses could look to in their own searches for environmental stewardship and sustainability."[32]

The decades from the 1980s then, stand out for the growth of much more vigorous articulations, especially in the United States, of the case that capitalism, whether natural, conscious, or something else, could play a positive role in providing solutions to environmental problems. It was an optimism born in an era when belief in liberal capitalism and market forces was at its peak. These views spoke to a more mainstream consumer psychographic—the green consumer—which provided the basis for the creation of substantial green business enterprises, as well as a growing interest of conventional business in sustainability.

The coming of age of organic food

The rising scale of green business was exemplified by the growth of the organic food market. Before the 1980s sales of organic food were held back by the fact that prices were typically higher than for conventional food. This created a vicious circle whereby only radical activists shopped in organic food stores, as they were motivated by concerns other than prices. In the rare cases that conventional retailers stocked organic food, they would hide it in the least prominent locations in a store, as the sales volume and profit margins did not justify a prime location. Low demand in turn provided no incentives for farmers to convert to organic growing. This situation now changed. "No longer the cuisine only of sandal-clad environmentalists, organic food is coming of age," concluded an article in *The New York Times* responding to the sudden growth of the American market in 1996. "It is clearly big business."[33]

The global market for certified organic food and drink had reached $15 billion by then. By 2014 it was estimated at $80 billion. This was an enormous shift. It was still only a small share of the estimated $4 trillion in global food retail sales, although this included developing countries where food was much less processed than in the West, even if not certified as organic. Nevertheless, whatever progress was made in healthier eating lifestyles, it was dwarfed by the growth and scale of the global obesity and diabetes epidemics driven by consumption of processed and fast foods: by 2013 one-third of the world's population was overweight or obese.[34] Eating organic still remained largely the preserve of the more affluent consumers in the Western world. The United States accounted for 43 percent of the global market, and Europe a further 38 percent.

Yet there was no simple correlation between incomes and eating organic food, as shown by variations between rich countries. In the United States by 2014 organic food accounted for 1.2 percent of the total food market, and per capita annual spending on it was $102. In Germany, the world's second largest market, per capita spending was $124 annually, and organic food amounted to 4.4 percent of food sales. Swiss per capita organic food consumption rose from $49 in the late 1990s to $279 in 2014, which was the highest in the world, and from 2 percent to 7.1 percent of total food sales; Danish per capita consumption rose over the same period from $60 to $217, and the share of total food sales from 2.5 percent to 7.6 percent. While those two countries ate proportionally more organic food than any other, per capita spending elsewhere was significantly lower: it was $44 in Britain and $11 in Japan in 2014.[35]

The growth of organic food markets after 1980 was both driven and enabled by the expansion of retail and distribution businesses, which made buying organic food both possible and desirable, and which reduced price premiums. Two distinctive paths can be seen in how the market grew in different countries. In the first, the growth of the market was driven by natural foods retailers and wholesalers. These were definitely not the mom-and-pop businesses or the Reform Houses of the past. Although many such stores remained, market growth was driven by a handful of firms which became very big. They created enticing retail experiences and organized complex supply chains. In the second path, large conventional retailers, especially cooperatives, shaped the growth of the market.

The United States was an example of the first path. During the 1970s and 1980s a new generation of entrepreneurial ventures emerged from existing clusters of organic food businesses and consumers—especially around Boulder, Colorado, a countercultural cluster. Wild Oats, for example, started as a conventional retailer based in Boulder in 1984. The founders, Libby Cook and Mike Gilliland, had no initial interest in organic food, but sensed a good market after also opening a natural foods store. They changed their business name to Wild Oats, and began fast expansion. Sales approached $1 billion by 2000.[36]

It was Whole Foods Market and its co-founder John Mackey which drove the consolidation of the American organic food market. In 1978, Mackey and his then-girlfriend Rene Lawson Hardy borrowed $45,000 from family and friends to open a natural foods store in Austin, Texas under the original name of Safer Way. Alongside many organic food entrepreneurs of the time, Mackey was involved in the counterculture movement in the late 1960s: he dropped out of college six times and lived in a commune studying Eastern philosophy and religion, yoga and meditation, and ecology. His new store struggled, but after two years Mackey persuaded his father and a customer to invest more money to open a bigger, 10,000-square-foot store called Whole Foods Market. He got several smaller local organic grocers to join him, and the venture took off.[37]

Mackey was characteristic of the new cohort of green entrepreneurs in his desire to combine a social mission with the pursuit of profits. He expanded outside of Texas. By 1991, the company operated twelve stores and had total annual sales of over $92 million. Mackey initially struggled to raise a lot of capital, being told by one venture capitalist that his business was "just a bunch of hippies selling food to other hippies," but in 1992 Whole Foods Market successfully went public, as did Wild Oats four years later.[38]

The public flotation provided the financial resources for Mackey to begin rolling up the highly fragmented natural foods retailing sector. He built a corporate culture far removed from the earnest natural food stores of the past. Unlike his hippie predecessors Mackey was not prepared to let organic values stand in the way of reaching a wider market. He sold non-organic products and paid special attention to making shopping a pleasant experience for consumers with foods beautifully displayed in a fashion which a previous generation of organic retailers would have regarded as blatantly consumerist.[39] By 2000 Whole Foods, which had acquired many competitors, accounted for one-third of the $6 billion American organic food market. Wild Oats held a further $836 million.[40] The two retailing giants owned 220 stores, while the remaining 12,250 natural foods stores were independent retailers. Natural foods stores as a whole accounted for over two-thirds of the organic food market.[41]

Whole Foods drove the expansion of the American organic food market. It sourced organic foods on an industrial scale to meet growing demand. These practices were not without their complexities. Whole Foods often sourced from large organic farms, whether in California or across the world, greatly raising its carbon footprint compared to buying locally. Corporate policies contained an ethical dimension, including giving 5 percent of profits to charitable causes and paying living wages to its staff, but Mackey resolutely opposed unionization.[42] Yet there were other practices which were ethically challenging. In 2007, while Whole Foods was in the middle of a $565 million takeover bid for Wild Oats, it was revealed that Mackey had spent eight years posting on *Yahoo! Finance* message boards under an alias criticizing Wild Oats, while praising his own firm and even his own personal haircut. After completing the acquisition, Whole Foods itself was sued for anti-competitive behavior by the Federal Trade Commission and had to put twelve Wild Oats stores and one Whole Foods store up for sale.[43]

In the big picture, Whole Foods Market was a major driver of making organic food a routine shopping experience for middle-class American consumers able to pay its premium prices. It expanded the market for organic food, if not organic values, far beyond niche ecologically interested consumers. Its success was symbolized by the belated entry into the organic market in the 2000s of conventional retailers, discussed further in Chapter 9. In 2015, for the first time ever, conventional grocery stores accounted for over half of all sales of organic food in the United States.[44]

Similarly, in Germany a new generation of dynamic entrepreneurs in natural foods also drove market expansion, while conventional supermarkets, as in the United States, were slow to enter the business and accounted for less than a quarter of the German organic food market in 2000.[45]

Rapunzel, whose foundation was discussed in Chapter 3, developed as a large organic wholesaler. It grew rapidly during the 1980s, from its initial base in a farmhouse making muesli and nut butter, and survived the founding couple's divorce in 1987, with Joseph Wilhelm carrying on the business. In 1985 Rapunzel began a long-term organic farming project in Izmir, Turkey which supplied the company with organic figs, nuts, and other crops.[46] By 1995 Rapunzel supplied about 450 retail outlets in Germany, and five years later sales reached $60 million. A wide purchasing network extended to thirty countries, and it also exported many products outside Germany.[47] Sales reached $200 million in 2015. In 1990 Rapunzel became publicly listed.[48] Yet Wilhelm's embrace of the capital market was distinctly less enthusiastic than Mackey's.[49] In 2011, concerned about the continuity of environmental principles upon the eventual retirement of the founder, he took the company private. "The soul [of the company] can easily be lost in a sale," he noted.[50]

If Rapunzel grew out of the counterculture roots of organic farming, the natural foods retailer Alnatura was guided by the anthroposophical tradition associated with Rudolf Steiner. The founder, Götz Rehn, attended an anthroposophical Waldorf school in Freiburg until the age of 12 and became interested in nature from an early age through spending time in his grandmother's garden and in the countryside around Freiburg, as well as through a gardening class at his school.[51] His family subsequently moved to Bochum, in the Ruhr industrial region, and he received both his undergraduate and doctoral degrees in economics, publishing his dissertation as a book in 1979. The book drew on anthroposophical, psychological, and management thought to develop a "counter-current model" of business organization which stressed that a company needed to understand its positive role in society in order for the individual employees to feel that they were part of a "legitimate" system.[52] Rehn himself had decided at the age of 21 to "do something meaningful" in business that "would not destroy the Earth and that would give regard to people." These views were strongly influenced by his strong and continuing interest in anthroposophy.[53]

Rehn's business career started conventionally as a manager for Nestlé for seven years, but felt his values were not aligned with the company.[54] He ultimately decided to pursue opportunities in organic food. While at Nestlé he had met a fellow anthroposophist, Götz Werner, who had founded a drugstore chain called DM. Werner in turn introduced him to another anthroposophist, Wolfgang Gutberlet, the founder of the Tegut supermarket chain, who was a strong believer in the market potential of organic foods.[55] Persuaded, and building on his experience in foods marketing, Rehn established the company which became Alnatura in 1984. Although both DM and Tegut were conventional businesses, they became early and major customers of Alnatura.

Rehn believed that a larger number of goods needed to be offered to consumers. Like Mackey, Rehn sought to break out of the traditional image of organic food, associated with the Reform Houses and the countercultural "Bio" shops in Germany, which he described as "chicken feed" and drab.[56] Rehn launched the first organic supermarket in Germany, in the city of Mannheim, in 1987. There were fifty supermarkets two decades later, large in size, and selling hundreds of own-brand products as well as other brands. Revenues reached $450 million by 2008.[57] There was global sourcing of organic products. In 1991 the company began a long-term relationship with Ibrahim Abouleish's Sekem enterprise, a firm whose history we will discuss later in this chapter. This Egyptian company supplied organic textiles and other products.[58]

Alnatura organized as a limited company in 1987, but Rehn declined to go public. He saw independence from shareholders as essential for Alnatura's success; it enabled him to treat capital as a means to "realize an idea" and to "develop the best products" rather than focus on making the greatest possible profits.[59] By 2015 revenues had reached $840 million, despite a change in ownership of Tegut, acquired by the Swiss cooperative retailer Migros, and a parting of the ways with DM, which introduced its own brand and dropped Alnatura products.[60]

In a number of other European countries, the organic food market was driven by conventional supermarkets and, especially, cooperatives, whose managements became converted to supporting organic foods, primarily because of the support of their individual members. This was the case in Denmark, where the consumer cooperative FDB (Fællesforeningen for Danmarks Brugsforeninger), exercised a powerful influence on the growth of the market. As in other European countries, there was a long tradition of organic farming in Denmark: an anthroposophical Biodynamic Association was founded in 1936. But the whole category remained marginal.[61]

In 1982 FDB began selling organic carrots, which were produced by a radical community of intellectuals and students, in response to the worries of their members about pesticides. Five years later FDB also began selling organic milk. In a culture where milk-drinking was especially widespread and important owing to the prominence of dairy farming in Denmark, this was a significant step as it began accustomizing parents to the idea that organic dairy products were good for children, who might have more difficulty than adults in processing toxins left over from synthetic pesticides or added hormones. Although organic milk was sold at a premium compared to conventional milk, it was in absolute terms not hugely expensive for many consumers, reducing one potential obstacle to purchases. Food purchased for children's consumption continued to make up a high proportion of organic sales in Denmark, and elsewhere.[62]

There were two further crucial moves, both involving the FDB. First, in 1989 lobbying by FDB and others led to the Danish government establishing a

Danish Organic Food Council for stakeholders to meet regularly. One out-come was the creation of the first official label for organic products. The red "Ø" label showed that a product was state-certified organic and thus estab-lished the credibility of organic food products.[63] Second, in 1993 FDB's Super Brugsen supermarkets lowered the retail price of organic food products by up to 40 percent and decided to sell organic products throughout the nation, not only in the capital city of Copenhagen. There were conflicts within the organization about taking such a radical the step, but the supporters of organic foods were facilitated by the democratic nature of the organization in which, in the last resort, commerical decisions could be made without regard to whether they would be profitable, at least in the short term.[64]

The cutting of prices drove sales of organic milk up 500 percent over the next few years.[65] Between 1996 and 2000, organic farmland in Denmark increased from 46,171 hectacres to 165,000 hectacres, representing 6.2 percent of total Danish farmland. Large supermarkets by then accounted for around three-quarters of sales of organic food, which represented between 2.5 and 3 percent of the total Danish food market, the largest per capita consumption in the world at the time.[66]

The Danish example showed that sharply reducing the price premium with conventional food was crucial if organic food was to expand from its niche position. When prices were not cut, huge surges in demand did not happen. In Britain, the large supermarket chain Safeway started making organic fruit and vegetables available as early as 1981, and the other large supermarkets includ-ing Asda and Sainsbury followed. By 2000 the big supermarkets accounted for around three-quarters of organic food sales in that country, but prices were not sharply reduced, and per capita consumption remained far lower than in Denmark.[67]

Studies of the "willingness to pay" for organic food revealed complex consumer motives for purchasing organic food. The case for organic food had traditionally rested on health concerns, including the rejection of pesti-cides and chemicals in the food chain, and more general beliefs that it had enhanced nutritional value, a claim that remains contested. Typically, and across countries, entry consumers for organic foods were better-educated than other consumers, and quite often the purchaser was a first-time pregnant woman or mother concerned about the health of her children.[68] By the 2000s advocates of organic food also connected it to efforts to reverse climate change on the grounds that organic agriculture used less energy than conventional systems: livestock emissions—a major cause of global warming—could be reduced as cattle grazed on high-quality forage; animal diets containing plants found in pastures might yield less enteric methane. Organic farming seemed to result in more fertile soil, and to lock away more carbon. However, research on impact was ongoing, and contested, and a lot depended on the precise type of organic and conventional farming being compared.[69]

Studies of the consumers of organic food, and other sustainable consumer products, regularly reported both heterogeneity and national differences. Arguments about both health and wider environmental benefits could motivate consumers to buy organic food, but the relative weight given these motives varied from country to country.[70] One study of why German consumers were more willing to buy organic food than their British counterparts, for example, found common consumer attitudes in the two countries about food safety and healthiness, but that British consumers did not link eating organic food with wider concerns about the natural environment, while Germans did.[71] In some countries, institutional arrangements and consumer values seemed to make the task of building an organic market harder than in others. For example, in Norway and the Netherlands, two European countries where per capita consumption of organic foods remained low, a widespread belief that government food safety standards were effective seems to have added to the challenges faced by organic food companies wanting to convince consumers to pay more for organic food.[72]

In New Zealand, another country with low per capita consumption despite developed-country per capita incomes, organic entrepreneurs ran up against the widespread belief that the country was a natural paradise whose food was already healthy and safe. The New Zealand government had a long-running strategy to promote tourism on the basis of the country's unspoilt natural environment.[73] As organic markets grew elsewhere after 1980, pioneering organic retailers in New Zealand encountered skepticism that existing food was unhealthy. "The perception was that we were green," noted two biodynamists who established one of the first organic food stores in Auckland in 1984. "We were not."[74] Meanwhile, neither of the two conventional supermarket chains which dominated New Zealand, nor the dominant dairy industry cooperative Fonterra, nor the New Zealand government, demonstrated any interest in organic food, partly out of concerns that promoting it would raise doubts whether the country's vast agricultural exports were as clean as marketing suggested.[75]

In Japan, another country with low organic food consumption, deep-seated feelings which were hard to change also help to explain the limited growth of the organic food market. The country's desire for modernization after World War II created a strong and collective disregard for past traditions. There was a traditional word for organic called "yuki," which meant "organic compound," but the concept became especially associated with radical and left-wing movements, like the activists who opposed building Tokyo's new airport at Narita during the 1960s and 1970s. When a new generation of entrepreneurs sought to develop organic businesses beginning in the 1980s, they needed to recreate the category by seeking inspiration from Europe, rather than drawing on past Japanese traditions which had unfavorable connotations for many consumers.[76] Creating such a category was not helped by the absence of any legal definition of organic food before 2003.[77]

Kohei Takashima, who founded an online retailer called Oisix in 2000, responded to the challenges by seeking to emphasize the safety of organic food, and by using e-commerce. A former McKinsey consultant who "wanted to do something good for society," Takashima thought there was a potential match between the internet and food purchases, as both were very personal. The firm's logo promoted "Foods safe enough for farmers to feed their own children." Takashima received funding from a large trading company, and started a search for farmers to supply organic food, at first being greeted with incredulity. There was no fee to join the service, and a core market developed of working mothers with small children or pregnant women. From selling only twenty lines of vegetables at its start, within a decade Oisix sold 3,300 different items. It opened a Hong Kong operation in 2009.[78] It made a successful IPO in 2013, and annual revenues had reached $170 million by 2014.[79] Oisix was one of several e-commerce organic food companies which grew the Japanese market. Although Japanese consumers purchased and ate only 5 percent of the organic food that their American counterparts did, half of Japan's organic fruits and vegetables were sold online, compared to 3 percent in the United States.[80]

Organic food, at least certified organic, remained a tiny niche in the developing world, but a definite one. The organic food market in China tripled between 2007 and 2015 to reach just over 1 percent of total food consumption as consumers reacted to numerous food contamination scandals. These foods were usually imported for sale to affluent Chinese, typically with children, who were prepared to pay a premium of up to 50 percent for organic products. Specialty stores opened in the country's biggest cities, but the real growth, as in Japan, was in online retailing companies.[81]

Often, the entrepreneurs behind the new organic businesses in developing countries saw the growth of the market in the West and judged it to be a matter of time before their own markets developed. This was the case in Turkey, where organic farming had been promoted by Rapunzel in the 1980s. In 1999 City Farm was established with the aim of creating a domestic market for organic food. The founders, a Turkish man and his American wife, had lived in the United States, and thought they could replicate the success of Whole Foods Market, but they ran into financial difficulties. In 2002, City Farm was taken over by the large Sabancı business group. Ayhan Sümerli, a former executive with Unilever-owned Lipton Tea in Turkey, was hired to run the group's food businesses, mostly small firms like City Farm, but the business did not gain traction. City Farm lost an estimated $10 million between 2002 and 2010.[82]

In 2010 Sümerli acquired the organic retailer, which had annual sales of $3 million and one shop, in a management buyout. Familiar with organic food from his work for Unilever in Germany, he based his business model primarily on Alnatura and was convinced that the Turkish market would develop along German lines. "Turkey is following the EU with a lag of ten years," he later remarked, optimistically, and "with widespread technology this can go down to five."[83]

Within three years Sümerli expanded sales to $10 million and eight shops, and also sold products through big Turkish retailers. Through his previous jobs with European multinationals, Sümerli had contacts with many agricultural suppliers, with whom he worked to persuade them to convert to organic production. By 2013 he had 400 suppliers, four-fifths of which were small farms between 10 and 20 acres in size. Like earlier organic pioneers, Sümerli also invested in building the legitimacy of the sector: he became the chairman of the Organic Food Producers Association, a trade association, and sought good relations with relevant government ministries.[84]

The scaling of the organic food market was remarkable given the industry's history. Purposeful entrepreneurs like John Mackey, Götz Rehn, and Kohei

Takashima drove the growth of the organic market in their respective countries by making the consumer experience more attractive, and building efficient supply and logistics systems. The cooperative FDB did the same in Denmark through radical price cuts. Even in countries where high-income consumers could pay a premium price for organic food, let alone in emerging markets like Turkey, building business was not easy. Whole Foods Market showed that access to capital markets could permit fast and rapid growth, although in Germany Rehn and, eventually, Wilhelm both opted for slower growth rather the pressures of answering to capital markets. Scaling had consequences beyond increased eating of organic food. The pioneers of organic foods were motivated by a broad social and environmental vision, and they made efforts to convince their initially skeptical customers to share this vision. In mainstream supermarkets, and large natural foods supermarkets, consumers were offered plentiful organic food, but rarely the wider vision.

Branding organic foods

The creation of successful organic food and drink brands, rare before the 1980s, was important in the growth of the organic food market. It expanded the category, raised its profile, and offered opportunities for selling in conventional channels. In this section, we will see some of the factors which successful brands shared and which may account for their success.

One of the most readily observable facts about organic brands is that they typically clustered in certain categories: different brands of organic yogurt, for instance, have emerged in countries around the world. A second is that many of the new start-ups behind organic brands were based in the United States. The country's entrepreneurial spirit and, arguably, the relative ease of finding external funding are partial explanations for the United States being a world leader in launching successful organic brands. But there is also a backlash effect at work: the extreme degree of industrialization of agriculture and the use of growth hormones and other scientific interventions in the United States made it easier to make the case for organic foods. A final common factor was that, if a brand was successful in proving that there was a market for its products, it was often acquired by a larger, often conventional, company. These new exit opportunities made some, although not all, founders rich, but left others disappointed.

Among the most successful brands were those created by organic retailers themselves, including the 365 Everyday Value brand launched by Whole Foods Market in 1997. In other cases, entrepreneurs launched specific organic food and drink brands. This was the case in yogurt, a food which had only become popular in most American and Western European diets after the 1950s. In the 1980s the first organic yoghurt brands appeared in the United States. Perhaps the most prominent of these brands that played a key role in creating the category was Stonyfield Farm. The brand originated in 1983 when Gary Hirshberg and Samuel Kaymen, both environmental activists, founded the business in New Hampshire. Kaymen began making yoghurt to fund a school he had been running to teach organic agriculture, while Hirshberg had been director of an ecological research group. They began with seven cows grazing on land free of pesticides and chemical fertilizers. They attracted as an early angel investor Josh Mailman, the son of a famous New York investor and philanthropist, who formed part of a group interested in using their inherited wealth to promote social good.[85]

Hirshberg and Kaymen initially drove their yogurt into Boston, stocked supermarket shelves, and gave away free cartons to interested shoppers, while avoiding advertising. The firm also gave out free yoghurt at non-profit events such as the annual Earth Day. It was not until 1992 that they made any profits. By 1998 sales had surpassed $40 million, and it was one of the largest brands of organic yoghurt in the United States. In 2001 France's Danone Groupe, a large French manufacturer of conventional yoghurt, acquired a 40 percent stake in the business and full control two years later.[86]

Baby food also grew as a large organic category. The European pioneer was the long-established German company Hipp, which progressively shifted to organic food under the chairmanship of Claus Hipp. Claus, who replaced his father as head of the firm in 1967, worked on his grandmother's Swiss farm as a child and knew the organic pioneer Hans Müller well. He later reflected that these years shaped his ecological ideologies, although it was not until 1993 that every product was organic. Like his father, Claus was personally committed to Christianity, and argued that it stood at the heart of the brand's integrity. "A religious anchoring is advantageous," he maintained in 2013. "If one were only to act ecologically on marketing grounds, then it would not work. It must come from within, from the heart, to succeed."[87] The company found itself a regular recipient of awards for being the most sustainable company in Germany.[88]

The concept of organic baby food was unknown in the United States until the 1980s, when Earth's Best was launched by the twin brothers Ron and Arnie Koss. The market was dominated by three large conventional firms, Gerber, Beech-Nut, and Heinz. The brothers had got the idea of baby foods while working in natural foods stores in upstate New York in the 1970s, when they noticed that all the organic products were for adults. By 1984 they had moved to Vermont, and they decided to venture into the baby food business. "I am an environmentalist," Ron Koss later observed. "I started Earth's Best because I have a connection to this planet, and I have a love of nature."[89] Arnie wrote later of their "multidimensional imagining" that organic baby food would lead to a broader paradigm shift in which the "chemically dependent agribusiness paradigm was reduced in its prominence."[90]

They persuaded a local business to sign a bank loan for them, and eventually raised over $1 million to begin production of an organic apple puree baby food in 1987. Even so, they continued to struggle to raise funds because the baby food business was capital-intensive. Perishable ingredients needed to be bought a year in advance when they were in season and frozen. Although sales had risen to $3.5 million in 1989, there were constant cash flow problems. That year they sold the majority of the business to venture capitalists. In a pattern familiar in the American industry, the new owners brought in a professional chief executive, and by the middle of the 1990 both brothers had been forced out of the company. By then the firm had revenues of $8 million and annual losses of $7 million.[91]

The firm's head office was moved to Boulder, Colorado, and the manufacturing contracted to a California fruit processor. All the former staff were dismissed, an event which Arnie Koss described as "like a death" to him.[92] By 1995 the firm had sales of nearly $24 million, though was still loss-making, and in 1998 it was sold to Heinz for $30 million. The twin brothers received $51,000 each and were left angry at the behavior of the venture investors, but they were also proud that Heinz and the other conventional baby food manufacturers were finally selling organic products themselves. "We had dragged Goliath into the arena," Arnie noted.[93]

The growth of these and other successful organic food and drink brands indicated the growing consumer interest in organics after 1980. Creating such brands remained a struggle, one which attracted people motivated by strong ecological and socially responsible agendas. Because of the financial difficulties of launching new brands in a still emerging market, the typical outcome was that, with the exception of tightly held family businesses such as Hipp, large conventional companies eventually acquired pioneering organic brands. This pattern, and its consequences, are examined further in Chapter 9.

From farm to market

The growth of organic food consumption was reflected in the expansion of organic farming. By 2014 there were an estimated 43 million hectares of organically farmed land in the world, although by then Europe and North America only accounted for 27 percent and 7 percent of this amount, respectively, and in those regions there were considerable differences between countries. Austria, Switzerland, and Sweden had converted between 12 percent and 20 percent of their agriculture to organic. In the United States, although it had the third-largest amount of organic farmland, it only accounted for 0.6 percent of the country's total farmland.[94]

It was no easy matter for farmers to convert to organic. The slow process of developing certification standards, discussed in Chapter 6, was a challenge. As the 1980s began, government agricultural programs were almost universally hostile to organic farming and instead continued to focus on scale and technological progress, which were seen as vital to national food supplies, and raising farm incomes. Conventional farmers were openly hostile, too.

Beginning in the late 1980s, agricultural polices underwent a striking reversal, which proved to be a significant factor in the subsequent growth of organic agriculture. This shift occurred first in Europe, as policy-makers in some countries, responding to pressure from voters, began to view organic agriculture as a force for environmental and social good rather than as an annoyance. In 1987 Denmark introduced financial support for producers who wanted to convert to organic agriculture, a policy shift which resulted in a strong surge in land under organic cultivation. Sweden, which had already introduced a levy on pesticide use in 1986, became the first country to provide subsidies for the continuation of organic production, not just conversion, in 1989. In 1992 the European Union launched a program that obliged all member states to provide grants for converting to, or continuing with, organic farming methods.[95] Over the following decades other governments also began to support conversion to organic agriculture, either for ecological reasons, or because it was seen as a growing market segment.

There was no such policy shift in the United States at federal or state level. The policy priority remained providing vast federal subsidies for commodity crop producers. Farmers were pressured to scale, and focus on a single commodity.[96] This focus primarily reflected certain idiosyncratic features of the American political system, which gives some regions—the farming states of the Great Plains, for example—formidable influence beyond their relative population size. In 2010, one estimate was that US farmers produced 32 percent of the world's corn supply on 84 million acres of farmland. The government-owned Commodity Credit Corporation dispersed large farm subsidies—around $7 billion in 2015—primarily to growers of corn and soy. The resulting availability of huge amounts of corn contributed to the nation's obesity problem, while the massive use of chemical fertilizers involved had multiple adverse environmental impacts. There were no subsidies for conversion to organic agriculture.[97]

Organic farmers in the United States, then, had to rely on themselves if they wanted to develop a viable business. "We had a hard time getting our stuff in to the distributors, or at least at a good enough price to make it worthwhile," Jim Cochran, who established the first commercial organic strawberry farm in California in 1983, later observed. "So we had to develop our own markets pretty much customer by customer."[98] Cochran's first encounter with organic occurred when he was a student at the University of California at Santa Cruz and saw Alan Chadwick's organic garden there. He became a strong social activist and supporter of labor unions. After working as a business manager for a cooperative of large, conventional strawberry farms, Cochran rented four acres of land at Davenport on the coast north of Santa Cruz to experiment with organic growing, and selling. "Nobody in the business had any clue that the customer wanted fruit that tasted good and wasn't sprayed," he later noted.[99]

Health scares often provided temporary opportunities for Cochran and other small organic farmers, reinforcing the backlash effect in the United States. In 1988 a health scare occurred related to the use of Alar, a growth regulator used to ripen apples, prompting a two-thirds growth in American organic produce sales in one year. Many supermarkets, especially in California, stocked organic fruit and vegetables for the first time, though most of them withdrew them subsequently because of consumer resistance to the much higher prices and irregularity of supplies.[100] It took Cochran a long time to develop a business selling his strawberries at his own farm, at farmers' markets, and to natural foods stores in San Francisco—five years just to become profitable. Then it was not until the 2000s, when Whole Foods Market became the farm's biggest buyer, that the company achieved stability.[101]

Organic farmers pursued a number of alternative strategies to build distribution and retailing outlets. One approach was community-supported agriculture, or CSA. This began in the early 1960s in Germany and Switzerland, when groups of farmers and consumers, primarily influenced by Rudolf Steiner's biodynamic philosophy, began to form cooperative partnerships to promote ecologically sound, and socially equitable, agriculture. A fundamental premise was that growers and consumers shared the risks and benefits of food production, with members paying at the onset of the growing season for a share of the anticipated harvest. Once harvesting began, they received weekly shares of vegetables and fruit in vegetable box schemes. An important figure in globalizing the concept was Jan Vander Tuin, who had worked on a biodynamic farm in Zurich. In 1984 he introduced the concept to the United States through a contact with Robyn Van En, who owned a small biodynamic farm in Massachusetts. Beginning with a small apple orchard, Van En and a small group around her combined Steiner's ideas with those propounded in Schumacher's *Small Is Beautiful*, one of whose arguments was the need to produce locally what was consumed locally. Van En became a passionate advocate of CSA in North America. In 1992 she founded CSA North America, a non-profit clearinghouse to support CSA development.[102]

CSA projects spread particularly in California. Among the most prominent exponents was Michael Ableman, who as a young man aspiring to be a professional photographer, had become involved in a southern California farm commune in the 1970s, before he took a job grafting orange trees at Fairview Gardens, near Santa Barbara. This was a remnant of a much larger farm established in the 1890s, which had become surrounded by suburban developments. When the manager left, Ableman took over the role, staying for two decades and saving the 12-acre farm from real estate developers. The farm became a role model for CSA agriculture.[103]

Cooperatives sometimes evolved into for-profit ventures. This was the case with the organic food box business developed by Thomas Harrtung and Søren Ejlersen in Denmark. In 1984, the 23-year-old Harrtung inherited his parents' farm in Jutland. He had studied at Copenhagen's Agricultural University but had intended to work in an aid agency before his parents died early. He introduced sustainable forest management, which he had studied at university, in the forested part of his land but followed conventional farming practices on the farmed part until 1994, when he began noticing the disconnect between his forest management and the conventional farm. A turning point came in 1996 when he attended the IFOAM scientific conference in Copenhagen and heard speeches by leading American organic farmers. Over the following years Harrtung combined his active participation in the Lutheran Church with a progressive espousal of Steiner's beliefs. "My religion became part of the gasoline for taking risk in the business as far as we possibly could," he observed. "We are biodynamic farmers now and believe there is a spiritual aspect to man and his interaction with land, sun and rain."[104]

Harrtung launched a cooperative at his farm in the following year, as did Søren Ejlersen. They soon brought their farms together and, concerned about the slow and cautious decision-making of their cooperative, took the business private and launched the firm of Aarstiderne (translation: The Seasons) in 1999. They stopped focusing on their local markets and began taking boxes of their products to the much larger market of Copenhagen. From the beginning each box also included menus and an innovative system of online ordering was introduced, eventually reaching tens of thousands of customers. In 2001 the firm secured funding from Triodis, the Dutch-based sustainable bank.[105] This provided funds for expansion, although there were missteps, including an unsuccessful experiment opening physical shops in Copenhagen. Still, by 2015 the firm had sales of $69 million and was delivering to well over 40,000 customers.[106]

A fully commercial path was exemplified by Drew and Myra Goodman, the founders of Earthbound Farms. Although they were both born on the Upper East Side of Manhattan, they first met when they went to college in California, at Santa Cruz and Berkeley respectively. Both developed strong ecological views. While Drew studied environmental science, Myra transferred to study international relations at Berkeley after her sophomore year abroad in India left her "outraged" and "anxious to change the world."[107] In 1984, aged 24 and 20 respectively, they started selling raspberries on a roadside stand grown from a house and garden plot in the Carmel Valley, which Myra's parents had bought as an investment property. Drew had worked with a group associated with Chadwick at UC Santa Cruz, but neither he nor his wife knew much about organic agriculture before the venture began. They did, however, share a dislike of pesticides.[108]

After two years they began selling pre-washed salads bagged for retail sale, after hearing from local chefs that they could sell baby heads of lettuce for the same price as full-size ones, enabling them to grow more of them on a small plot. "We sold in local gourmet markets," Myra Goodman later remembered. "It was hard at first because they would only take our salad as 'guaranteed sales' which meant they wouldn't pay us anything unless our salads sold." The Goodmans were persistent and flexible. The first profits were made only at the end of 1987. In 1993 they contracted with Costco, the membership warehouse, to supply conventional bagged salad mix, employing crops grown on land still going through the mandated three-year transition to organic. Costco declined to have organic written on the labels, in view of consumer perceptions that organic was expensive and not tasty. The Goodmans decided not to object, and this proved the making of the company. Sales increased tenfold in one year. By 1999 Costco wanted the labels to specify organic.[109]

The Goodmans also worked hard to expand their supplies. A partnership in 1995 with a large conventional salad grower transitioning to organic increased their supply, and enabled the Goodmans to focus on processing, marketing, and distribution. Partnerships with large-scale, Salinas Valley-based farmers with winter operations in Arizona and Mexico enabled Earthbound Farm to greatly expand supplies. Earthbound Farm was able to reduce the price differential between organic and conventional salads, while also delivering new income streams from conventional agriculture. Another marketing alliance in 2000 enabled entry to the citrus, avocado, and tropical fruit business. By the early 2000s Earthbound Farm's annual sales had reached $300 million, the signature organic salad mix was available in more than 70 percent of supermarkets in the United States, and it was the largest organic produce brand in North America.[110]

Earthbound Farm was one of many large organic farms which developed in California. They supplied the growing demand generated by Whole Foods Market and equivalent successful organic retailers, but their growth was not universally welcomed. The area had seen the pioneering stages of the organic movement in the United States, but the large organic farms which developed seem to have little in common with the radical and alternative views of their predecessors. By the 1990s California had more organic farmland than anywhere else in the world, but by 1997 just 2 percent of Californian growers grossed more than 50 percent of the total value of organic production. Critics talked of an "organic-industrial complex."[111]

The largest expansion of organic production was not in California, however. Organic production became globalized, and production was increasingly divorced from consumption. By 2014 the largest regional source of organic food production was Australia and the Pacific Islands, which accounted for 40 percent. There were 2,567 certified organic businesses in Australia by then, about half of them classified as small, some of them long-established, like the Melbourne-based organic wholesaler Kadac, but many others were attracted to organic food more recently, and included very large firms.[112] Latin America accounted for a further 15 percent of organic production, Asia for 8 percent, and Africa for 3 percent. Over one-quarter of organic production, therefore, was in the developing world, which also accounted for 86 percent of all individual organic producers.

The globalization of the organic food chain was far removed from the world of production and consumption being in harmony as envisaged by Steiner. The resulting transport costs had a negative impact on greenhouse gas emissions, which was partially mitigated by the positive gains from lower use of chemicals and pesticides. Within the broader definition of sustainability, however, there were new opportunities for organic farmers in developing countries.

Sekem, the business built by Ibrahim Abouleish, provides one example. Born in Egypt, Abouleish studied chemistry and pharmacology in Austria and stayed as a researcher, becoming an Austrian citizen.[113] In 1975, on a visit to Egypt, he was shocked by the environmental degradation and poverty. He had read the works of Rudolf Steiner, and in 1977 he returned to Egypt and purchased from the state 70 acres of desert land in Belbes, 37 miles northeast of Cairo. There he established Sekem, taking its name from the hieroglyphic meaning "vitality of the sun," to develop biodynamic farming.[114] Abouleish had strong religious and philosophical motivations. "Anthroposophy has no link with religion," he noted later, "it is just a philosophy, but it does help you understand the world you live in. Religion brings ethics and morals. I cannot function without the one or the other...My religion Islam needs more entrepreneurs, entrepreneurs that are able to explain religion in a modern way so they are not considered as greedy people, but as a factor of development, a sustainable development."[115]

Abouleish and a local villager began reclaiming desert and making it cultivable. This was a long-term project which involved planting some 120,000 trees. Abouleish sought finance from an Islamic bank, which took a 40 percent equity holding, but the relationship soured badly, causing long-term difficulties raising funds. He also ran into opposition from the country's Ministry of Agriculture, which believed biodynamic agriculture would spread disease in the country.[116]

Abouleish sought foreign markets. He employed his knowledge of pharmacology to start making medicinal products. In 1981 Sekem sent its first shipment of medicinal herbs and food ingredients to the United States. Two years later it began selling herbal remedies on the local market. This developed into a business which packed organically certified herbal teas, dairy products, oils, spices, honey, dates, organic coffee, juices, and preserves for consumers in Egypt and abroad. In 1986 Abouleish worked with the German Development Bank and a German natural medical products company called Dr. Schaete to create ATOS Pharma, a joint venture to research and develop medicines from natural sources. Six years later ATOS began manufacturing and selling natural cosmetics under license from the organic products company Weleda.[117]

Abouleish also began selling organic food locally during the early 1980s. As there were no certified organic foods in the national market at all, Abouleish created awareness through slowly building contacts with journalists. He also sought to progressively widen the scope of the crops he grew organically. In 1988 he and a Greek partner set up another company called Libra to produce and sell both locally and internationally organically grown crops. He drove the creation of an industry association, the Egyptian Biodynamic Association, which pioneered the growing of biodynamic cotton from 1991. In that year Sekem began collaborating with Alnatura to produce natural fabrics. Sekem also extended its own agricultural business. In 1994 Libra began to grow 1,000 acres of cotton biodynamically, based on intensive cooperation between scientists, manufacturers, and farmers. Trained and experienced advisors helped small-scale farmers, weekly visiting different regions to answer questions and solve urgent problems such as insect development. In 1996 a disagreement between Abouleish and his partners on what constituted organic led him to withdraw from Libra and found a new company called Hator to produce and pack fresh fruit and vegetables.[118] The venture flourished, and survived subsequent upheavals. By 2010 Sekem cultivated over 780 hectares of land,

86 percent of which had been reclaimed.[119] Four years later overall revenues were $41 million, nearly a quarter derived from exports, with a business spanning biodynamic farming and organic cotton, and including extensive investments in schools and other social facilities.[120] From the 1980s, Sekem built an extensive school system extending from kindergarten to higher education aimed at "trying to teach our youth from a very young age the importance of respecting the environment they live in."[121]

Between the 1980s and the 2010s, organic farming expanded from experimental ventures in Switzerland, California, and the Egyptian desert to become a global industry which included large enterprises spread around the world. The whole concept of organic farming was mainstreamed by people such as Cochran, the Goodmans, and Abouleish, who were prepared to invest ahead of proven demand and distribution networks. The process involved multiple challenges, from developing new farming techniques to inventing new concepts, such as pre-washed salad bags, to pioneering new ways of e-commerce. Persuading the public to buy was perhaps the biggest challenge. Over time, especially as the numbers of organic food consumers grew and natural foods stores expanded their reach, these challenges were overcome, but new dilemmas arose, especially concerning the legitimacy of relying on large organic farms engaged in long-distance trade.

The mainstreaming of natural beauty

Although the natural beauty industry began to escape from its marginal niche a little later than organic foods, it soon followed a similar arc of growth. By 2014 the world natural and organic personal care market had reached $30 billion in global sales. This growth was transformational, though natural remained modest compared to the overall world beauty market, which expanded from sales of $162 billion in 1998 to reach $460 billion in 2014.[122]

As in the growth of organic food, the expansion of natural beauty reflected in part the expansion of the category of the green consumer in Europe and the United States, but there was nothing automatic about this growth. It continued to demand hard work building the category and explaining its legitimacy to a skeptical world. Pioneering figures such as Anita Roddick and Horst Rechelbacher, whom we met in Chapter 3, continued to enhance their appeal to ecologically concerned consumers by associating purchases of their brands with wider environmental causes, thereby fostering legitimacy. In 1990 The

Body Shop Foundation in Britain was established as a charity which funded human rights and environmental protection groups. In 1992 Rechelbacher was one of the three original founders of Business for Social Responsibility, an association advocating for corporate responsibility.[123]

There remained, however, formidable challenges beyond the usual ones of coming up with enticing new brands and reaching new customers. There was no sudden rush by conventional outlets, whether department stores for expensive products or drugstores and pharmacies for mass brands, to welcome small niche brands with little proven market. However, both The Body Shop and Aveda showed that this roadblock could be overcome through creating other channels, such as franchised stores and beauty salons, respectively, which could both reach and educate consumers.

Some new firms were strongly committed to biodynamic and organic traditions. In 1983 Bernard Chevilliat, a bee keeper and biologist, launched the Melvita organic brand in Lagorce, France. This venture and equivalents built small, niche markets of committed consumers. Some new ventures, especially in the United States, became the basis for much bigger brands, which became pioneers of reaching consumers in new ways. This was the case of Bare Escentuals, founded in San Francisco in 1976 by Diane Richardson, who saw a potential for mineral cosmetic products without preservatives. She began by importing clay pots of mineral blush from India. Under the subsequent leadership of Leslie Blodgett during the 1990s, the firm broke down traditional distribution channels, sharply segmented between mass and premium brands, by pursuing a multi-channel strategy. Particularly innovative was the novel and successful use of the QVC home shopping network.[124]

Blodgett was installed by a private equity investor who had invested in 1990 as the original business hovered towards insolvency. She later managed an IPO in 2006, by which time revenues had reached $400 million.[125] This was an indication of a new interest in natural beauty by conventional firms, which first began to use the word "natural," and later to establish or buy up green brands, a trend examined further in Chapter 9. As in food, natural beauty was no longer the preserve of affluent consumers in Europe and the United States. As discretionary incomes rose in Asia and Latin America, consumers began to be attracted to brands which looked relevant to them, which used local ingredients, and which drew on local beauty traditions. In countries in which manufacturing quality standards were often sub-optimal, the idea of a product avoiding chemicals also proved attractive. Local firms, in turn, perceived a competitive edge against the powerful European and American brands which dominated the global industry. This was the strategy of the Chinese beauty company Shanghai Jahwa, which in the late 1990s launched the Herborist brand, formulated using herbal ingredients traditionally used in Chinese medicine. By 2014 it was one of the top ten fastest-growing global brands and had already entered European markets.[126]

In Brazil a cluster of local brands developed which evolved a strong environmental and social agenda, although originally paying little if any regard to relying on plant ingredients. These included O Boticário, founded by Miguel Gellert Krigsner in 1977, which grew rapidly inside and subsequently outside Brazil by employing a franchising strategy. In 1990 Krigsner created a foundation, funded by 1 percent of the cosmetic company's annual gross income, to invest in social and environmental causes. Fundação O Boticário de Proteção a Natureza became one of the country's leading environmental NGOs.[127]

The largest firm in this cluster was Natura, which had its origins in 1969 when Antônio Luiz Seabra opened a small laboratory and cosmetics store in the city of São Paulo. The company adopted a direct-selling model to better reach consumers. Guilherme Leal and Pedro Passos joined Seabra, and in 1989 the whole business was consolidated as Natura Cosméticos. By 2005, when the firm made an IPO, it had revenues of $1.5 billion and employed 480,000 sales consultants.[128]

Natura demonstrated a strong environmental awareness from the beginning. Seabra placed cosmetics within the context of the importance of relationships between people, communities, and the environment. These views were formalized in the early 1990s with an emphasis on "well being/being well," and a growing commitment to social and environmental sustainability. Seabra offered, as had Anita Roddick previously, an explicit critique of the beauty industry beyond the nature of the ingredients employed. The industry, he argued, had "overpromised things to the customers, especially exaggerating aging and death fears." Manipulative advertising was, he argued, a "cultural crime." Instead, Seabra saw cosmetics as a means to heal a broken world. "It can be a way for people to express their emotions, their feelings, and a growing concern about the Earth's preservation and their quest for a harmonious development of human potential."[129]

The company's values were transmitted through its sales consultants and through multiple institutional initiatives. In 1998 Leal co-founded an NGO called the Ethos Institute of Business and Social Responsibility to help companies manage their businesses in a socially responsible fashion. In 2000 the company launched the Ekos brand, a landmark product line made from Brazilian raw materials gathered by sustainable methods. Testing on animals stopped shortly afterwards. In the same year the company also became the first in the world to practice "integrated reporting," which tried to report the company's financial, social, and environmental performance in one report. In 2007 Natura launched a strategy to become a carbon-neutral company.[130]

By 2015, as revenues approached $3 billion, Natura held 14 percent of the Brazilian market and employed one and a half million sales consultants. Businesses had been launched in neighboring countries, including Mexico and Colombia, as well as a small symbolic presence in Paris, the world's beauty capital. Greenness was not, however, necessarily an international comparative advantage. The strong ideological views of the founders helped to limit its international expansion. For example, the firm declined to invest in China or any firm which sold in China, which had become the world's second biggest beauty market and for which Natura's accessibly priced brands were a good fit, because the country mandated testing of cosmetics on animals.[131]

The growth of the natural beauty market, and the emergence of prominent firms which seemed to successfully combine making profits with a commitment to sustainability, were big changes compared to the past. Yet success coexisted with ambiguity. Issues of legitimacy arose, as shown in Chapter 9, when iconic brands were acquired by the big conventional beauty companies. It was, however, less the ownership of such brands, which was well-hidden from consumers, than the meaning of natural beauty itself which continued to generate considerable consumer confusion, and to complicate any assessment of whether the environmental impact was positive or otherwise. As Chapter 6 explores, there was a prolonged and contested process of certification, reflecting profound differences on definitions. While organic foods typically became highly regulated, beauty products were not. The category came to include products ranging from those formally certified as organic to so-called "naturally-inspired" products. "Natural" acquired many associations beyond the ingredients used, including the avoidance of animal testing, and support for a wide range of social and environmental issues. Most products labeled "natural" still contained some synthetic fragrances, artificial dyes, or petroleum by-products, sometimes serving as preservatives since plant-based preservatives had poor anti-microbial and anti-fungal properties. The very use of the term "natural" acquired distinctly idiosyncratic qualities. Petroleum, animal products, and alcohol were "natural" products, for example, but not in the sense understood by the consumer, let alone by the green movement.

Beyond the confusion surrounding the meaning of natural beauty, it was not clear how far the industry could be regarded as a driver of sustainability. Although conventional cosmetics and hair dyes had a long history of incorporating some harmful chemical ingredients, and others whose effects were unknown, there was no case for saying that all natural ingredients were safe, and there was no evidence that all (as opposed to some) chemically synthesized ingredients posed health risks. If the entire multi-billion dollar beauty industry converted exclusively to natural ingredients tomorrow, the sheer quantity of plants needed to produce tiny amounts of certain ingredients would result in huge areas of land being devoted to cosmetics ingredients, presumably at the cost of cultivating food. Moreover, as Rodale among other early green entrepreneurs argued, the entire beauty industry was a prime example of the very consumerism which incentivized people to buy heavily advertised and attractively packaged brands rather than consider the environmental costs of their decisions.

During these decades, then, a group of talented entrepreneurs, passionate about social and ecological issues in their motivation, mainstreamed the natural beauty market. They built brands which responded to the health and environmental concerns of a growing consumer segment. In a complete break from the past, the more successful of these businesses were financially profitable, enabling further growth as they accessed capital markets and investors. Some founders became rich, and some funded environmental and social NGOs, including ones established by themselves. It was an achievement based on an evolving and multi-faceted view of what natural beauty meant. For some it was more about natural ingredients, for others about protecting biodiversity, for others avoiding animal testing, and for others social responsibility. This made for a diffuse market category, but as beauty was an industry with a large customer base, especially but not only among women, it helped diffuse at least the language of environmentalism more broadly. It also provided the base for passionate environmental advocates, beginning with Roddick and Rechelbacher, who exercised an influence far beyond the beauty industry.

Greener buildings

As the second wave of environmentalism had taken hold, some architects had achieved considerable success as environmental activists, but less success at securing clients to commission their designs. After 1980, there was a significant mainstreaming of ecological architecture as triple-glazed glass, natural ventilation, and other ecological design features transitioned from the niche to the mainstream. Sustainability became entrenched in major schools of architecture. As Chapter 6 discusses, the development of environmental building certification was one driver of this mainstreaming. In a 2012 survey of 803 architects, engineers, contractors, building owners, and building consultants located in sixty-two countries, 28 percent of firms reported that they were focusing their work on sustainable design and construction by doing at least 60 percent of their projects green.[132]

This diffusion of ecological architecture was neither automatic nor immediate. Indeed, during the 1980s the impetus given to more sustainable architecture from rising prices of fossil fuels in the previous decade faded alongside falling oil prices. There was a notable cooling of interest in the subject among the members of the American Institute of Architects (AIA).[133] There were setbacks for some pioneers. Malcolm Wells's Earthships ran into legal problems with municipalities and individual clients who complained about quality. In 1990 he voluntarily gave up his New Mexico architecture and construction licenses after a dispute with clients.[134] Sim Van der Ryn retrospectively wrote of his disillusion after the election of President Ronald Reagan in 1980, and the replacement of Jerry Brown by a Republican administration in California two years later. "After years of success implementing my ideas and thought experiments," he observed, "nothing seemed to be working. I felt despair and hopelessness."[135]

Nevertheless, noteworthy institutional entrepreneurship laid the basis for a further diffusion of ecological concepts in the built environment. A first mover in this process was the fourth Aga Khan, who in 1976 established an award for architecture designed to create public awareness of Islamic culture. From the beginning, juries considered context, social and economic factors, and environmental impact as important criteria. The Aga Khan Award became, one study of ecological architecture observed, "an arbiter of a new, socially and environmentally based consciousness."[136]

Another important case of institutional entrepreneurship came in 1982 when the physicist Amory Lovins and his wife, Hunter Lovins, began the

Rocky Mountain Institute in Colorado in 1982 as a research center focused on energy efficiency. Amory Lovins had come to national prominence in 1976 when he published an article in the journal *Foreign Affairs* about two alternative paths for the country's energy strategy. The first was steadily increasing reliance on fossil fuels and nuclear fission, which he condemned as having serious environmental risks. The alternative, which he called "the soft path," favored increasing use of wind power and solar power, along with increased commitment to energy conservation and energy efficiency.[137] The Institute developed out of the house the couple built, dubbed the "Banana Farm," which used one-tenth the energy of a typical US house of its size. Lower utility bills quickly offset the higher construction costs, saving money on heating and cooling within a year. Both the Lovins became influential public intellectuals, while the Institute became a powerhouse of ideas and concepts, including criteria for ecological architecture that embraced such principles as using the largest possible proportion of regional resources and materials.[138]

Within the architectural profession, there was an evolving understanding of what was needed to be sustainable. An AIA Committee on the Environment (COTE) was formed in 1989.[139] Three years later COTE produced, with funds from the Environmental Protection Agency, the influential *Environmental Resource Guide* of 1992, a pioneering attempt to use life-cycle analysis to assess the effectiveness of building materials. In 1992 Susan Maxman, the principal of her own architectural firm, SMP Architects, participated in the UN Earth Summit conference at Rio de Janeiro as the AIA president-elect. As the first-ever female AIA president, she set sustainability as the theme for the following year's World Congress held with the International Union of Architects in Chicago. This meeting produced a Declaration of Interdependence for a Sustainable Future which developed a wide-ranging vision rather than focusing on particular technical issues. Sustainable design, the Declaration noted, "integrates consideration of resource and energy efficiency, healthy buildings and materials, ecologically and socially sensitive land-use, and an aesthetic sensitivity that inspires, affirms and ennobles."[140]

The AIA became an institutional setting in which a number of female architects, in particular, advocated environmental agendas. Gail Lindsey was another leading female architect, who started an important stimulus to green design, the COTE Top Ten Green Projects award, in 1997. She established her own environmental design consultancy in North Carolina, traveling and lecturing widely to make the case for more sustainable design.[141] In the mid-2000s, the percentage of women involved in COTE was nearly double the percentage of women in the AIA overall.[142]

Ecological ideas were disseminated at international events by radical architects who combined their practices with institutional entrepreneurship. These included the New Zealand architect Tony Watkins, a proponent of vernacular architecture. He was active, for example, at the Second United Nations Conference on Human Settlements (known as Habitat 2), held in Vancouver in 1996, which focused on "social development and environmental protection" in human settlements.[143] Watkins was instrumental in getting the "peaceful cities" concept adopted at that conference, where he also persuaded the organizers to pedestrianize the conference space, so that government officials and people from environmental NGOs could mix freely.[144]

The design of innovative buildings also raised the profile of ecological architecture. Among the early icons of energy-efficient buildings was the New York head office building of the Environmental Defense Fund, opened in 1984, and designed by the young architect William McDonough. In 1992 McDonough published *The Hannover Principles: Design for Sustainability*, in response to a commission by the German city of Hannover which was hosting the World Trade Fair. The book codified many basic principles of sustainable architecture.[145] Conventional, star architects, such as Norman Foster, began to design buildings incorporating technology to reduce environmental impact, and clients emerged to commission them.[146] Foster's Commerzbank building in Frankfurt was described as the world's tallest environmentally conscious high-rise tower when it was completed in 1997, being almost 1,000 feet high. Foster had been highly influenced by Buckminster Fuller, whom he first met in 1971. "He was an extraordinary conscience," Foster later recalled, "in the sense that he was the first, I think, to identify the fragility of the planet."[147]

Both Foster and Fuller influenced a new generation of architects. These included Peter Busby, a Canadian whose environmental interests had grown during the oil crises of the 1970s and after reading Ian McHarg's *Design with Nature*. He interned with Foster in London and met Buckminster Fuller before returning to Canada to open his own firm in Vancouver in 1984. From the beginning Busby was concerned to focus on environmental principles but still found securing commissions to be initially tough. He sought business from universities which he felt were more open to innovation, and lectured and promoted the idea. "I developed a very strong brand," he observed, "and when my clients come to me they know what they're going to get. They are going to get a green building."[148]

Busby's business remained a boutique Vancouver business committed to sustainability until 2004, when it merged with the much larger San Francisco architecture practice of Perkins + Will. Two years earlier the American firm had approached Busby after deciding that if they wanted a distinctive profile as a global architecture firm, they needed a strong capability in sustainable design. During an eighteen-month courtship, Busby was persuaded that scaling in a larger firm offered an opportunity to effect change. He insisted that all ninety principals for the firm pass their LEED accreditation exams, as he would not be "the green guy sitting in the corner." After every principal had passed, he sold his company to Perkins + Will and then used the money to become a significant shareholder in the larger firm.[149]

An increasing number of ecological architects were also active outside North America and Europe, typically using local materials and local craftsmen. In South Asia, the work of Geoffrey Bawa, a Sri Lankan lawyer turned architect, was characterized by sensitivity to site and context. He built private houses and hotels, but also public buildings including a national Parliament building. In 2001 he became the first non-Muslim to win the Aga Khan Award.[150]

The rediscovery of the local was also a feature of the work of Jimmy Lim in Malaysia, which fell into the tropical architecture tradition. Born in Penang, Malaysia, he was educated in Australia but returned to Kuala Lumpur in 1978 to establish CSL Associates, concentrating on residential design. Lim traced his interest in sustainable architecture back to his Chinese immigrant grandparents, who were poor and who always urged their family to "be frugal and never waste," and to his formal training in Sydney between 1964 and 1968, which emphasized the use of the environment when designing buildings. When he started his business, he struggled to attract clients. Finally he started experimenting with his own house to serve as a demonstration of what could be achieved.[151] Lim's search to combine modern and traditional architecture resulted in celebrated projects such as the Salinger House, built in 1992 using traditional methods with local materials and a minimum of technology.[152] He developed an underlying philosophy which he called the Architecture of Humility. "We humble ourselves to Nature and all that is part of the Universe."[153]

Although Lim initially found gaining commissions difficult, in the late 1990s he began receiving commissions for high-rise towers. He developed a new style for tropical skyscrapers combining traditional styles, which he called ecological towers. This brought him into direct competition with his fierce local rival Ken Yeang. Yeang earned a Ph.D. in ecological design from Cambridge University, began practicing in 1975, and specialized in skyscrapers featuring "sky courts" full of greenery; he uses building height to harness solar energy and wind for effective natural ventilation.[154] Yeang wrote a series of influential books about how to build environmentally friendly skyscrapers for large cities. In a book on *Eco Skyscrapers* first published in 1995, he noted that the skyscraper was one "of the most un-ecological of all building types," but that it would not be superseded any time soon, and that the task of designers was to "mitigate its negative environmental impacts and to make it as humane and pleasurably habitable for its inhabitants as possible."[155]

It was in East Asia, however, that some of the most radical ecological visions emerged. The Broad Group, founded by Zhang Yue in Hunan, China, in 1988, evolved from a manufacturer of central air conditioning systems to a manufacturer of prefabricated buildings which could be assembled rapidly and contained high levels of insulation, quadruple-glazed windows, and highly efficient heating, cooling, and power systems. In 2015 he completed a 57-floor, 800-apartment building as offices and housing for families of employees of Broad in Changsha. "Environmental protection is more important than profit," Zhang noted, "and energy conservation is more important than sales."[156] Broad was, however, not representative of the Chinese industry as a whole. The country experienced a vast building boom from the 1990s, and had reached 15 percent of the world construction market by 2010, but only a tiny percentage of new buildings were environmentally friendly.[157]

Green architects could still not transform the built environment by themselves. They continued to form only one component of complex ecosystem, which included urban planners, property developers, and builders. China's real estate boom, for example, was driven by multi-billion dollar firms such as SOHO China.[158] In construction, global giants, such as Balfour Beatty and Skanska, coexisted with millions of small, privately owned companies motivated primarily by cash flow and profitability. Few builders cared about the long term. Even construction firms anxious to employ sustainable technologies were constrained by their role as service providers which followed specifications decided by others.[159]

As ever, buildings needed to be commissioned. This continued to be a challenge because green buildings were more expensive to build, if cheaper to maintain and heat over the longer term. In the United States, during the 1980s and 1990s many greener buildings were initially commissioned by state and city governments. The federal government also invested heavily in promoting energy-efficient buildings through schemes such as the Energy Star program launched by the Environmental Protection Agency in 1992. As concerns about global warming intensified, large corporations also increasingly sought certification for big office buildings.[160] Green buildings were heavily concentrated in commercial real estate in large cities: a survey in 2015 found 62 percent of office buildings greater than 500,000 square feet had green certification, compared to less than 5 percent of all office buildings with less than 100,000 square feet.[161]

The mainstreaming of ecological architecture was a significant achievement. Visionary architects, institutional entrepreneurship, and the willingness of some governments and corporations to commission greener office buildings were all part of the explanation of how this happened. The change was real, but also its meaning and scale were open for debate. Calling a building sustainable if it was located in a city created out of the desert was highly problematic. Even without such ambiguities, most of the world's built environment remained the opposite of sustainable.

The eco-tourism boom

Between 1980 and 2015 international tourism grew to be a $7 trillion industry. There were 1.2 billion international tourist arrivals in the latter year. The growth reflected the growing discretionary incomes and leisure time of the world's middle class, alongside continued falling travel costs, but it especially reflected the re-entry of China into the global economy and its growing wealth. In 1980 there were virtually no Chinese international tourists. In 2015 China was by far the largest source of tourist spending, estimated at $165 billion. The United States and Germany followed with $112 billion and $92 billion, respectively.[162] The industry was an enormous generator of jobs, serving as the largest employer in the world, and as a source of enormous and well-documented environmental damage. This damage was threefold:

physical, including from construction and deforestation; pollution, including from solid waste, sewage, and travel; and depletion of natural resources, especially water and land. An average-size golf course in Thailand and other tropical countries consumes 1,500 kg of chemical fertilizers, pesticides, and herbicides per year and uses as much water as 60,000 rural villagers.[163]

It was within the context of this environmental degradation that eco-tourism emerged as a separate and commercially viable part of the burgeoning global tourism market. Unlike the vast conventional industry, it sought not simply to limit environmental impact, but to contribute positively to sustainability. It was, as Chapter 4 explored, not entirely new. Tourist businesses had enabled consumers to look at nature since the modern industry began. From the 1960s Lars-Erik Lindblad and his counterparts created tourist businesses which sought to greatly limit negative environmental impacts. This approach was now given a formal name, and a set of principles was articulated to define it.

The origins of the term "eco-tourism," sometime between the 1960s and the 1980s, are vague.[164] However, as Chapter 6 explores, formal institutionalization began after The International Ecotourism Society (hereafter TIES) was launched in 1990 as the world's first international non-profit organization dedicated to eco-tourism as a tool for conservation and sustainable development. It developed the now widely accepted definition of eco-tourism as "responsible travel to natural areas that conserves the environment and improves the well-being of local people."[165] Twelve years later the category was further legitimized when the United Nations proclaimed the International Year of Ecotourism.

The formalization of the concept of eco-tourism was accompanied by growth of its customer base far beyond ecologically committed consumers and towards a broader group of consumers seeking interesting ways to see nature while feeling good, or at least not guilty, about their trip. In the *Green Consumer Guide* in 1989, Elkington and Hayes devoted a chapter to green tourism, providing a list of addresses of environmentally friendly travel agencies and other providers of environmentally friendly vacations.[166] A TIES profile of the "average" eco-tourist a decade later described them as between 35 and 55 years old; equally male and female; mainly traveling as couples rather than as families or alone; over 80 percent college graduates; and willing to spend more than regular tourists on average.[167]

While eco-tourism evidently evolved from being a luxury industry serving an elite niche into a much broader industry, the porous boundaries of the tourist industry defied attempts at quantification of the market. It was very difficult to draw boundaries between formal eco-tourism and other activities involving nature. An estimate of the size of the total eco-tourism market in 1989 ranged from $10 billion to $200 billion.[168] By 2015 some sources claimed eco-tourism to represent one-quarter of the global tourist market, but in reality it remained a very diffuse category, made even more confusing by the bevy of other categories which were in use, including ethical, pro-poor, responsible, and sustainable.[169]

Entrepreneurs played a leading role in building the eco-tourism market, with governments sometimes in a supporting role, especially when the category demonstrated a proven ability to attract tourists. Often governments were more interested using revenues from the tourist business to build the infrastructure, such as airports and modern roads, needed to grow conventional tourism attracting large numbers of people. The businesses involved in eco-tourism were as heterogeneous as the consumers. Long-established luxury businesses like Abercrombie & Kent and Lindblad Expeditions coexisted with tens of thousands of small travel agents, owners of lodges and hotels, and others. Many were small businesses in developing countries; some were based in the West and operated in Africa, Asia, and Latin America, as well as Europe and North America. It was, and remained, a highly fragmented industry, as was tourism as a whole. Like other industries, the greener the business, the harder it was to be commercially viable. Even as the concept of eco-tourism attracted public attention from the 1990s, most entrepreneurs faced skepticism, the challenges of running businesses in regions with poor infrastructure, and the perennial problem of cash flow.

There was no such thing as a typical eco-tourist business or entrepreneur. Often their entrepreneurial careers were haphazard and opportunistic, resting on personal preferences for a particular location, which transitioned into a for-profit business. For example, the New York entrepreneur Stanley Selengut created what may have been the first ecologically positive beachside resort at Maho Bay on St. John in the US Virgin Islands, building over time an international reputation. Learning about the island's appeal from the Rockefellers, who had donated most of the island to the nation in 1956 for conservation, Selengut in 1976 negotiated a 35-year lease for 14 acres of hilly land on Maho Bay abutting the national park. He was, at first, interested in building a traditional beach house but was discouraged by park service officials who had seen over-development on the other islands and worried about the adverse environmental impact.[170]

Selengut conserved his land by avoiding the traditional clear-cutting approach, and instead constructed a tented camp and raised wooden walkways. There were eighteen tents to begin with, with wooden frames and mosquito netting, which became Selengut's first resort on the property, the Maho Bay Campground.[171] It was not immediately profitable, but numbers of guests grew, especially after a *New York Times* travel article on Maho Bay Campground praised its sustainability. Maho Bay grossed $3 million annually by 1993.[172]

The early camp did not use alternative energy or employ composting toilets, but Selengut adopted these in new developments during the early 1990s. After hosting a National Park Service workshop which generated a set of guidelines on sustainable architecture in 1991, Selengut began construction of Harmony Resort, luxury hotel condominiums which boasted solar- and wind-powered temperature regulation, electricity generation, and water heaters, and were constructed principally from recycled materials. The Concordia Eco-Resort, built on tents overlooking Salt Pond Bay, followed. Selengut became a frequent speaker at eco-tourism conferences. He was notable, among other things, for his constant assertion that eco-tourism could be a profitable business.[173]

As the eco-tourism market developed, a strong clustering effect was observed, as was earlier seen in Chapter 4 in the case of Switzerland. The case of Costa Rica, which had become the world's leading eco-tourism destination by the 2000s, ahead of such forerunners as Kenya and the Galapagos Islands, is illustrative. By then many of its one million tourists each year were eco-tourists for at least part of their time.[174]

Costa Rica's ability to benefit from the global surge of eco-tourism was not too surprising. It had warm weather, nice beaches, was conveniently located near the large US and Canadian markets, and relatively accessible, with a modern international airport near the capital San José opening in 1957. The country's tourism ministry provided incentives and tax breaks after 1985 and encouraged foreign investment for luxury tourist resorts. Costa Rica also had a long-standing and well-functioning democracy, and abolished its army in 1948 after a brief civil war. By the 1970s it had invested substantially in health care systems and education, achieving the highest literacy rate in Latin America. The country was an oasis of peace and stability at a time when Central America was otherwise overrun by guerrilla conflicts, government-supported death squads, and ruthless gangs. If such stability was a draw for tourists, whether green or not, the country was also open to foreigners who wanted to buy businesses. There were no restrictions on foreign people or corporations buying property, providing the potential to act as a host economy for expatriate, especially American, investors and entrepreneurs.[175]

These institutional factors favored all types of tourism, but some specific factors helped eco-tourism. Like its neighbors, it had enormous biodiversity and wonderful rainforests. Foundational work on biodiversity had been performed by non-profit scientific organizations, local and foreign, which had helped prompt the government to found a national park system in 1969, funded by the government and international philanthropic support. The parks had no facilities for visitors, but they had the potential to become a significant draw for private tour companies, making it worth investing to operate tours. Both expatriate and local Costa Rican entrepreneurs became active in developing such businesses from the 1970s. They were motivated by a love of nature and/or ecological views: given that the market was unproven and difficult at the beginning, this was not an activity likely to attract people hungry for large profits. Each group of actors shared the emergent consensus that for-profit businesses could help sustainability rather than disrupt it.[176]

Many small tour companies were instrumental in facilitating the development of the market. The founders were both expatriate Americans and Costa Ricans.[177] In 1978 Costa Rica Expeditions, which would become the first travel agency and tour operator specializing in eco-tourism in the country, was established by Michael Kaye. Born and raised in Manhattan, he spent much of his childhood visiting the American Museum of Natural History and Central Park near his home and the wilderness on family vacations. After high school he began rafting in the American West in the early 1960s, eventually establishing his own rafting company in California and becoming engaged in environmentalist campaigns.[178]

In the course of exploring new rafting opportunities, Kaye met his future wife in El Salvador, and they eventually settled in Costa Rica. Kaye launched a premium rafting business, targeted initially at North Americans. Like Selengut and other pioneers of eco-tourism, he believed that a profitable business model was fully compatible with sustainability, and he scaled his activities accordingly. Kaye expanded by diversifying into hotels, beginning in Tortuguero in 1986, thanks to securing financing from a US-backed private bank.[179] Five years later, when *Travel and Leisure Magazine* was eager to recognize an eco-tourism company, Costa Rica Expeditions received the magazine's first award in this category; fortuitously, the magazine asked the advice of a journalist who knew Kaye personally. In an evolving business model, Kaye took advantage of the new opportunities for direct marketing provided by the internet: he became a partner in one of Costa Rica's first internet service providers in 1994.[180]

Another pioneering tour company, which shared Kaye's vision of combining profits and sustainability, was Horizontes Nature Tours, founded in 1984 by Tamara Budowski and Margarita Forero, both then aged 24. Budowski was the daughter of a prominent forest biologist whose work frequently took the family abroad for research in the wild.[181] Both Budowski and Forero broke with family expectations in order to work in the travel business. They met at a college which offered a new degree program in tourism; Budowski later studied marketing in Miami, where she was alerted to the problems of mass tourism development.[182] In Costa Rica, they struggled to get a conservation-oriented travel company started. Lacking capital, they initially secured an outbound-only license. They finally broke through by forming an alliance with Sergio Miranda, a family friend of Forero who was beginning to develop the Marenco private reserve near Corcovado National Park, and who also owned a hotel. This arrangement, and Miranda's financial resources, allowed Budowski and Forero to bring eco-tourists into the country, first by offering nature tours of the national parks to the wholesale travel trade, primarily in the United States, in 1986.[183]

Horizontes initially focused on group business from the United States and Canada by creating tours for conservation and educational organizations. Such groups made up about 75 percent of their business in 1992, at which time the firm had expanded to employ twenty-eight full-time staff, a majority of them women. It donated to numerous local causes, including the national zoo, as well as scientific and conservation organizations, and offered a free training course to forty guides working for other companies to improve their biological and ecological knowledge.[184]

If tour companies like Horizontes were important in getting eco-tourists to the country, the creators of lodges and other forms of accommodation gave them somewhere to stay. Private nature reserves were by then the main attraction. Serendipity played a large role in the emergence of the first lodges. An early example was the Savegre Mountain Lodge. This originated in 1954 when brothers Efraín and Federico Chacón, who worked on a coffee plantation, got lost and ended up finding a beautiful location in the mountains. They returned with their families and created a farm. Access was only possible on foot or horseback, and they supported themselves through agriculture and selling cheese off the farm. Tourism started thanks to Efraín introducing a few trout into the river, and it became a fishing destination. In 1971 the first cabins were built for visitors.[185]

It was at that time that the area was visited by two orchid-hunting Harvard botanists, who happened to remark in print on the large population of birds known as resplendent quetzals. These scientists and others, Efraín Chacón later recalled, "told [him] about how important it was to keep the environment and also [he] saw some people's interest in nature." The quetzals proved a huge attraction. In 1982 faculty and students from Southern Nazarene University in Oklahoma began visiting the area. Eight years later they created a field station to enable longer visits. In time, eco-tourism reshaped the family's business. In the mid-1980s they shut down their cattle farming. The founder's son Marino recalled that they would have needed to cut more trees for farming, but "people were showing up here to look at the trees and the birds and quetzals."[186]

Another early eco-lodge was also the work of individuals who had no initial commitment to conservation. The founder, an American expatriate named Jack Ewing, was a farmer who worked for North American cattle exporters, meat-packers, and ranchers in Costa Rica. By 1976, Ewing was the general manager of a 330-hectare property with beachfront on the Pacific Ocean, known as Hacienda Baru. He grew increasingly interested in the surrounding jungle and its wildlife. After seeing an ocelot shot, Ewing banned hunting on his property. "In the 1970s I certainly didn't consider myself an environmentalist," Ewing later reflected. "But once I prohibited hunting, I got a reputation as being an environmentalist."[187] In 1988, after a tourist had offered to pay for a tour of the rainforest, the Ewings began offering tours, which within three years had become profitable.[188] Subsequently Ewing built cabins at Hacienda Baru for overnight stays, and diversified from rainforest tours to canopy and bird-watching tours, and tours focusing on the pre-Columbian heritage of the area.[189]

The success of these, and hundreds of other small entrepreneurial ventures, turned the whole country of Costa Rica into a green brand. This lowered entry barriers for new ventures, which could focus on establishing the credibility of their own firms; the argument and the infrastructure were by now in place to support tourism. Tourism became Costa Rica's principal source of foreign exchange in 1993, surpassing bananas. The category was estimated to employ 10 percent of Costa Ricans in 2000, many in rural areas. A virtuous circle of investment, ecological education, and sound environmental policies drove the recovery of Costa Rica's forests, which had been restored to cover more than 40 percent of the country's land area by 2002.[190]

Trade-offs, however, were also apparent. Even the most environmentally sensitive international tourists arrived chiefly by fossil fuel-burning jets. And even so-called "soft" nature tourists seek comfortable accommodation. Many traveled to Costa Rica because it had become fashionable and had little interest in nature beyond beaches. One highly critical study talked of the overlap between eco-tourism and what the authors called "ego-tourism," consisting of people who want to emphasize their social status through where they travel, feeling "exempt from the criticism levelled at much Third World tourism."[191]

These new types of consumer created opportunities for boutique hotels and luxury eco-lodges, but as the expansion of the internet in the 1990s opened up new travel booking options, the challenge for such businesses was to remain committed to sustainability. Although ego-tourists were often quite affluent, they more often as not used internet comparison shopping sites, which focused primarily on price.[192] Michael Kaye, for instance, noted that consumer purchasing patterns and company reviews reflected no desire to put sustainability at a level with price or comfort.[193] During the early 2000s, Tamara Budowski took real lack of interest of the new eco-tourists, the building of more and more golf courses, the polluting practices of cruise ships and the commercialized killing of sharks and other animals in Costa Rica as a sign that, "despite all the efforts," eco-tourism "wasn't working." She continued to run her business until 2008, but found herself troubled by it and retired to seek new horizons in esoteric religion and the global eco-village movement.[194]

Meanwhile, as in other industries, once the eco-tourism market had been proven, conventional firms and travel associations sought to join the party. By the late 1980s the conventional tourist associations had already endorsed eco-tourism. In 1991 the American Society of Travel Agents, the largest travel trade association, established an Environmental Committee. Four years later major industry bodies led by the World Travel & Tourism Council (made up of major airlines, hotel chains, and cruise lines), the United Nations World Tourism Organization (including government tourism ministries and others such as NGOs), and the Earth Council, responded to the Earth Summit in Rio with a document called "Agenda 21 for the Travel and Tourism Industry," which made strong claims about how properly conducted tourism could help the natural environment.[195] Conventional corporations are eager to call themselves green and eco-friendly. "Much of what is marketed as eco-tourism," one leading authority on the industry concluded in 2008, "is simply conventional mass tourism wrapped in a thin veneer of 'green.'"[196]

The premise of eco-tourism aligns with that of the Romantic era—that visiting nature can restore our humanity. The rise of eco-tourism as an industry showed that it was possible to make a profit doing it, but how far and how much it contributed to a sustainable world was another matter.

Conclusion

The achievements of green entrepreneurs in this era were remarkable. Organic food and natural beauty evolved as mainstream markets. Deserts literally bloomed with organic agriculture. It became normal to include sustainable elements in office buildings in the world's largest cities. Green skyscrapers were built. Eco-tourism became a mainstream category of the global tourism industry. Green entrepreneurship globalized. Entrepreneurs offered Turkish consumers the opportunity to buy organic food, and Brazilians natural beauty products. Across industries, the gap in acceptance and purchase with conventional businesses appeared, finally, to be closing. All these industries had their roots in older concerns about human health and respect for nature, but their advocates were effective in bringing out their relevance to key contemporary issues led by climate change and loss of biodiversity.

A singular achievement was the diffusion of the concept that making money and saving the planet were genuinely compatible. Within the wider context of the reemergence of liberal capitalism and the decline of state intervention, green entrepreneurs made the case for the importance of sustainability and the ability of the private sector to provide solutions. Although they were diverse in their views and their roles, John Elkington, Paul Hawken, Götz Rehn, Antônio

Luiz Seabra, Amory and Hunter Lovins, Jimmy Lim, Tamara Budowski, and their counterparts were powerful public advocates for the importance of sustainability in different settings. They were, in many cases, well ahead of policy-makers, consumers, and conventional business in their arguments. Their actions and writings were enormously important in legitimizing green business—and whole categories from organic foods to eco-tourism. Compared to the past, ecological concerns were no longer considered bizarre.

Nevertheless, creating and growing green firms remained a tough proposition. Markets still needed to be made rather than served. Organic foods businesses, for example, needed to work hard, and purposefully, to make their products accessible and attractive to consumers. They had to overcome common perceptions that organic food was not tasty, or that shopping organic was for idealist radicals and not for the masses. Whether eco-tourist businesses or ecological architects, green entrepreneurs continued to need to explain their cases, and the need to pay premium prices, to prospective consumers. Clustering was, as a result, especially important at the initial fragile stages of growth. In organic foods, clusters like Boulder, Colorado provided sources of initially committed consumers and employees. In Costa Rica, it provided a national brand image which drew more customers and attracted more entrepreneurs, whether local or expatriate.

A number of businesses could and did expand far beyond geographical clusters. However, products and services remained, for the most part, priced at a premium over their conventional counterparts. They sometimes competed against other hugely subsidized competitors, as in American agriculture. They continued to have to compete against products and services whose environmental externalities were not included in their prices, as in the case of conventional building, or cheap vacations sold on travel websites. When a handful of highly successful businesses gained access to investors and capital markets, the policies which came along with the funds were rarely compatible with the aspirations of many green entrepreneurs, as the experiences of the Koss brothers, Roddick, Rehn, and others suggest.

Meanwhile success, as measured by greater mainstreaming, was accompanied by the emergence of a new set of challenges, related in part to scaling, and especially to how scaling was achieved. The sustainability benefits of scaling differed between industries. While the expansion of organic retailing and farming enabled many more consumers to eat food without chemicals or additives, for example, it typically occurred through the transportation of organic food over great distances. If scaling occurred through the use of local products, the downsides were far fewer. Enjoying and learning about nature and generating income for local communities were clearly much more positive outcomes for the natural environment than a mega beach resort created by destroying forests. While this was a plus for biodiversity, if people traveled large distances to such eco-resorts and governments built bigger airports to facilitate such traffic, it was a minus for climate change.

In the case of natural beauty, scaling enabled more consumers to choose not to put chemicals into their bodies, but it also consumed more plants which could have been used for food. More fundamentally, as natural beauty became one marketing position in a portfolio of beauty brands, the whole exercise simply reinforced consumerism, by making even ecologically concerned consumers feel justified in making purchases. The most eco-friendly make-up is, after all, no make-up.

In contrast, scaling had a much more positive impact in green architecture and construction. As buildings and cities were major drivers of global warming and other negative environmental consequences, the more the built environment incorporated higher environmental standards, the better. It was not scaling itself but the standards used to define sustainability which could be problematic.

In all industries, there was a problem that scaling was typically achieved by some dilution of the most rigorous ecological standards. This was, on the one hand, seemingly the only way to attract more consumers and clients, and on the other hand a potentially dangerous slippery slope. As niches moved towards the mainstream, and conventional firms added green brands to their portfolios, the meaning of sustainability also became blurred. The creation of certification and standards, examined in Chapter 6, were an attempt to avoid such blurring and to secure legitimacy, but they did not always succeed. Indeed the scaling of businesses raised new questions about what sustainability really meant. Legitimate questions were asked whether industrial organic farming, or a giant skyscraper housing a leading bank, were sustainable in a legitimate sense of the word. We will see in the remaining chapters how institutional entrepreneurship, new sources of finance, government policies, and the sudden greening of conventional business responded to these challenges.

Notes

1. Jani Actman, "Exxon Valdez Oil Spill Devastated Killer Whales," *National Geographic*, January 26, 2016.

2. *Report of the World Commission on Environment and Development: Our Common Future* (New York; United Nations 1987), p.16.

3. Ramachandra Guha, *Environmentalism: A Global History* (New York: Longman, 2000), pp.140–1.

4. Carrie A. Meyer, "Opportunism and NGOs: Entrepreneurship and Green North–South Transfers," *World Development* 23, no. 8 (1995), pp.1277–89; Guha, *Environmentalism*, p.141.

5. Frank Uekötter, *The Greenest Nation? A New History of German Environmentalism* (Cambridge, MA: MIT Press, 2014), pp.99–100.

6. Russell J. Dalton, *The Green Rainbow: Environmental Groups in Western Europe* (New Haven: Yale University Press, 1994).

7. Al Gore, *Earth in the Balance: Ecology and the Human Spirit* (Boston: Houghton Mifflin, 1992).

8. Cary Coglianese and Ryan Anderson, "Business and Environmental Law," in Pratima Bansal and Andrew J. Hoffman (eds.), *The Oxford Handbook of Business and the Natural Environment* (Oxford: Oxford University Press, 2012), pp.140–60.

9. Spencer R. Weart, *The Discovery of Global Warming* (Cambridge, MA: Harvard University Press, 2003), pp.157–8.

10. Forest Reinhardt, Gunnar Trumbull, Mikell Hyman, Patia McGrath, and Nazli Zeynep Uludere, "The Political Economy of Carbon Trading," Harvard Business School Case No. 9-710-056 (rev. April 27, 2011).

11. Stephan Schmidheiny, *Changing Course: A Global Business Perspective on Development and the Environment* (Cambridge, MA: MIT Press, 1992).

12. Livio D. DeSimone and Frank Popoff, *Eco-Efficiency: Business Link to Sustainable Development* (Cambridge, MA: MIT Press, 1997).

13. Sandra Waddock, *The Difference Makers* (Sheffield: Greenleaf, 2008), pp.175–8.

14. <http://johnelkington.com/about/personal/education>, accessed January 3, 2016.

15. John Elkington with Tom Burke, *The Green Capitalists* (London: Victor Gollancz, 1987).

16. John Elkington, *Cannibals with Forks: The Triple Bottom Line of 21st Century Business* (Oxford: Capstone Publishing, 1997).

17. John Elkington and Julia Hailes, *The Green Consumer Guide: From Shampoo to Champagne, High-Street Shopping for a Better Environment* (London: Victor Gollancz, 1988).

18. Elkington and Hailes, *Green Consumer Guide*, p.3.

19. Monica M. Emerich, *The Gospel of Sustainability: Media, Market and LOHAS* (Champaign, IL: University of Illinois Press, 2011).

20. Andrew Gilg, Stewart Barr, and Nicholas Ford, "Green Consumption or Sustainable Lifestyles? Identifying the Sustainable Consumer," *Futures* 37 (2005), pp.481–504.

21. Waddock, *Difference Makers*, pp.181–2.

22. Ibid., p.186.

23. Matthew J. Kiernan, *Investing in a Sustainable World* (New York: Amacom, 2009), pp.221–3.

24. John Elkington, *The Zeronauts: Breaking the Sustainability Barrier* (London: Routledge, 2012).

25. Paul Hawken, *The Magic of Findhorn* (New York: Harper & Row, 1975). Findhorn was started in 1962. During the 1990s Findhorn became central in the eco-village movement. <http://www.ross-jackson.com/rj/21987/41762/>, accessed April 30, 2014.

26. Paul Hawken, *The Ecology of Commerce* (New York: HarperCollins, 1993), p. xiii.

27. Ibid., p.xv.

28. Paul Hawken, Amory Lovins, and L. Hunter Lovins, *Natural Capitalism: Creating the Next Industrial Revolution* (Boston: Little, Brown and Company, 1999), pp.273–5, 277–9.

29. Review of *Natural Capitalism*, in *The Economist*, November 13, 1999.

30. Gary Hirshberg, *Stirring It Up: How to Make Money and Save the World* (New York: Hyperion, 1999).

31. John Mackey and Rajendra Sisodia, *Conscious Capitalism: Liberating the Heroic Spirit of Business* (Boston: Harvard Business School Press, 2013); John Mackey and Justin Fox, "The HBR Interview: Whole Foods CEO John Mackey," *Harvard Business Review* (January 2011).

32. Yvon Chouinard, *Let My People Go Surfing* (New York: Penguin, 2005), pp.61–76.

33. "A Widening Popularity Brings Acquisitions," *New York Times*, October 26, 1996.

34. <http://www.ers.usda.gov/topics/international-markets-trade/global-food-markets/global-food-industry.aspx>, accessed April 1, 2016; Marie Ng et al., "Global, Regional, and National Prevalence of Overweight and Obesity in Children and Adults during 1980–2013: A Systematic Analysis for the Global Burden of Disease Study 2013," *The Lancet* 384, no. 9945 (August 30, 2014), pp.766–81.

35. FiBL and IFOAM, *The World of Organic Agriculture 2016* (February 2016), <https://shop.fibl.org/fileadmin/documents/shop/1698-organic-world-2016.pdf>, accessed July 1, 2016.

36. John R. Wells and Travis Haglock, "Wild Oats Markets, Inc.," Harvard Business School Case No. 9-707-438 (rev. April 3, 2008).

37. Christopher Marquis, Marya Besharov, and Bobbi Thomason, "Whole Foods: Balancing Social Mission and Growth," Harvard Business School Case No. 9-410-023 (rev. September 28, 2011).

38. Beth Kowitt, "Wholefoods Takes Over America," *Fortune*, April 28, 2014, p.74.

39. Marquis et al., "Whole Foods"; Samuel Fromartz, *Organic, Inc.: Natural Foods and How They Grew* (Orlando: Harcourt, 2006), pp.241–5.

40. Wells and Haglock, "Wild Oats."

41. FAO, *World Markets for Organic Fruit and Vegetables—Opportunities for Developing Countries in the Production and Export of Organic Horticultural Products* (2001), <http://www.fao.org.ezp-prod1.hul.harvard.edu/DOCREP/004/Y1669E/y1669e00.htm>, accessed April 30, 2014.

42. Mackey and Sisodia, *Conscious Capitalism*, pp.158–9.

43. Marquis et al., "Whole Foods."

44. Angel González, "Largest Organic Grocer Now Costco, Analysts Say," *Seattle Times*, April 4, 2016; FiBL and IFOAM, *World of Organic Agriculture*, p.250.

45. FAO, *World Markets.*

46. <http://www.rapunzel.de/bio-demeter-haselnuesse-aprikosen-feigen-sultaninen-tu erkei.html>, accessed August 2, 2016; Eva Wonneberger, *Die Alternativebewegung im Allgäu: Landkommunen, Biohöfe und andere Initiativen* (Wangen: FIU Verlag, 2008), p.141.

47. Rapunzel Naturkost AG, "Lagebericht über das Geschäftsjahr 1990" (January 1, 1991); Anon., "Big Bang im Naturkostladen," *Lebensmittel Zeitung*, August 16, 1996.

48. Handelsregister Bekanntmachungen, Ausgabe-Nr. 0179, "Rapunzel Naturkost Aktiengesellschaft," January 1, 1990.

49. Joachim Schalinski, "'Bio Gourmet' treibt Rapunzel," *Lebensmittel Zeitung*, October 5, 2007.

50. Christiane Langrock-Koegel, "Jetzt seid ihr dran," *Enorm Magazin* (March 2015), <http://enorm-magazin.de/jetzt-seid-ihr-dran>, accessed February 2, 2016.

51. Michael Gassmann, "Der Rauswurf bei dm war für uns enttäuschend," *Die Welt*, November 16, 2015.

52. Götz Rehn, *Modelle der Organisationsentwicklung* (Bern and Stuttgart: Verlag Paul Haupt, 1979), p.322.

53. Sebastian Balzter, "Der Körner-König: Alnatura-Gründer Götz Rehn," *Frankfurter Allgemeine Zeitung*, June 7, 2015; Gassmann, "Der Rauswurf."

54. Anon., "Anthroposophie und die Wirtschaft, interview with Götz Rehn," *Süddeutsche Zeitung*, January 17, 2011.

55. Balzter, "Der Körner-König."

56. Anon., "Naturkost als Chance," *Lebensmittel Zeitung*, February 21, 1997.

57. Ugesh Joseph, *The "Made in Germany" Champion Brands* (Burlington: Gower Publishing, 2013), p.244; Marius Sienel, *Der deutsche Gesundheitsmarkt: Risiken und Potenziale für den Handelsmarkt der Zukunft* (Hamburg: Diplomica Verlag, 2015), p.57.

58. Lauran FitzPatrick, "Farming Firm Tackles Egypt's Problems in a Visionary Way," Agence France Presse, December 8, 2003.

59. Anon., "Anthroposophie und die Wirtschaft," interview with Götz Rehn, *Süddeutsche Zeitung*, January 17, 2011.

60. Jochen Remmert, "Mit eiserner Hand ausgelistet," *Frankfurter Allgemeine Zeitung*, January 23, 2016; Jens Heisterkamp, "Götz Werner und Götz Rehn versöhnen sich," *Info3 Magazin*, February 15, 2016, <http://www.info3-magazin.de/goetz-werner-und-goetz-rehn-versoehnen-sich/>, accessed March 8, 2016; Anon., "Drogeriekette vs. Biohändler: Alnatura Chef und dm-Gründer beenden Streit," *Der Spiegel*, February 16, 2016.

61. The predecessors of the Merkur Bank in Denmark had opened an anthroposophical organic food retailer in 1974. See Lars Pehrson and Henrik Platz, "Fra Græsrod til Professionel Bankvirksomhed," in Lars Pehrson et al. (eds.), *Merkur 25 År* (Copenhagen: Merkur Bank, 2007), p.10.

62. Interview with Karsten Korting and Thomas Roland (FDB), Copenhagen, May 22, 2012.

63. *Organic Market in Europe* (2011), p.97, <https://www.fibl.org/en/shop-en/article/c/market/p/1558-organic-market.html>, accessed June 9, 2015.

64. Interview with Korting and Roland.

65. Ibid.

66. FAO, *World Markets*.

67. Ibid.

68. Hanne Torjusen, Lotte Sangstad, Katherine O'Doherty Jensen, and Umni Kjærnes, *European Consumers' Conceptions of Organic Food: A Review of Available Research* (Oslo: National Institute for Consumer Research, 2014).

69. Rodale Institute, "Reversing Climate Change Achievable by Farming Organically," April 23, 2014, <http://rodaleinstitute.org/reversing-climate-change-achievable-by-farming-organically>, accessed March 8, 2016; Tamat Haspel, "Is Organic Agriculture Really Better for the Environment," *The Washington Post*, May 14, 2016.

70. Renée Shaw Hughner, Pierre McDonagh, Andrea Prothero, Clifford J. Shultz II, and Julie Staton, "Who Are Organic Food Consumers?" *Journal of Consumer Behaviour* 6 (2007), pp.275–304.

71. Susan Baker, Keith E. Thompson, Julia Engelken, and Karen Huntley, "Mapping the Values Driving Organic Food Choice: Germany vs. the UK," *European Journal of Marketing* 38, no. 8 (2004), pp.995–1012.

72. Arie Hollander, "'Tegen Beter Weten In.' De Geschiedenis van de Biologische Landbouw en Voeding in Nederland (1880–2001)," Utrecht University Ph.D., 2012.

73. Geoffrey Jones and Simon Mowatt, "National Image as a Competitive Disadvantage: The Case of the New Zealand Organic Food Industry," *Business History* 58, no. 8 (2016), pp.1262–88.

74. Interview with Juliet Lamont and Rodnie Whitlock (Ceres), Wellington, January 25, 2012.

75. Jones and Mowatt, "National Image."

76. Interview with Yasushi Tamura (Mavie), Tokyo, May 24, 2010.

77. Interview with Kohei Takashima (Oisix), Tokyo, May 31, 2010.

78. Ibid.

79. Annual Report Oisix, 2014.

80. Schuyler Velasco, "Is Food the Future of Entrepreneurial Japan?" *Christian Science Monitor*, December 10, 2013.

81. Kimberly Wright, "Going Organic: Investing in China's Growing Health Foods Market," *China Business Review*, <http://www.chinabusinessreview.com/going-organic-investing-in-chinas-growing-health-foods-market/>, accessed June 3, 2016.

82. Interview with Ayhan Sümerli (City Farm), Istanbul, July 3, 2013.

83. Ibid.

84. Ibid.

85. Lisa Katayama, "Doughnuts to Dollars: How a Business Scion's Son Went from Burning Man to Angel Investing," <http://www.fastcompany.com/1707100/doughnuts-dollars-how-business-scions-son-went-burning-man-angel-investing>, accessed May 15, 2016.

86. Nancy F. Koehn, Nora N. Khan, and Elizabeth W. Legris, "Gary Hirshberg and Stonyfield Farm," Harvard Business School Case No. 9-312-122, October 2012.

87. Interview with Claus Hipp, Pfaffenhofen an der Ilm, February 25, 2013.

88. <http://vmfgroup.com/en/Media-center/Press-releases/HiPP-selected-once-again-the-most-sustainable-company-in-Germany>, accessed July 2, 2016.

89. Carol Marie Cropper, "Bringing Up Baby with Its Parents on the Sideline," *New York Times*, May 5, 1998.

90. Ron and Arnie Koss, *The Earth's Best Story: A Bittersweet Tale of Twin Brothers Who Sparked an Organic Revolution* (White River Junction, VT: Chelsea Green Publishing, 2010), p.x.

91. Ibid., parts 4 and 5, and p.336.

92. Ibid., p.337.

93. Ibid., pp.344, 350–1.

94. FiBL and IFOAM, *World of Organic Agriculture.*

95. Susanne Padel and Nic Lampkin, "The Development of Governmental Support for Organic Farming in Europe," in William Lockeretz (ed.), *Organic Farming: An International History* (Wallingford: CABI, 2007), pp.94–102.

96. Janet McGarry, "Organic Pioneers Reflect on 40 Years of CCOF," January 22, 2013, <http://www.cuesa.org/article/organic-pioneers-reflect-40-years-ccof>, accessed May 4, 2016.

97. Amelia Urry, "Our Crazy Farm Subsidies, Explained," *Grist,* <http://grist.org/food/our-crazy-farm-subsidies-explained>, accessed April 20, 2015.

98. Interview with Jim Cochran by Ellen Farmer, December 10, 2007, UC Santa Cruz Library, Oral History Collection, <http://library.ucsc.edu/reg-hist/cultiv/cochran>, accessed June 14, 2015.

99. Patrick Connors, "Way Beyond Organic," <http://newfarm.rodaleinstitute.org/features/2005/0405/swanton/index.shtml>, accessed April 19, 2015.

100. William B. Tate, "The Development of the Organic Industry and Market: An International Perspective," in Nicolas Lampkin and Susanne Padel (eds.), *The Economics of Organic Farming: An International Perspective* (Wallingford: CABI, 1994), pp.22–3.

101. Connors, "Way Beyond Organic."

102. Rodale Institute, "The History of Community Supported Agriculture, Part I Community Farms in the 21st Century: Poised for Another Wave of Growth?" <http://newfarm.rodaleinstitute.org/features/0104/csa-history/part1.shtml>, accessed June 2, 2012.

103. Michael Ableman and Alice Waters, *On Good Land: The Autobiography of an Urban Farm* (San Francisco: Chronicle Books, 1998); Michael Ableman, Cynthia Wisehart, and Sam Bittman, *From the Good Earth: A Celebration of Growing Food Around the World* (New York: Abrams, 1993), p.12.

104. Interview with Thomas Harrtung, Barritskov, May 22, 2013. For IFOAM, see Chapter 6.

105. See Chapter 7.

106. Lisa Abend, "Thomas Harttung," *Time Magazine,* September 22, 2009; <http://www.proff.dk/firma/aarstiderne/humleb%C3%A6k/postordrefirmaer/13589851-2/>, accessed May 5, 2016.

107. Interview with Myra Goodman, Carmel, March 15, 2012.

108. Interview with Drew Goodman by Sarah Rabkin, April 22, 2009, UC Santa Cruz Library, Oral History Collection, <http://library.ucsc.edu/reg-hist/cultiv/good man>, accessed March 15, 2016; Fromartz, *Organic, Inc.*, p.125; Ben Harris, "Earth Mother," *Tablet*, October 11, 2011.

109. Interview with Myra Goodman.

110. Fromartz, *Organic, Inc.*, pp.132–8; Julie Guthman, *Agrarian Dreams: The Paradox of Organic Farming in California* (Berkeley: University of California Press, 2004), pp.29, 157.

111. Guthman, *Agrarian Dreams*, chapter 3.

112. FiBL and IFOAM, *World of Organic Agriculture*; Australian Organic Market Report 2014, <http://www.organicknowledge.com.au/uncategorized/australian-organic-market-report-2014/>; <https://www.kadac.com.au/about-us>, accessed August 28, 2015.

113. Ibrahim Abouleish, *SEKEM: A Sustainable Community in the Egyptian Desert* (Edinburgh: Floris Books, 2005), p.43.

114. Ibrahim and Helmy Abouleish, "Garden in the Desert: Sekem Makes Comprehensive Sustainable Development a Reality in Egypt," *Innovations: Technology, Governance, Globalization* 3, no. 3 (2008), p.94.

115. Interview with Ibrahim Abouleish, October 5, 2011.

116. Abouleish, *SEKEM*, pp.87–91, 98–9.

117. Ibid., 155–8.

118. Abouleish, "Garden in the Desert," p.103.

119. Celia de Anca, *Beyond Tribalism: Managing Identities in a Diverse World* (Basingstoke: Palgrave Macmillan, 2012), p.206.

120. Sekem Sustainability Report, 2014.

121. Interview with Abouleish; Abouleish, *SEKEM*, pp.167–70.

122. The United States, China, and Brazil accounted for well over one-third of the entire market in 2014. Euromonitor International, "Natural Segment Continues to Outpace the Overall Beauty Market," October 2, 2014; Global Cosmetics Industry, "Natural Segment Continues to Outpace the Overall Beauty Market," <http://www.gcimagazine.com/mar ketstrends/segments/natural/Natural-Segment-Continues-to-Outpace-the-Overall-Beauty-Market-277942301.html>, accessed July 14, 2015.

123. <http://www.businesswire.com/news/home/20140217005451/en/Beauty-Industry-Loses-Icon-Horst-Rechelbacher-Founder#.U5DUu6PD-Uk>, accessed January 2, 2016.

124. Leslie Blodgett, "How I Did It: Leslie Blodgett of Bare Escentuals," *Inc.com*, July 1, 2010, <http://www.inc.com/magazine/20100701/how-i-did-it-leslie-blodgett-of-bare-escentuals.html>, accessed October 23, 2016.

125. Interview with John Hansen (J. H. Partners), Cambridge, MA, February 17, 2012.

126. Geoffrey Jones, *Beauty Imagined: A History of the Global Beauty Industry* (Oxford: Oxford University Press, 2010), p.330; John Deighton, Leora Kornfeld, Yanqun He, and Qingyun Jiang, "Herborist," Harvard Business School Case No. 9-511-051 (rev. October 1, 2014).

127. "Challenges and Opportunities for Sustainable Cosmetics in Brazil," *Brazil Beauty News*, September 30, 2014, <http://www.brazilbeautynews.com/challenges-and-opportunities-for-sustainable,306>, accessed October 23, 2016.

128. Geoffrey Jones and Ricardo Reisen de Pinho, "Natura: Global Beauty Made in Brazil," Harvard Business School Case No. 9-807-029 (October 20, 2012).

129. Ibid.

130. Ibid.; Robert G. Eccles, George Serafeim, and James Heffernan, "Natura Cosméticos, S.A.," Harvard Business School Case No. 9-412-052, November 2011 (rev. June 2013).

131. Geoffrey Jones, "The Growth Opportunity That Lies Next Door," *Harvard Business Review* 90, nos. 7–8 (July–August 2012), pp.141–5.

132. McGraw-Hill Construction, *World Green Building Trends* (2013), <http://www.worldgbc.org/files/8613/6295/6420/World_Green_Building_Trends_SmartMarket_Report_2013.pdf>, accessed April 26, 2016.

133. James Steele, *Ecological Architecture: A Critical History* (London: Thames & Hudson, 2005), p.36; Kira Gould, "AIA/COTE: A History within a Movement," <http://www.aia.org/practicing/groups/kc/AIAS077347>, accessed July 2, 2016.

134. The AIA finally reinstated the license of Wells in 2007. Steel, *Ecological Architecture*, p.149.

135. Sim Van der Ryn, *Design for Life* (Layton, UT: Gibbs Smith, 2005), p.124.

136. Steele, *Ecological Architecture*, p.11.

137. Amory B. Lovins, "Energy Strategy: The Road Not Taken," *Foreign Affairs* (October 1976); Amory B. Lovins, *Soft Energy Paths* (New York: Ballinger, 1977).

138. Jeffrey Ball, "The Homely Costs of Energy Conservation: An Environmental Pioneer Raises the Bar on a Green-Energy Experiment, but Can His Latest Innovations Help the Rest of Us?" *Wall Street Journal*, August 7, 2009.

139. Gould, "AIA/COTE."

140. Olfemi Majekodunmi and Susan A. Maxman, "Declaration of Interdependence for a Sustainable Future," <http://www.comarchitect.org/webhelp/declaration_of_interdependence_for_a_sustainable_future.htm>, accessed January 2, 2016.

141. Stephani L. Miller, "Sustainability Champion Gail A. Lindsey Dies," *Residential Architect*, February 18, 2009.

142. Kira Gould and Lance Hosey, *Women in Green: Voices of Sustainable Design* (Bainbridge Island, WA: Ecotone, 2007), pp.vi–vii.

143. <http:/www.unhabitat.org/declarations/ist-dec.htm>, accessed July 28, 2015.

144. Interview with Tony Watkins, Auckland, January 27, 2012.

145. <http://www.mcdonough.com/wp-content/uploads/2013/03/Hannover-Principles-1992.pdf>, accessed February 4 2015.

146. Steele, *Ecological Architecture*, pp.123–33.

147. BBC Dream Builders, Interview with Norman Foster by Razia Iqbal, <http://www.fosterandpartners.com/media/1028028/NF-BBC-Dream_Builders_transcript.pdf>, accessed June 4, 2016.

148. Telephone interview with Peter Busby, December 9, 2011.

149. Ibid.

150. "Life of Geoffrey Bawa," <http://www.geoffreybawa.com/life/introduction>, accessed October 23, 2016.

151. Telephone interview with Jimmy Lim, July 6, 2011.

152. Steele, *Ecological Architecture*, pp.213–19.

153. Interview with Jimmy Lim.

154. Ken Yeang, *The Green Skyscraper* (New York: Prestel, 1999).

155. Ken Yeang, *Eco Skyscrapers* (Mulgrave, Australia: Images Publishing, 2007), p.20.

156. Christopher Marquis, Nancy Hua Dai, and Lynn Yin, "Chairman Zhang and Broad Group: Growth Dilemmas," Harvard Business School Case No. 9-412-095 (rev. June 24, 2015); Lloyd Alter, "Broad Sustainable Building Completes World's Tallest Prefab, 57 Stories," *Treehugger*, March 9, 2015.

157. Interview with Noel Morrin (Skanksa), February 25, 2010.

158. Geoffrey Jones and Amanda Yang, "Zhang Xin and the Emergence of Chinese Philanthropy," Harvard Business School Case No. 9-317-045 (September 23, 2016).

159. Interview with Noel Morrin (Skanksa), February 25 2010.

160. "The Federal Commitment to Green Building: Experiences and Expectations" (2010), <https://archive.epa.gov/greenbuilding/web/pdf/2010_fed_gb_report.pdf>, accessed July 2, 2016; Building Design and Construction Magazine, "The White Paper on Sustainability: A Report on the Green Building Movement," <https://archive.epa.gov/greenbuilding/web/pdf/bdcwhitepaperr2.pdf>, accessed July 3, 2016.

161. CBRE, National Green Building Adoption Index, 2015, <http://www.cbre.com/.../green-building-adoption-index-2015.pdf>, accessed February 8, 2016.

162. World Tourism Organization, "International Tourist Arrivals Up 4%, Reach a Record 1.2 Billion in 2015," January 18, 2016, <http://media.unwto.org/press-release/2016-01-18>, accessed March 4, 2016.

163. United Nations Environment Program, "Tourism's Three Main Impact Areas," <http://www.unep.org/resourceefficiency/Business/SectoralActivities/Tourism/Fac tsandFiguresaboutTourism/ImpactsofTourism/EnvironmentalImpacts/TourismsThree MainImpactAreas/tabid/78776>, accessed June 4, 2016.

164. Ross Dowling, "The History of Ecotourism," in Roy Ballantyne and Jan Packer (eds.), *International Handbook on Ecotourism* (Cheltenham: Edward Elgar, 2013), pp.19–20.

165. Martha Honey, *Ecotourism and Sustainable Development* (Washington, DC: Island Press, 2008), p.6.

166. Elkington and Hailes, *Green Consumer Guide*, pp.272–99.

167. TIES, Ecotourism Statistical Fact Sheet (2000), <http://www.active-tourism. com/factsEcotourism1.pdf>, accessed January 27, 2016.

168. David Weaver, Bill Faulkner, and Laura Lawton, *Nature-Based Tourism in Australia and Beyond: A Preliminary Investigation* (CRC for Sustainable Tourism, 1999), <http://www. sustainabletourismonline.com/82/nature-based-tourism/nature-based-tourism-in-australia- and-beyond-a-preliminary-investigation>, accessed August 1, 2016.

169. Center for Responsible Travel, "The Case for Responsible Travel: Trends & Statistics" (2015), <http://www.responsibletravel.org/resources/documents/2015% 20Trends%20&%20Statistics_Final.pdf>, accessed August 6, 2016.

170. Jack Boulware, "Paradise Lost?" *American Way*, September 15, 2008.

171. Lynda Lohr, "Stanley Selengut Reflects on 37 Years of Maho Bay Camps," *St. John Source*, April 25, 2013.

172. Ibid.; Honey, *Ecotourism*, p.62.

173. Honey, *Ecotourism*, pp.72–5.

174. Geoffrey Jones and Andrew Spadafora, "Entrepreneurs and the Co-Creation of Ecotourism in Costa Rica," Harvard Business School Working Paper No. 16-136 (2016).

175. Ibid.

176. Ibid.; Honey, *Ecotourism*, 170–2.

177. Jones and Spadafora, "Entrepreneurs," Table 1.

178. Ibid.; Interview with Michael Kaye by Andrew Spadafora, June 5, 2014, Creating Emerging Markets Project (hereafter CEM), Baker Library Historical Collections, Harvard Business School, <http://www.hbs.edu/businesshistory/emerging-markets>.

179. Ibid.

180. Ibid.

181. Interview with Tamara Budowski, Escazu, June 6, 2014; Interview with Tamara Budowski by Royal G. Jackson, September 21, 1992, Royal G. Jackson Papers, Series II.1, Oregon State University Special Collections.

182. "Ana Margarita Forero," in Camilo Rodríguez Chaverri, *Mujeres pioneras del turismo en Costa Rica* (San José: Maya & PZ Editorial, 2006), pp.140–6.

183. "Tamara Budowski," in Chaverri, *Mujeres pioneras*, p.154.

184. Interview with Tamara Budowski, June 6, 2014; Jones and Spadafora, "Entrepreneurs."

185. Jones and Spadafora, "Entrepreneurs."

186. Interview with Efrain Chacón, June 17, 2014.

187. Interview with Jack Ewing by Andrew Spadafora, June 3, 2014, CEM, Baker Library Historical Collections, Harvard Business School, <http://www.hbs.edu/businesshistory/emerging-markets>; Jones and Spadafora, "Entrepreneurs."

188. Interview with Jack Ewing, June 3, 2014.

189. Jones and Spadafora, "Entrepreneurs."

190. Honey, *Ecotourism*, p.162; Ina Porras, David Barton, Adriana Chacón-Cascante, and Miriam Miranda, *Learning from 20 Years of Payments for Ecosystem Services in Costa Rica* (London: International Institute for Environment and Development, 2013), pp.8–9.

191. Martin Mowforth and Ian Munt, *Tourism and Sustainability* (London: Routledge, 2009), pp.126–30.

192. Interview with Jim Damalas by Andrew Spadafora, June 4, 2014, CEM, Baker Library Historical Collections, Harvard Business School, <http://www.hbs.edu/businesshistory/emerging-markets/>.

193. Interview with Michael Kaye, June 5, 2014.

194. Interview with Tamara Budowski, June 6, 2014.

195. Honey, *Ecotourism*, pp.26–8.

196. Ibid., p.68.

6

Building Green Institutions

The growth of green business from the 1980s onward was accompanied by the advent of standards and certification schemes. Their aim was to define what sustainability actually meant in specific contexts, and to codify it. Defining sustainability distinctly for each sector proved to be a challenging exercise given that the concept was inherently multi-dimensional and because scientific knowledge and the measurability of results kept evolving, fluid in time. It also required significant value-judgments about the relative importance of various factors, some of which bore little relation to the usual considerations of profit and loss. The effort to define sustainability, and to set the appropriate metrics, exposed many of the fault lines which lay at the heart of the tensions between profits and sustainability.

This chapter covers three major themes in the development of working models of sustainability. The first is how standards and certification came into being in the industries covered here. There was certainly nothing new about standards per se. The concept of voluntary standards had emerged with industrialization in the nineteenth century as engineers worked towards agreement on technical specifications for things like nuts and bolts. If every manufacturer or every country made nuts and bolts in different sizes, few things would be built, or at least few would be built cheaply and safely. In 1901 the British Standards Institution became the first national standards body. In 1947 the International Organization for Standardization (ISO) was founded as an NGO headquartered in Geneva. Not surprisingly, given the challenges of reaching agreement on even the most straightforwardly mechanical standards, the ISO shied away from defining less tangible concepts like sustainability for a long time. Although problems of the natural environment had been first raised at ISO in 1968, it was only in 1996 that organization issued the first of its ISO 14000 series of environmental management standards.[1] In other words, the

ISO had issued 13,999 previous standards before getting around to defining standards for environmental sustainability. The various voluntary standards discussed in this chapter were, for the most part, well ahead in time of ISO 14000, or at least contemporary with it.

As the historical literature on the setting of standards has stressed, the process is always contested and full of "conflicts and contingencies."[2] In the context of industries inhabited by entrepreneurs with strong ideological views, the development of environmental/sustainability standards was going to be difficult, all the more so as a growing number of conventional firms turned their attention to green matters more from a focus on profits than from environmental zeal. It required building coalitions between multiple stake-holders, at a time when the very terms of engagement had yet to emerge. This chapter looks at the green institutional entrepreneurs who drove the standards-setting process and who were important shapers of sustainable business.[3]

A second major theme of the chapter is the different ways that standards and certification advanced across different industries. It was much easier to organize effective standards and certification in some industries than in others. The form standards took also varied widely. In many instances, the promoters of standards secured some acceptance by establishing a non-profit organization, or by securing governmental involvement to lend credibility or provide enforcement powers. Remarkably different mixtures of private certi-fication and government involvement occurred.

The third theme is whether standards and certification help explain the expansion of these industries after 1980. Their advantages were, in theory, considerable. Certification bestows legitimacy, making it easier for govern-ments to justify supporting green firms, and might even in time offer a path to persuade policy-makers to price environmental externalities into competitor conventional products. Certification was also an implicit form of communi-cation with consumers to increase their confidence in products and services, and to differentiate products from the offerings of conventional competitors. If consumers were to be asked to pay a premium price, as they typically were even as green business expanded, standards both offered something beyond a single company's assertion and could reduce the barriers of high search and information costs. Finally, the commercial benefits flowing from certification offered the prospects of attracting more external finance and, thus, providing resources to scale.

Nevertheless, certification sometimes proved to be a mixed blessing. Some industries, such as natural beauty, suffered from late development of standards and confusion and conflicts between different standards. The more successful case in construction illustrated some of the trade-offs in creating broad coalitions—and in creating institutions that could be gamed.

Certifying organic food and agriculture

Earlier chapters have shown that organic agriculture, at least in Europe, was far ahead of the other industries considered in this book in considering the need for, and executing, standards and certification. The biodynamic movement's Demeter trademark survived the Nazi era in Germany, in part by collaboration with the regime. It continued as the only international organic food trademark even despite the disruptions of World War II and the Cold War. In Germany, a new organization, the Demeter-Bund, was founded in 1954 to regulate the use of the trademark, offer advisory services, and establish quality controls to ensure standards were met. By the 1960s, such advisory services were provided regularly outside Germany, especially in Mediterranean countries. National organizations began to build closer links. In 1972 a meeting of European representatives of Demeter agreed on internationally binding guidelines for biodynamic products. This agreement created standards for processing, packaging, and labeling.[4] The standard spread outside Europe after 1980. In the United States, Demeter was founded in 1985 as a non-profit organization, and it obtained a registered trademark for "Biodynamic" soon afterwards. By 2016 Demeter International consisted of a network of individual certification organizations in forty-five countries.[5]

There were other attempts at certification in Europe after World War II, but they either failed to gain traction or remained highly localized. It was only in the late 1960s and the early 1970s that the British-based Soil Association formulated a set of organic standards and a certification system that secured wider acceptance.[6] These were also years when the local and fragmented industry in the United States saw attempts at standards and certification. In the mid-1960s Walnut Acres and another farm-to-market company, Shiloh Farms, created in-house programs to ensure that the ingredients they purchased were grown in accordance with their own standards. Walnut Acres used its own certifying and labeling program for three decades. In 1971 Jerome Rodale's *Organic Gardening and Farming* magazine started an organic certification program in California in response to a surge of interest in the subject after the first Earth Day. The Rodale standards required a 3 percent minimum humus content in soil, verifiable by an independent laboratory test. Shortly after his death, his son discontinued the program in 1973 after concluding that the firm could not manage it, even though it only had ninety farmers signed up, mostly in California.[7]

Although discontinued, the Rodale standards created momentum. Reluctant to abandon certification, fifty-four farmers around Santa Cruz who had signed up to them started their own certifying body, California Certified Organic Farmers (CCOF). They visited farms to check that crops were being grown organically.[8] Elsewhere, the Northeast Organic Farming Association was founded in Vermont and New Hampshire in 1971. In 1977 it developed its first certification standards. There was some modest governmental support. In 1973 the state of Oregon had passed the first state organic food regulation in response to reports of fraudulent claims of being organic. The California Organic Food Act in 1979 introduced a state-mandated certification program, which legally defined organic practices, but it had no budget and made no provision for enforcement. The CCOF had to pursue infractions in the courts on its own.[9] For the first twelve years it functioned as a volunteer-run certification program, with members inspecting each other's farms using guidelines derived from Rodale's standards.[10]

The turning point for institution-building in organic agriculture came in 1980, and it happened in Europe. The first key development was the launch of an international standard. This emerged from the French biodynamic organization Nature et Progrès (N & P), whose origins were discussed in Chapter 3. Roland Chevriot, the President after 1970, was a visionary for organic agriculture with a strong international outlook. N & P sent people to the fringe meetings at the United Nations Conference in Stockholm in 1972.[11] In the same year a meeting in Versailles attracted several thousand people.[12] Chevriot's invitation letter to the event noted that "the food quality and ecology crisis is no longer a national problem, but an actual international concern."[13] N & P released its first set of guidelines for organic agriculture in France, but Chevriot wanted to internationalize them. At the Versailles conference, he took the initiative to launch International Federation for Organic Agriculture Movements (IFOAM), persuading the Soil Association, the Swedish Biodynamic Association, the Soil Association of South Africa, and Rodale Press of the United States to sign up along with N & P.[14] IFOAM initially operated out of borrowed space from N & P, and faced a huge challenge seeking standardization as each national organization had its own ideas about standards. Yet by 1980 the first draft of organic standards was in place. In 1986 the organization was sufficiently established to hire its first full-time employee.[15]

The IFOAM standards signaled a transition away from a system which had rested on personal relationships between farmers and consumers, and among farmers themselves. It moved instead towards transferring the powers of verification to a separate certification and inspection system. In a movement which had been based on strong values, it began to make formal rules the primary form of regulation. Verification overtook zeal as the cost of entry.

This transition opened up the potential to democratize the market for organic food, by providing consumers who were not personally acquainted with organic gardening and farming with information to understand what the product was, and to have confidence that it was legitimate. Over time, IFOAM also widened its scope. As Asian and then Latin American societies joined from the 1980s, IFOAM's agenda expanded to reflect their concerns, including social justice and development. IFOAM laid claim to be the representative of the world organic movement. In 1992 it participated in the UN Food and Agriculture Organization's Rio Conference in Brazil. In the IFOAM General Assembly in São Paulo that year a chapter on social justice was added to the organization's Basic Standards.[16] Years later, it worked to refocus the organic movement as a solution to climate change.[17]

Standards are not Platonic ideals. They are the result of men and women working together to codify words and measurements by which phenomena in the physical world can be judged to be acceptable or not acceptable, the same or not the same. This work often requires compromises between competing interests and disparate visions. Sometimes, competing standards appear, as when groups of people in different places do this work separately, either oblivious of each other's efforts or because they do not accept the other group's legitimacy. The effort to define organic food internationally raised the possibility that competing standards might arise.[18] It also made more pressing the need for certification and enforcement to guarantee that the standard had indeed been followed.

Governments offered a potential solution to this latter issue. Private standards began to coexist with public regulation, although with wide variations between countries. Once more it was France which had a long history of defining standards for food and drinks such as champagne, which took the lead.[19] A pivotal French law, Loi d'Orientation Agricole, passed in 1980, officially recognized the existence and validity of organic agricultural techniques and established a requirement for formal supervision of organic produce and products by an independent party.[20]

The French standards were based on those drafted by N & P in 1972, which defined the substances that would be allowed for use in organic farming, as well as for processing and preservation of organic foods. The Ministry of Agriculture created the distinctive green and white logo AB (*agriculture biologique*) in 1985, which was placed on all certified organic produce originating in the country. Another law in 1988 protected the use of the term "agriculture biologique" for use only by those certified by independent organizations.[21]

Certification required further organizational innovation. In 1978 the Association des Conseillers Indépendants en Agriculture Biologique (ACAB) was established by a group of agricultural engineers and professors at agricultural schools and designed to advocate the cause of organic agriculture in French agricultural institutions. Claude Aubert, a close associate of Roland Chevriot, was one of the founders, and the organization was closely associated with N & P.[22] Subsequently N & P began employing ACAB for independent monitoring and supervision to protect its brand.[23] After the French organic laws were passed, ACAB, which had always been split between members who offered advisory services and those who carried out inspections and were known as the "independents," found itself in a unique place as the first certification body accepted by the French authorities. The organization served as both an advocate for organic agriculture and a provider of certification services.[24]

During the 1980s several other European governments came to be involved in organic standards, or developed logos for organic products. Public policy motivations ranged widely from enthusiasm for environmental and social benefits to wanting to support what was seen as a potentially lucrative infant industry.[25] Lobbying was important too. In Denmark campaigning by organic farmers and the cooperative retailer FDB encouraged the Danish government to develop the red "Ø" label, which, as Chapter 5 noted, was so important in the growth of the organic food market in that country.

A further layer of complexity was added as regional integration in Europe resulted in a new set of public agencies becoming involved. This affected both the process of certification and the standards themselves. In 1989 the European Committee for Standardization, a non-profit organization established in 1961, turned its attention to certification. European Standard 45011 on product certification set the standards for what could be deemed a competent certification system for any sector. This meant that certification systems wishing to operate at either the national or European level would have to conform to the requirements of 45011.[26] For bodies like the ACAB, this meant substantial changes in its market and its business model, because the new standard required a separation of advisory and inspection services, thereby rendering ACAB's business model obsolete, and N & P's comparable services as well.[27]

The unexpected consequence was the creation of a large, for-profit certification company. The director of ACAB was William Vidal, an agriculturist who had become interested in organic agriculture in the 1970s.[28] In 1991 he reorganized ACAB's inspection and certification business into the independent limited liability company called ECOCERT, in which he was a shareholder.[29] The new venture moved quickly to seize the new opportunities for the provision of certification services, benefiting from its official accreditation by the French government and legitimacy in the organic community owing to its association with ACAB.[30] Twenty years later ECOCERT held a market share of 65 percent in the certification of organic producers and 60 percent for processors in France.[31]

Vidal drove a rapid diversification of ECOCERT beyond both organic food and France. It diversified into the certification of cosmetics, perfumes, and textiles. It expanded internationally. Opening the first international subsidiary in Portugal in 1994, it expanded rapidly, acquiring large US and Swiss certifiers in 2011 and 2015. By 2016 it had revenues of $49 million and had affiliates in twenty-four countries.[32] Although organic certification became the basis for a successful business, the consequences were more contested. Blaise Hommelen, who had helped found ECOCERT and directed its Belgian office, complained that Vidal had changed the rules to centralize control, which he characterized as a "coup d'état." In 2007 he and others left and established a competitor, Certisys. N & P was equally critical of ECOCERT becoming a pure for-profit business. The organization opted to use only state certifiers, and not private certification even if accredited by state officials.[33]

European integration also significantly impacted standards themselves. In 1991, the European Union produced its own set of organic standards for organic crop production, certification, and labeling in the entire EU. As they also applied to imports into the region, they came to have a significant global impact. They were also progressively extended beyond crops, beginning with livestock.[34] However, again, definitional issues were raised. The EU standards were heavily influenced by IFOAM, which represented European organic producers through an EU group which lobbied extensively,[35] but it differed from some national standards. In France the government modified its own standards in 1995 to bring them in line with the EU's, and at the same time dropped N & P as a certifying organization. This displeased activists who considered that the EU standards were a step backwards. N & P responded with a new set of guidelines and their own certification standards in 1995. The group became known as the "boycotters," representing organic farmers who refused to obtain the government certification.[36]

Tensions regarding standards were associated with generational changes. In Denmark large numbers of farmers converted to organic farming following the market growth encouraged by the red "Ø" label. Many of these newcomers lacked the strong ideological views of earlier organic farmers, being less opposed in principle to conventional agriculture. The two groups divided during the 1990s over the question of whether the organic farmers association, Landsforeningen Økologisk Jordbrug, should advance stricter private standards than those set by the government and the EU, or whether they should aim for parity with national and international standards.[37]

A general pattern across the EU was that most organic farmers who converted during the 1980s and 1990s adhered to private standards, but most converting after 2000 chose to be certified by their national regulations.[38] Most European countries established national organic regulations based on the EU rules, which required that operators be certified either to national regulation or to the standards of a private body, where these are at least equivalent. In two countries with national regulations, most farmers chose to be certified to a single private standard. This was the case in Switzerland, where over 90 percent were certified by Bio-Suisse, an NGO, and Britain, where over 60 percent of organic farmers were certified to Soil Association standards. As both these standards were well known to consumers, large retailers encouraged labeling of organic products with them.[39]

In Sweden, there was no national regulation at all. Instead a private standard-setting body called KRAV (Association for Control of Organic

Production) set standards. This was formed in 1985 by four organic farming organizations. This timing happened because individual members of the cooperative KF, the largest retailer of food in Sweden, pressured the organization to sell organic foods. To achieve this, KF sought a single association of organic farmers with whom to partner. KRAV was originally described as representing "alternative" farmers but sought to open its membership to other organizations, including conventional farmers. Standards were negotiated as more members joined. This caused friction with original members, and in 1989 the Biodynamic Association and several other founders left. Sweden's biggest dairy, Arla, was initially hostile to the whole concept of organic food, but media and public criticism of not selling organic milk led to it joining KRAV in 1991 and launching its own eco-labeled milk. As KRAV expanded, the word "alternative," associated with a political ideology and the Green Party, was replaced by "organic." In 1993 the Swedish government authorized KRAV to audit organic agriculture to make sure it met EU standards, although KRAV's own standards were stricter. The organization came to include organic and conventional farmers, large retailers and food companies, trade unions, and many others, and claimed 98 percent of Swedish consumers were aware of the KRAV trademark.[40]

In the United States in the 1980s, the momentum towards creating standards and governmental involvement took a different pace and form than in Europe. By the end of the decade over thirty individual states had laws on organic agriculture, but this left many other states entirely unregulated, with producers free to define whether or not they were organic themselves. This coexisted with proliferating private certification as organic farmers and local non-profits, many of them explicitly anti-capitalist, introduced multiple certification schemes, few of them effectively enforced. In 1985 CCOF was finally able to hire its first paid member of staff but soon ran into financial difficulties, and the organization only survived through a $10,000 donation from The Grateful Dead, the prominent Californian countercultural musical group. CCOF undertook a major lobbying role in the state. Working with Sam Farr, a former Peace Corps volunteer in Latin America and then a member of the California State Assembly and strong supporter of organic agriculture, they successfully lobbied for passage of the California Organic Foods Act of 1990. This law finally added enforcement to the legal definitions of organic practices established in 1979, although third-party certification was still voluntary.[41]

It took a considerable effort to develop more national organic standards. In the fall of 1985, in Albany, New York, a group of farmers met and structured the concept of a farmer-owned and farmer-controlled association. This initial meeting set the cornerstone for the Organic Crop Improvement Association (OCIA), a member-owned, non-profit organization. Three years later a group of Peruvian farmers joined the organization, attracted by the concepts of farmer-to-farmer networking and crop improvement, beginning the spread of the organization to Latin America and later elsewhere.[42] This became the first chapter-based certification program to operate under a single set of standards throughout the United States and Latin America, but as it allowed local autonomy in decision-making, there continued to be a wide divergence of practice within the organization.[43]

It was at this time that IFOAM organized a meeting of North American organic certifiers and businesses to consider developing global standards. From this meeting the Organic Foods Production Association of North America, which later changed its name to the Organic Trade Association (OTA), was created in 1985 to represent growers, distributors, and processors in the United States and Canada. However, there continued to be conflicts over competing and inconsistent certification systems, which some felt could only be overcome by legislation at the federal level.[44] Finally, the Organic Foods Production Act of 1990 was passed as Title 21 of the Food, Agriculture, Conservation, and Trade Act of 1990. It called for the establishment of the National Organic Program (NOP) and National Organic Standards Board (NOSB) within the US Department of Agriculture (USDA), finally backing the "certified organic" claim with federal legislation.

Unlike Sweden's KRAV, the US government as represented by the USDA was under no obligation to accept NOSB's recommendations. There were also a smaller number of parties represented in NOSB, and they were all related to the organic movement. A vice-president of Whole Foods Market sat on the board, as the only retailer, providing the company unique access to shaping the rules. The USDA strictly defined organic as a marketing label; in contrast to Europe, there was no recognition of any health or environmental benefit.[45] There was an adversarial relationship between the organic movement and the USDA, and between organic and conventional farming. In 1997 there was an uproar among activists over proposed standards, including those for genetically modified organisms (GMOs), resulting in the creation of a new lobbying group, the Organic Consumers Association, in 1998 by Ronnie Cummins, a long-time radical political activist and bitter opponent of genetically modified food.[46] In 2000 came the issue of the "Final Rule" of the NOSB which required anyone involved in growing and processing organic food to be certified by the USDA. The standards prohibited the use of pesticides and synthetic fertilizers, and it regulated crop rotation practices and the genetic manipulation of crops and animals. The announcement of the standards was hosted by Whole Foods.[47]

Organic standards became firmly established, along with most other public policies in the United States, as a contested battleground between interest groups with limited trust in each other. As in Europe, government support for organic standards was also not the end of the story. The role of interest groups in regulations and enforcement was seen by many as a problem, especially the lobbying by large conventional food groups.[48] The USDA used certifying agents to enforce certification requirements on farms in audits, but these agents came from a diverse group of non-profit groups, like the CCOF, state-run agencies, and large farms, all of whom sometimes subcontracted certification. Farmers paid the certifiers to certify them, and certifiers competed for the business. The system provided incentives for maximum flexibility in interpreting standards, if not worse.[49]

The more the market grew, the more discrepancies were uncovered. Between 2005 and 2014, thirty-eight of the eighty-one USDA certifying agents failed on at least one occasion to uphold basic USDA standards.[50] There were multiple tensions between, on the one hand, smaller organic farmers and societies representing them, and, on the other hand, large-scale "industrial organic" businesses. The Cornucopia Institute, a Wisconsin-based farm policy institute, made repeated disclosures of large, certified organic farms which were visibly not following rules and regulations.[51]

If there was ambiguity about the process of organic certification in the United States, consumers were also presented with other certificates to choose from. The Natural Products Association (NPA) had been in existence since 1936 as a non-profit representing manufacturers and retailers. It had started with a focus on health foods but expanded over time to dietary and other foods, cosmetics, and other products. In 2008, the NPA launched its own certification—the Natural Standard for Personal Care. Neither the FDA nor the USDA had rules or regulations for products labeled "natural" and the term was widely used. In 2009 another body, NSF International, a US-based public health and safety standards organization founded in 1944, published a new American National Standard for personal care products containing organic ingredients, called NSF/ANSI 305.[52]

There was also the Fair Trade movement, which had diverse but primarily European origins, and developed its first labels during the late 1980s around a fictional Dutch character, Max Havelaar, who served as an advocate for exploited coffee pickers. In 1997 Fairtrade International, based in Germany, was created to bring uniformity. Although it was concerned more with process and social justice than organic certification, there was also a significant overlap with organic standards in that fair prices, as defined by the organization, were meant to encourage sustainable production.[53] Sales of Fair Trade labeled coffee, as well as other products, soared from the late 1990s. The Starbucks coffee chain displayed the Fair Trade USA logo on its advertisements, even though, critics noted, only one-tenth of its products were fair trade certified.[54]

The simultaneous spread of organic certification and the growth of organic agriculture after 1980 lend credence to the argument that such institutionalization facilitated the organic food market. Certification enhanced credibility among consumers and farmers, assisted the entry of governments to support the sector or even subsidize it, and facilitated international trade. It is less clear if the marked differences in standards setting and certification within the EU, and between it and the United States, had a major impact compared to other determining factors behind organic consumption. It is evident that clear and trusted standards, like Sweden's KRAV label, were positives in growing an organic market. Conversely, weak or confusing standards were not helpful to expanding the market. This was one factor, among several, in the limited growth of the organic market in New Zealand.[55]

As organic farming and consumption spread globally, so did organic certification. By 2015 some eighty-seven countries had national organic certification. A number of the Asian and Latin American national standards were endorsed by IFOAM, including those of Argentina, China, Costa Rica, India, and Turkey, though many were not.[56] However, in countries where legal institutions were weak and fraud prevalent, certification could not be insulated from bad operators. There was evidence of widespread fraudulent labeling.[57] In Turkey, İpek Hanımın Çiftliği (İpek Hanım's Farm), to give just one example, sold directly from its own farm, but did not certify its products because it considered the certification process in the country to be corrupt. Organic certificates might "be credible in other countries of the world," the founder's son Can Turhan observed in 2013. "Organic agriculture is not a profitable business if you do it properly. But it can be very profitable if you bend the rules. One of the most common ways of bending the rules (in Turkey) is getting an organic farming certificate for a small portion of land...the government does not check the rest of the land plots. And you can use whichever chemicals you want in these areas."[58]

But the main challenge to organic labeling wasn't fraud. There was a deeper issue: the setting of standards forced a discussion of what organic meant. As it meant different things to different people, competing visions of sustainability, represented by words like "organic," "natural," and "Fair Trade," became codified. Certification was also an open-ended process, as new issues emerged over time, such as whether hydroponic foods, grown using irrigation to deliver nutrients, could be certified organic.[59] Certification exposed, but did not resolve, the social construction of the concept of sustainability in organic food.

It was not surprising, given the nature of the challenge in codifying standards, that persistent green institutional entrepreneurs, such Roland Chevriot and Jerome Rodale, played formative roles in their initial stages. As governments became involved, beginning in Europe, the process of standardization and certification became co-organized by a mixture of private and public agencies, and competing standards multiplied, reflecting the impact of lobbying, different political systems, and different ways the organic movement had evolved.[60] The impact on the growth of organic agriculture was broadly positive. Although it is challenging to tease out the exact impacts of standards on the growth of organic food compared to other factors, a rule of thumb was that standards which were clear, widely known, and respected encouraged organic consumption and agriculture, and those that were confusing or weakly enforced did not. Scaling necessarily raised new complexities, highlighted by the fact that certification became a lucrative business for for-profit companies, and an activity which was gamed, in both developed and emerging markets.

Certifying beauty

Natural beauty took off as a business even before its standards emerged. During the 1980s and 1990s the industry grew quite rapidly, even though it remained small compared to the giant conventional industry. This growth occurred while the industry was almost entirely devoid of certification, beyond the Demeter trademark used by the small biodynamic ventures such as Weleda. Yet when certification efforts did start, the results were not very positive.

The first efforts at certification came from within the biodynamic movement. A key figure was the Swiss-born Rodolphe Balz, who had graduated in sociology and geography and then taught as a professor, before moving to France to become a farmer, buying an abandoned farm. He joined N & P, became a member of their board of directors, and helped draft the first standards for organic agriculture in 1981.[61] While these standards became foundational, Balz ran into more trouble when he turned his attention to beauty.

Balz was interested in the therapeutic values of plants and essential oils, and was heavily influenced by his mother, who had grown medicinal and aromatic plants in her yard and had prominent naturopaths as friends. It was this interest which led him towards personal care. In 1986 Balz launched Sanoflore Laboratory in a small village in southeast France. He specialized at first in the organic production of aromatic and medicinal plants, and organic shampoos, shower gels, and massage oils before, in the mid-1990s, launching his first organic cosmetics, although he found few takers, as few consumers knew what the term meant. Balz himself saw building a business as "a double necessity." He needed "to make money to survive," he observed, but he also needed "to protect the environment where my children and grandchildren will live."[62]

In 1995 Balz tried to get the makers of organic cosmetics to confer on a set of shared standards. As he later noted, there were twenty-five small laboratories at the first meeting, but only three at the next. He was unable to advance the project. He felt it was important to make the attempt because the natural and organic beauty industry was not only growing in scale by then but also in diversity. In France there was a distinction between natural and organic (or "bio" as it was known) cosmetics. Most products labeled "natural" still contained some synthetic fragrances, artificial dyes, or petroleum by-products. Elsewhere too, even the iconic green brands of the era made some use of non-organic ingredients for preservative and other purposes. Balz later recalled his own encounter with Anita Roddick of The Body Shop. "The Body Shop was a good idea originally," he later critically observed, "they were marketing geniuses, and the woman, the owner was really nice and approachable, she had great ideas, and a lot of ethics, but her ethics were focused more on people than the composition of her products. She didn't know much about natural really and even less about bio." Body Shop products at that time, Balz opined, "if you only looked into their composition, were absolutely disgusting."[63]

Balz resumed the ideal of creating a standard in 2000. He contacted ECOCERT, and finally gathered momentum. He and seven other bio-cosmetics producers drafted the very first set of guidelines specifically for bio-cosmetics. At the same time he launched the first association for bio-cosmetic professionals, called COSMEBIO.[64] In 2003 ECOCERT launched the first standards for natural and organic cosmetics in France. The standard specified both the use of ingredients from renewable resources and their manufacture by environmentally friendly processes, including whether packaging was biodegradable or recyclable. The ECOCERT label required that a minimum of 95 percent of all plant-based ingredients in the formula and a minimum of 10 percent of all ingredients by weight had to come from organic farming. For the natural cosmetic label, a minimum of 50 percent of all plant-based ingredients in the formula and a minimum of 5 percent of all ingredients by weight must come from organic farming. An onsite audit was conducted annually by an ECOCERT auditor.

ECOCERT and four other private organic and natural cosmetics organizations—COSMEBIO, BDIH of Germany, ICEA of Italy, and the Soil Association of Britain—also began working towards a common standard, but it was only in 2010 that the COSMOS standard was agreed. The natural standard specified that no more than 5 percent of the total product could be synthetic. The organic label required that at least 95 percent of the physically processed agro-ingredients were organic. An NGO was formed in Brussels to administer the COSMOS standards.[65]

The long delay in creating this standard resulted in the alternative standard NaTrue being founded in 2007. The principal drivers were Moritz Aebersold, a director of Weleda, and Julie Tyrrell, an expert on cosmetics regulation who had previously worked for the European Cosmetics Association and Estée Lauder. It was initially intended that NaTrue would translate what was hoped would be new EU regulatory standards into internationally agreed definitions and minimum requirements for manufacturers. But hopes for EU regulatory clarification of the definitions for cosmetics were in vain, and fearing COS-MOS might lead a race to the bottom, NaTrue launched its own standards in

2009. NaTrue's ambition to build a global label, however, suffered from the familiar problem that definitions of organic raw material differed so widely. In 2014 it finally adopted the IFOAM technical definition.[66]

In the United States, there was no private certification of natural beauty products. The USDA requirement that 95 percent of ingredients should be organic was considered problematic by many within the industry because cosmetics required synthesized chemicals, such as emulsifiers. The result was conflict. In 2008 the Organic Consumer Association filed a lawsuit against twelve cosmetics companies saying that they were advertising their products as organic even though they had no certified organic ingredients. In the following year this group and Dr. Bronner's filed another lawsuit against bodies such as ECOCERT, which required only 10 percent of ingredients to be organic in order to obtain certification, claiming they should stop organic certification if products could not be certified under USDA standards.[67]

Beginning in 2009, NaTrue also became the first independent certifier outside the United States to attempt to negotiate agreements with US standards bodies for international harmonization and definition of the ambiguous term "natural" that included the US market.[68] This proved to be a contentious process, as NaTrue was able to come to an agreement with NSF International, but not with the country's Natural Products Association. The NaTrue/NSF collaboration, based on NaTrue's own rules and not NSF's, was intended as the basis for the establishment of an official ANSI-ISO standard (American National Standards Institute, the US representative of ISO, the International Organization for Standardization).[69] The NPA publicly complained about further consumer confusion.[70]

Even so, the confusion around certification did not stop the growth of the natural beauty market, broadly defined. Beauty was an industry which grew relentlessly, worldwide, and a portion of that market was suspicious of putting chemical ingredients in their bodies and welcomed alternatives. However, certification probably worsened, rather than relieved, the identity crisis faced by natural beauty. Companies that made the effort, and accepted the higher expense, of using plants grown without pesticides, synthetic fertilizers, or genetic modification found themselves at a disadvantage on costs and without a way to differentiate their product offerings.[71] In 2014 a NaTrue report to the European Parliament stated that only three-quarters of women surveyed in Europe, the core natural beauty market, had some understanding that there was a difference between organic and natural cosmetics, and only one-quarter had a clear perception what that difference was.[72]

These considerations made many firms skeptical about certification. Instead, they sought to assure consumers that they were primarily but not entirely natural, avoiding harmful chemicals, but seeking to be effective. The existence of varying national standards played into that decision. "We're a predominantly Australian brand," Sam McKay, a former chief executive of Jurlique, observed, "but we're focused on growing internationally. And when you look at Europe, the US, Asia and Australia, there is no global certification standard in terms of organic, natural or even biodynamic beauty products."[73]

Natural beauty came late to certification, but there was no shortage of green institutional entrepreneurs. Unlike organic food, government standards were rare beyond the USDA organic standard. Private certification proved difficult because of a lack of common definitions. Natural beauty grew as an industry despite, rather than because of, certification.

Architecture and construction

The creation of green building standards and certification systems, which had its origins during the 1980s and grew to fruition during the 1990s, was much more complete than in natural beauty. This greater success may reflect a greater range of actors, many of them less passionately ecological than some of the green entrepreneurs in beauty. The standards grew as a result of a complex interaction between architects, conventional property developers, public agencies, and NGOs.

The process of institutionalization and certification began once again in Europe, but unlike the industries discussed earlier in this chapter, co-creation between public and private actors appeared early in the process. The pioneering building assessment and certification system was the Building Research Establishment Environmental Assessment Method (BREEAM), launched in Britain in 1990. This had its origins, at least partly, in a long-standing government agency known as the Building Research Establishment (BRE). In the wake of the 1973 oil crisis, this agency became focused on energy efficiency, including in buildings. However, it was able to achieve little traction in the property development and construction industries.[74]

BRE's early endeavors were reinforced by a private architectural design and energy consulting firm called Energy Conscious Design founded in 1980. The founders, Richard Ferraro, David Turrent, and John Doggart, were architects with an interest in solar energy. Doggart had worked with architect Richard Rogers in the late 1960s and then served as energy consultant for the "New Town" of Milton Keynes, experimenting in solar power.[75] The three men came together as they shared a desire to establish an architectural firm explicitly based on low-energy design.[76]

Like BRE, the new firm found few interested in its ideas. It was renamed ECD Partners (hereafter ECD) in 1984, adopting an abbreviation "to mask our activities to a skeptical private sector," as Ferraro put it.[77] Among the few clients was BRE, which commissioned ECD to write a report on the potential for industry acceptance of a new building energy label.[78] ECD published the results of its study in 1990. It showed that between the early 1970s and the late 1980s, the percentage of firms in the property industry believing that energy conservation in buildings was an important issue had risen from 45 percent to 75 percent, and suggested that there was strong support for a labeling program.[79]

During the late 1980s a number of property developers involved in London's Canary Wharf redevelopment project, especially Stanhope Properties, Greycoat, and Olympia & York, became interested in the idea of building commercial buildings that incorporated effective environmental improvements, especially low-energy performance. Ron German, one of Stanhope's executives, and John Doggart of ECD concluded that they could progress best if a government agency was involved, and they reached out to BRE.[80]

BRE, ECD, and the property developers worked together to produce the initial version of BREEAM. From the outset, the standard was focused not only on energy efficiency and resource scarcity, but also on broader environmental challenges, including the effects of chlorofluorocarbons (CFCs), used in aerosols and air conditioning. There was also attention paid to the emerging issue of the need to control the greenhouse gases generated by buildings.[81] BREEAM was intended as a green label, not a rating system. Although it initiated the practice of operating on a point system, it did not attempt to make these points comparable across categories and add them up for a total score. It was designed for commercial office buildings, and office buildings were BREEAM's initial clients. In was an entirely voluntary system for developers, who used it either to understand best practices or to highlight their achievements to the market.[82]

The first version was a design-stage assessment tool, and had an immediate impact. BREEAM issued green label certificates for over eighty buildings comprising 25 percent of total British new office space in its first year, and within two years had reached nine million square feet of new office space.[83] Versions of the certification for new houses, supermarkets, and other retail space followed. In 1993 BREEAM introduced an overall building score certification ranging from Pass to Good, Very Good, and Excellent. Assessments, and subsequently certifications, were at first primarily conducted by ECD.[84]

Considerable effort was made to respond to the substantial skepticism of many conventional developers and builders that certification was not worth their time and money. BREEAM sponsored award schemes which builders and developers could enter and use for marketing purposes.[85] Further steps to secure legitimacy were taken after BRE was privatized in 1997 and sold to an in-house management team backed by almost a hundred stakeholder organizations and firms which included scientific bodies, environmental organizations, architects, developers, and engineering firms.[86] The Foundation for the Built Environment (later renamed BRE Trust) was established to serve as the non-profit owner for BRE. It sought to balance members from the various sectors of the building industry, as well as academia.[87] In 1998 a major new version of BREEAM for new and existing office buildings was issued, which integrated transportation and building site issues into a building's overall environmental impact.[88]

BREEAM was soon extended to retail, educational, and other buildings. During the 2000s it was licensed to various independent certifying entities to create national green building schemes elsewhere in Europe. The scheme retained close links with both the British government and the European Union. BREEAM was widely adopted for government buildings. After 2006, when Britain adopted the European Union's Directive on the Energy Performance of Buildings, which required member states to reduce greenhouse gas emissions below 1990 levels in new buildings and to introduce energy performance certificates, BREEAM's Ecohomes system was turned into the Code for Sustainable Homes as a national regulatory requirement for homes built using public funds.[89] By 2015 BREEAM had more than 250,000 certified buildings and more than one million registrations across its global operations.[90]

Although BREEAM was pioneering, it did not remain unique. In 1996 certification systems were created in France, Canada, and Hong Kong, but it was in the United States that the most widely known green building certification was created. The Leadership in Energy and Environmental Design (LEED) system was launched in 1998. The US Green Building Council, a unique collaborative entity, both promoted LEED and helped spread the green building movement by exporting the idea of national green building councils.

As in Britain, certification emerged in part from long-established public agency concerns. By the 1970s the long-established Center for Building Technology of the US Commerce Department's National Bureau of Standards was conducting research on energy efficiency, much like the BRE.[91] From 1973 the Center cooperated with the National Conference of States on Building Codes and Standards, a non-profit organization established by state governors, to develop criteria for evaluating buildings' energy usage. These were subsequently adopted by key associations of building engineers and ANSI as a voluntary standard for new buildings dealing with heating and ventilation, lighting, electrical distribution, and water systems.[92] Also involved in early initiatives were non-governmental standards-setting bodies interested in building efficiency, especially the American Society for Testing and Materials (ASTM).[93] All of these efforts faced the challenge of dealing with a highly fragmented industry, notorious for structural rigidity and conservatism.

It was the 30-year-old real-estate developer David Gottfried who moved building certification forward in 1991. At the time, Gottfried was working for development and construction companies owned by his cousins Diane and Jim Katz in Washington, DC. Their firm had just taken on renovating the Environmental Defense Fund headquarters when he visited the site. Gottfried was prone to environmental idealism thanks to his California upbringing and sought out like-minded thinkers. Excited about the emergence of BREEAM, he attended a meeting of the recently formed COTE and listened to a team of architects discuss the soon-to-be-published *Environmental Resource Guide*, whose importance was noted in Chapter 5. He subsequently attended the 1992 AIA national convention, and returned from it with a new sense of purpose.[94]

In the course of his research, Gottfried connected with Mike Italiano, a partner at a Chicago law firm who specialized in environmental law and who had advised the ASTM in establishing an environmental committee in 1990.[95] Gottfried, advised by Italiano, attempted to diversify his cousins' firm into environmental consulting, but this generated little business. Even Worldwatch, an environmental research institute founded in 1974, rejected their bid for development and construction of a proposed new headquarters in favor of a cheaper, but not environmentally informed, bid.[96]

Gottfried and Italiano tried to launch an environmental consulting business in 1992, but that fell through when they failed to get an expected government contract, and they switched to creating a new non-profit organization to promote green buildings. They persuaded several environmentally inclined supplier companies, including the heating and air-conditioning company Carrier (owned by the United Technologies Corporation, a multi-billion dollar engineering company and defense contractor), to join the venture as dues-paying members by laying out a program of developing environmental standards. Sixty firms and non-profit organizations became founding members in 1993. Rick Fedrizzi of Carrier became the chairman, and Gottfried was the first employee. The organization took the formal name of the U.S. Green Building Council (USGBC) several months later. The central USGBC strategy was to include members across industrial sectors, as well as environmental organizations, in the hope of securing consensus among key stakeholders.[97]

This consensus approach had its downsides. The prominence of green building product suppliers in the USGBC caused suspicions of conflict of interest. The AIA initially declined to become involved.[98] Financial difficulties in collecting pledged dues caused Gottfried to resign in 1994, after he had paid the USGBC's expenses out of pocket for six months without drawing a salary.[99] He returned to run USGBC in 1996 as a client of a San Francisco consulting company, WorldBuild Technologies, which he had started in the meantime.[100] He and the Council gained experience working alongside the non-profit Public Technology, Inc. on an EPA-funded set of guidelines for best practices. This was published in 1996 as the *Sustainable Building Technical Manual*, in which Gottfried made the business case for green building on the basis of life-cycle cost analysis.[101] This was the key to making green building attractive to profit-focused entities.

The USGBC developed the new rating system LEED, which was piloted in 1998. A more sophisticated version, known as LEED 2.0, was launched two years later. In between, in 1999, Christine Ervin was hired as president and chief executive. She had previously worked at the World Wildlife Fund and in Oregon state government on environmental issues, and between 1993 and 1997 had been US Assistant Secretary of Energy, responsible for promoting clean energy technologies.

The energetic and well-connected Ervin drove the expansion of LEED, despite an initially skeptical marketplace. Realtors, for example, doubted the ability to market LEED-certified new buildings to tenants. Yet during her five-year tenure, Ervin expanded the USGBC from the three-person staff and 200 members she inherited fifty staff and 5,000 member firms. Hundreds of volunteers drafted LEED rating systems for commercial interiors, existing buildings, health care, schools, neighborhood developments, and other markets. The US government's General Services Administration, which owned a huge portfolio of federal buildings, became an early adopter. They were joined by municipalities and state governments. Washington, DC and Boston were the first cities to introduce LEED-based requirements, in 2006 and 2007 respectively. In 2008, California became the first state to adopt a statewide green building code.[102] There were over 10,000 LEED certified projects in 2011, one-third in buildings owned by the public sector.[103] The USGBC prospered alongside its main product, with its budget surpassing $100 million in 2007.[104] By 2014, there were 185,000 people in building-related industries holding LEED professional credentials, and 3 billion square feet of total building space had been LEED certified. Ninety percent of these buildings were located in the United States.[105]

The Green Building Council model spread to other countries. A first World GBC conference was held in 2002, at which the USGBC promised $25,000 to seed a formal international organization.[106] In 2015 the World Green Building Council included national green building councils in seventy-five countries.[107] By then China (including Hong Kong and Macao) and Taiwan had become the second largest region for LEED after the United States, with 1,657 LEED projects in mainland China and a total of 1,961 LEED projects in the region as a whole. SOHO China, the country's largest commercial property developer, was a prominent public supporter of the certification scheme.[108]

BREEAM and LEED were joined by other smaller certification schemes in particular countries and cities, such as HK-Beam, launched in Hong Kong in 1996, Haute Qualité Environnementale (HQE) launched in France in 1996, and the Tokyo Green Building Programme, launched in 2002. There were significant variations between countries in their engagement with green building, but with interesting variations from other industries. Germany, for example, only came up with its own standard, Deutsche Gesellschaft für Nachhaltiges Bauen (DGNP), in 2008. In 2012 it was estimated the green share of total building activity was 52 percent in Britain, 48 percent in the United States, but only 28 percent in Germany.[109]

Building certification schemes as a whole stand out as much more widely adopted and impactful than their counterparts in beauty. Yet there were parallels in the uncertainties and skepticism regarding what was being certified. Critics argued against both LEED and BREEAM that they failed to measure post-construction performance, for instance of carbon emissions, to see if tenant behavior changes expectations expressed in the certification rating.[110] LEED's point system, touted for its flexibility, also attracted critics, especially among ecological architects. "You can do something truly dreadful," one landscape architect noted, "and still meet all of LEED's criteria."[111] As in other certification systems, the use of metrics in the standards provided the opportunity for gaming of the system. There were also incentives to developers and builders to game it because certification could be, and was, used in marketing. Environmental activists talked explicitly of "LEEDwashing."[112] The Green Building Councils, although non-profits, needed to earn revenues in order to fund the organization, and therefore had no incentive to make standards so rigorous that certification was too difficult to obtain. Finally, at best, the certificate schemes captured only a part of the problem. Critics noted that a new home could receive a top LEED certification even if it was an oversized house (often known in the United States as a McMansion), built in an environmentally stressed area like a desert, and with no access to public transit.[113]

The green building certification schemes created after 1990 were significant innovations. They owed a lot to the successful institution-building of certain individuals, including the people who drove BREEAM forward, and, in the United States, David Gottfried and Christine Ervin. They had to overcome major skepticism in the industry, and they did that with smart strategies which co-opted conventional property developers and builders into the mission, alongside architects and environmentalists. They provide a valuable case study of how to align incentives among multiple stakeholders. It helped, too, that there were some powerful green consumers in the industry in the form of government agencies prepared to act as lead purchasers whose early support yielded a powerful demonstration effect. The process also raised important questions about outcomes. The institutionalization of building performance was a major influence encouraging architects and builders to think harder about sustainability than they had previously. Equally, the need to make the certification schemes relevant to conventional business, and to align incentives with them, required keeping compliance costs low. The question was whether this represented the necessary start of a journey in which standards would become ever more stringent, or whether it created an imagined sustainability which only incrementally limited the damage the built environment was doing to the natural environment.

Eco-tourism: sampling nature or trampling it?

The substantial growth of eco-tourism after 1980 was also accompanied by institutionalization. Its distinctive features made it a challenging industry in which to introduce standards and certification: it was highly fragmented, and the service it offered was by definition highly local. In some respects, standardization was almost a threat to the whole purpose of eco-tourism, which was to preserve and enhance local environments and communities, not standardize them like international hotel chains. There were also multiple parties with a stake in the industry. Although eco-tourism was an industry begun by small green entrepreneurs, once a market segment was identified, it attracted some very large conventional hotel chains and travel agencies. Tourism was also an industry in which national governments, all the more urgently in developing countries, were closely involved because of its importance generating revenue and large-scale employment. For the same reason, NGOs and international aid agencies also became interested in standards-setting in eco-tourism. This made for a combustible mix. Although significant attempts were made to develop definitions, the industry ended up with a confusing and contradictory set of standards.

A key figure in the first attempts to build institutions was Megan Epler Wood. Once again the story involved a strong element of serendipity. Epler Wood, an American liberal arts major with a strong interest in media, had become interested in nature when she was 21, after her best friend took her trekking along the Appalachian Trail. She was hired after graduation by the still-small American branch of the World Wildlife Fund which was eager to expand its media presence. In 1986 a Fulbright Scholarship enabled her to go to Colombia to make a documentary about a remote private reserve in the Andean cloud forest. She was struck by the burning forests all around the site and the need to generate revenues for the local people. On her return, she persuaded the National Audubon Society to give her a contract to make a documentary about eco-tourism. She began filming in Kenya, Belize, and Montana. Then the unexpected happened: the beer company sponsor behind the documentary withdrew after criticism of its environmental practices.[114]

Epler Wood was left with worldwide contacts made during the filming, but no documentary. At this stage she decided to found an organization dedicated to promoting eco-tourism. Understanding that she lacked credibility as a young documentarian, she persuaded a prominent Kenyan conservationist, David Western, one of the few authors to publish academic papers on the subject at the time, to join the endeavor and become president of the planned venture. Western, the son of a gamekeeper who had grown up in Tanzania, was an early pioneer of the concept of using tourist revenues for conservation purposes, and was then the head of the New York Zoological Society's Wildlife Conservation Center in East Africa.[115] Epler Wood and Western raised funds from American philanthropists, including from Liz Claiborne and the Merck family. In 1990 the International Ecotourism Society (TIES) was launched as the world's first international non-profit dedicated to eco-tourism as a tool for conservation and sustainable development.[116]

TIES began by trying to provide basic definitions of the industry. In 1991 Western convened the first TIES board meeting with experts from around the world. The result was the definition of eco-tourism as "responsible travel to natural areas that conserves the environment and improves the well-being of local people."[117] A TIES meeting in 1994 hosted by Stanley Selengut on St. John in the US Virgin Islands resulted in the formulation of "eco-lodges" as a concept. The meeting included architects and landscape architects, one of whom, Hitesh Mehta, went on to publish a definitive set of guidelines for eco-lodges.[118]

Eco-tourism was an industry which faced major issues of legitimacy. The tourism industry as a whole was widely considered in environmentalist circles as a destroyer of natural environments rather than a preserver of them. A core claim that eco-tourism was a legitimate and valid tool for sustainable development was met, and continues to be met, with skepticism. Despite the diffusion of the belief that profits and sustainability were compatible, it required a leap of faith for many to believe that transporting affluent Western consumers to remote villages and tropical rainforests would not do more harm than good.

Epler Wood sought to overcome this skepticism by bringing the various interested parties together in TIES. She worked to ensure that membership included environmentalists, academics, and business, both green and conventional, and that it included both Western and local firms. Many of the first members were founders of entrepreneurial firms such as Richard Ryel, an early pioneer of adventure travel with his firm International Expeditions based in Alabama, and Kurt Kutay, the founder of Seattle-based Wildland Adventures. Kutay, who had conducted research in national parks in Costa Rica, was instrumental in recruiting local firms, such as the tour operator Horizontes in Costa Rica, as well as Western businesses.[119]

Epler Wood was not convinced that certification as such would help the industry. She believed that certification schemes were prone to encourage a focus on checklists, but others sought to take this route. A Green Globe program emerged from discussions at the Earth Summit in 1992. It was managed by the World Travel and Tourism Council, the World Tourism Organization, and the Earth Council, which represented environmentalist NGOs. Epler Wood was discouraged that the initial focus was on creating a global network, which led to certificates being given away without due diligence.[120]

Green Globe remained the only global certificate, but other schemes proliferated. By 2008 there were between sixty and eighty separate "green" tourism certification programs, mostly covering one region or country.[121] There were strong incentives for national governments and others to engage in certification as it offered a path to accessing international funding. As the argument that eco-tourism could facilitate sustainable development gained traction, international agencies also became interested in supporting it. By the mid-1990s, for example, the United States Agency for International Development had invested in over one hundred projects with some eco-tourism component, which involved more than $2 billion in funding.[122] The availability of plentiful international aid was, in this industry as elsewhere, a recipe for misaligned incentives and rent-seeking.

As the Costa Rican industry took off, and the original pioneers scaled their businesses and were joined by followers, there was also a scramble to more clearly define the industry. Richard Holland and Chris Wille of the NGO Rainforest Alliance developed voluntary guidelines for eco-tourism enterprises in Costa Rica and distributed them in 1990. These consisted of a code of responsible tourist conduct with a commitment to environmental education. Company compliance was to be monitored by student volunteers in exchange for publication in a "recommended" list.[123]

The largest effort at developing standards and certification for sustainable tourism in the country came in a cooperative effort between 1994 and 1997 between the government's Costa Rican Tourism Institute (ICT), the industry, NGOs, and the country's leading business school, INCAE. The group included ICT's Vice-President, Bary Roberts, a pioneering entrepreneur in eco-tourism who had started in the business in the late 1970s.[124] The first version of the resulting "Certification for Sustainable Tourism" (CST) was made available for hotels in 1997, and for tour operators in 2001. It offered on-site inspections by accredited auditors to verify performance in such areas as water and energy consumption, emissions, waste management, effect on flora and fauna, and impact on the local community. More than one hundred hotels had applied for CST certification by 2001.[125] Despite its popularity, CST was also criticized. Roberts and others were disappointed when a change of government led the ICT to take full ownership of the CST, closing out the partnership with business and environmental NGOs.[126] Critics complained that the CST assisted larger companies at the expense of more innovative smaller ones, and that its requirements were unnecessarily expensive and time-consuming.[127]

Epler Wood's distrust of certification in eco-tourism led her to retire from the presidency of TIES in 2001 and establish her own consultancy with a focus on promoting a triple bottom-line approach in the industry. Her successor Martha Honey opted to pursue certification. TIES joined with the Rainforest Alliance to create an accreditation system for sustainable tourism and certification. The certification process proved a lengthy one, and there were few takers. "Far too few people in the industry got involved," Epler Wood noted. "It was a very NGO-led process, with not enough business participation. So it led to some of the greenest businesses doing it, and the rest not."[128] TIES itself struggled to retain coherence. By 2016 it lacked even a physical office.

Absent an industry institution capable of creating and imposing standards, the numbers of certification schemes proliferated. In 2008 the Rainforest Alliance, whose tourism department was based in Costa Rica, the United Nations Environment Programme, the United Nations Foundation, and the United Nations World Tourism Organization founded the Global Sustainable Tourism Council in an attempt to bring some cohesion. It issued criteria which were the minimum, not the maximum, which businesses, governments, and destinations should achieve to approach social, environmental, cultural, and economic sustainability. The criteria were designed to be adapted to local conditions, and supplemented by additional criteria applying to the specific location and activity. Epler Wood remained skeptical of the whole effort. "It's all about compliance officers," she concluded. "It has to be about leadership, about understanding business's responsibility, and not about hiring a compliance officer."[129]

Confused, conflicting, and weak certification clearly had no impact whatsoever on the growth of eco-tourism. If its size was really near one-quarter of the $7 trillion worldwide tourist industry, as some estimates cited in Chapter 5 suggest, it could lay claim to be the largest green industry. Yet the fact that there was no agreed estimate of the size of the industry because its identity was so poorly defined marked the failure of institutionalization in this industry, despite the work of people such as Epler Wood and David Western. The fragmented and local nature of the industry was partly responsible for this. The intervention of many national governments, aid agencies, and NGOs was another problem. Whatever the cause, the proliferation of certificates, almost all of them voluntary and primarily prized as marketing tools, provided little legitimacy to the industry. Indeed, more so than the other industries, certification was probably a force for delegitimization.

Conclusion

The decades since 1980 witnessed a search for the means to define more clearly the value of green products and services in ways which would lead consumers to buy them, governments to support them, and others to follow them. Standards and certification were seen as the path to credibility.

Growing environmental awareness and the rise of the green consumer facilitated the spread of standards and certification. These trends encouraged large conventional firms, from the Arla retailer in Sweden to property developers in London, to become engaged because there was a perceived emergent consumer segment. They also encouraged governments to become involved in supporting private standards or setting their own. It was not an easy path. Among the unconverted, there was widespread skepticism as to whether there really was a market value for a greener building, that eco-tourism could genuinely be a significant force for development, and so on. Institutional entrepreneurs such as Roland Chevriot, Rodolphe Balz, David Gottfried, Megan Epler Wood, the hard-working farmer volunteers of the California Certified Organic Farmers, and many others, were critical to starting conversations, assembling initial resources, and building coalitions.

Except in the case of eco-tourism, which was probably the least successful case, Europeans took the first initiatives in standards. The biodynamic Demeter trademark, and its certification process, was the first mover, but when the new wave of institutionalization and certification started during the second wave of environmentalism, IFOAM, ECOCERT, and BREEAM were ahead of their American counterparts, both in timing and in internationalization. This was partly a question of geographical scale; small-scale organic farmers in California and New England were a great distance away from each other, which made sharing concerns and setting standards all the more difficult. In organic foods and other products, national governments, other public agencies, and the EU became more closely involved in setting and supporting standards and certification.

Institutionalization required building coalitions among multiple stakeholders. The wider the coalition, the more successful was the certification in terms of membership and industry acceptance. This was evident in the cases of BREEAM and LEED building certifications, and also in some organic food certifications, like KRAV. However, the trade-off was making sure compliance costs were not too high. Standards and certification needed to be set at such a level that they were seen as being within reach of most participants. They had to be attractive enough that the NGOs who administered them would be funded. Audit fees themselves were problematic, as they restricted certification to firms able and willing to spend the money. Standards and certification sometimes created misaligned incentives and the potential for gaming. For-profit certification companies and private certifiers paid by clients were not incentivized to enforce standards with the utmost rigor, although they needed to protect their reputation and credibility. Standards and certification also provided the tools for the growth of "eco-business" and greenwashing, as we will see in Chapter 9.

Conversely, however, the conflicting, weak, or confusing certifications which emerged in natural beauty did little to counter the diffused identities of those industries, and in the case of eco-tourism may have made it worse. In an industry which sold primarily in a local market, as in the case of food, it mattered less if one country had a KRAV standard and another Bio-Suisse. In an industry such as eco-tourism, in which there was a great deal of international travel, fragmented standards had a lot more potential to cause consumer confusion, yet global certification schemes were so general that their real-world value was questionable.

The challenge of certification in these industries went right to the heart of the whole concept of green or sustainable industry. Once the concept had to be codified, the multiple alternatives in the domain of sustainability were exposed, as were the difficulties in identifying suitable metrics to define them. Certification shed light on the contested meaning of sustainability. USDA certification of organic, for example, made no mention of any health benefit, either to individuals or the planet, while for others the whole point of avoiding pesticides was the damage done to people and the soil. It was, as a result, not a coincidence that the biodynamic movement was decades ahead in certification, as it has a unified point of view and an ideology shared among its membership. Once certification was extended to wider constituents, who did not share strong ideological beliefs and were responsible to shareholders for making profits, the process of setting metrics typically, perhaps inevitably, started with the lowest common denominator. When compliance officers replaced values, certification turned out to have considerable downsides.

Notes

1. Craig N. Murphy and JoAnne Yates, *The International Organization for Standardization (ISO): Global Governance through Voluntary Consensus* (London: Routledge, 2009), pp.77–81. The "14000 series" consists of thirteen individual standards numbered non-consecutively. The number of such ISO certifications rose from 36,000 in 2001 to 110,000 in 2005.

2. Andrew L. Russell, *Open Standards and the Digital Age* (Cambridge: Cambridge University Press, 2014), p.16.

3. The importance of institutional entrepreneurship is explored in Julie Battilana, Bernard Leca, and Eva Boxenbaum, "How Actors Change Institutions: Towards a Theory of Institutional Entrepreneurship," *Academy of Management Annals* 3, no. 1 (2009), pp.65–107.

4. Herbert H. Koepf and Bodo von Plato, *Die biologisch-dynamische Wirtschaftsweise im 20. Jahrhundert: Die Entwicklungsgeschichte der biologisch-dynamischen Landwirtschaft* (Dornach: Verlag am Goetheanum, 2001), pp.220–8.

5. "Biodynamic Agriculture at a Glance," <http://www.demeter-usa.org/downloads/Demeter-At-A-Glance.pdf>, accessed August 1, 2016.

6. Otto Schmid, "Development of Standards for Organic Farming," in William Lockeretz (ed.), *Organic Farming: An International History* (Wallingford: CABI, 2007), p.154.

7. Julie Guthman, *Agrarian Dreams* (Berkeley: University of California Press, 2004), p.112.

8. Interview with Janet and Grant Brians, July 19, 2007, in UC Santa Cruz Library, "Cultivating a Movement."

9. History of the CCOF, <http://www.ccof.org/images/logo.gif>, accessed February 13, 2015.

10. Interview with Janet and Grant Brians; Janet McGarry, "Organic Pioneers Reflect on 40 Years of CCOF," January 22, 2013, <http://www.cuesa.org/article/organic-pioneers-reflect-40-years-ccof>, accessed May 4, 2016.

11. Roland Bechmann, "Une Seule Terre: Stockholm 1972," *Aménagement et Nature* 26 (June 1972), pp.34–5.

12. Arlette Harrouch, "Le rôle de Nature et Progrès dans l'histoire de la bio en France: Témoignage d'une actrice engagée," *Nature et Progrès* 44 (November–December 2003).

13. IFOAM Founding Letter, <http://infohub.ifoam.bio/sites/default/files/page/files/founding_letter.pdf>, accessed July 5, 2016.

14. "Le Congrès de Versailles, 3, 4, 5 Novembre 1972," *Nature et Progrès* 9, no. 4 (January–March 1973).

15. Bernward Geier, "IFOAM and the History of the International Organic Movement," in Lockeretz (ed.), *Organic Farming*, pp.175–85.

16. Michael Sligh and Thomas Cierpka, "Organic Values," in Lockeretz (ed.), *Organic Farming*, pp.37–8.

17. <http://www.ifoam.bio/en/core-campaigns/climate-change-campaign>, accessed July 4, 2016.

18. Bernhard Freyer, Jim Bingen, and Milena Klimek, "Ethics in the Organic Movement," in Bernhard Freyer (ed.), *Re-Thinking Organic Food and Farming in a Changing World* (Dordrecht: Springer, 2015), pp.13–44; Schmid, "Development of Standards."

19. Darren Halpin, Carsten Daugbjerg, and Yonatan Schwartzman, "Interest-Group Capacities and Infant Industry Development: State-Sponsored Growth in Organic Farming," *International Political Science Review* 32, no. 2 (June 2011), pp.147–66.

20. <http://www.natureetprogres.org/nature_et_progres/histoire_nature_progres.html>, accessed July 8 2015.

21. <http://www.penser-bio.fr/Historique>, accessed July 8, 2015.

22. Laure Bonnaud and Nathalie Joly, *L'alimentation sous contrôle: Tracer, auditer, conseiller* (Dijon: Educagri, 2012), p.112.

23. <http://www.natureetprogres.org/nature_et_progres/histoire_nature_progres. html>, accessed June 22, 2015.

24. Bonnaud and Joly, *L'alimentation*, p.113.

25. Susanne Padel and Nic Lampkin, "The Development of Governmental Support for Organic Farming in Europe," in Lockeretz (ed.), *Organic Farming*, pp.96–7.

26. See Richard Gould, "EN 15267, A New Unified Testing and Approval Scheme for Automated Measuring Systems," <http://www.eu-etv-strategy.eu/pdfs/ETV_ AMS_scheme_and_potential_framework_web.pdf>, accessed August 7, 2016.

27. Bonnaud and Joly, *L'alimentation*, p.113.

28. Gaëlle Richard, "Ecocert, géant du label bio," *Sud-Ouest*, October 24, 2013, <http://www.sudouest.fr/2013/10/24/ecocert-geant-du-label-bio-1208751-2461.php>, accessed June 14, 2014.

29. Anon., "Ecocert leader de la certification bio," press release, Chambre de Commerce et d'Industrie de Gers, November 2010, <http://www.gers.cci.fr/ac tualites/ecocert-leader-de-la-certification-bio.html>, accessed June 14, 2014.

30. Bonnaud and Joly, *L'alimentation*, p.114.

31. Ibid., p.115.

32. <http://www.ecocert.com/sites/default/files/u3/ECOCERT_PR_certifica tion BiodiversityCommitment_EN.pdf>, accessed September 3, 2014. The US certifier was Indiana Certified Organic and the Swiss was the IMO Group.

33. Anon., "Label AB: Un business pas bien bio," weblog entry of *Courant Libre*, a service of L'Agence Française de Développement, August 4, 2009, <http://courantlibre. solidairesdumonde.org/archives/2010/week25/index-1.html>, accessed June 8 2014.

34. Padel and Lampkin, "Development," p.97.

35. Peter Gibbon, "European Organic Setting Organizations and Climate-Change Standards," *OECD Global Forum on Trade*, June 9–10, 2009, <https://www.oecd.org/ tad/events/42850898.pdf>, accessed June 10, 2014.

36. Interview with Richard Marietta, Paris, June 8, 2011; Harrouch, "Le rôle de Nature et Progrès."

37. Kirsten Bransholm Pedersen, Bente Kjærgård, and Birgit Land Pedersen, "Økologiske værdier under forandring?" in Forbrugerrådet, *Værdier til salg— forbrugernes forventninger og krav til den økologiske fødevareproduktion* (Copenhagen: Forbrugerrådet, 2009).

38. Gibbon, "European Organic Setting Organizations."

39. Ibid.

40. Magnus Boström and Mikael Klintman, "State-Centered Versus Non-State-Driven Organic Food Standardization: A Comparison of the US and Sweden," *Agriculture and Human Values* 23 (2006), pp.163–80. KRAV Market Report 2016, <http://www.krav.se/sites/www.krav.se/files/krav_market_report_2016_eng_webb.pdf>, accessed July 29, 2016.

41. McGarry, "Organic Pioneers."

42. <http://www.ocia.org/about-ocia>, accessed May 5, 2016.

43. Brandon H. Lee, "The Infrastructure of Collective Action and Policy Content Diffusion in the Organic Food Industry," *Academy of Management Journal* 52, no. 6 (2009), p.1249.

44. Grace Gershuny, "Conflicts over Organic Standards," September 23, 2010, <http://social-ecology.org/wp/2010/09/conflicts-over-organic-standards>, accessed October 23, 2016.

45. Kathleen Merrigan, "The Role of Government Standards and Market Facilitation," in OECD, *Organic Agriculture: Sustainability, Markets and Policies* (Wallingford: CABI, 2003), p.277; Boström and Klintman, "State-Centered."

46. Ronnie Cummins, *Genetically Engineered Food: A Self-Defense Guide for Consumers* (New York: Marlowe, 2000).

47. Christopher Marquis, Marya Besharov, Bobbi Thomason, and Leah Kaplow, "Whole Foods: Balancing Social Mission and Growth," Harvard Business School Case No. 9-410-023 (August 29, 2009).

48. Bruce A. Scholten, *U.S. Organic Dairy Politics: Animals, Pasture, People, and Agribusiness* (New York: St Martin's Press, 2014).

49. Peter Laufer, *Organic: A Journalist's Quest to Discover the Truth behind Food Labeling* (Guildford, CT: Globe Pequot Press, 2014).

50. Caelainn Barr, "Organic-Farming Boom Stretches Certification System," *Wall Street Journal*, December 9, 2014.

51. Cornucopia Institute, "Regulations Not Being Enforced—Watchdog Asks for USDA to Remove Program Management," December 11, 2014, <http://www.cornucopia.org/2014/12/investigation-factory-farms-producing-massive-quantities-organic-milk-eggs/#more-14709>.

52. <http://www.nsf.org/consumer-resources/green-living/organic-certification/personal-care-products-containing-organic-ingredients/>, accessed May 6, 2014.

53. Alex Nicholas and Charlotte Opal, *Fair Trade: Market-Driven Ethical Consumption* (London: Sage, 2004); Matthew Anderson, *A History of Fair Trade in Contemporary Britain* (Basingstoke: Palgrave Macmillan, 2015).

54. Laura Raynolds and Michael Long, "Fair/Alternative Trade: Historical and Empirical Dimensions," in Laura T. Raynolds, Douglas L. Murray, and John

Wilkinson (eds.), *Fair Trade: The Challenges of Transforming Globalization* (London: Routledge, 2007), pp.15–32; Kathryn Wheeler, *Fair Trade and the Citizen Consumer: Shopping for Justice?* (New York: Palgrave Macmillan, 2012); Keith R. Brown, *Buying into Fair Trade: Culture, Morality, and Consumption* (New York: New York University Press, 2013), pp.9–10, 14.

55. Geoffrey Jones and Simon Mowatt, "National Image as a Competitive Disadvantage: The Case of the New Zealand Organic Food Industry," *Business History* 58, no. 2 (2016), pp.1262–88.

56. FiBL and IFOAM, *The World of Organic Agriculture 2016* (February 2016), <https://shop.fibl.org/fileadmin/documents/shop/1698-organic-world-2016.pdf>, accessed July 1, 2016, pp.141–2.

57. Laufer, *Organic.*

58. Telephone interview with Can Turhan, August 19, 2013.

59. Stephanie Strom, "What's Organic," *New York Times*, November 15, 2016.

60. In 2015 the International Directory of Organic Food Wholesale and Supply Companies listed 45 separate schemes, 38 of them based in Europe. <http://www.organic-bio.com/en/labels/>, accessed May 19, 2016.

61. Interview with Rodolphe Balz, April 13, 2011; Rodolphe Balz, *The Healing Power of Essential Oils* (Twin Lakes, WI: Lotus Light, 1996).

62. Interview with Rodolphe Balz, April 13, 2011.

63. Ibid.

64. Ibid.

65. Amy B. Olson, "Non-State Market Driven Governance: A Case Study in Organic and Natural Personal Care Products," Walden University Ph.D., 2010.

66. Andrew McDougall, "Natrue Adopts IFOAM Definition for Acceptance of Organic Raw Materials," August 12, 2014, <http://www.cosmeticsdesign-europe.com/Regulation-Safety/Natrue-adopts-IFOAM-definition-for-acceptance-of-organic-raw-materials>, accessed, July 8, 2015.

67. Euromonitor International, "Natural Beauty Goes Mainstream, but Organic Beauty Stand-off Continues" (March 15, 2010).

68. Olson, "Non-State Market Driven Governance," p.66.

69. Lötzerich-Bernhard, interview with Julie Tyrrell.

70. Anon., "New Standard for Natural Personal Care Products," *WholeFoods Magazine*, February 24, 2011, <http://www.wholefoodsmagazine.com/news/main-news/new-standards-natural-personal-care-products>, accessed June 4, 2015.

71. Mintel, "Natural and Organic Personal Care—Europe," December 2010.

72. Michelle Yeomans, "Consumers Still Struggle with the Difference Between Natural and Organic," November 18, 2014, <http://www.cosmeticsdesign-europe.

com/Market-Trends/Consumers-still-struggle-with-the-difference-between-natural-and-organic>, accessed August 2, 2015.

73. Interview with Sam McKay (Jurlique), Boston, MA, January 18, 2013; Geoffrey Jones and Andrew Spadafora, "Jurlique: Globalizing Beauty from Nature and Science," Harvard Business School Case No. 9-314-087 (March 24, 2014).

74. Roger Courtney, "Building Research Establishment: Past, Present, and Future," *Building Research and Information* 25, no. 5 (1997), pp.285–91; telephone interview with Alan Yates (BRE Group), November 21, 2014.

75. <http://www.superhomes.org.uk/the-team>, August 5, 2015.

76. Anon., "Environment '90: ECD Partnership Enjoys Success as the Industry Turns to Energy-Efficient Design," *Construction News*, April 12, 1990.

77. David Nicholson-Lord, "Healing the Sick; Architects Have Finally Seen the Light and Are Putting It into Their Buildings," *The Independent* (London), November 10, 1991.

78. Anon., "Environment '90."

79. Christopher Warman, "Energy Efficiency Keynote of 1990s," *The Times*, January 19, 1990.

80. Telephone interview with Alan Yates (BRE), November 21, 2014.

81. Roger Baldwin, Stan Leach, John Doggart, and Miles Attenborough, *BREEAM 1/90: An Environmental Assessment for New Office Designs* (Garston, UK: BRE, 1990).

82. Interview with Alan Yates; Nicholson-Lord, "Healing the Sick"; Anon., "ECD Partnership."

83. Nicholson-Lord, "Healing the Sick"; Anon., "Green Test for Broadcasting House," *The Times* (London), February 12, 1992.

84. Interview with Alan Yates.

85. Anthea Masey, "The Green House Blues," *Mail on Sunday*, April 30, 1995; David Nicholson-Lord, "Reading the Green Gauge," *The Independent*, June 9, 1996.

86. Courtney, "Building Research Establishment," p.289.

87. Ibid., p.290; <http://www.bre.co.uk/page.jsp?id=1712>, accessed June 15, 2015.

88. Roger Baldwin, Alan Yates, Nigel Howard, and Susheel Rao, *BREEAM 98 for Offices* (Garston, UK: BRE, 1998).

89. Thilo Ebert, Natalie Essig, and Gerd Hauser, *Green Building Certification Systems* (Munich: DETAIL/Institut für internationale Architektur-Dokumentation, 2011), p.31; Mike Scott, "Insulation Will Not Be Enough to Hit Targets," *Financial Times*, April 18, 2008.

90. <http://www.breeam.org/about.jsp?id=66>, accessed October 23, 2016.

91. Institute for Applied Technology, *The Center for Building Technology: A Perspective* (Washington, DC: U.S. Government Printing Office, 1976).

92. Jim Heldenbrand, "Design and Evaluation Criteria for Energy Conservation in New Buildings," <http://nvlpubs.nist.gov/nistpubs/sp958-lide/260-265.pdf>, accessed June 2, 2016.

93. Ibid., pp.262–3.

94. David Gottfried, *Greed to Green: The Transformation of an Industry and a Life* (Berkeley: Worldbuild Publishing, 2004), pp.3–9, 53–8.

95. Ibid., pp.61–3.

96. Ibid., pp.70–3.

97. Ibid., pp.87, 98–101, 109–12; Lee Scopel, "U.S. Green Building Council's President Discusses Past, Future of LEED System," *Daily Journal of Commerce* (Portland, OR), September 23, 2002.

98. Gottfried, *Greed*, pp.123–4.

99. Ibid., pp.134–5.

100. Ibid., p.165.

101. Public Technology, Inc., *Sustainable Building Technical Manual: Green Building Design, Construction, and Operations* (Washington, DC: Public Technology, Inc., 1996).

102. Christine Ervin, "Market Transformation: The Green Building Story," <http://www.christineervin.com/downloads/Christine_Ervin_chapter.pdf>, p.112, accessed June 4, 2016.

103. Ibid., p.115.

104. Gottfried, *Greed*, pp.177–8; David Gottfried, *Explosion Green: One Man's Journey to Green the World's Largest Industry* (New York: Morgan James, 2014), p.241.

105. <http://www.usgbc.org/leed>, accessed August 5, 2016; <http://www.usgbc.org/articles/three-billion-square-feet-green-building-space-leed%C2%AE-certified>, accessed August 5, 2016. There were also over 20,000 USGBC members by 2009. Ebert, Essig, and Hauser, *Green Building*, pp.39, 41.

106. Gottfried, *Greed*, pp.211–14, 219–22.

107. <http://www.worldgbc.org/worldgbc/become-member/members/>, accessed June 2, 2016.

108. "LEED in Motion: Greater China," February 2015, <http://www.usgbc.org/resources/leed-motion-greater-china>, accessed February 8, 2016.

109. World Building Council, "Will Europe Stay Competitive in the Global Green Building Market," September 16, 2013, <http://www.worldgbc.org/regions/europe/ern-blogs/general/will-europe-stay-competitive-global-green-building-market>, accessed June 5, 2016.

110. Jerry Yudelson, *Green Building Trends: Europe* (Washington, DC: Island Press, 2009), p.28.

111. Kira Gould and Lance Hosey, *Women in Green: Voices of Sustainable Design* (Bainbridge Island, WA: Ecotone, 2007), p.110.

112. Lloyd Alter, "The Four Sins of LEEDwashing: LEED Green Buildings That Perhaps Aren't Really Green," *Treehugger*, March 17, 2009.

113. Kaid Benfield, "As Good and Important as It Is, LEED Can Be So Embarrassing," January 18, 2013, <http://switchboard.nrdc.org/blogs/kbenfield/as_good_and_important_as_it_is.html>, accessed July 4, 2016.

114. Interview with Megan Epler Wood, March 26, 2015, Cambridge, MA.

115. Western later took over the Kenyan Wildlife Service after its former head, the controversial Richard Leakey, was dismissed in 1994. On Leakey, see Graham Boynton, "Richard Leakey: What Does Angelina Jolie See in This Man?" *The Guardian*, April 30, 2015.

116. Interview with Megan Epler Wood.

117. Martha Honey, *Ecotourism and Sustainable Development* (Washington, DC: Island Press, 2008), pp.6–10, 15–16.

118. Hitesh Mehta, Ana L. Báez, and Paul O'Loughlin, *International Ecolodge Guidelines* (Washington, DC: International Ecotourism Society, 2002).

119. Interview with Megan Epler Wood.

120. <http://www.greenglobeint.com/about/history>, accessed July 16, 2015; interview with Megan Epler Wood.

121. Honey, *Ecotourism*, pp.113–14.

122. Ibid., p.17.

123. Interview by Royal G. Jackson with Richard Holland, August 28, 1992, Royal G. Jackson Papers. Series II.1, Oregon State University Special Collections.

124. On Roberts and Tikal Tours, see Geoffrey Jones and Andrew Spadafora, "Entrepreneurs and the Co-Creation of Ecotourism in Costa Rica," Harvard Business School Working Paper No. 16–136 (2016).

125. Amos Bien, "Environmental Certification for Tourism in Central America: CST and Other Programs," in Martha Honey (ed.), *Ecotourism & Certification: Setting Standards in Practice* (Washington, DC: Island Press, 2002), pp.147–9; Interview with Bary Roberts by Andrew Spadafora, June 9, 2014, CEM, Baker Library Historical Collections, Harvard Business School, <http://www.hbs.edu/businesshistory/emerging-markets/>.

126. Interview with Bary Roberts.

127. Bien, "Environmental Certification," p.150; Interview with Jim Damalas by Andrew Spadafora, June 4, 2014, CEM, Baker Library Historical Collections, Harvard Business School, <http://www.hbs.edu/businesshistory/emerging-markets/>.

128. Interview with Megan Epler Wood.

129. Ibid.

7

Can Finance Change the World?

Before the 1980s the possibility that the financial system could contribute to environmental sustainability would have been seen as, at best, implausible. Banks and other financial institutions were associated with profit-seeking, not sustainability. Yet putting together the financial resources to start and grow a business was one of the most fundamental challenges faced by green entrepreneurs. Start-ups serving unproven markets and technologies—sometimes motivated by non-mainstream philosophies—faced special challenges, especially since the financial services industry had never incorporated sustainability into its business models. Stephan Schmidheiny, the founder of the Business Council for Sustainable Development, and his co-author noted in *Financing Change*, published in 1996, that there were "reasons to believe" that financial markets "encourage short-term goals, undervalue environmental resources, discount the future, and favor accounting and reporting systems that do not reflect environmental risks and opportunities."[1]

The core problems related to how risk and opportunity were assessed. It was difficult to quantify environmental benefits and risks—and that much more difficult to quantify their impact on the financial performance of portfolio companies or bank clients. Greener businesses often required long-term investment horizons because they were developing new technologies or searching for a new consumer segment. The misalignment between time horizons was magnified as concepts of shareholder capitalism and agency theory became fashionable from the 1980s, creating institutional shareholder pressures on chief executives of public companies to focus on quarterly earnings. As capital markets became globalized from the 1980s, technological developments, such as computerized high-frequency and algorithmic trading, favored transactions over long-term investment. Even absent such structural shifts, the lack of disclosure by most listed companies of any meaningful information about their environmental, social, and governance information impacts meant that purposeful allocation of capital to support sustainability was very challenging.[2]

As the environmental and social costs of conventional businesses went largely unaccounted, their financial performance typically looked better compared to green firms. There was a widespread belief that greener businesses financially underperformed because there was a trade-off between profits and sustainability. Industries such as tobacco, alcohol, and fossil fuels were widely perceived in financial markets as amongst the most profitable investments.[3] Empirical evidence corroborated the view that mutual funds that included so-called "sin stocks" performed very well.[4]

This was a major issue as, especially in higher-income economies, growing numbers of people became investors in firms, primarily through their pension funds. As financial assets became an increasingly important part of household balance sheets, the value of securities and the profits that underpinned price mattered. Money managers and institutional investors, whatever their personal beliefs about sustainability, were obligated by fiduciary duty to seek the best financial return.[5] Even the investment officers of environmental organizations and endowments, such as Nature Conservancy and the United Nations Environment Programme (UNEP)'s pension fund, declined to invest their funds according to sustainable criteria.[6] This view of fiduciary duty, Schmidheiny and Zorraquín noted, was "at the core of arguments to exclude soft or non-financial factors, such as the environment or social goals, in investment decisions."[7]

Difficulties in fund-raising were a recurrent theme in the capital-intensive solar industry, even in the United States which had the deepest capital markets and by far the largest venture capital industry. The PV solar pioneers of the 1970s found it impossible to raise funds from banks and venture capitalists, and were left with the large oil companies. Even in much less capital-intensive industries such as organic food and natural beauty where reliance on family, friends, and savings could start a business, scaling required much more access to cash which was very difficult to secure for a long period. Beyond the United States, funding opportunities were far fewer. In Japan, venture capital firms were usually affiliates of large banks and insurance companies. They were typically highly risk-averse, and as the founder of the organic food retailer Oisix, discussed in Chapter 5 discovered, they would only lend to companies which had an established revenue stream.[8]

When external funding was raised by green entrepreneurs, they often faced a clash of values. "The two to three million in bridging was the beginning of the carving up of Earth's Best," Arnie Koss wrote about the first venture capital investment in his organic baby foods business. "The investor pecking order would now constantly be reshuffled by the introduction of revolving advantageous stock positions, shareholder rights, voting trusts warrants, options, and first rights of refusal."[9] The venture capitalists, he added, were "the bad guys in this story."[10] For Paul Hawken, the most serious downside of venture capital was its tendency to push companies to scale too quickly so they could exit with a profit. Fast growth, he noted, tended to lead to many ventures failing, often literally, but also ethically. Large investments of external capital, he noted in his book *The Ecology of Commerce*, "tend to take over their beneficiaries, both in real terms and in the values they represent."[11]

By then the first discussions had begun about how to engage the conventional financial system on sustainability issues. Large commercial banks had already been drawn unwillingly into this domain as US court cases began to suggest that they might be held responsible for toxic waste issues.[12] In 1991 UNEP launched a financial initiative in association with a small group of commercial banks, including HSBC and Deutsche Bank, designed to raise the banking industry's awareness of the environmental agenda. In the following year, in the context of the Earth Summit in Rio, this group and UNEP called for an integration of environmental concerns into banking strategies. By the end of 1992, twenty-three of the world's leading commercial banks, representing $1.5 trillion in combined assets, had signed the UNEP statement. By then, the term "sustainable banking" had also come into use, having first been used in the context of multilateral development banks.[13] In 1995 UNEP signed a voluntary agreement with a group of large insurance and reinsurance companies which pledged to help achieve a sound environment.[14]

The reality behind such pledges was another matter. In 2016 a review of twenty-five large US, Canadian, and European banks by the Rainforest Action Network, Sierra Club, and other environmental groups found that collectively they invested a combined $784 billion over the previous two years in Arctic drilling, Canadian oil sands mining, coal mining, and coal-fired power plants.[15] The British government, acknowledging the low involvement of investment banking in financing environmental projects, launched its own UK Green Investment Bank in 2012, which could only invest in infrastructure projects which met specified green purposes. It invested in sixty-six infra-structure projects and seven funds over the following four years before being privatized.[16]

Overall, the glacial progress of the greening of conventional finance was apparently confirmed by the fact that UNEP felt obliged to publish an extensive report in 2015 designed "to advance a step change in the financial system's effectiveness in mobilizing capital towards a green and inclusive economy."[17]

The focus of this chapter is not the greening of conventional financial institutions, but rather the attempts to address the perceived misalignment between green businesses and the conventional financial system through creating new types of financial institutions. Rudolf Steiner was the inspiration of this idea. In 1919 he proposed the foundation of "a bank-like institution that would in its financial activities serve economic and spiritual enterprises, which are oriented towards the goals as well as the attitude of the anthroposophically-oriented worldview." He envisaged that such a bank would not aim at profit-maximization but, rather, would assist other anthroposophical enterprises both financially and with guidance in their operations through being a direct par-ticipant in managing them.[18] However, over fifty years would pass before the first such formal institutions were created.

This chapter looks at how green entrepreneurs, starting in the 1980s, envisaged a financial system that could support green businesses in innovative ways rather than, as Hawken suggested, undermine them. Unlike the previous chapters in Part II, which proceeded through a range of industries, this one focuses on only one: banking and finance. It looks at how innovations in banking, investing, and venture capital gave birth, improbably, to key concepts of sustainability like environmental reporting and impact investing. Although banking had seemed at odds with sustainability, the view emerged that sustainability itself would not be sustainable as a real-world business practice without the involvement of the finance industry.

Sustainable and social banks

Beginning in the 1970s, and accelerating after 1980, a number of alternative banks were established, some inspired by the ideas of Steiner. These institu-tions predated by two decades or more the UNEP Financial Initiative launched in 1991. This new type of financial institution came to be called "social banking," although terms such as "sustainable," "ethical," and "alternative" banking were also used, reflecting that they typically concentrated on sustainability in the broadest sense of the word. A working definition, provided by Olaf Weber, is that such banks "exclusively offer financial products and services that have a positive impact on society, the environment, or sustainable development."[19]

In 2014 the Global Alliance for Banking on Values (GABV), a worldwide association of social banks formed five years earlier, had twenty-five members with a total balance sheet of more than $50 billion. It was a disparate group which included microfinance institutions based in emerging markets; BRAC, the world's largest NGO, based in Bangladesh; two California-based banks which focused on lending to low-income communities; and a number of European banks, with assets totaling $16 billion, which had mixed ecological and social objectives, which will be the main focus of this section. They included the Germany-based Gemeinschaft für Leihen und Schenken (GLS) Bank (with assets of $2.2 billion), the Dutch-based Triodos Bank ($6.7 billion), and the Danish-based Merkur Bank ($0.2 billion).[20] There were more social banks around the world, perhaps as many as 600, but the GABV probably represented the largest of them. It was a tiny part of the global financial system. Total banking assets in United States alone were $15 trillion in 2014.[21]

The first two social banks in Europe were founded in Germany and Britain in 1974, both of them influenced by Steiner's philosophy. The origins of the German bank lay in an encounter on a tram in the city of Bochum between a lawyer, Wilhelm Ernst Barkhoff, and an anthroposophist attempting to finance a new Waldorf school in 1956.[22] Barkhoff had been born into a poor Catholic family, joined the Nazi party, and fought in World War II on the Russian front after his legal studies were ended. He emerged from the war with a skepticism about both church and state but a strong conviction about the need for citizens to help improve society. A long-time associate once described him as "a funny mixture of true conservative Catholic and total revolutionary."[23]

Barkhoff found his first encounter with anthroposophists unusual, but he soon warmed to the idea of trying to finance the school. He used his connections with the local branch of Commerzbank, the large commercial bank, to get funding for the school and subsequently for an expansion. He achieved a better interest rate by pooling the credit of the students' parents. Barkhoff engaged in community projects from the late 1950s, and often spoke about the need for a new kind of bank whose purpose was not to make money from money but to provide socially useful goods. Working with an employee at his legal practice, he formalized their school project system in 1961 by setting up a non-profit trust institution which supported more schools. The system, in cooperation with Commerzbank, earned the trust a commission on each new customer it drew for the bank.[24] Barkhoff was not sympathetic to the student movement's goals to use the state to improve society, preferring instead "a social initiative of citizens themselves."[25] In 1967 he organized a credit guarantee association, formed with over a thousand people, which allowed members to guarantee or backstop loans to other members through putting up the collateral for their loans required by mainstream banks.[26]

Seven years later Barkhoff formed GLS as a mutually-owned cooperative bank. The membership and deposits grew out of the preexisting membership in the trust and the credit guarantee association.[27] It was small: the bank had just over $800,000 on its balance sheet after a year. Anthroposophy motivated the venture, but the immediate motivator was the perceived need to finance the Waldorf schools and biodynamic farms which needed capital.[28] Barkhoff led the bank until he retired in 1981.

GLS operated differently than conventional banks. It charged interest on its loans by tabulating its annual operating costs and spreading them across its clients. Depositor-members offered GLS borrowers the use of their capital cheaply, or even in some cases for free.[29] The low- or no-yield savings account, adopted by subsequent social banks in Europe, was based on the assumption that there were "green depositors" who would forgo interest on their savings so as to pass the cost-savings on to the projects the bank was financing. At the beginning, about 20 percent of GLS depositors adopted a no-interest savings account, while the others accepted below-market interest rates.[30]

GLS screened the institutions to which it lent to ensure a match of values, and aimed at maximum transparency. The bank published details of its projects to depositors, eventually after 1980 in their newsletter, along with the amount of the loan, and sought input from depositor-members concerning what sorts of projects they preferred to finance.[31] Although GLS began with a broad social agenda, as environmental concerns rose amongst its German members, it became progressively more formally ecological. It had financed Demeter-certified biodynamic farming from early days.[32]

In 1989, the bank set up the first fund to finance wind-power projects in Germany.[33]

The British equivalent of GLS was Mercury Provident, also established in 1974 by anthroposophists. Like GLS, it was a cooperative with a full banking license. It also initially lent to organic farmers, but over time the portfolio included small recycling operators, a wind farm, and Steiner-inspired education and health projects. However, its balance sheet never passed $18 million, partly because it strictly avoided lending outside the anthroposophical community. In 1994 it was acquired by the Dutch-based Triodos Bank, which was by then four times larger.[34]

The Triodos Bank, which grew to be Europe's largest social bank, was formed in 1980 with $600,000 in share capital, and was part of a new wave of social banks in that decade. Its origin lay in a study group established in 1968 by four Dutch professionals for a heterogeneous set of people including anthroposophists, religious believers, and admirers of the small-is-beautiful concept of E. F. Schumacher. They discussed how money could be used more consciously and transparently. They were aware of the GLS Bank but from the beginning sought to engage with people beyond the anthroposophist community. A non-profit foundation was established in 1971. In 1980 they secured a full banking license and began operating as Triodos Bank.[35]

The name Triodos signified Steiner's "threefold path." Steiner's "threefolding" concept divided society into economic, legal/political, and cultural components which needed to be treated holistically. The founders of Triodos saw its threefold task as supporting social, cultural, and environmental goals and institutions. They aimed to promote development in these three areas at a reasonable profit.[36] The Preamble to the Bank's Articles of Association stated that "Triodos Bank is—entirely freely—associated with the philosophy initiated by Rudolf Steiner, anthroposophy."[37] Before 1999, executive board members had to be "inspired" by Steiner's anthroposophy, and they had to be approved by anthroposophical and Christian associations, but they did not formally need to belong to a Steiner organization. Like GLS, the bank supported schools, music venues, and other cultural institutions, alongside entrepreneurs in social and ecological businesses with lending aligned with anthroposophical principles and practices rather than systematized data-driven criteria.[38] "Profit is not an objective in itself," noted Peter Blom, who became CEO in 1997 after working with the bank since 1980.[39]

There was also significant experimentation as Triodos, originally just a commercial lender, launched small venture capital funds. In 1980 it created the first green fund in Europe, the biodynamic agriculture fund. Others followed in wind and solar energy. In 1998 the separate funds were rolled into Triodos Green Fund. Triodos worked to hire professionals with relevant industry experience, which both helped make the funds successful, and encouraged others to launch such funds.[40]

The bank was also active in encouraging a tax incentive scheme for individuals in the Netherlands, which was introduced in 1995, that raised the attractiveness of investment in green funds there and contributed to the success of its own offerings. At the time, Triodos controlled nearly the entire Dutch market for green funds, which was a mere $14 million; by 2010, it had $800 million under management, and the green funds class based in the country had grown to almost $10 billion.[41] Triodos also entered the broader Socially Responsible Investment (SRI) fund market, whose development is discussed in the following section. The earliest and best-known SRI fund, Triodos Meerwaarde Fonds, was founded in 1997 and co-managed with Anglo-Dutch insurer Delta Lloyd. Traded on the Amsterdam stock exchange, it was one of the Netherlands' first SRI funds.[42]

The leaders of Triodos sought to expand their business without losing their values. This was not a straightforward matter, as the bank expanded in scale and geographically, opening elsewhere in Europe, beginning with Belgium in 1993 and Britain in 1995. It hired bankers trained at conventional institutions for their expertise, but it limited executive salaries and did not pay bonuses.[43] Triodos worked hard to insure that the bank's committed depositors remained actively involved in determining where their money should go. Like GLS, the company placed an unusual emphasis on transparency in publishing its loan portfolio.[44]

Although Triodos was established as a limited company, it was deliberately not listed on the stock exchange. Instead, shares are held by the Foundation for the Administration of Triodos Bank Shares (SAAT). The foundation's board voted all of the shares and was tasked with doing so in the interests of all the bank's stakeholders; investors in the bank purchased depositary receipts from SAAT at a price based on net asset value. The SAAT board was in turn elected by the holders of depositary receipts, and the receipt holders themselves are limited to 1,000 votes and 10 percent of issued receipts.[45] The design was explicitly meant, as the bank's head of public affairs noted, to "avoid the short-termism of being listed on a stock exchange."[46]

Triodis's impact was, for its size, significant. Its investments in wind energy in Denmark and Germany in the 1990s played a significant role in the industry's growth.[47] It facilitated the often fragile early stages of growth of multiple green firms. A case in point was the Danish organic foods retailer Aarstiderne, to which it extended credit at a crucial time to assist in its expansion. In 2001 it took a 20 percent stake in the company in return for $2 million plus the provision of loans, which provided the funds needed for the business to expand.[48] Along with GLS, Triodos also lent to the Egyptian organic producer Sekem, and in 2007 both banks took $3.4 million equity stakes in it.[49] As a business institution, Triodos performed well. It was almost untouched by the 2008 financial crisis, earning a return on equity between 4.5 percent and 5.6 percent between 2007 and 2012.[50]

Triodos was the largest of a cluster of social and ecological banks in Europe which emerged in the 1980s. Merkur Andelskasse (Merkur Cooperative Bank) was started in the city of Aalborg in Denmark in 1982. Its origins lay with a small cooperative retail store called Aurion that sold biodynamic products, one of whose employees wanted to open a bakery to add on to the business. Lars Pehrson and his colleagues reached out to GLS to discuss financing, and they were so impressed by their encounter that they resolved to found a Danish equivalent. They made use of a 1934 law which allowed the formation of a savings and loan organization so long as it was a closed association in a particular geographic area and relinquished the right to advertise. The original members contributed their own savings. In 1985, when the European Union harmonized banking law among its members, Merkur was grandfathered in as a fully-fledged financial institution.[51] After the large FDP price cuts for organic food in 1987, the bank received funding from the GIAA Trust established by Canadian-born Ross Jackson and his Danish wife Hildur, which financed many conversions to organic farming in the country.[52] By 1997, the bank had total assets of $27 million and had financed over 500 projects, of which about one-fifth were in biodynamic and organic farming. Assets had risen to $411 million by 2015.[53]

Finally, the Ecology Building Society, formed in Yorkshire in Britain in 1981, was a small for-profit cooperative building society, with assets of $227 million in 2014. This mutually owned mortgage lender originated when a local solicitor named David Pedley, who had strong environmentalist views and owned a small organic farm, struggled to secure a mortgage on a property as he did not want to modernize it but keep the fittings as they were. The new institution was built up by people with self-sufficiency and environmentalist views, and links to the Ecology Party (a forerunner of the Green Party). Although Pedley left the organization just after it started, a talented team of Jim Walker, Gus Smith, Tony Weekes, Bob Lowman, and later Paul Ellis and Pam Waring was successful in raising money from members, many of whom were Quakers, to finance building projects which upheld ecological principles. The initial seeking of funds had to happen at very local level. Weekes later recalled that much of his time was spent "attending things like green fairs and green festivals and various other alternative organizations to try and say, look this is something different."[54]

The Ecology Building Society demonstrated that relatively small size did not rule out having an impact. It was instrumental in opening up a whole category of property lending on self-build properties, which the conventional banking sector would not finance, and so created a market for green building products in Britain as a result.[55] The bank also worked with ecological builders. In the early 1990s it sponsored a book written by an architect on the ecological renovation of buildings. Subsequently, it helped form the Passivhaus Trust, the British branch of the organization supporting the Passivhaus ("passive house" in English) low-energy design standard which had been developed in Germany in the early 1990s.[56]

During the 1970s and 1980s, then, green entrepreneurs, many of them inspired by Rudolf Steiner's philosophy, created banks which offered an alternative to conventional banking. They provided a new source of finance for entrepreneurs building green businesses, especially, but not only, in organic agriculture and renewable energy and in niche areas such as ecological building products and homes. The pioneers considered here were followed by others: Alternative Bank Schweiz (ABS) in Switzerland was founded in 1990, Ekobanken in Sweden was founded in 1996, Banca Etica in Italy in 1999, and New Resource Bank in San Francisco in 2006. However, these banks remained, in the context of the global financial system, minnows, besides being primarily confined to Western Europe. Their limited size had at least two causes: because the banks restricted themselves to other anthroposophical businesses; and because they generally restricted themselves to lending to businesses whose values they shared. Financing depended on green depositors being willing to accept lower or no interest in order to do social good; this greatly limited the deposit base. Green savers were rarer than green consumers. Within the broader category of social banks, it was the microfinance institutions, such as BRAC and Grameen Bank, which grew enormously in scale and impact. However, these banks had shown that viable alternative banking institutions could be built, as their robustness during the 2008 financial crisis indicated.

Socially responsible investing

Like social banking, SRI (socially responsible investing) grew from the 1980s through the efforts of a number of dynamic entrepreneurs, some of them very values-driven, and others representing a more hybrid mix of conventional and values-driven financiers. The primary characteristic of SRI was exclusionary investment, or avoiding companies or entire industries deemed socially irresponsible, although in the 1990s it also became associated with strategies to promote positive changes in society. Unlike social banking, there was a strong American presence in the formative stages of the industry. Also unlike social banking, women were prominent in shaping the industry.

The historical origins of SRI are often traced back to Christian sects such as the Quakers and Methodists in eighteenth- and nineteenth-century Britain and the United States, who abstained from investing in what they judged morally reprehensible businesses such as slavery and alcohol.[57] SRI-type investing strategies continued in the twentieth century. In Britain, the Church of England started screening according to ethical criteria with its first equity investing activity in 1948.[58] The first retail mutual fund to offer ethical and social screens in the United States was probably the Foursquare Fund, started in Boston by Christian Scientists in 1962, which screened out companies producing alcohol, tobacco, and pharmaceuticals.[59] In the United States especially, shareholder activism became an important contributor to the ideas behind ideologically driven SRI. During the civil rights era of the 1960s, some firms were targeted by activists securing proxy votes to enable them to attend annual general meetings where they pushed for more black employees. The beginnings of the divestment movement from apartheid-era South Africa in the 1970s were shareholder activist campaigns to persuade firms to divest.[60]

Shareholder activism provided the context for the emergence of a number of new ventures during the 1970s. In 1969 Alice Tepper Marlin, a financial analyst and anti-Vietnam War activist, founded the non-profit Council on Economic Priorities (CEP) to provide research for investors and "disseminate unbiased and detailed information on the practices of U.S. corporations in four major areas: minority employment, effect on the environment, defense production and foreign investment."[61] CEP's second report, published in 1970, was a study of the environmental performance of the pulp and paper industry, which attempted to show investors objectively—without political advocacy—that the most polluting companies were also poorer performers on financial grounds.[62] There were others who shared Tepper Marlin's ideas, and combined them with for-profit businesses. In 1971 two Methodist ministers, Luther Tyson and J. Elliott Corbett, founded the Pax World Fund, headquartered in Portsmouth, New Hampshire, which combined the traditional screens against alcohol, tobacco, gambling, and armaments with an anti-Vietnam war identity.[63]

During the 1970s, a decade when environmental concerns began to achieve much more public prominence, there emerged a new category of entrepreneurs: conventional financiers who became interested in sustainability issues. In 1972 the mainstream New York investment firm Dreyfus & Co. added its own screened mutual fund, the Dreyfus Third Century Fund, which placed a greater emphasis on the natural environment than Pax. Howard Stein, who had become president of the brokerage house seven years earlier and was one of the pioneers of the mutual fund industry, saw the fund as a way of promoting his liberal political values, which included vocal opposition to the Vietnam War.[64]

During the 1980s this phenomenon of conventional financiers investing in SRI intensified. The first of this wave, the Calvert Social Investment Fund (CSIF), emerged from Calvert Investments, which had been established in 1976 in Washington, DC by D. Wayne Silby and John G. Guffey, Jr., classmates at the Wharton School. They had over $1 billion in assets under management by 1982.[65] Silby was a self-described "grateful product" of the 1960s who loved meditation. After attending a meditation retreat in which the Buddhist principle of "Right Livelihood," or integrating one's work with one's values, was discussed, Silby decided to allocate capital to create a filtered fund on condition that he "wasn't betting the ranch."[66] This was the origin of CSIF in 1982, which Silby intended would promote "human rights, environmental-ism, and equality."[67] Silby gathered well-known environmentalists and civil rights figures for its advisory council, including Robert Rodale and Amory Lovins.[68] Silby and Guffey sold the entire Calvert Group to Acacia Mutual Life Insurance in 1984, but retained their board memberships at CSIF.[69]

CSIF did not perform as well as the S&P 500 index during the 1980s, although it did much better in the late 1990s.[70] By 2000, Calvert had the largest family of SRI funds in the world, making up $2.4 billion of the company's $6.7 billion in total assets, with 220,000 shareholders.[71] Silby himself went on to co-found in 1987 with Josh Mailman, another active believer in Buddhist meditation and the angel investor who helped fund Stonyfield Farms, the non-profit Social Venture Network, designed as a platform to connect entrepreneurs who wanted to use business to create a more values-driven and sustainable world.[72]

At the same time as CSIF got underway in 1982, Joan Bavaria founded Franklin Research and Development Corporation (FRDC). While figures such as Howard Stein and Wayne Silby can be regarded as conventional financiers with a strong social consciousness, Bavaria was a values-driven green entre-preneur who became a formative influence both on the evolution of SRI and on reporting standards for corporate sustainability. She was a powerful expo-nent of the need to engage conventional business in environmental issues, but without compromising her core values.

Bavaria's importance as a green entrepreneur might have been hard to predict from her early career. Born in a small town in rural western Massa-chusetts, she developed an early love of nature and animals, but it was her ambition to be an artist which initially motivated her. She moved to Boston as a 17-year-old student at the Massachusetts College of Art, from which she eventually dropped out. In 1967 as a divorced mother of two children, one of whom was hospitalized with scarlet fever leaving her with large bills, she used a family connection to get a job as a secretary's assistant at the Bank of Boston. Curious and hardworking, she impressed her superiors and within eighteen months had been promoted to investment officer, an unusual step not only because she had started as a secretary but also because only four of the Bank's investment professionals were female. She later commented that she thought her appointment reflected the management's recognition that women could be paid less than men for doing an equally good job.[73]

Serendipity then came into play. The Bank of Boston's management assigned Bavaria to work with its wealthy female clients. She encountered a number who inquired how their money was being used. One client who had inherited wealth asked Bavaria how much of the world's wealth was being used to do good for society, "because she was feeling guilty about the money."[74] This interaction started Bavaria along the path of thinking how wealth could have an impact beyond generating financial returns. Another incident encouraged her transition into an activist. Trying to manage her work–life balance, she started a lunch-hour exercise class for fellow employees in her building. When the Bank decided that it needed the space for other uses, she protested the decision, even to the extent of gaining media coverage for it. Although the space was not returned, the Bank did agree to offer employees free membership in a health facility. This incident triggered a life-long concern for employment practices, particularly as they affected women. As she later remarked, "sometimes to make changes you have to find pressure points that are not always in the rules."[75]

In 1975, Bavaria, suspecting she would hit a glass ceiling at her bank because of being a woman, moved to Franklin Management, an investment house in Boston. She continued to receive requests from clients, including the pension fund of the University of California at Berkeley, who wanted to invest in firms screened for positive social and environmental impact. After seeing that returns on her screened accounts were higher than those earned on unscreened accounts, she approached Don Falvey, whose family owned Franklin Management and whom she later married, to form a separate SRI group, called Franklin Research and Development.

Despite facing skepticism inside and outside Franklin, Bavaria pushed ahead with the idea that she could both provide investors with a competitive return and achieve a positive ecological impact. She wanted, she later observed, "to look at capitalism in a multidimensional way."[76] FRDC screened out companies that polluted water and air, as well as those that made liquor, tobacco, and military goods or did business in South Africa.[77] It published a monthly newsletter called *Franklin's Insight*, one of the few publications on the SRI industry, which carried profiles of both attractive and controversial companies.[78] Beyond screening, Bavaria pursued dialogue with the managers of large corporations to convince them, in person, of the need for more sustainable practices. In 1982 FRDC was spun-off as a separate company and organized as a cooperative owned by its employees. FRDC, Bavaria told Stephanie Leighton when she joined the company in 1990—she would later become a partner—was about "social change through financial services."[79] By the end of 1988, it had a small but respectable $162 million in assets under management but lagged 2 percent in annualized returns against the S&P since inception.[80] It attracted a loyal investor base: two-thirds of FRDC's investors were high net worth individuals, and the remainder churches and small foundations.[81]

Bavaria created the CERES organization in 1989, to which she devoted much of the rest of her life and which we will examine in the next section. She continued to lead FRDC, whose assets had risen to $570 million by 1999. She changed its name to Trillium Asset Management that year in acknowledgment both of its pursuit of a triple bottom line, and its distinctively female leadership. "As a majority woman-owned firm at the time," a senior vice-president of Trillium later noted, "we chose a non-masculine image—a flower."[82]

Within the context of the male-dominated finance industry, Bavaria and her colleagues formed part of a cluster of women who took leading roles in the development of SRI, both in the United States and elsewhere. Some of these women worked for a time at FRDC. This was the case of Amy Domini. She began working as a typist in a brokerage firm in Cambridge, Massachusetts in 1973 and eventually became the company's first female broker. After receiving inquiries from clients about the possibility of avoiding certain stocks or actively promoting social or environmental goals through investing, she co-authored a book entitled *Ethical Investing* with her then-husband Peter Kinder, a lawyer, in 1984. While promoting the book, she came to the conclusion that to make her case, better data were required on both corporate social and environmental performance and the performance of SRI investors. She worked briefly at FRDC before settling in 1987 at another Cambridge firm, conducting much the same corporate accountability research as at FRDC. Kinder left his job entirely, and the couple built a business at home turning publicly available records into company audit reports. In 1990 they were joined by Steven Lydenberg, a long-time employee at Franklin, and founded KLD Research & Analytics, with an office in Harvard Square.[83]

In 1990 KLD launched an index of socially screened large-cap companies, designed to provide more rigorous measures of investing sustainably, and so make SRI appear professional in the finance industry. The index did not sell well, though eventually it became a symbol and a reference point. Domini attempted to sell mutual funds based on the index to the major fund managers, but without success. Consequently, in 1991 she launched what became Domini Social Investments to invest herself.[84] The firm grew slowly but successfully. The two companies separated when Domini and Kinder divorced in 1998. KLD, still run by Kinder, continued to expand its ratings, offering indices according to market capitalization, climate risk, and other categories.[85] Domini Social Investments' flagship fund, the Domini Social Equity Fund, was an index fund from the outset but was converted into an actively managed fund in 2006. It consistently underperformed the S&P 500.[86]

Women were also formative figures in SRI beyond the United States. Among them, Tessa Tennant was particularly influential both in her home country of Britain and in Asia. In 1988 she established the Jupiter Ecology Fund, which was among the first in a small wave of specifically green British funds; it became the most influential. Tennant had studied environmental science at the University of London and volunteered at the Green Alliance, an environmental think tank which had been founded in 1979. It was located close to the City of London, where many financial institutions were clustered around the Bank of England. "I kind of became super aware of the fact," she later recalled, "that the City was not engaged in the conversation (about the environment) at all. And yet it was quite clear that it was shareholders and investors that called the shots in the strongest possible way with companies . . . in terms of what got financed."[87]

Tennant was aware of the first SRI fund established in Britain. This was the Friends Provident Stewardship Fund, launched in 1984, after a decade-long struggle against government regulators by Charles Jacob, the investment manager of the Methodist Church, to establish a unit trust which screened out companies regarded as unethical.[88] Tennant was more intrigued by the development of SRI in the United States, which she visited in the fall of 1987. After an internship she landed at FRDC, she returned impressed and determined to follow the same path.[89] Coming from a wealthy family and having married into the aristocratic and eccentric Tennant family, she had the connections and contacts needed to start something in London.[90]

In fact, soon after Tennant returned to Britain she was approached by Derek Childs, a director of the then-leading merchant bank Warburg and a fund manager of its investment company, who had learned of her visit to see

SRI in the United States. Childs had invested successfully in a number of green technology companies and had begun to consider creating a green fund because it provided the opportunity, as Tennant later described, "to make money and do something good for the environment." Tennant used her experience at FRDC to write a prospectus for the new Merlin Ecology Fund, which became the flagship for Merlin Fund Management, founded in that year. Childs served as fund manager, where he broke from the precedent at the time by taking a quasi-private equity approach of investing in green enterprises at a very early stage and before they were listed. Tennant focused on solving data and methodology issues of evaluating company environmental importance which created widespread cynicism concerning SRI.[91] The pursuit of investment opportunities in companies that held out the promise of genuine environmental improvements became a permanent feature of the Fund. Instead of simply screening for sin stocks, the Ecology Fund became motivated by, in the words of Charlie Thomas, the manager of the Fund after 2000, "the investment opportunity around environmental companies."[92]

The fund was renamed the Jupiter Ecology Fund in 1989 after Merlin was acquired by Jupiter Asset Management. Changes in management led Tennant and her team to move to another fund in 1994. By that date, the Ecology Fund still had assets of only $15 million, but it had reached $164 million by 2003. Thomas noted that even then they were still regarded as "the wacky greens. The tree huggers."[93] Unlike many of the pioneering funds, Jupiter Ecology became a resounding financial success. One of its largest investments was in Denmark-based Vestas, the leading global wind energy company. By 2012 it had returned 460 percent since inception and significantly beat its benchmark index, the IMA Global Growth index. In that year the Fund's assets exceeded $650 million.[94]

Meanwhile Tennant found that she was unable to induce her new firm, NPI, to prioritize environmental investments. She persuaded her employers to let her go to Asia on her own account to try to establish a sustainability fund. She had become convinced that the pace of investment in the region was so great that it was critical to encourage green investment. "Sustainability had got to take hold there *fast*," Tennant observed, "otherwise it would just make anything in Europe and America just look a joke."[95] In 2001 she and David St Maur Sheil established the Association for Sustainable and Responsible Investment in Asia as a non-profit environmental consultancy based in Hong Kong and dedicated to promoting corporate responsibility and sustainable investment practice.

It was in Japan, however, where the concept of SRI developed first in Asia and where the first fund was launched in 1999. A key figure in the creation of the Fund was Mizue Tsukushi. While still a child she had converted to Catholicism and later, with her husband, who had worked in a labor union, she spent a year journeying on land from Asia to France, being shocked by the poverty of India. Returning to Japan after getting pregnant in Paris, she began working as a secretary for a French engineering company in Tokyo, and then for the oil company Total, before in 1988 moving to a Belgian-owned bank. After entering finance, she began to feel that finance had a real potential to improve the world. "It's true that the financial world makes rich people rich," she later remarked, "but it's a kind of know-how, and I thought if I could understand it, I could use it for poor people."[96]

In 1990 Tsukushi moved to the Tokyo office of the Union Bank of Switzerland and became interested in the concept of SRI, especially after meeting Tessa Tennant in 1997 when she came to the conference which led to the Kyoto Protocol on climate change. When Tsukushi's plans to launch a fund within her bank were frustrated, she established The Good Bankers Co. in 1998 with the idea of launching an SRI fund.[97] During the following year a study group, almost entirely of women, was formed to consider how finance could be used to enhance sustainability.[98]

The prospects for launching an SRI fund in Japan seemed low given the low risk profile of Japanese investors. Most individuals held assets in cash or bank deposits, with only 10 percent holding shares. Many regarded investing in shares as a form of cheating by seeking to make money without working. Even pension funds invested in bonds rather than shares. Nevertheless, the timing was propitious for Tsukushi. The Kyoto conference had raised the profile of environmental issues, as had the launch of Toyota's Prius model, the first mass-produced hybrid automobile, in 1997. The concept of a fund attracted the attention of Nikko, Japan's third largest brokerage firm. The Nikko Eco Fund was jointly developed by The Good Bankers Co., and the Nikko Securities Group, and launched in August 1999.

The Nikko Eco Fund was an immediate success. It expanded to 23 billion yen (over $200 million) in only ten days. It broke through traditional barriers to investment in equities by reaching a new demographic. An estimated

99 percent of the subscribers to the Fund were individual investors, largely women and young people. Assets surpassed 100 billion yen ($880 million) within four months, a level which it had taken Jupiter Asset Management seven years to reach. The success was temporary. The bursting of the dot.com bubble in 2001 resulted in the Japanese stock market as a whole falling very sharply. Eco-funds were sharply criticized as being almost fraudulent. It proved difficult to regain traction, although the market did not disappear. In 2010 the market size of Japanese eco-funds was estimated at 400 billion yen ($4.5 billion).[99]

The prominence of female entrepreneurs in SRI in the United States, Britain, and Japan was noteworthy. Mariko Kawaguchi, a member of the study group behind the Nikko Eco Fund and an economist with the Daiwa Institute of Research, offered one explanation for why women appeared more prominently as actors in green finance. She drew attention to the general employment position of women in financial services. "In other industries," she noted, management is "very male dominated. It is men who get the chance to demonstrate their green concerns. In finance there were more women, but mostly in marginal roles, with men dominating the main power positions. In such marginal roles, woman have more freedom to do radical things."[100]

By the time the Nikko Fund was launched, SRI, unlike the situation two decades earlier, had an established niche, and one which continued to attract new entrants who could by then mobilize considerable resources in support of their endeavors. This was the case of the Swiss banker Reto Ringger who in 1995 launched his own financial firm, called Sustainable Asset Management (SAM), designed to "combine the principles of sustainability with financial markets."[101] Ringger perceived that there was a disconnect between the short time horizons of investment managers and the needs of pension funds to plan for decades into the future, and that long-term risks, such as climate change, needed to factor into decisions on investments. He believed that the more sustainable a company was, the more valuable it would become over time. Ringger sought, in other words, to demonstrate for all to see that profits and sustainability were positively correlated.

Securing initial funding from Swiss Re, the giant reinsurance company which was itself increasingly concerned about the impact of environmental shocks on its business,[102] Ringger constructed an index which would enable the monitoring of the price performance of sustainable companies over time.

Ringger partnered with Dow Jones, the American financial firm, to launch the Dow Jones Sustainability Index (DJSI) in 1999. Shortly thereafter Ringger established a fund based on the index and became an active asset manager.[103] The DJSI became widely used by both conventional and SRI fund managers. In its first few years it performed worse than the Dow Jones Industrial Average but matched broader indexes. By 2010 global assets invested according to the DJSI were over $8 billion. A whole family of other indexes was created.[104] Ringger sold his own holding in SAM in 2008 to the Dutch bank Robeco. Two years later he founded a private wealth management company, Globalance, which helped high net worth individuals invest in sustainability and strove to show clients as transparently as it could the ecological and social footprint of their investment portfolios.[105]

By 2014 global SRI assets were estimated to have reached $21.4 trillion, of which $6.57 trillion were in the United States and $13.6 trillion in Europe. The latter figure reflected Europe's catch-up in a business initially pioneered in the United States, as institutional investors, who accounted for 94 percent of assets in this class, allocated some of their vast funds to SRI.[106] SRI assets reached the trillions because their investment portfolios contained companies far larger than, say, Aarstiderne or Sekem. Their scale reflected the spread of sustainability language and practices to large conventional corporations, a trend which we will see more fully in Chapter 9. In 2004, when Paul Hawken's non-profit research organization Natural Capital Institute assembled a database of 602 SRI funds throughout the world, it found the cumulative investment portfolio of the combined funds was broadly the same as those of conventional mutual funds. The report concluded that "most SRI mutual funds allow practically any publicly-held corporations" to be included in their portfolios. Pax World Funds, to give one of many examples, had large shareholdings in the automotive manufacturer General Motors and Corn Products (later Ingredien), the manufacturer of the fructose syrup used in soft drinks which many blamed for contributing to increasing obesity and diabetes.[107]

Beyond such apparently odd investments, Hawken's primary complaint was that there was no transparency (or accountability) in screening and portfolio selection. This left investors unable to understand the rationale for the selection of certain firms. There appeared a strong bias in portfolio selections towards large, globalized corporations.[108] Critics pointed to misaligned structuring of SRI indexes. They used screening to evaluate the composition of an index, but then tracked changes in the share values of firms, rather than their sustainability performance.[109] There was some evidence that the threat of being excluded from an SRI index resulted in an improved sustainability performance, but this did not remove the doubts concerning how sustainability was being measured.[110] Hawken himself went into partnership with Baldwin Brothers, a Massachusetts-based independent advisory firm, to create Highwater Global Fund, intended as a fund for wealthy individuals. Screening was performed by Hawken and his team. Pharmaceutical companies and banks were excluded from the fund. Excluding banks greatly assisted the fund's performance following the 2008 financial crisis. Also excluded was Whole Foods Market due to its global supply chain and John Mackey's unusual messages about his competitor on a Yahoo! Message board.[111] Highwater remained a small fund.

SRI evolved over these decades, then, from being seen as "wacky" to becoming a $21 trillion niche in the investment world. It was largely co-created by a cluster of values-driven women, such as Joan Bavaria, Amy Domini, Tessa Tennant, and Mizue Tsukushi—many of them self-made—and a group of conventional male financiers like Howard Stein, Derek Childs, and Reto Ringger who sensed that there was a market to be served, and had a desire to do something positive. SRI was conceived as a means to reward sustainability strategies by conventional firms, but as it developed as a financial product, financial returns seemed to be prioritized over sustainability returns. The screening process was often so general that it seemed almost any company could be identified as sustainable. Arguably the uncertainty about the impact of SRI was one factor which led to the replaying of the single issue divestment strategy which had been used against apartheid South Africa. During the 2010s philanthropic foundations, churches, cities, and even Norway's sovereign wealth fund, the world's biggest, began divesting shareholdings in coal and, in some instances, other fossil fuels, in the hope of generating faster progress away from such fuels. The outcome, along with the frequent assertion that such divestment could be financially beneficial, remained to be seen.[112]

CERES and the Global Reporting Initiative

Joan Bavaria's creation of the Coalition for Environmentally Responsible Economies (or CERES) in 1989 was a major step in the process of building networks of businesses committed to sustainability, as well as developing metrics to measure it. In her pursuit of multi-dimensional capitalism, Bavaria set her insights on creating institutional frameworks to advance the mission of sustainability beyond FRDC itself. Her first move was the foundation of the Social Investment Forum (SIF) in the mid-1980s, which became the principal industry association for social investment professionals, and which started off meeting in the Boston offices of FRDC. In 1988 the SIF executive board began discussing the lack of hard information on many environmental issues, at least beyond pollution regulation. A process of connecting with environmental movements around the United States began, and committee members were tasked with developing a set of principles regarding corporate conduct on environmental matters to echo the Sullivan Principles on investments in apartheid-era South Africa.[113]

This work was underway when the *Exxon Valdez* oil spill occurred in March 1989, providing a catalyst which enabled Bavaria to drive the project forward. She was convinced that getting the metrics right was key to being able to use wealth to secure environmental and social improvements, because the right metrics could demonstrate that there was an economic as well as an ethical case to be made for sustainable investment. Bavaria had a talent for convincing people to join her endeavors, and she recruited as co-founder of CERES Denis Hayes, who had been the coordinator of the first Earth Day. His participation provided a source of legitimacy for CERES with environmentalist activists.[114]

A set of "Valdez Principles," subsequently renamed the CERES Principles, were released in the summer of 1989. They asked corporations to stop air and water pollution, conserve energy, market safe products, pay for damage to the environment, and make public reports on their progress.[115] Bavaria's self-stated aim was to "catalyze the release of standardized information on environmental performance, using the model of the Financial Accounting Standards Board." CERES aimed to work with companies on drafting a model environmental report that would provide the necessary data but not disclose proprietary business information. Signatories of the principles paid fees for the cost of CERES's monitoring and verification of compliance.[116]

It proved hard to get the project off the ground. By the end of 1990 CERES's membership included the California and New York City pension funds, hundreds of church groups under the umbrella of the Interfaith Center on Corporate Responsibility, and some environmental groups, including the Sierra Club, Friends of the Earth, and the National Audubon Society. There was no rush of corporate signatories to the Principles.[117] Aveda was the first privately-owned company to sign the CERES Principles, in 1989. Tom's of Maine and Ben & Jerry's followed, but larger firms were much slower to join.[118] Bavaria's recruitment of the California and New York pension funds, who were major institutional investors, provided her with some voice in corporate boardrooms.[119]

Bavaria initially ran both FRDC and CERES, but in 1996 she hired as executive director Bob Massie, an Episcopalian priest in the town of Somerville, next to Cambridge, Massachusetts. As a student Massie had been a prominent anti-apartheid activist. He had subsequently written a doctorate at the Harvard Business School on morality and large corporations, and lectured at Harvard Divinity School, where he had met Bavaria after he had invited her as a guest to a class on the institutional relationships between churches and corporations. Bavaria liked both Massie's track record in shareholder activism and his training at the Harvard Business School, and was also interested in his connections with religious activists. Massie accepted the position even though CERES had only enough money to pay six months of his salary.[120] Bavaria remained as chair of the organization until 2001.

CERES was important both in itself and because it served as a catalyst for the development of environmental reporting. In the late 1990s it set out with the Boston-based NGO Tellus Institute to establish sustainability reporting as a common practice worldwide, which came to fruition as the Global Reporting Initiative. "Measuring your performance above and beyond your legal requirements was considered completely insane," Massie, who drove the idea along with Allen White of Tellus, later remarked.[121] It was certainly considered insane in corporate America. Massie and White found it almost impossible to generate significant interest. White later described American business as "very defensive, and very litigious."[122]

Massie and White widened the scope of their search for partners. They assembled people from NGOs and accounting organizations, and in 1998 UNEP formally joined as a partnering institution. A steering committee, drawing members from Europe, Japan, India, and the United States, was formed to develop sustainability reporting guidelines. In 1998 John Elkington, who was recruited to the committee, advised that they expand the project beyond environmental reporting to wider social sustainability issues.[123] This set the work on a trajectory different from CERES. In 2000 the first version of the reporting Guidelines was established; in 2001 GRI became an independent organization based in Boston; and in 2002 a second version of the Guidelines was published encompassing ninety-seven reporting indicators. GRI was incorporated as an NGO based in Amsterdam. A third generation of Guidelines followed in 2006, and a fourth in 2013.[124]

During its first decade the GRI guidelines were used as a basis for more than 4,700 voluntary corporate reports in over seventy countries.[125] By 2008 nearly all of the 100 largest companies in Britain and Japan, and three-quarters of the largest US companies, had issued such reports, although the take-up of the idea was far less common elsewhere.[126] By 2016 GRI had hundreds of organizational stakeholders, including NGOs, educational institutions, and companies. Among the last, the core Gold Community of GRI, a grouping of stakeholders, included green company stalwarts, such as GLS, Triodos, and Natura, but also many large conventional corporations.[127] Overall GRI has had more of a global impact than CERES, which came to influence some of the largest US corporations, but still had less than seventy companies signed up in 2016.

Once more, as in the case of SRI, it was less straightforward to assess the overall impact of GRI on environmental sustainability. As in the case of certification programs and SRI screening, environmental reporting raised challenging issues concerning what was being reported. Environmental accounting was voluntary and not standardized, which made comparisons between companies difficult. Many studies noted selective disclosure of information.[128] It was not reassuring, in this respect, that members of the Gold Community of GRI included the German automobile manufacturer Volkswagen, which would acknowledge in 2015 that at least 11 million of its vehicles were equipped with software that was used to cheat on emissions tests in the United States.[129] It was noteworthy that it was virtually unknown for a company to report a deterioration in its environmental performance. Even if all reporting was done in good faith, the boundaries of what was reported typically covered only a limited range of corporate activities. Banks, for example, did not report the environmental impact of their borrowers' actions. If a bank financed, say, a mountain-top removal mining project, it did not factor in its reporting.

The information contained in GRI reports was also rarely related to the wider performance of corporations. The concept of "integrated reporting" aimed to more fully integrate financial and environmental reporting. The

Danish pharmaceutical company Novo Group was an early mover. At the beginning of the 1990s, it had been criticized by consumer and environmental advocates, including Ralph Nader and John Elkington, for the effects of its detergent enzymes and its use of genetically engineered organisms. The company invited its critics to examine its practices, both to revise the mistakes in their criticisms and to suggest ways of improving its environmental performance. The result was a long process which led, in 2004, to the company publishing a pioneering integrated report.[130] The first US company to issue an integrated report was the unlikely case of the United Technologies Corporation, the aerospace, defense, and construction company, in 2008. There was, however, no sudden breakthrough. The integrated reports issued by firms showed, once more, considerable variability in both the type of information reported across firms and by the same firm over time.[131]

The creation of CERES and the development of environmental reporting, then, represented further attempts, like SRI, to engage conventional business, and to provide a route and a language to shift business towards greater environmental sustainability. Bavaria's insight that developing metrics was essential if capital markets were to be recruited to the cause of sustainability was profound. The strategy rested on an optimistic assumption that the right metrics would demonstrate that profits and sustainability were compatible, and that there was not a massive trade-off. Environmental reporting went from being considered insane to being mainstreamed within two decades. This very speed, however, was indicative that the pain threshold for corporations reporting their environmental impact appeared limited.

Venture capital and impact investing

The provision of venture capital or private equity was a third means, alongside social banking and SRI, that finance services could use to support businesses seeking to make a positive ecological impact. Triodos and other social banks experimented with venture funds beginning in the 1980s. They were joined by other institutions, which took a diverse range of organizational forms, spanning venture capital and private equity investing. In 2007 a former McKinsey consultant coined the phrase "impact investing" to describe the phenomenon which he defined as seeking to make investments which sought "financial returns while also intentionally addressing social and environmental challenges."[132] Unlike SRI, impact investing did not cover buying shares of established companies or trying to affect big business environmental strategies at all, but instead involved taking a major stake in start-ups or early-stage companies, especially, if not always, in the developing world.

Like Joan Bavaria, these investors argued that sustainability could be profitable, and believed that if it was, the huge wealth available in global capital markets could be tapped to support sustainability. They were quite small, and although not in microfinance, they sought to provide capital for businesses which were much smaller than those which typically attracted venture capital funding. Many of the ventures had roots in international development.

An early mover in the United States, the Global Environment Fund, was established in Washington, DC in 1990. It used a private equity model of investing in entrepreneurial companies which sought to reduce the environmental impact, especially in energy and waste, of established conventional industries, broadly through incremental innovation. By 2016 the fund had invested $1 billion in over sixty companies across Africa, Asia, and Latin America, as well as in the United States and Central Europe.[133]

An ultimately less successful, model was adopted by Philip LaRocco and Christine Eibs Singer, who formed a new firm called LaRocco Associates in New Jersey in 1990. They had both previously worked at the Port Authority of New York and New Jersey, where they saw how public–private partnerships could be highly productive, but they both felt constrained by working in a governmental bureaucracy. LaRocco, a self-described "over-the-hill hippie," was motivated to help find a solution to global poverty, though over time he became more concerned with environmental impact. If people were divided into three categories—greedy bastards, bleeding hearts, and tree-huggers—La Rocco later observed, he was a bleeding heart who had subsequently become more of a tree-hugger.[134]

LaRocco Associates was a small firm which conducted consulting, research, and project management for international development clients and foundations. It was commissioned by the Rockefeller Foundation to assess the possibilities for private finance from, in Singer's words, the "global north" to create "environmental benefits in the global south."[135] The project concluded that the best way to address the challenges of both the environment and poverty was to focus on delivering renewable energy to the poor in developing nations, as the lack of energy appeared to be a driver of poverty. If supplied in the form of fossil fuels, there would be a major environmental cost.[136]

The Rockefeller project became the basis for E+Co, which LaRocco and Singer founded as a non-profit in 1994, and which within two years had absorbed LaRocco Associates. The new venture aimed to use capital from multiple sources to support small private enterprises in delivering off-grid, small-system renewable energy to underserved rural populations, as an alternative to the giant grid-based electrification projects development banks typically preferred. LaRocco and Singer imagined a hybrid of venture capital, public finance, project finance, and microfinance.[137]

Initially, LaRocco and Singer believed that E+Co's role would be limited to providing seed capital and demonstrating the profitability and viability of smaller businesses in renewable energy in so-called "frontier" markets—then exiting when conventional firms could take over.[138] However, there were acute issues executing the business model. As financial returns remained low in the market generally, E+Co sought capital from public sources, including philanthropic foundations and the multilateral development banks, in the form of grants and low-interest revolving loans. This public funding was problematic as it emerged that many such donors expected clear-cut start and end dates, which was not a good fit with start-up firms. Some donors disliked subsidizing for-profit businesses, and withdrew their support when enterprises showed signs of success. E+Co also struggled to exit investments as conventional lenders were unwilling to invest in them.[139]

As the venture got underway, LaRocco estimated that one out of five portfolio companies in which the firm invested would fail outright, three would stay small, and one would grow substantially and be financially successful.[140] His solution to such perceived high risk was diversification. E+Co invested in multiple technologies, from solar to hydro to cook stoves, and in many countries. By 2002, E+Co had a $9 million loan and equity portfolio with sixty-two active investments in more than twenty countries. These were overseen by a highly decentralized network of regional offices, run by local staff.[141] In 2009, when LaRocco retired as CEO, E+Co had $37 million of assets: over two-fifths of its investments in Asia and almost a further two-fifths in Africa. Over 70 percent of lending was to solar, biomass, and hydro-electricity.[142]

E+Co's policies generated considerable excitement. The *Financial Times* named it Sustainable Investor of the year in 2008: the runner-up was Sustainable Asset Management.[143] In that year E+Co reported it had supported 194 enterprises and that this support had facilitated clean energy access to 78 million people. However, managing such a decentralized and diversified business was tough, and seemed to depend heavily on LaRocco and Singer keeping the show on the road. When LaRocco retired and new members joined the board, primarily from conventional finance, the strains became apparent. Singer left the firm. In 2012 the decision was taken to wind E+Co down. Its portfolio investments in Africa were absorbed by a new for-profit private equity entity, while those in Latin America and Asia were taken over by other private equity firms.[144]

A set of financial institutions also emerged out of the Nature Conservancy. An atypical NGO, the Nature Conservancy was highly decentralized. Under the presidency of John Sawhill, a former McKinsey partner, after 1989 it began experimenting with market-oriented approaches to conservation.[145] In the course of protecting an area of the Virginia coastal shoreline that it had bought in 1969, the Conservancy in 1995 launched a for-profit company called the Virginia Eastern Shore Sustainable Development Corporation, aimed at helping to create fifty small businesses, primarily in eco-tourism, organic agriculture, and crafts, and to become profitable after four years. It struggled to combine making profits with pursuing sustainability. After a few years it became evident that green start-ups pursuing a triple bottom line were unable to become profitable against conventional incumbents in a short period of time. The firm was dissolved in 1999. It was noteworthy that a number of similar endeavors in the 1990s, such as USAID's ambitious Biodiversity Conservation Network, which financed forty-eight conservation-minded small businesses in Asia and the Pacific, largely floundered because of execution problems.[146]

As the meltdown of the Virginia experiment was underway, the Nature Conservancy, under Patricia Léon's leadership, also formed the EcoEnterprises Fund, designed as a ten-year fund, jointly with the Inter-American Development Bank. Tammy Newmark was hired to manage the fund after a career in Wall Street which had left her dissatisfied with the impact on communities of the finance industry.[147] Following her MBA at Wharton, where she wrote a thesis about the ability of entrepreneurs in developing countries to compensate for lack of capital through creativity, she held appointments at institutions which supported entrepreneurs addressing environmental problems, including the International Finance Corporation, before being approached to run the EcoEnterprises Fund.[148]

Although it had the support of the Conservancy and the Inter-American Development Bank's Multilateral Investment Fund (MIF), Newmark needed more capital. She worked with both foundations and individual donors in the Social Venture Network, but encountered widespread skepticism about the idea of a for-profit entrepreneurial conservation fund run by a non-profit. It was still shy of the desired capitalization when the fund was launched in 2000. Over the course of the fund's ten-year life, Newmark and her all-female investment team deployed $6.3 million in investments in twenty-three entre- preneurial companies based in ten Latin American countries. Like E+Co, EcoEnterprises offered not just capital but assistance in business planning. However, unlike E+Co, it stayed focused on one region, and invested heavily in screening, drawing on the resources of the Nature Conservancy and NGOs.[149] A number of the firms in which EcoEnterprises invested became considerable success stories, both in business terms and in providing income for rural communities. It invested in four eco-tourism projects (after reviewing 120), including one in Costa Rica, where the Fund was based. Among the successes was the Ecuadorian firm Terrafertil, which became a leading global supplier of organic golden berries, a native Andean fruit, and which developed a successful business selling dried tropical fruits, snack mixes, and juices under the label Nature's Heart throughout Latin America, the United States, Europe, and Asia.[150]

By 2009, Newmark could claim that her portfolio companies had generated 2,000 jobs and $290 million in revenues, and yielded an environmental benefit of 1.3 million acres of land preserved according to habitat and biodiversity criteria.[151] At the close of the fund's operating period, which included the outbreak of the global financial crisis, EcoEnterprises had not succeeding in making a profit, but it had broken even, excluding operating costs, and had demonstrated proof of concept. In its new iteration established in 2010, EcoEnterprise Partners II, capitalized at $20.5 million, the fund became independent of the Nature Conservancy.[152] By 2016 the second fund, still managed by Newmark, was almost fully invested. However, proof of concept was not matched by emulation. After fifteen years, the investors behind EcoEnterprises Fund were the same group of dedicated institutions and private individuals, and no equivalent fund had been launched.[153]

Although diverse in their backgrounds and approaches, then, LaRocco, Singer, and Newmark and their counterparts in the emergent industry of impact investing shared a belief that deploying capital to support green entrepreneurship could be an important means to facilitate sustainability. The path to achieve this proved not to be straightforward. There were hybrid organizational forms, including collaboration with NGOs and multilateral institutions. There were complete failures, such as the Virginia Eastern Shore Sustainable Development Corporation, and many problems in execution.

These ventures were faced with challenging issues of identifying the right companies to invest in and how to effectively manage their portfolios, which some managed far better than others. There was a major issue, especially for for-profit models, that green companies were not typically ones that became profitable quickly, because they continued to face the challenges of doing things in new ways, and in ways that did not involve rent-seeking from the Earth's resources. EcoEnterprises were among the institutions which proved that viable business models could be built. Yet proof of concept was not accompanied by a rush of new ventures and huge capital flows into sustainability, which remained a niche rather than a mainstream investment domain. While luminaries in the world of finance compared the emergent sector of impact investing to the early stages of the venture capital industry in the 1960s and 1970s,[154] in practice it remained more of a vision than a reality.

Conclusion

From the 1980s, then, there were multiple attempts to create a set of institutions which would recruit finance to assist the business of sustainability. They addressed a major issue: the assembly of financial resources and managerial capabilities to start and grow a business was one of the most fundamental challenges faced by green entrepreneurs, both in developed and certainly even more so in emerging economies. They were poorly served by conventional financial institutions which, by their very nature, doubted that sustainability was compatible with profitability or that wider definitions of profitability could be meaningful in the real world.

A reimagining of the role of financial services was the common thread which linked social bankers beginning with Barkhoff, SRI exponents such as Bavaria, and impact investors such as Newmark. Although they were heterogeneous in their motivations, ambitions, and achievements, they shared a common vision that finance could help rather than hinder sustainability. The radical nature of much of the experimentation might have reflected the fact that, unlike many other categories discussed in this book, women were prominent among the most formative influences. This cohort of women combined the boldness of their vision for the role of finance with patient and effective execution, often involving collaboration or consultation with different parties. For Bavaria, the self-taught asset manager who not only created a prominent socially responsible investment company but also an industry association and CERES, these traits were foundational.

The outcomes from these endeavors were positive, but not yet transformational. New financial products were created to deliver capital and address risk in green businesses, but they had yet to become mainstream. GLS, Triodos, and the other social banks both demonstrated the viability of an alternative means of conducting commercial banking and assisted multiple small green ventures to do business. Yet social banking remained marginal in the wider universe of commercial banking. FRDC, Good Bankers, and other pioneers overcame skepticism to create a trillion-dollar SRI industry, which also spawned influential institutions, including CERES, environmental reporting, and sustainability indexes. Yet SRI funds only accounted for a fragment of total investment funds, and the execution of many such SRI funds was such that the industry symbolized in many ways the contested nature of sustainability. Environmental reporting voluntarily spread widely to many large corporations, yet there were many uncertainties concerning what was being reported and how to interpret it. Finally, a small number of impact investors, although successfully facilitating many hundreds of green ventures, especially in emerging markets, remained a tiny part of the financial world.

As the financial crisis in 2008 demonstrated, the global financial system as a whole remained the opposite of sustainable, despite the calls since the 1990s for banks to integrate environmental concerns into their strategies. The green entrepreneurs in finance mapped out alternative paths, but the jury was out as to whether and how the financial industry as a whole would follow them—beyond using the language of sustainability. While harnessing financial markets in the cause of sustainability offered compelling new opportunities, there appeared to remain a shortage of significant green investors and green depositors who were willing to fund the exercise.

Notes

1. Stephan Schmidheiny and Federico Zorraquín, *Financing Change: The Financial Community, Eco-Efficiency, and Sustainable Development* (Cambridge, MA: MIT Press, 1996), p.4.

2. Siobhan Cleary, *Stock Exchanges and Sustainability*, United Nations Environment Programme, Inquiry into the Design of a Sustainable Financial System, Working Paper, December 2015, <http://unepinquiry.org/wp-content/uploads/2015/12/Stock_Exchanges_and_Sustainability.pdf>, accessed July 17, 2016.

3. Schmidheiny and Zorraquín, *Financing Change*, p.90; Matthew J. Kiernan, *Investing in a Sustainable World: Why Green Is the New Color of Money on Wall Street* (New York: AMACOM, 2009), chapter 2.

4. Harrison Hong and Marcin Kacperczyk, "The Price of Sin: The Effects of Social Norms on Markets," *Journal of Financial Economics* 93 (2009), pp.15–36.

5. John H. Langbein and Richard A. Posner, "Social Investing and the Law of Trusts," *Michigan Law Review* 79 (1980), pp.72–112; Stephen Viederman, "Fiduciary Duty," in Cary Krosinsky and Nick Robins (eds.), *Sustainable Investing: The Art of Long-Term Performance* (London: Routledge, 2008), pp.189–99.

6. Kiernan, *Investing*, chapter 3; Interview with Matthew Patsky, Boston, December 3, 2013; Interview with Ross Jackson, Birkerød, October 31, 2013.

7. Schmidheiny and Zorraquín, *Financing Change*, p.82.

8. Interview with Kohei Takashima, Tokyo, May 31, 2010.

9. Ron and Arnie Koss, *The Earth's Best Story: A Bittersweet Tale of Twin Brothers Who Sparked an Organic Revolution* (White River Junction, VT: Chelsea Green Publishing, 2010), p.231.

10. Ibid., p.308.

11. Paul Hawken, *The Ecology of Commerce* (New York: HarperCollins, 1993), p.150.

12. Schmidheiny and Zorraquín, *Financing Change*, p.13.

13. Raymond F. Mikesell and Lawrence F. Williams, *International Banks and the Environment: From Growth to Sustainability: An Unfinished Agenda* (San Francisco: Sierra Club Books, 1992).

14. Jan Jaap Bouma, Marcel Jeucken, and Leon Klinkers (eds.), *Sustainable Banking: The Greening of Finance* (Sheffield, UK: Greenleaf Publishing, 2001), pp.390–400; "Events and Initiatives That Have Shaped the Role of the Banking Sector in Sustainable Development," <https://www.iisd.org/business/banking/sus_timeline.aspx>, accessed January 8, 2016.

15. "Shorting the Climate: Fossil Fuel Finance Report Card 2016," <http://www.ran.org/shorting_the_climate>, accessed August 11, 2016.

16. Terry Macalister, "Green Investment Bank Could Be Snapped up by Foreign Buyers," *The Guardian*, March 2, 2016.

17. United Nations Environment Programme, Inquiry into the Design of a Sustainable Financial System, *The Financial System We Need*, October 2015, <http://apps. unep.org/publications/index.php?option=com_pub&task=download&file=011830_en>, accessed June 27, 2015.

18. Steiner quoted in Christoph Lindenberg, *Rudolf Steiner: Eine Biographie*, vol. 2: *1915–1925* (Stuttgart: Verlag Freies Geistesleben, 1997), p.699.

19. Olaf Weber, "Social Banks and their Development," *European Financial Review*, October 21, 2014, <http://www.europeanfinancialreview.com/?p=3507>, accessed August 18, 2015.

20. Roland Benedikter "Social Banking and Social Finance: Building Stones Towards a Sustainable Post-Crisis Financial System?" *European Financial Review*, February 12, 2012, <http://www.europeanfinancialreview.com/?p=2027>, accessed May 2, 2016.

21. <https://research.stlouisfed.org/fred2/series/TLAACBW027SBOG>, accessed March 8, 2016.

22. Caspar Dohmen, *Good Bank: Das Modell der GLS Bank* (Freiburg: Orange Press, 2011), pp.16–17.

23. Ibid., p.27.

24. Ibid., pp.17–18, 23.

25. Ibid., pp.15–16.

26. Ibid., p.22.

27. <https://www.gls.de/privatkunden/english-portrait/>, accessed August 13, 2015.

28. Dohmen, *Good Bank*, pp.38–9.

29. Ibid., pp.13, 25; Eva Schneeweiss, "GLS Bank: Successfully Sustainable," in Heiko Spitzeck, Michael Pirson, and Claus Dierksmeier (eds.), *Banking with Integrity: The Winners of the Financial Crisis?* (Basingstoke: Palgrave Macmillan, 2012), p.111.

30. Dohmen, *Good Bank*, p.13.

31. Schneeweiss, "GLS Bank," 109; Dohmen, *Good Bank*, p.11.

32. Dohmen, *Good Bank*, p.139.

33. Ibid., p.66.

34. Paul Gosling, "Ethical Banks to Merge," *The Independent*, January 30, 1994; Interview with Paul Ellis, Pam Waring, Gus Smith, Jim Walker, and Tony Weekes, Silsden, November 8, 2013.

35. Interview with Thomas Steiner, Zeist, November 4, 2013.

36. Katrin Käufer, *Banking As If Society Mattered: The Case of Triodos Bank* (Cambridge, MA: MIT CoLab, 2011), p.55, <https://colab.mit.edu/sites/default/files/

Banking_as_if_Society_Mattered.pdf>, accessed October 8, 2015; Rebecca Henderson, Kate Isaacs, and Katrin Käufer, "Triodos Bank: Conscious Money in Action," Harvard Business School Case No. 9-313-109 (June 20, 2013).

37. *Articles of Association of Triodos Bank, N.V.* (Zeist: Triodos Bank, n.d.), Preamble, <http://docplayer.net/14936460-Articles-of-association-of-triodos-bank-n-v.html>, accessed August 10, 2016.

38. Henderson, Isaacs, and Käufer, "Triodos Bank," pp.5–7; Käufer, *Banking*, pp.44–6; Frank Jan de Graaf, "Triodos Bank—Mission-Driven Success Pays Off: From Dutch Enfant Terrible to European Business Leader," in Spitzeck, Pirson, and Dierksmeier (eds.), *Banking*, p.161.

39. <http://www.triodos.com/en/about-triodos-bank/what-we-do/our-expertise-overview/sustainable-banking/peter-blom/>, accessed July 14, 2016.

40. De Graaf, "Triodos Bank," p.165; Henderson, Isaacs, and Käufer, "Triodos Bank," pp.7–8.

41. Theo van Bellegem, "The Green Fund System in the Netherlands," in Bouma, Jeucken, and Klinkers (eds.), *Sustainable Banking*, pp.234–44; Käufer, *Banking*, pp.60–2.

42. Käufer, *Banking*, pp.26.

43. De Graaf, "Triodos Bank," p.165; Käufer, *Banking*, pp.48ff.

44. Käufer, *Banking*, p.68.

45. Ibid., p.58.

46. Interview with James Niven, Zeist, November 8, 2013.

47. Henderson, Isaacs, and Käufer, "Triodos Bank," pp.4, 8, 13.

48. Interview with Thomas Harrtung, Barritskov, May 22, 2013.

49. Dohmen, *Good Bank*, p.152; "Triodos und GLS Bank take 5m euro holding in Sekem Group," March 4 20,07, <http://www.nna-news.org/cgi-bin/dada/mail.cgi?fla vor=archive;list=news;id=20070304152002>, accessed June 8, 2016.

50. Henderson, Isaacs, and Käufer, "Triodos Bank," pp.4, 8, 13.

51. Lars Pehrson and Henrik Platz, "Fra Græsrod til Professionel Bankvirk-somhed," in Lars Pehrson et al. (eds.), *Merkur 25 År* (Copenhagen: Merkur Bank, 2007), pp.10–12.

52. Ibid., p.14; Interview with Ross Jackson, Birkerød, October 31, 2013; Pehrson, "Merkur fylder 30 år," *Pengevirke*, March, 2012, p.25.

53. Lars Pehrson, "Merkur gennem 15 år," *Sociale Penge*, March 1997, p.30; Merkur Andelskasse, Årsrapport 2015.

54. Interview with Tony Weeks, Silsden, November 8, 2013.

55. Interview with Paul Ellis, Silsden, November 8, 2013.

56. Interview with Tony Weekes, November 8, 2013. The book was Edward Harland, *Eco-Renovation* (Cambridge: UIT, 1993).

57. Russell Sparkes, *Socially Responsible Investment: A Global Revolution* (Chichester: John Wiley, 2002), chapter 2; Peter D. Kinder, Steven D. Lydenberg, and Amy L. Domini, *Investing for Good: Making Money While Being Socially Responsible* (New York: HarperBusiness, 1993), p.12; Steve Schueth, "Socially Responsible Investing in the United States," *Journal of Business Ethics* 43, no. 3 (2003), p.189.

58. Sparkes, *Socially Responsible Investment*, p.51; <http://www.churchofengland.org/media/36534/gambling.pdf>, accessed August 1, 2016; <http://www.eccr.org.uk/module-htmlpages-display-pid-18.html>, accessed July 2, 2016.

59. Myra Alperson et al., *Better World Investment Guide*, Council on Economic Priorities (New York: Prentice Hall, 1991), pp.2–3; Harvey D. Shapiro, "Doing Well While Doing Good," *New York Times*, August 7, 1983; Thomas Watterson, "Prospects for the Smaller Fund: Greater Opportunity and Risks," *Christian Science Monitor*, May 16, 1986.

60. Kinder, Lydenberg, and Domini, *Investing for Good*, chapter 5.

61. Sparkes, *Socially Responsible Investment*, p.280; Steven D. Lydenberg, *CEP's First Decade* (New York: Council on Economic Priorities, 1980), p.5.

62. David Vogel, *Lobbying the Corporation: Citizen Challenges to Business Authority* (New York: Basic Books, 1978), p.132.

63. Amy L. Domini, with Peter D. Kinder, *Ethical Investing* (Reading, MA: Addison-Wesley, 1984), pp.134–5; Sarah M. Gantz, "Luther E. Tyson, 85, Applied Social Activism to Mutual Fund Investing," *Boston Globe*, May 22, 2008.

64. Anon., "Dreyfus Premier Third Century Approaches the Third Millennium," November 24, 1999, <http://www.socialfunds.com/news/save.cgi?sfArticleId=87>, accessed July 27, 2015.

65. Sam Brownell and Sara Herald, "The Story of Calvert," in Cary Krosinsky (ed.), *Evolutions in Sustainable Finance* (Hoboken, NJ: John Wiley, 2011), p.91; Anon., "Pioneers of Social Investing: John G. Guffey and D. Wayne Silby," *Wharton Alumni Magazine* (Spring 2007), <https://www.wharton.upenn.edu/wp-content/uploads/125anniversaryissue/guffey-silby.html>, accessed August 12, 2016.

66. Anon., "Creating an Impact on Investing: D. Wayne Silby, W'70," *Wharton Club of New York Magazine* (Winter 2013), p.16.

67. Brownell and Herald, "The Story of Calvert," p.92.

68. Jill Lawrence, "Socially Concerned Investors Are Offered Variety of Funds," *Reading Eagle*, November 29, 1983.

69. <http://www.wharton.upenn.edu/125anniversaryissue/guffey-silby.html>, accessed July 6, 2015. Calvert is today a subsidiary of Ameritas Life Insurance Corp.

70. Peter D. Kinder, Steven D. Lydenberg, and Amy. L Domini, *Social Investment Almanac* (New York: Henry Holt, 1992), p.398: Sparkes, *Socially Responsible Investment*, p.91.

71. Sparkes, *Socially Responsible Investment*, pp.91–2.

72. <http://www.svn.org/who-we-are/about-svn>, accessed October 8, 2015.

73. Interviews with Pat Davidson, March 5, 2016, and Chris Clark, March 17, 2016, cited in Geoffrey Jones and Seema Amble, "Joan Bavaria and Multi-Dimensional Capitalism," Harvard Business School Case No. 9-317-028 (September 6, 2016).

74. Sandra Waddock, *The Difference Makers: How Social and Institutional Entrepreneurs Created the Corporate Responsibility Movement* (Sheffield, UK: Greenleaf Publishing, 2008), p.69.

75. Quoted in Jones and Amble, "Joan Bavaria," p.3; Interview with Cheryl Smith and Stephanie Leighton (Trillium), Boston, December 3, 2013.

76. Jones and Amble, "Joan Bavaria," p.4.

77. Stan Hinde, "Joan Bavaria's Crusade for the Environment," *Washington Post*, December 23, 1990.

78. Kinder, Lydenberg and Domini (eds.), *Social Investment Almanac*, pp.245–7; see also Domini, with Kinder, *Ethical Investing*, pp.65–6.

79. Interview with Stephanie Leighton.

80. Jones and Amble, "Joan Bavaria," p.9.

81. Interview with Cheryl Smith.

82. Ibid.

83. Waddock, *Difference Makers*, p.92.

84. Ibid., pp.85, 94–5, 97–9.

85. Ibid., p.99.

86. Colm Fay, "Domini and BP," in Krosinsky (ed.), *Evolutions*, p.83; Jennifer F. Cheng, "Domini Social Investments: A CSR Case Study," Graduate School of International Relations and Pacific Studies, University of California at San Diego (Fall 2007), p.17; <https://www.domini.com/domini-funds/fund-performance>, accessed June 8, 2016.

87. Telephone interview with Tessa Tennant, February 6, 2014.

88. Craig Mackenzie, "Ethical Investment and the Challenge of Corporate Reform: A Critical Assessment of the Procedures and Purposes of UK Ethical Unit Trusts," University of Bath Ph.D., 1997.

89. Interview with Tessa Tennant.

90. Tom Willis, "The Final Days of London Bohemian Henry Tennant," *Evening Standard*, February 23, 2011.

91. Interview with Tessa Tennant.

92. Interview with Charlie Thomas (Jupiter Ecology), London, November 7, 2013.

93. Ibid.; Mark L. Trevitt, "Jupiter Ecology," in Krosinsky (ed.), *Evolutions*, pp.17–19.

94. Trevitt, "Jupiter Ecology," pp.11, 24–5.

95. Interview with Tessa Tennant.

96. Interview with Mizue Tsukushi (The Good Bankers), Tokyo, April 18, 2014.

97. Ibid.

98. Interview with Mariko Kawaguchi (Daiwa Institute of Research), Tokyo, April 17, 2014.

99. Mizue Tsukushi, "Women's Finance Initiative Activities Japanese Economy: SRI's Growth Potential in Japan," *Japan Spotlight* (May/June 2010).

100. Interview with Mariko Kawaguchi.

101. Reto Ringger, "A Vision of a Sustainable Bank," TED Talk, October 23, 2010, <http://www.youtube.com/watch?v=hw5fk-ko-k4>, accessed July 14, 2016.

102. Neils Viggo Haueter and Geoffrey Jones, "Risk and Reinsurance," in Neils Viggo Haueter and Geoffrey Jones (eds.), *Managing Risk in Reinsurance: From City Fires to Global Warming* (Oxford: Oxford University Press, 2017).

103. Thomas O. Murtha and Ashley Hamilton, "Sustainable Asset Management," in Krosinsky (ed.), *Evolutions*, p.55.

104. Ibid., pp.53–7; Alois Flatz, Lena Serck-Hanssen, and Erica Tucker-Bassin, "The Dow Jones Sustainability Group Index," in Bouma, Jeucken, and Klinkers (eds.), *Sustainable Banking*, p.232.

105. Murtha and Hamilton, "Sustainable Asset Management," pp.54–5.

106. Global Sustainable Investment Alliance, "Global Sustainable Investment Review," 2014. In contrast, in the United States individuals accounted for a quarter of SRI investors.

107. Paul Hawken, "Socially Responsible Investing" (October 2004), <http://community-wealth.org/sites/clone.community-wealth.org/files/downloads/report-harkin.pdf>, accessed July 2, 2016.

108. Ibid., pp.21–3.

109. Oren Perez, "The Green Economy Paradox: A Critical Inquiry into Sustainability Indexes," *Minnesota Journal of Law, Science & Technology* 17, no. 1 (2016).

110. Aaron K. Chatterji and Michael W. Toffel, "How Firms Respond to Being Rated," *Strategic Management Journal* 31, no. 9 (2010), pp.917–45.

111. Alixis van Gelder, Dean Martucci, and Erika Kimball, "Highwater Global," in Krosinsky (ed.), *Evolutions*; Marc Gunther, "Paul Hawken's Winning Investment Strategy," *Huffington Post*, April 17, 2010.

112. Daniel C. Apfel, "Exploring Divestment as a Strategy for Change: An Evaluation of the History, Success, and Challenges of Fossil Fuel Divestment," *Social Research: An International Quarterly* 82, no. 4 (2015), pp.913–37; "World's Biggest wealth Fund excludes 52 Coal-related Groups," *The Guardian*, April 15, 2014.

113. Joan Bavaria, "CERES and the Valdez Principles," in Kinder, Lydenberg, and Domini (eds.), *Social Investment Almanac*, p.138; Waddock, *Difference Makers*, p.130.

114. Halina S. Brown, Martin de Jong, and Teodorina Lessidrenska, "The Rise of the Global Reporting Initiative: A Case of Institutional Entrepreneurship," *Environmental Politics* 18, no. 2 (2009), pp.182–200; Jones and Amble, "Joan Bavaria."

115. Bavaria, "CERES," pp.139–40.

116. Ibid., pp.140–1; Christopher McKenzie, "Environmental Investing: A Suggestion for State Legislation," in Kinder, Lydenberg, and Domini (eds.), *Social Investment Almanac*, p.42.

117. Hinde, "Joan Bavaria's Crusade."

118. <http://www.ceres.org/about-us/our-history>; Waddock, *Difference Makers*, p.131.

119. Sparkes, *Socially Responsible Investment*, p.61.

120. Bob Massie, *A Song in the Night* (New York: Doubleday, 2012), p.218; Jones and Amble, "Joan Bavaria," p.12.

121. Jones and Amble, "Joan Bavaria," p.10.

122. Waddock, *Difference Makers*, p.188.

123. Ibid., pp.191–2.

124. Brown, de Jong, and Lessidrenska, "The Rise"; Joel Gehman, "The Global Reporting Initiative: 1997–2009," *SSRN Electronic Journal* (February 2011), doi: 10.2139/ssrn.1924439, accessed May 15, 2016.

125. David L. Levy, Halina S. Brown, and Martin de Jong, "The Contested Politics of Corporate Governance: The Case of the Global Reporting Initiative," *Business & Society* 49, no. 1 (2010), p.88.

126. Christopher Marquis, Michael W. Toffel, and Yanhua Zhou, "Scrutiny, Norms, and Selective Disclosure: A Global Study of Greenwashing," *Organization Science* 27, no. 2 (March–April 2016), pp.483–504.

127. <https://www.globalreporting.org/network/GOLDCommunity/Pages/default. aspx>, accessed May 28, 2016.

128. Ans Kolk, "A Decade of Sustainability Reporting: Developments and Significance," *International Journal of Environment and Sustainable Development* 3, no. 1 (2004), pp.51–64; Levy, Brown, and de Jong, "Contested Politics"; Marquis, Toffel, and Zhou, "Scrutiny, Norms, and Selective Disclosure."

129. Guilbert Gates, Jack Ewing, Karl Russell, and Derek Watkins, "Explaining Volkswagen's Emissions Scandal," *New York Times*, April 28, 2016.

130. Colin Dey and John Burns, "Integrated Reporting at Novo Nordisk," in Anthony Hopwood, Jeffrey Unerman, and Jessica Fries (eds.), *Accounting for Sustainability: Practical Insights* (New York: Earthscan, 2010), pp.216–17.

131. Robert G. Eccles and George Serafeim, "Corporate and Integrated Reporting: A Functional Perspective," in Susan Albers Mohrman, James O'Toole, and Edward E. Lawler (eds.), *Corporate Stewardship: Achieving Sustainable Effectiveness* (Sheffield, UK: Greenleaf Publishing, 2015).

132. Antony Bugg-Levine and Jed Emerson, *Impact Investing: Transforming How We Make Money While Making a Difference* (San Francisco: Jossey-Bass, 2011), p.5.

133. Michael Kennedy, Debra McCoy, William F. Meehan, and Paul Pfleiderer, "Managing Value at the Global Environment Fund," Stanford Graduate School of Business Case F-285, February 2, 2013; <http://www.globalenvironmentfund.com/category/portfolio>, accessed June 1, 2016.

134. Interview with Phil LaRocco, Syracuse, December 10, 2013.

135. Christine Eibs Singer, "Impact Investing in Energy Enterprises: A Three-Act Play," *Innovations*, Special Edition for SOCAP11 (2011), p.84.

136. Ibid., pp.84–5.

137. Ibid., pp.86–7; Interview with Phil LaRocco; Scott Baron and George Weinmann, "Innovations in Energy: E+Co's Investment in Tecnosol," in C. K. Prahalad (ed.), *The Fortune at the Bottom of the Pyramid* (Upper Saddle River, NJ: Wharton School Publishing, 2005).

138. Baron and Weinmann, "Innovations in Energy," pp.14–15.

139. Ibid., pp.16–18; Singer, "Impact Investing," pp.87, 91, 93; Interview with Phil LaRocco.

140. Interview with Phil LaRocco.

141. Baron and Weinmann, "Innovations in Energy," p.19; Interview with Phil LaRocco.

142. E+Co Annual Report 2009.

143. John Willman, "Brazilian Bank Wins Sustainable Award," *Financial Times*, June 4, 2008.

144. David Bank, "E+Co Avoids Liquidation—Barely—And Emerges Persistent," <http://www.huffingtonpost.com/david-bank/eco-avoids-liquidation-ba_b_1932503.html>, accessed August 10, 2016.

145. Tammy Newmark and Michele Pena, *Portfolio for the Planet: Lessons from 10 Years of Impact Investing* (London: Earthscan, 2012), p.8; Alice Howard and Joan Magretta, "Surviving Success: An Interview with the Nature Conservancy's John Sawhill," *Harvard Business Review* (September–October 1995).

146. Brian Babson, Peter Plastrik, and Richard Turner, "Lessons from the Life and Death of the Virginia Eastern Shore Sustainable Development Corporation," <http://www.washingtonpost.com/wp-srv/nation/shoulders/n2s1_independentreport.pdf>, accessed December 18, 2015; William Ginn, *Investing in Nature: Case Studies of*

Land Conservation in Collaboration with Business (Washington, DC: Island Press, 2005), pp.157–66.

147. Newmark and Pena, *Portfolio*, p.14–15.

148. Ibid., p.122.

149. Ibid., pp.25ff., 124.

150. Ibid., pp.4, 42–5; Dan Weil, "EcoEnterprises Fund Grows Its Sustainable VC Investments in Latin America," in Thomson Reuters World Trade Executive, "Venture Equity Latin America 2013 Year-End Report," pp.6–7; European Investment Bank, "10 Things You Need to Know about the EIB and Climate Finance," <http://www.eib.org/projects/priorities/climate-action/road-to-paris/10-things-you-need-to-know-about-the-eib-and-climate-finance.htm>, accessed June 4, 2016.

151. Tammy Newmark, "Green Venture Capital," *Americas Quarterly* 3, no. 4 (Fall 2009), p.96.

152. Newmark and Pena, *Portfolio*, pp.138–9; <http://www.womenyoushouldknow.net/earth-day-women-investing-in-our-environment>, April 20, 2012, accessed July 8, 2015.

153. Paola Pedroza, "EcoEnterprises Fund: Impact Investment at its Best," February 10, 2016, <http://www.fomin.org/en-us/Home/FOMINblog/Blogs/DetailsBlog/ArtMID/13858/ArticleID/3353/EcoEnterprises-Fund-Impact-investment-at-its-best.aspx>, accessed June 4, 2016.

154. Sir Ronald Cohen and William A. Sahlman, "Social Impact Investing Will Be the New Venture Capital," *Harvard Business Review*, January 17, 2013.

8

The Green Team: Government and Business

Environmental issues rose higher on the agendas of politicians and governments after the 1980s. Previously, and with the notable exception of nature conservation schemes, governments had more often been a driver of environmental degradation rather than a provider of solutions. Motivated by the need to encourage economic development and facilitate rising incomes, governments had massively subsidized high-yield agriculture by any means necessary, including the widespread use of pesticides. The same motives—development and growth—had led to huge subsidies for fossil fuels and nuclear energy. In the case of waste, the municipalities which largely set the rules for the industry preferred landfills to recycling, a choice which went wholly unquestioned before the 1960s.

After 1980 government policies became, broadly speaking, much more supportive of green industries—with a hodgepodge of different policies around the world. We saw in Chapter 5 the case of organic agriculture where European willingness to subsidize conversion to organic agriculture provided a stark contrast with the absence of such support in the United States. This disparity typified a broader trend. While the United States had taken a lead in new environmental legislation beginning in the 1960s, Western Europe had by 1990 replaced the United States in passing proactive environmental legislation. This shift reflected broad political developments in the two regions. As suggested by the political scientist David Vogel, one factor was the sudden politicization and polarization of many environmental issues in the United States, with one of two main parties—the Republicans—resistant to regulation. The decision of President George W. Bush to unilaterally withdraw from the Kyoto Protocol after assuming office in 2001 was indicative of the

Republican Party's emergent position. It was shaped by strong lobbying by oil, coal, and automobile companies, as well as the lack of interest in environmental issues of Christian conservatives and gun owners, which became two of the Party's most influential groups.[1]

This policy division between important components of the American political system and Europe resulted in, and was associated with, other differences. Metrics of risk assessment came to vary. Notwithstanding the steady rise of environmental activism, the United States began in the 1980s to require higher levels of scientific evidence to justify new regulations. In contrast, the EU included the precautionary principle in the Maastricht Treaty in 1992, enabling the enacting of regulations even if some uncertainties on the scientific evidence endured.[2]

This chapter examines the cases of waste management and the wind and solar energy industries after 1980. It shows that the policy differences between the United States and Europe in balancing business interests and environmental action endure to the present day and, indeed, contribute to the disparate outcomes between the two regions. In both regions, and elsewhere, there was more governmental intervention, beyond the municipal level, helping to drive the growth of large multinational waste management companies. However, in many European countries policy-makers prioritized recycling far more than at the national level in the United States, where recycling and waste recovery levels remained low compared to many developed countries. In renewable energy, today's wind and solar industries were the creations of policy-makers in the United States during the 1980s, but policy support for renewable energy since then has usually been greater and more consistent in Europe.

In both cases governments became shapers of markets and co-creators of the rapidly expanding recycling and renewable energy industries. This governmental role was a critical factor in the growth of these industries, as entrepreneurial endeavors to develop these industries had been previously handicapped by the vagaries of recycling markets and the huge fixed costs incurred in introducing new solar and wind technologies. Public policy alleviated some of the huge challenges of risk management in industries exposed to unexpected price swings caused by exogenous factors, especially in overall energy prices. Subsidies, feed-in tariffs, tax breaks, legislation to promote recycling, and other policies promoted investment in new technologies by giving businesses the confidence that profitability could be combined with sustainability. The shortcomings and contradictions of apparently green businesses, and the governments charged with regulating, will become apparent, as will the lack of linearity in developments with the American squandering of its early eco lead of the 1960s.

These industries also provide striking evidence of the Janus-face of government policy. The availability of attractive contracts and subsidies generated rent-seeking behavior; even without such behavior, distorted outcomes were frequent. Because subsidies were set for certain time periods, public policies encouraged short-term strategies rather than long-term investment horizons, something which became a major problem in renewable energy. As large corporations became central actors in these industries, the adoption of green rhetoric also became a convenient means of securing tax breaks and other favors, whilst also gaining societal legitimacy. Governments emerge as shapers of markets, as facilitators of sustainable businesses, but also as disruptors of them. Importantly, also, whatever the support for green strategies, public policies as a whole still remained chronically lopsided with few attempts, for example, made to price environmental externalities into fossil fuels, plastics, and other environmentally damaging industries.

Global waste as big business

The role of new legislation in prompting the growth of big waste businesses from the 1960s was a theme of Chapter 4. Government intervention intensified after 1980, along with the shift from local and city policies to national regulation. As the problem of global warming entered public discussion, the negative environmental consequences of poor waste management took on a starker cast. The methane released by the organic fraction of the waste stream at landfills was recognized as a substantial contributor to greenhouse gases. The rise of waste in policy-makers' priorities laid the basis for a further scaling of large waste firms. The large national waste companies which grew in many countries had a new set of laws to obey—laws that, thanks to their lobbying efforts, they helped write.

In the United States, revelations about the lingering effects of decades-old toxic waste dumping at Love Canal in New York State in 1978 further raised awareness of the health risks of hazardous waste disposal absent environmental controls.[3] In the wake of this toxic discovery, the United States passed the Comprehensive Environmental Response, Compensation, and Liability Act of

1980, the "Superfund" law, which empowered the Environmental Protection Agency (EPA) to clean up such toxic sites and to compel responsible parties to perform cleanups or reimburse the government for EPA-led cleanups. The trade association, the National Solid Waste Management Association, was an active lobbyist on all federal waste legislation during the 1970s and afterwards, working especially to make sure that federal involvement in financing waste management would not lead to subsidization of the municipalities' programs.[4]

The primary focus of policy-makers in the wake of the second oil price rises of the late 1970s, encouraged by the industry, was mass incineration and conversion to energy. Previously, huge capital-intensive incineration plants had struggled to find markets for their electricity, but the advent of feed-in tariffs at that time, as we will see in the next section, made them appear more viable. The number of plants rose from 60 in 1980 to 110 by 1987. The ownership of waste-to-energy plants was highly concentrated with four large firms holding half the market. Waste Management invested in Wheelabrator, one of the four firms, in 1988, and took majority control two years later.[5] Recycling, in contrast, was more often a matter of public relations by public officials and companies than undertaken for positive environmental impact. In the early 1990s President Bill Clinton's proposals to elevate the EPA to cabinet status was derailed by conservative amendments in Congress, as were plans to revitalize the Superfund through a tax on oil and chemical businesses.[6]

Absent national policies, a wide variety of waste disposal practices developed in the United States. Interest in waste-to-energy generally declined during the 1990s, partly because of concerns about the environmental impact of the dioxins and other toxic chemicals released from burning waste, and because no one wanted large incinerators located near them. In 2016 there were eighty-six facilities in the United States, across twenty-five states, mostly in the northeast.[7] A patchwork of state and municipal recycling laws developed, which can be traced back to municipal curbside recycling programs in Massachusetts and on the West Coast in the 1980s, combined with some states mandating consumers paid a five-cent deposit per beer and soft drink bottle, recouped by returning the item for recycling.[8] The creation of new curbside municipal recycling programs grew fastest between 1994 and 2000, when 6,108 new programs were initiated.[9]

The structure of the American industry continued to evolve towards control by large corporations. The share of municipalities in industry revenues fell from 35 percent to 22 percent between 1992 and 2011.[10] In 2016 the two largest waste management companies accounted for almost 40 percent of the revenue of the solid waste industry in the United States. Waste Management alone held 16.7 percent, and a second company, Republic Services, held a further 12.5 percent.[11] Both these companies had by then also made extensive multinational investments across the world.

The journey of these two firms to such a commanding position did not unfold in straightforward fashion. Dean Buntrock's Waste Management acquired hundreds of small companies during the 1980s, and by the end of decade had revenues of over $6 billion, making it the biggest waste disposal firm in the world.[12] Although the firm increasingly employed environmental-ist language in its marketing, there was much in their business models that was not sustainable. During the 1980s the company paid over $40 million in fines, penalties, and out-of-court settlements relating to alleged violations of envir-onmental laws at its dump sites. The acquisition of firms in hazardous waste, which had appeared an attractive option after the federal regulatory response to the Love Canal scandal made this area seem like a profitable opportunity, ultimately proved very damaging as costly lawsuits soon followed.[13]

Amidst growing shareholder complaints, Buntrock left the company in 1997. It soon emerged that the firm had engaged in major accounting frauds, inflating its profits by $1.7 billion. Buntrock and his colleagues were indicted by the SEC for fraud, although the case was eventually settled with no admission of guilt.[14] Meanwhile, in 1998 it was acquired by a smaller com-pany. The new venture kept the Waste Management name.[15] Although cor-porate governance and environmental practices were subsequently improved, lawsuits against the company continued.[16]

In the 1980s Waste Management's major competitor was still Browning-Ferris Industries which also grew as a multi-billion dollar company through acquisitions, and also ran into legal difficulties after buying a firm engaged in the Love Canal cleanup.[17] In 1999 it was acquired by a smaller firm, Arizona-based Allied Waste Industries and private equity firms, for $7 billion.[18] In 2008 it changed ownership again when it was acquired by its smaller com-petitor Republic Services to create the second-largest waste company in the United States.

In aggregate, the system of giant corporations and highly fragmented local governance resulted in a waste management system in the United States which relied much more on landfills than affluent European countries, such as Germany and Sweden. Denmark and the Netherlands were other northwest European countries with little landfilling, along with Japan, although Britain, southern European countries, such as Italy and Spain, and Eastern European countries, such as Hungary and Poland, equaled or exceeded the rate in the United States.[19]

These and other national differences are shown in Figure 8.1, which presents data on how selected countries disposed of their municipal waste in 2011. By that year global municipal waste had reached 1.3 billion tonnes per

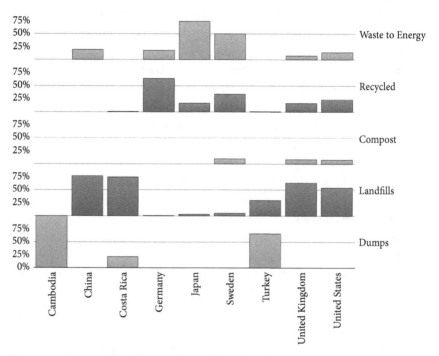

Figure 8.1 Municipal solid waste disposal in selected countries, 2011 (%)

Note: For most countries there are residual "Other" categories which are not shown here. The largest case is Germany where the Other category is 17.98 percent, and represents incineration without energy recovery.

Sources: Daniel Hoornweg and Perinaz Bhada-Tata, *What a Waste: A Global Review of Solid Waste Management* (Washington, DC: World Bank, 2012), Annex L, <https://openknowledge.worldbank.org/handle/10986/17388>, accessed July 20, 2016; for China, *China Statistical Yearbook 2012*, <http://www.stats.gov.cn/tjsj/ndsj/2012/indexeh.htm>, accessed July 20, 2016; Germany, Statistisches Bundesamt, *Abfallbilanz 2013* (Wiesbaden, 2015), p. 25.

annum. Figure 8.1 includes both some of the world's biggest generators of waste—total municipal waste generation in tonnes per day was 624,700 in the United States and 520,548 in China—and smaller waste generators—3,260 tonnes per day in the eco-tourism hub of Costa Rica.[20] A word of warning is necessary about the numbers presented here: municipal waste reporting was full of inconsistencies between countries. Although dumps and landfills are shown as two categories, for example, the reality was more of a spectrum stretching with porous borders from open-dumping to sanitary landfilling.[21]

There were some similarities, amid important differences, between the waste management industries in the United States and Germany. The Waste Management Law of 1986, which moved Germany towards a greater emphasis on recycling, gave private companies, which had more experience in that area than municipalities, an advantage, and there were specific recommendations to hire private firms if they were more effective.[22] German cities began to turn their waste collection departments into arm's-length companies, either owned by the city or by the city in partnership with a private company. This development, along with the increased cost of compliance with environmental regulation, economies of scale in environmental technologies, and the opportunities opened by the need to provide efficient waste services in the formerly Communist East Germany following reunification in 1989, provided a stimulus for further growth of large waste management businesses.

A wave of consolidation swept the German waste business between 1989 and 1993. The country's large electrical utilities acquired many of the largest waste companies. RWE bought most of Trienekens in 1989, and VEW acquired a quarter of Edelhoff in 1992 and the remainder two years later.[23] Not all of these mergers had happy endings. Trienekens was caught in a massive corruption scandal involving the bribing of local politicians in Cologne to ensure that the firm's tender for an over-sized incineration plant was accepted. In the wake of this scandal, RWE acquired entire ownership.[24] The Rethmann business also grew, diversifying into hazardous waste treatment, water filtration, and recycling, and into foreign countries.[25] In 2004 Rethmann bought the remainder of the RWE waste management division, which was merged with its own waste business and renamed Remondis. It became the market leader in Germany and was active in thirty-four countries by 2015 with sales of US$7.5 billion.

While the growth of large firms, and instances of corruption, appeared to be a common characteristic in both the United States and Germany, the legislative framework for waste management differed considerably. It was national rather than state in Germany, and recycling was strongly encouraged. The 1986 law allowed the federal government to promulgate nationwide ordinances on particular kinds of waste. The most important of these was the Packaging Ordinance of 1991 which introduced "producer responsibility," mandating that primary, secondary, and transport packaging of goods be returned to its original producers, at their expense, for reuse or reprocessing.[26] The ordinance had an "escape clause" in the form of an alternative to the primary packaging deposit system if private provision could meet comparable recycling rates to those envisioned under the command-and-control approach. The escape clause was a deliberate ploy by the Christian Democratic environment minister, Klaus Töpfer, who wanted to work with business to devise a workable system where the private sector would pay for collection and recycling of packaging collectively. The companies involved, both the packaging industry and the waste companies, were active participants throughout the legislative process.[27]

This legislation created the "Dual System," so-called because it supplemented community collection services for most other types of waste with collection of packaging-only wastes by a consortium of several hundred private manufacturers, packagers, retailers, and waste management firms.[28] The consortium incorporated a private non-profit joint stock company called Duales System Deutschland AG (DSD) which licensed the right to use a "green dot" symbol on packaging materials for a fee designed to cover the cost of collection and delivery. The fee did not cover the costs of recycling itself, expected to be recouped by the resale of secondary materials.[29]

The scheme got off to a troubled start. The closeness between the government and the big waste companies attracted critical attention from activists.[30] DSD, however, flourished. In 1995 it helped create a Europe-wide organization, composed of its equivalent "producer responsibility" organizations elsewhere, which licensed out the green dot symbol, which became widely adopted outside of Germany.[31]

The German waste management industry continued to have a more collaborative relationship with the German government. After the 1991 Packaging Ordinance, the next major legislation was the Kreislaufwirtschaftsgesetz

(KrWG), or recycling economy law, passed in 1994. The KrWG replaced the 1986 law and expanded the producer responsibility concept contained in the packaging ordinance more broadly to many other types of waste, while emphasizing recycling over incineration or landfilling.[32] The major German industry association, the BDE (German Waste Management Federation, which the VPS—discussed in Chapter 4—had been renamed in 1986) worked closely with Töpfer, helping to ensure that the introduction of producer responsibility both required private firms to take more account of the environmental costs of the waste generated by their products, and encouraged more privatization.[33]

Elsewhere in Europe, privatization and the growth of large firms were general trends, but with many variations in structures and outcomes. In Sweden, there was heavy investment in municipal incineration plants for electric power, especially for district heating, the favored system in Sweden whereby heating was produced from a centralized source and then distributed to individual households. Twenty plants processed nearly 50 percent of Sweden's household waste by the early 1980s.[34] From the 1980s there was also considerable emphasis on recycling. In 1994 an Ecocycle Law was passed, mandating producer responsibility for the collection and processing of packaging waste.[35] Swedish manufacturers developed a self-regulatory organization and non-profit enterprises to collect their wastes. Five non-profit producer-led recycling enterprises established the equivalent of DSD in the form of REPA Registret AB, to which eventually thousands of Swedish packaging producers, manufacturers, and retailers paid a fee based on the amount and type of packaging they were responsible for.[36]

In Britain, government polices mandating privatization and compulsory tendering led to rapid consolidation from dozens of small regional ventures, and the entry into the industry of large utilities. Four companies controlled over a quarter of collection contracts by tonnage by the 2000s.[37] Instead of a DSD-type of organization, British policies focused on tax incentives to discourage landfills and encourage recycling. This proved ineffective in reducing producers' generation of waste, and if anything led to an increase in illegal dumping.[38] As Figure 8.1 shows, Britain ended up with even more landfilling than the United States, less recycling, and less waste-to-energy.

During the 2000s EU policy-makers were far ahead of their American counterparts in responding to the mounting problem of electronic waste. In

2003 the EU introduced the Directive on Waste from Electrical and Electronic Equipment in response to the amount of electronic waste being deposited in landfills, and to increase the amount of electronic waste being recycled. This was an extension of the producer responsibility principle introduced in the German packaging ordinance. Manufacturers of electronics were mandated to collect and recycle them, either taking them back themselves or joining collaborative arrangements. The EU was joined by ten other countries, including Japan, South Korea, and China, in mandating electronics recycling, but there was no equivalent national legislation passed in the United States.[39] Instead individual states, beginning with California in 2003, passed their own laws requiring producer responsibility for recycling products. By 2013, thirty-two states had enacted such legislation, of varying levels of stringency.[40] Some manufacturers and retailers, including Dell and IBM, launched voluntary programs. In 2010 some 27 percent of US e-waste was recycled. The EU equivalent was 37 percent.[41]

Japan's waste management industry took a different form than those of the West. Before 1980 the country was a laggard in waste management. As the country's fast economic growth got underway in the 1950s, the volume of garbage mounted with few environmental controls. Municipal waste was either dumped or put in landfills. The first legislation on industrial waste appeared only in 1970, and illegal dumping and other poor practices, especially concerning soil contamination, were rampant. While pollution incidents had prompted some regulations over water and air, soil contamination was entirely ignored.[42]

As elsewhere, household waste management was the responsibility of municipalities. The system charged municipal staff with making regular collections and taking them to municipally owned facilities, originally landfills. Larger waste items, such as discarded furniture, were collected by a large number of small companies in return for a fee. This was, and has remained, an activity for tens of thousands of small firms. There was no equivalent to the integrated waste management companies of the West, even as environmental regulations intensified. In 2015 there were almost 20,000 such firms registered to conduct household waste, many of them small, family-owned businesses. The industrial waste market was equally fragmented with tens of thousands of companies. There were still almost 140,000 companies engaged in it in 2015, although some larger companies had developed by then.[43]

The municipalities began shifting towards incineration in the 1960s. Over time Japan became the world leader in incineration and waste-to-energy technology, disposing of three-quarters of its waste in that fashion (Figure 8.1). After dioxin levels in Japan rose to high levels in the 1990s, there was also a heavy investment in cleaner technologies. Furnaces, many located in city centers, were sometimes designed by architects, and included sports and other facilities for local citizens, heated by the electricity generated.[44]

During the 1990s national legislation, beginning with the Basic Environment Law of 1993, began to shape the waste management system. In 1995 the first law was passed mandating recycling by municipalities. Other laws followed mandating the producer responsibility principle and recycling of home appliances, construction materials, and food waste.[45]

As new legislation was put in place, the prospect of profits for businesses that could supply new services grew. As in Germany, the writing of these laws included a great deal of industry involvement. Mamoru Mitsumoto, the founder of the Takeei Corporation which grew to be one of the larger firms in construction waste, recalled how he was closely involved in the industry association in the 1990s, and was in constant dialogue with both the Ministry of Health, which supervised waste management, and the Ministry of Construction. He was, as a result, "able to foresee what kind of legislation would be enacted."[46]

Executives from Dowa Holding recalled a similar involvement in shaping the development of soil contamination legislation. Dowa, a long-established mining and smelting company, entered recycling and waste management on a small scale in 1977, and much more extensively after one of its executives had recognized both the scale of Waste Management Inc.'s business and environmental legislation such as the Superfund during a visit to New York in 1994.[47] Some in Japan had expected the country would follow American practices on issues such as industrial waste management, soil contamination, and recycling. "We were able to imagine there might be quite a large market," Hirokazu Yoshikawa, Dowa's executive in charge of environmental management noted, "but we had no idea how many products would be recycled or whether we could collect sufficient amounts of products for recycling."[48] During the early 2000s Dowa worked closely with the Japanese government to develop legislation, modeled on the American example. In 2003 the Japanese equivalent of the US Superfund legislation was enacted to deal with soil contamination.

"Our strategy was to bring up the invisible market to the surface by legislation," Yoshikawa later noted, "and to get the market once it became visible."[49]

Outside the developed world, formal waste management systems were largely absent before 1980, and many countries still rely *de facto* on unregulated dumping and lack environmental control. The lack of rules and systems became a major problem as some countries experienced fast economic growth after 1980, resulting in rising amounts of waste. China's growth over three decades to being the world's second largest economy resulted in a huge waste mountain. As we can see in Figure 8.1, China and other countries outside the developed world—Cambodia, Costa Rica, and Turkey being representative cases—have waste outcomes heavily skewed towards landfills and dumps. Many sites classified/categorized/claimed as landfills in the developing countries were more like dumps than the carefully regulated sanitary landfills in the West.

As waste mountains grew, struggling municipalities across Africa, Asia, and Latin America often turned to Western waste companies such as Waste Management and France's Veolia. These two firms grew as giant multinational businesses, with market capitalizations of $28 billion and $11 billion respectively in 2016.[50] Locally owned firms grew rapidly in some countries. In China, what became for a time the largest private sector waste company was founded in 1993 by Yen Yibo, a former government engineer with a degree in environmental engineering. Sound Environmental Resources began by engaging in industrial waste water treatment in Beijing, and grew as an integrated waste management company, which listed on the Singapore Stock Exchange in 2006 and later on other exchanges in China. Despite competing against many state-owned firms, as well as affiliates of foreign multinationals, two decades after its foundation it had a market capitalization approaching $7 billion and managed seventy water treatment, sewage treatment, urban domestic waste treatment, and industrial waste treatment plants in China. During 2015 widespread allegations of massive fraud led to the firm being delisted.[51]

China typified many of the challenges in waste management in emerging economies. In 2015 the country produced 300 million of the 1.4 billion tons of solid waste in the world, most of it in towns. It was largely collected unsorted and put in landfills or sent to incinerators, which were poorly regulated and typically spewed toxic fumes. Landfills and incinerators were located in the poor outskirts of towns, adding pollution to poverty. There was, however, some recycling alongside these distressing figures: up to 5.6 million informal collectors hand-picked anything of value in the garbage.[52] Many other countries also had scavengers working in the informal sector, an activity which provided key income for very poor people, as well as being quite effective in recycling. One estimate was that 15 million people worldwide worked as scavengers. They were sometimes well organized: Latin America was estimated to have around 1,000 scavenger cooperatives and associations in 2015.[53]

When municipal governments contracted out their own services to modern firms, including multinational affiliates, recycling rates often fell in developing countries as scavengers were squeezed out, but there were other environmental benefits. For example, the city of São Paulo in Brazil had two of the world's largest landfills, in which private companies under contract to municipalities dumped waste. Waste disposal accounted for one-quarter of the country's greenhouse gas emissions in 2005. The city then contracted with a company called Biogas, owned by Brazilian and Danish companies, to install thermo-electric power plants to burn the methane emitted by the decaying waste from the landfills to produce cleaner energy. By 2010 waste disposal only amounted to 5 percent of greenhouse gas emissions, and considerable energy was generated.[54] Modern sanitary landfills and incinerators delivered health benefits and reduced greenhouse gases, but they did not necessarily raise recycling rates, and they reduced employment for the very poor.

As globalization and the spread of consumer societies after 1980 resulted in more and more waste, governments turned to private business to solve the problem, even while retaining overall control over what the businesses did. The result was increasingly profitable opportunities, whether for small entrepreneurs or global companies like Waste Management. Waste and recycling suddenly emerged as an attractive business for venture capital, private equity, and wealthy angel investors. In Germany DSD was acquired by the US private equity firm KKR in 2006. It was subsequently sold to its managers and the British private equity firm Solidus Partners four years later. In the United States, both Republic Services and Waste Management emerged as attractive companies for Bill Gates, the software billionaire. By 2014 Gates held one-quarter of the shares of Republic Services, while the Bill and Melinda Gates Foundation, their charity arm, held 4 percent of Waste Management.[55]

Yet the problem of waste has not come close to being even remotely solved by the second decade of the twenty-first century. While only a few in the West live near unsanitary dumps, much of the world still does. A handful of developed countries, including Germany, Japan, and Sweden, became advanced in recycling waste and recovering energy. The producer responsibility system, originating in Germany from a close dialogue between the government and industry, was among the more successful government policies introduced.

The consequences of waste for climate change and for the health of billions of people have proven severe. Governments and municipalities made the rules and awarded the contracts—and bear ultimate responsibility for sub-optimal outcomes. Government's role has been both necessary and the cause of further problems, for as the markets grew, there were plentiful opportunities for firms to co-opt green images while engaging in gray practices to secure contracts. Indeed, some of the best environmental outcomes occurred in countries such as Germany and Sweden where businesses worked, not solely in pursuit of the bottom line but in tandem with governments to craft effective waste policies. In most other cases, profits have been prioritized over sustainability, and public/private collaboration seems to have encouraged sub-optimal environmental outcomes more than the opposite.

The rise of renewable energy

In 1980 both wind and solar energy capacity remained tiny, and largely confined to the United States with Denmark and Japan having minimal wind and/or solar capabilities. As Figure 8.2 indicates, in that year wind and solar were inconsequential as sources of electricity in even those countries, let alone anywhere else. Combustible fuels (coal, oil, and natural gas) provided over 70 percent of the electricity in the three countries, including 100 percent in Denmark. Nuclear energy and hydro power supplied the residual in Japan and the United States.

By 2014 much had changed. A great deal more electricity was being generated compared to 1980; in the United States generation rose from 2,286 to 4,368 gigawatts (GW) over the period, in Japan from 552 to 1,082 GW, and in Germany from 437 to 640 GW. By 2014 China's electricity generation was 5,431 GW, and India's 1,193 GW. But there were also significant shifts in energy sources. Denmark had two-fifths of its electricity derived from wind power, Germany 9 percent, and Sweden 7 percent. The US share of wind was at 4 percent. In India and China—where data are not available for

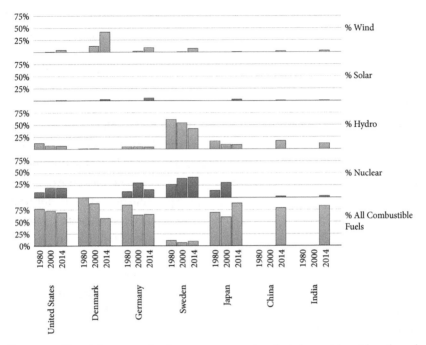

Figure 8.2 Electricity generation by energy source in selected countries at benchmark dates, 1980–2015 (percentage shares)

Sources: OECD: International Energy Agency, IEA Electricity Information Statistics; China and India: *Energy Statistics Yearbook*, United Nations 2013.

1980 and 2000—wind energy represented around 2.5 percent. The use of solar power had also grown in these countries, although less so than wind. In Germany it supplied over 9 percent of electricity, and 2.4 percent in Japan, but only 0.6 percent in the United States, and 0.1 percent in China. The continued importance of combustible fuels in the United States and China, the world's two biggest economies, was noteworthy. In Japan, the third biggest economy, reliance on combustible fuels even temporarily increased after the country's nuclear electricity-generating capacity was for a time entirely shut down after a meltdown at a plant at Fukushima in 2011.[56] Moreover, such figures entirely miss the huge and continued use of fossil fuels, primarily petroleum, in heating and motor vehicles. The widespread use of electric cars, and the development of the new battery technologies needed to make them truly viable, remained visions of the future which were far from becoming realities.

324

The story of these countries fitted a broad general pattern of only a very slow movement to the use of wind and solar energy, with only a handful of countries more advanced in the process. In the world as a whole, wind provided 2.3 percent of electricity and solar a mere 0.4 percent in 2014. Coal alone still generated 40 percent of the world's electricity: the proportions were 39 percent in the United States, 71 percent in India, and 76 percent in China. In addition, natural gas (22.5 percent), hydro (16.2 percent), and nuclear (10.9 percent) remained larger generators of world electricity than wind and solar.[57] Each has adverse environmental impacts. Nuclear power yields no greenhouse gas emissions, but the waste generated remains a huge environmental hazard, as are the catastrophic risks posed if reactors have a meltdown. Natural gas emits half as much CO_2 as coal to generate the same amount of electricity, but generates significant emissions of methane, which is also a greenhouse gas. Hydropower does not directly generate emissions, which is why Central and Latin America—where more than half of all electricity came from hydro and a further quarter from natural gas—had the lowest emissions in the developing world. Yet the building of large hydro dams often destroyed natural habitats and harmed indigenous communities, as well as releasing carbon as trees and plants were swept away for reservoirs.

The contested meaning of sustainability was very evident as energy strategies were debated and governments allocated growing resources to shifting energy mixes as climate change concerns rose. Some interests made the case that hydroelectric power and even, implausibly, natural gas fell into the category of clean energy.[58] Wind and solar were evidently renewable, unlike natural gas, and clean in that they had no direct greenhouse gas emissions. This does not mean that they do not have adverse environmental impacts as their scale increases. Scarce metals are used to make solar panels. They and windmills are made in industrial processes which leave carbon footprints. The waste substances in making crystalline silicon for solar energy include tetrachloride, a toxic substance that reacts violently with water, and the greenhouse gas sulfur hexafluoride, used to clean the reactors used in silicon production. Solar plants and windmills occupy large areas of land, disrupting local flora and fauna. Birds die flying into windmills. Located in rural areas, solar plants and windmills also need vast transmission lines built to connect to grids. While wind and solar energy are renewable, windmills and solar panels are not, and disposing of them poses major challenges.[59]

In the last resort, whatever was achieved for renewable energy in particular countries, it needs to be remembered that public policy at the global level has failed. Global emissions of carbon dioxide more than doubled between 1973 and 2012: in the latter year, China accounted for 26 percent of them and the United States for the second-largest share at 16 percent.[60] Still, considering its zero starting point, the growth in both the solar and wind industries was substantial after 1980 and was accompanied by major shifts in the geographies where products were made and the energy used. In 1980 world annual production of photovoltaic solar cells was 7 megawatts (MW), and cumulative production was 20 MW. These cells were largely made and used in the United States. By 2013 the respective numbers were 44,646 MW and 184,186 MW respectively: 60 percent were made in China and 22 percent more in Japan and Taiwan. Turning to use, in 2013 Germany (25 percent) and China (13 percent) had the highest installed capacity in the world. The United States was in fifth place use-wise with 8 percent. Two years later China passed Germany to become the country with the largest amount of solar power at 43,200 MW.[61] There was a similar transformation in the amount of wind energy generated and the geography. In 1980 cumulative installed wind capacity was 8 MW in the United States and 5 MW in Denmark, and little elsewhere. In 2014 global cumulative capacity was 368,597 MW. China (31 percent), the United States (17 percent), and Germany (10 percent) had the highest installed capacity.[62] Change was afoot, and the shift to renewable energy was accelerating rapidly, but not yet at a pace at a global level to match the emergent crisis of climate change.

First renewables boom in the United States

The following sections look at three sequential waves of public policies and their impacts on business. Each wave of public policy shifted the balance between profits and sustainability. Government support made investing in wind power profitable for the first time and, at times but not always, did the same for solar power. In the process, these industries grew beyond the narrow preserve of values-driven entrepreneurs. The power of public policy to create a market and to scale an industry was vividly displayed. Yet the downsides of public policy were equally evident in spectacular boom and bust cycles.

Between 1980 and 1990 there was a remarkable growth in wind capacity in the United States from 8 MW to 1,484 MW, which represented over three-quarters of total world capacity of 1,930 MW. US annual solar photo-voltaic production was lower but grew substantially, from 2.5 MW to 14.8 MW. New government polices drove this growth.

Beginning in the late 1970s, legislation passed during the presidency of Jimmy Carter in the United States marked the start of this new era. The context was the second rise in oil prices associated with the advent of the Islamic Republic in Iran. While the first oil price rises in 1973 had stimulated limited interest in wind and solar energy, this time it was different. In part this new interest was a response to a nuclear meltdown that occurred in March 1979 in a reactor of the Three Mile Island Nuclear Generating Station in Pennsylvania. This was the first major accident at a civilian nuclear plant; it caused a huge public outcry, and was followed by a sharp and sustained fall in new nuclear plant construction.[63] In June President Carter announced a target that renewable energy would supply 20 percent of American electricity by the end of the century. Carter's focus was on solar power. "Every advance in making electricity directly from the sun decreases our reliance on uncertain sources of imported oil," he noted in a published letter to Congress.[64] In 1979 Carter announced a new $3 billion program of research into solar power, which included installing a showcase solar heater at the White House.[65]

Unlike earlier government efforts to develop new technologies under the auspices of NASA, the new policies aimed at stimulating demand for alternative energy. The 1978 Energy Tax Act offered a 30 percent investment tax credit for residential consumers for solar and wind energy equipment and a 10 percent investment tax credit for business consumers for the installation of solar, wind, and geothermal technologies.[66] More critically, the Public Utility Regulatory Policies Act (PURPA) of 1978 opened the door to competition in the electricity supply by requiring utility companies to buy electricity from "nonutility facilities that produce electric power," including renewable power plants. This deregulated energy generation markets in the United States for the first time since the 1930s. The legislation was the origin of feed-in tariffs which, although they varied widely, shared the basic principle of offering grid access on the basis of long-term contracts which reflect the costs of renewable energy. This was an absolutely critical development as entrepreneurial providers of renewable energy had previously been unable to sell their products to utilities which dominated the supply of electricity in the United States.[67]

The PURPA legislation left the utility commissioners of individual states to implement the rules. There was very little uptake, except in the state of California, the haven of hippies, organic farmers, and environmental activists, which had already banned oil as a fuel for electricity generation and had stopped the construction of coal-fired power plants due to concerns about air pollution.[68] Further momentum came when the Governor, Jerry Brown, was persuaded to lend support to renewable energy as part of the program of the Office of Appropriate Technology headed by the architect Sim Van der Ryn, as we saw in Chapter 3.

Van der Ryn recruited Tyrone Cashman, whom he had first encountered at the Green Gulch Farm Zen Center community outside San Francisco in 1977, to head the renewable energy department. Cashman, who had studied at one time to be a Jesuit priest, had strong ecological concerns. He had completed a Columbia University Ph.D. dissertation in philosophy on "Man's Place in Nature" in 1974 and subsequently spent time at the New Alchemy Institute in Woods Hole, Massachusetts, a center for radical research on small-scale sustainable technologies, including in organic agriculture, aquaculture, and energy. He helped build a small wind turbine for New Alchemy clients in Ottawa and became enthusiastic about wind energy as a solution to pollution.[69]

Cashman was given autonomy to develop state policies to support wind and solar energy in addition to executing federal policies. In a later interview, he observed that he decided to throw "a stick of dynamite to break open a vicious cycle that was killing us. Nobody wanted to invest in new energy technologies. What we did was make it so seductive that they would invest—even if the wind turbines didn't work."[70]

Cashman deployed several "sticks of dynamite." The California state legislature was already considering proposals aimed at energy conservation, which included the idea of state income tax credits for installing small solar heating systems for a house or swimming pool. Cashman secured the inclusion of wind energy in the legislation. This enabled investors in wind power systems to receive a 25 percent deduction for investments made between 1981 and 1985, in addition to the 25 percent deduction already given from federal income taxes. Investors in small systems, like a solar heating provision, received a 50 percent state income tax credit.[71] Most importantly of all, the Interim Standard Offer 4 contract (hereafter ISO4) introduced in 1983 aimed to provide non-utility developers of wind energy long-term price certainty which would help them obtain financing. The feed-in tariff contracts, based on estimated long-term costs, offered a fixed price for ten years followed by twenty years of floating prices.[72] Almost all new wind capacity came under these contracts. Although California's tax credits for wind energy declined from 25 percent in 1985 to 15 percent in 1986, and then disappeared, the ISO4 contracts continued through the following decade.[73]

Both the length of the California contracts and the fixed energy prices for the first ten years provided a guaranteed income stream. Previously, banks had not been willing to finance wind developers. Wind developers could now use the contracts to raise finance. Capital raising was also facilitated by state-sponsored resource studies, which provided clear evidence of the availability of the wind, even if the state was far from the windiest in the country. The conditions were set for the so-called California wind boom. Thousands of windmills were installed at three windy mountain passes: east of San Francisco at Altramont Pass, northeast of Los Angeles at Tehachapi Pass, and outside Palm Springs at the San Gorgonio Pass. By 1990, most US wind capacity, and at least over three-quarters of the world's, was installed in California, where wind energy produced 1.1 percent of California's electricity at that time.[74]

While supportive government policies were key to the boom, it was entrepreneurs and firms who undertook the massive task of building wind farms. Four entrepreneurial start-ups—US Windpower, Fayette, FloWind, and Zond Systems—were key to the initial stages of growing the Californian industry. They accounted for more than half of installed capacity by the mid-1980s.[75] Promoting sustainability coexisted with taking advantage of the many financial incentives. Russell Wolfe and Stanley Charren, who as Chapter 3 noted had founded the world's first wind farm in New Hampshire, moved the headquarters of their firm US Windpower from New Hampshire to Livermore, near Altamont, in 1981. Fayette was run by John Eckland, a CIA veteran who had become interested in alternative energy through concerns about future energy security. He purchased a small Pennsylvania-based wind company in 1977, and he moved it to Altamont in 1981. James Dehlsen, a serial entrepreneur, founded Zond systems at Tehachapi in 1980. He sold his successful fluid lubricant firm to fund the business, having become convinced of both the need for renewable energy after having read Amory Lovin's work on soft energy paths and the economic feasibility made possible by the tax incentives.[76]

The problem, which became apparent as the wind farms were being put into operation, was that many turbines were poor quality. A perceived need to capture subsidies fast reinforced the competitive structure of the American wind industry, which saw—especially compared to the emergent Danish industry—limited cooperation on standards and testing. Companies resisted quality standards when they were proposed, partly because they feared such standards would require costly design modifications to machines they wanted to sell quickly.[77] In 1986, sixty US firms produced turbines, but within three years, this had fallen sharply as poorly managed firms struggled under the costs of repairs, warranty issues, and complaints. Fayette and FloWind had failed by the early 1990s.[78]

Indeed, it was the Danish industry which gained most from the Californian wind boom. The Danish firms, enjoying considerable governmental support in their home market, offered three-bladed upwind machines derived from the Gedser mill design—now modernized with the addition of fiberglass blades. They had certification from the Danish test center at Risø along with statistics that showed their designs were more reliable than their US counterparts. Zond responded to the failures of American models by buying three thousand machines from Vestas for its Tehachapi farms during the first half of the 1980s.[79] By 1992, Danish firms had supplied 43 percent, and Japanese firms a further 4 percent, while US firms had supplied 49 percent of the 15,856 turbines installed in California.[80]

Boom was soon followed by bust. After President Ronald Reagan succeeded Carter in 1981, he rejected recommendations of the Solar Energy Research Institute suggesting that the United States could implement a program to increase its share of renewables in energy production, and cut the agency's staff by two-thirds. Spending was increased on nuclear power.[81] Reagan ordered the removal of solar panels from the White House in 1986 when the roof was renovated. Federal tax incentives expired at the end of 1985. In California, Jerry Brown was replaced by George Deukmejian, a Republican, as Governor in 1983. Subsidies for renewables were reduced. This policy shift reflected both Republican support for conventional energy interests and a fall in the world price of oil, which had peaked in 1980 at over US$35 per barrel, but fell to $10 per barrel by 1986.

California's wind industry was severely damaged in 1986. There were bankruptcies and financial turbulence across the industry.[82] Vestas went bankrupt. Zond alone provided 90 percent of its market and had to be reconstructed as Vestas Wind Systems in 1987—majority-owned by a Dutch investment fund.[83] US Windpower survived by diversifying into construction services and energy management services. It was renamed Kenetech Corporation in 1988 with revenues approaching $50 million. It built new turbines itself, being the world's second-largest turbine manufacturer at one stage and began diversifying outside California.[84] It was particularly successful at securing finance from institutional investors, helped by the support of the brokerage firm Merrill Lynch. In 1993, it became the first wind company to make an IPO when it raised almost $100 million. Technical problems with a new generation of machines contributed to bankruptcy in 1996.[85] Zond, the last survivor, began to develop its own turbines after 1990, but found the new technology was challenging and expensive. In 1997, James Dehlsen persuaded Enron, a natural gas producer and trader which was attracted to renewable energy by the opportunities to secure federal tax credits, to become majority owners. The business flourished under Enron. When Enron itself went bankrupt in 2002, the former Zond business became the basis for entry into wind energy of the giant conglomerate GE.[86]

In the case of the solar industry, PURPA and California's state tax credits were applied to an industry in which, in the United States, major oil corporations including Exxon, Mobil, Amoco, and ARCO had already invested in the entrepreneurial firms which had created the industry. By 1980, oil companies accounted for 70 percent of all the solar modules sold in the United States.[87] US-based companies accounted for 85 percent of world sales.[88]

The large US oil companies had the financial resources to scale the capital-intensive solar business, especially with the favorable policy regime. In the decade after 1977, ARCO invested over $200 million in the STI business it had acquired from Bill Yerkes, which was renamed Arco Solar. Yerkes estimated 90 percent was defrayed by tax credits.[89] With new funding, Yerkes created a research laboratory of 100 people in a new 10,000-square-feet production facility. In 1982, the company built the first privately funded central-station PV plant in the high desert near Hesperia in California. The plant, which was unmanned, fed electricity into the distribution grid of the Southern California Edison utility.[90] The firm's sales reached $40 million in 1988, and it became, for a time, the largest PV manufacturer in the world.

Yet there was more to growing a solar business than money. ARCO imported managers who had no understanding of solar technology and pursued technological options in thin-film silicon which Yerkes considered unviable. He left the firm in 1985, returning to his former employer Boeing. "The company was screwed up within two years after they bought it," Yerkes later commented. "We went from making cells for $10 a watt and selling them for $15 to making cells for $32 a watt and selling them for $5."[91] Five years later ARCO sold the solar business never having earned a profit.[92] In 1984 Exxon sold Solar Power to Solarex. Mobil sold its solar business to German-owned ASE ten years later. Solarex, in which Amoco had taken an investment, was one of the more successful ventures, in part because, as the co-founder Peter Varadi noted, the firm "made it a point to not work exclusively with government agencies" and instead to go "after costumers, where the real money is."[93] Yet during the early 1980s declining oil prices and the inability to raise funds led to Amoco's acquisition of the entire business in 1983. Varadi and his co-founder Joseph Lindmeyer left the company. Amoco retained the business until its own acquisition by the British oil company BP in 1999, though Varadi judged their management of it poor.[94]

Both the fluctuations in public policies and the presence of deep-pocketed oil companies added to the challenges faced by a new generation of green entrepreneurs, many of them in California, such as Ishaq Shahryar. Shahryar had arrived in the United States in 1956 on a scholarship from the government in Afghanistan. He enrolled at the University of California, Santa Barbara, studied chemistry, and eventually got a job at Spectrolab, where he developed the process of screen-printing cells on solar panels, which is still used today. Shahryar had vivid memories of his youth in Afghanistan, where he had had to study by candle or kerosene light when the electricity supplies went off, and he was convinced of the potential of solar to help the rural poor. "My goal was rural electrification," he later said, "a light for students to read by at night."[95] When Spectrolab was refocused on space, Shahryar resolved to found his own company, Solec International, in 1975.[96]

A two-decade search for funding followed. In 1981 Shahryar sold 80 percent of the company to a British glass company, which sold it five years later, almost pushing the company to bankruptcy. This fate was averted in 1987 when Solec provided the solar cells for a solar electric race car being built by the hair care entrepreneur and multi-millionaire John Paul DeJoria, an active supporter of environmental issues, who promptly invested $1 million in the venture.[97] Shahryar sought to survive by focusing on niche markets, such as solar panel systems for lighting bus shelters and streets, and using single-crystal silicons rather than more expensive, thin-film, technologies. By the mid-1990s Shahryar had a modest 2 percent of the US PV market, and it was profitable, but he still needed funds to build scale. He finally sold Solec International to the Japanese electronics companies Sanyo and Sumitomo.[98]

The most visionary business of this era was not in PV cells at all; it was solar arrays manufacturer LUZ, the brainchild of Arnold Goldman, a Rhode Island-born engineering graduate of the University of Southern California. After profitably selling his word processing company in 1977, he moved to Israel to write a book on philosophy and social theory. He envisioned the creation of a utopian city, which he named LUZ after the biblical city where Jacob dreamed of a ladder ascending to heaven. The city would consist of twelve component communities surrounded by a wall which would gather sunlight for energy.[99]

Although the concept of building utopia gained little traction, there was some Israeli government interest in solar energy thanks to the hostility of Arab oil producers to the country. Goldman formed LUZ International in partnership with an entrepreneur named Patrick François, a French-Israeli dual-national. They wanted to base LUZ's R&D and manufacturing in Israel but found little interest in funding the endeavor from the US venture capitalists they approached. Goldman finally secured some capital from the investors who had supported his earlier company and built a small solar energy collecting system, to produce steam and heat, with a computer control system to keep it aimed at the sun. A small industrial process-steam generator was built for a kibbutz. When this worked, LUZ started building three pilot industrial steam systems for textile companies in the southeastern United States. It turned out that this plan was not viable. The locations with the best sunlight, like California's deserts, had no industrial facilities which needed steam, whilst the areas with factories often had less sunlight.[100]

After learning that a subsidiary of Phillips Petroleum, which was also in the process-steam market, had obtained a contract from a utility, the Southern California Edison Company, to sell it power, Goldman decided to refocus on the California market. Between 1984 and 1990 LUZ raised $1 billion from investors and built nine reflective solar collectors in the Mojave desert, which focused sunlight on oil-carrying receiver pipes. The oil was heated as it circulated through the pipes to create the steam for a turbine generator. LUZ sold its electricity using the feed-in tariffs, and earned returns for its investors through careful use of federal solar tax credits. The credits, however, were renewed by the US Congress annually, which made long-term planning difficult, and to access them a new plant had to be put online by December 31 of a given year so that investors could use the tax credits their work generated. LUZ devoted considerable time to lobbying Congress each year to get the credits extended.[101] By 1990 LUZ had built and installed nine solar electricity generating (SEGS) plants in California, featuring almost 940,000 mirrors.

The fiscal support LUZ had received began to unravel. In 1989 Congress extended the solar tax credit for 1990 for only nine months, forcing a huge rush to complete a plant. As plans for a tenth project got underway, the exemption from California's property tax suddenly ended. In contrast to fossil fuels, the generation of electricity from solar required extensive equipment, which had been counted as assets and therefore not subject to property tax. Governor Deukmejian vetoed legislation to keep the exemption, "in his last few minutes in office," Goldman later observed. "It was absolutely ridiculous."[102] Unable to finance the tenth project which it was building, LUZ filed for bankruptcy in 1991. The SEGS remained in operation, selling their electricity to the Southern California Edison and serving as the world's largest solar site.[103]

The wind and solar industries came of age, then, mainly in California, and mainly because they received the kind of support which governments had long given to nuclear energy and coal. Enabled by feed-in tariffs to access the grid, and by a range of subsidies, both American and international firms found it possible, and attractive, to scale their businesses. Both the visionary green entrepreneurs and the big oil companies which invested millions of dollars in solar energy were important in overcoming the huge technological challenges of making solar and wind energy economically viable. The results were remarkable. Installed wind capacity in the world rose from 13 MW to 1,930 MW between 1980 and 1990: of the latter, 1,494 MW was in the United States and 343 MW in Denmark. The ramp-up of global PV production rose from 20 MW in 1989 to 275 MW in 1990—and reached 78,000 MW in 1995, of which 35,000 MW was in the United States.[104]

Yet the short-term nature of the policies created multiple inefficiencies. The embryonic American wind industry raced so hard to secure credits and subsidies that it built a weak technological base. In an industry where the United States was such an important market, the sudden withdrawal of government funding for the solar industry in the Reagan years sent a signal which led to the industry "coming to a virtual halt."[105] Goldman's SEGS turned out to be indestructible and still produce electricity to the present day, but his company ended up bankrupt. There would be no more thermal deployment until the 2000s.

The pattern of fluctuating public policies in renewable energy in the United States helps explain why leadership in wind and solar technologies and deployment moved away from the United States. There remained supportive policies, but few were consistent over the long term, and many were at state level. State governments introduced renewable energy standards that mandated utilities obtain set percentages of their electric power from renewable sources. By 2000 twelve states had such standards, and by 2015 the number had risen to twenty-nine, motivated by many factors, including the strength of the Democratic Party in state legislatures.[106] However, the growth of solar and wind energy was not facilitated by restrictions on transmitting electricity across state borders, and especially by the existence of three separate grids for the western and eastern parts of the country, and Texas. Policy fluctuations were symbolized by the saga of solar panels in the White House. Almost two decades after President Reagan had removed his predecessor's solar panels, in 2003 President George W. Bush brought 167 solar panels back to the White House, which were used for, among other things, heating the Presidential pool. In 2013 President Barack Obama installed more panels, to heat the President's residence.[107]

Second renewables boom in Europe

The second round of massive public policy support for wind and solar energy came in Europe from the 1990s, as concerns about climate change had by this time risen sharply to become central to policy-makers. A number of governments embarked on radical policies to support renewables and open the markets. Just as European governments began to promote innovative solutions to deliver environmentally sound methods of recycling packaging and other wastes, the center of gravity in the renewable energy business shifted away from the United States. In so doing, they also supported smaller and more visionary green entrepreneurial firms in the wind and solar businesses who were struggling to bring costs down.

Between 1990 and 2000 wind energy became dominated by Europe. There was a strong growth in installed wind capacity in pioneer Denmark, from 343 MW to 2,417 MW. More striking still was the sudden emergence from nothing of wind energy in Germany and Spain. By 2000 installed wind capacity was 6,113 MW in Germany and 2,235 MW in Spain. The three European countries accounted for over three-fifths of world capacity of 17,400 MW. The once dominant United States had increased wind capacity during the 1990s, reaching 2,578 MW, but now only represented 14 percent of the world capacity. Europe was not a large PV solar manufacturer. In 2000 the production of Germany, the only significant producer in the region, was only 8 percent of the annual world total of 277 MW. The two biggest producers were Japan at 46 percent and the United States at 27 percent. Yet in terms of installation, Germany's 76 MW accounted for 6 percent of world total of 1,250 MW, putting it in second place to Japan's 26 percent.

By the time of the California wind rush, the Danish government had become more supportive of the wind energy industry, which had previously grown in opposition to the government rather than because of it. In 1979 the government instituted a 30 percent investment subsidy for buyers of certified wind turbines. When this had little effect, subsidies were raised to 50 percent. Under voluntary agreements made between the utilities and wind turbine manufacturers, the utilities agreed to pay owner-users for wind power at a guaranteed minimum price, and to share between the utilities and the turbine owners the cost of connecting the turbines to the grid.[108] In the wake of vigorous social movements, Denmark passed a law prohibiting nuclear production on its territory in 1986, although the country imported electricity from a nuclear plant called Barsebäcks kärnkraftsverk, opened in 1975, in nearby southern Sweden.

Government support for the Danish industry grew even as it collapsed in California. By the late 1980s Denmark was setting formal targets for wind power growth as part of its strategy to reduce carbon emissions.[109] After the voluntary agreements between the utilities, manufacturers, and turbine makers broke down in 1992, the government introduced a feed-in tariff that maintained previous payments for wind power, though making wind turbine owners pay for connecting their turbines to the low-voltage grid. In 1991 subsidies for wind power producers were introduced. The powerful OVE organization continued to exercise a powerful influence shaping these policies.[110] In 1994, the government required municipalities to plan for future wind turbine construction and began offering subsidies for the replacement of older, inefficient, or loud turbines with new machines.[111] There was further innovation during these years—the first offshore wind farm was created at Vindeby in 1991.

By 2000 Denmark had almost as much total wind capacity as the United States, despite the obvious differences in country size, and it provided 12 percent of Danish electricity generation, the highest share in the world. A listing of the largest wind turbine companies in 1996 identified Vestas as the largest, accounting for one-fifth of all installed capacity, almost twice as much as the then nearly-bankrupt US Windpower. Other Danish firms were in third, fifth, sixth, and tenth places.[112] They dominated foreign markets rather than rely on support in their home market. By the 1990s Vestas exported 90 percent of the windmills it made and was active in thirty countries.[113] It listed on the Copenhagen Stock Exchange in 1998, and used its new capital to acquire Danish makers of components and other wind companies. In 1997 two other turbine makers, Micon and Nordtank, merged to create NEG Micon, which merged with Vestas six years later.

There were some parallels with the sudden expansion of the German wind energy. As was evident in the case of waste management, the 1990s saw growing environmentalist policies in Germany, which extended across political parties and reflected the strength of social movements. Political hostility to nuclear power, intensified by a major nuclear accident at Chernobyl in 1986, stimulated increased support for renewable energy.

Policy measures transformed the market for renewable energy. In 1990 the Electricity Feed Act, the first feed-in tariff legislation in Germany, required utilities to connect alternative energy generators to the grid, and buy their electricity at agreed rates set at 80 percent of the historical average retail price.[114] The introduction of a 1,000-roof program for PVs in 1990, under which the federal government provided 50 percent of the investment costs plus a further 20 percent from the state governments, provided a substantive breakthrough for solar energy as individual consumers could now generate their own electricity. This program served as a role model elsewhere. The

Japanese Thousand Roofs program, launched in 1994, was a major driver of Japan's growth to become the largest manufacturer in the world by 2000. Unlike in the United States, policy became more rather than less favorable in Germany over time, especially when a new government was formed between the Social Democrats and the Green Party in 1998. The Renewable Energy Sources Act in 2000 decoupled the feed-in tariff process from retail rates and instead based the process on the cost of production. Rates were fixed for twenty years. A new 100,000-roof program was put in place in 1999. By 2008 an estimated half-million German roofs had solar systems.[115]

Environmental activists were able to influence the growth of solar power too. Four large companies generated four-fifths of the country's electric power, while the remainder was generated by a thousand or so local electric utilities, typically owned by the towns which they served. While the large utilities were seeking to generate more power from waste-to-energy sources by buying waste management firms in the early 1990s, activists were able to influence the remaining local electric utilities. They lobbied city councils for a system whereby the private owners of solar power systems could feed the electricity they generated into the public grid, receiving sufficient revenues in return to maintain their systems and make a small profit. After several towns had taken this route, it was approved by the government of the state of North Rhine-Westphalia in 1994 and then spread. By 1997 forty-two German towns had such systems.[116]

A new generation of entrepreneurs had emerged in wind energy even before public policies became so favorable. In wind energy, the most prominent figure was Aloys Wobben. Trained as an electrical engineer, he had an epiphany in the early 1970s after hearing a lecture about the finite nature of fossil fuels.[117] With a friend, he built his first wind power plant in his back garden in 1975. He founded Enercon in 1984, and two years later sold his first wind turbine to a furniture dealer. Enercon's turbines were initially located around Ostfriesland in Lower Saxony, where they were made, and from the beginning the firm provided service maintenance. This service relationship provided feedback to Enercon, enabling it to continuously improve design. In 1992 Wobben created gearless windmills that functioned without hydraulics and were thus more environmentally friendly, as no oil was required to drive the machinery.[118]

Enercon's business remained small until the feed-in tariff legislation was passed, and then flourished. This was because the government not only opened markets for renewable energy but also favored local firms. Two-thirds of the support provided went to local companies rather than Danish suppliers, enabling the German firms to build scale in the market.[119] Wobben captured about one-third of the fast-growing German market for turbines and accounted for most of the German machines sold abroad. By 1996 Enercon already accounted for 8 percent of installed wind capacity in the world, making it the fourth-largest turbine firm. Wobben became a passionate public advocate for sustainability. "Our planet is already damaged," Wobben noted in an interview in 2004. "We have lost animal species, the state of the atmosphere is weak and we have to protect what is left. It should be immediately forbidden for everybody to increase emissions."[120] A second tier of turbine manufacturers also emerged, including the firms of Tacke, AN Wind, and DeWind, along with component manufacturers such as Winergy, which became one of the world's leading gearbox manufacturers.[121]

In solar, too, there was already a German business presence even before government policies turned favorable. The giant electrical company Siemens had undertaken research in solar since the 1950s. In 1990 it acquired ARCO Solar. Siemens closed down its domestic production in favor of its American plants and focused on supplying markets in the developing world. By 1996 Siemens Solar Industries accounted for one-fifth of the total installed PV capacity worldwide. Market share did not translate into profits, however. By 2001 Siemens had sold its affiliate to the oil company Shell. Five years later Shell sold its solar business to SolarWorld, a start-up launched in 1998 by Frank H. Asbeck, who twenty years previously had been one of the co-founders of what became the Green Party in Germany.[122]

Asbeck was one of a new cohort of German solar entrepreneurs. Reiner Lemoine, an aerospace engineer with an early commitment to radical ethical and environmental issues, was the most important. After graduating in 1978, he founded an engineering company in Berlin called Wuseltronik which built measuring devices for wind and solar applications. It was run as a collective on the basis of strong ethical principles, which included refusing to accept contract work from the army. In 1996 he co-founded another company, Solon, to assemble PV modules, which two years later became a public company with the corporate slogan "Don't leave the planet to the stupid." It was initially planned for Solon to make solar cells in its own factory in Berlin, but Lemoine could not raise sufficient capital. After finding that the solar cells which it then had to acquire from outside suppliers were of variable quality,

Lemoine and his colleagues left Solon to form their own specialist cell manufacturer, Q-Cells. This was an innovation in the traditional PV industry structure, which had always seen companies combine wafer manufacture, cell production, and module assembly.[123]

Although the German government's policies favored local firms, the influence of the booming German market was felt elsewhere. The German market, for example, reignited the American solar industry. First Solar, which became one of the world's largest PV manufacturers, originated as a venture started by the highly successful window glass inventor Harold McMaster in Arizona in 1984. Having sold his glass venture and become wealthy, he had the ambition to make thin film cells on a large scale, apparently motivated by a desire to reduce America's dependence on imported oil. Assembling the same research team as in his earlier venture, McMaster made considerable strides in increasing the efficiency of solar cells. In 1999 it was purchased by True North Partners, LLC, the investment arm of the Walton family, who owned the giant retailer WalMart, and renamed First Solar. The company grew rapidly on sales to Germany and went public in 2006.[124]

Europe was not only a story of national governments. Spain's fast growth in wind and solar energy manufacturing and installation was a result of EU policies. Before the 1990s there was little policy support for renewable energy in Spain, but this changed as the EU's regional development fund emerged as a subsidy for renewable energy projects. In 1997 the European Commission proposed that the EU should aim to reach a 12 percent share for renewable energy in electricity generation by 2010, which in turn released further funds to support renewable energy. The Spanish government passed the Electric Power Act, which initiated an aggressive feed-in tariff policy.[125] Many large cities in Spain passed regulations requiring the obligatory installation of solar PV on new buildings and some regional energy plans prioritized the use of PV.[126] By 2000 Spain had 2 percent of its electricity generated by wind energy, a higher percentage than Germany.[127] The engineering company Gamesa, owned by Iberdrola, Spain's second largest electrical utility, developed a large wind turbine business, initially employing Vestas technology.[128] Another engineering firm, Abengoa, based in Seville, grew as a large PV solar manufacturer under the influence of Felipe Benjumea, the son of the founder who, alarmed by global warming, shifted the company into renewable energies, initially serving foreign markets and then partaking of the domestic subsidy-driven boom.[129]

Europe ended up with striking differences between neighboring countries in energy mixes, largely unrelated to resource endowment. Northwest Europe as a whole had strong and steady westerly winds, but it was Denmark and Germany, not Sweden (or Britain and France, where both wind and solar energy remained marginal in 2000) which led the growth in wind energy. Germany's investment in solar was not driven by the country being exceptionally sunny. The strength of anti-nuclear and other social movements had a clear policy impact in Denmark and Germany, but Sweden had many environmental activists, and it ended up dependent on nuclear and hydro. Industrial structures formed part of the explanation of differences. Sweden, Britain, and France, like Germany but unlike Denmark and Spain, had capital-intensive industrial sectors which required a great deal of electricity, supplied constantly. Nuclear energy did not depend on the vagaries of wind and sun. Both Britain and France had nuclear weapons, which encouraged investment in civilian nuclear facilities. Nuclear energy supplied 76 percent of France's electricity in 2000, and 21 percent of Britain's. Both countries had giant state-owned electrical utilities which monopolized market entry, and favored nuclear power.[130]

Evident, also, were different perceptions across Europe of what clean and renewable energy was. An entrepreneur who started a wind farm business in France in 2002 later recalled that when he started talking about his project he was treated as a "utopian." "For most people in France," he added, "wind turbines were just a gadget...We have always been taught in school that nuclear energy is clean, and cheap, and readily available."[131] By the 1980s, there was a completely different perception of nuclear energy in Denmark, and in Germany where, after the Fukushima nuclear reactor meltdown in Japan in 2011, the government ordered the closing of all nuclear plants within ten years.[132]

This second wave of renewable energy policies reshaped the wind and solar industries. Europe emerged as the global center of innovation and dominant market in wind energy in particular, but was also a major force in solar energy. However, the ability of government policies to distort outcomes was evident. When the global financial crisis of 2008 led governments in Europe and elsewhere to reduce subsidies, European wind and solar industries were badly affected, especially as they were exposed to new Chinese competition. Vestas passed through a major crisis in 2012. The Spanish renewables industry's huge and heavily subsidized boom turned into a major bust as the global financial crisis severely hit Spain, causing subsidies to be cut. In 2016 Abengoa, which had debts of $14.5 billion, had to file for Chapter 11 bankruptcy protection for its US affiliate. In the same year Gamesa merged its wind energy business with that of Siemens, with the German company holding almost 60 percent of the equity.[133]

In Germany distortions arising from government policies became increasingly evident. Subsidies to solar resulted in massive adoption by private homes: by 2013 the state of Bavaria alone had more PV capacity than the entire United States. Yet the subsidies for solar cost half of all funding for renewables, while solar provided only one-fifth of the energy from renewables. As wind and solar generated power intermittently, and absent technologies to store energy on a large scale, coal and nuclear plants had to be kept running to guarantee a steady stream of electricity. The result was overproduction of power during daylight hours, driving down spot prices of electricity so much that German utilities had to close down power plants and scrap plans for new ones. The cost was borne by electricity users who paid some of the highest prices for electricity in Europe.[134]

Meanwhile the rapid growth of the Chinese industry, discussed next, decimated the German solar manufacturing industry, as it did much of the American. During 2011 and 2012 most of the German PV manufacturers, including Solon, Solar Millennium, and Q-Cells went bankrupt. The thin-film unit of Q-Cells was acquired by China's Hanergy Thin Film, and the remainder was acquired by the Korean conglomerate Hanwha.[135]

As in the case of California, the ability of public policies to create a market for renewable energy and national champions emerges clearly from the European renewable energy boom from the 1990s. A cohort of visionary green entrepreneurs including Reiner Lemoine and Aloys Wobben responded to, and benefited from, the new feed-in tariffs and subsidies. Green consumers, too, played their part in the growth of the industry by installing solar panels on their roofs. Yet the second renewables boom demonstrated visibly the distorting, costly, and sometimes perverse impacts of many supportive government policies.

Third renewables boom in China
The sudden rapid growth of wind and solar companies in China represented a third renewables boom in which, once again, public policy was central. In 2014 wind and solar energy was still less important as a source of electricity than in

the United States, yet that did not capture the seismic shift which had occurred. In 2000 the United States and Japan still dominated solar PV production. By 2015 China had become the biggest solar PV producer, and had the largest installed capacity in the world. The global average cost of solar panels fell from $9.70 per watt in 1980 to $3.03 per watt in 2005. Thanks the surging production of Chinese firms, it had reached 75 cents in 2015.[136] China's installed wind power capacity soared from 0.567 GW in 2003 to 91 GW in 2013. In 2010 China surpassed the United States in installed wind capacity.[137]

The first wind turbines in China were installed in the late 1980s as part of donor aid from Western countries.[138] In the mid-1990s, China's signing of international environmental treaties, especially the Kyoto Protocol, led to more foreign governments and bilateral agencies providing money and technological assistance to the Chinese government to help create a renewable energy program.[139] Western firms, led by Vestas and Gamesa, dominated the small wind turbine business in China at that stage, though they were obliged to take Chinese joint-venture partners.[140]

Mounting and extreme air pollution, reflecting China's position as the world's largest producer and consumer of coal, stimulated increased Chinese government support for renewable energy. China's first Renewable Energy Law, issued in 2005, defined its strategic priorities and responsibilities for the development of non-fossil energy sources. It targeted 15 percent of national energy consumption to be sourced from renewable energy by 2020. Renewable energy was subsidized by a fee charged to all electricity users of 0.029 cents per kilowatt-hour. The Renewable Energy Law was amended in 2009 to introduce a feed-in tariff which required grid companies to buy all the electricity produced by renewable energy generators.[141]

A number of Chinese firms, often state-owned, developed rapidly, although unevenly. They were helped by strict local content requirements and preference from state-owned Chinese electricity utilities. The share of foreign companies in wind turbine installations fell from 78 percent to 12 percent between 2004 and 2009.The number of Chinese companies among the global top ten turbine manufacturers went from zero to four between 2006 and 2010.[142] In 2015 Xinjiang Goldwind edged past Vestas, still recovering from its recent financial crisis, to become the largest wind turbine manufacturer in the world.

The origins of Xinjiang Goldwind went back to a wind firm founded in 1986 in one of the country's remote, but windy, central Asian provinces. It was supported by the local government and received a Danish grant. As so often in the industry, the person behind the venture, Wang Wenqi, found himself ridiculed for arguing that wind could become a serious energy source, but he gathered around him a group of believers including Wu Gang, who co-founded Goldwind in 1998. The company developed a strong engineering culture and a strategy of acquiring its technology through alliances with second-tier, often German, firms.[143] Its shares were floated on the Shenzhen stock exchange, and it raised almost $1 billion in a Hong Kong IPO in 2010. The largest shareholders were state-owned companies, and it received billions of dollars in a line of credit from the China Development Bank.[144]

China also made a rapid and game-changing entry into the solar industry. A "Golden Roofs" initiative also announced in 2009 provided a subsidy of $2.93 per watt for roof-mounted PV systems over 50 kilowatts which could cover over half of a system's installation cost. A feed-in tariff of $0.16 per kilowatt-hour was also established for PV power projects at the same time. Encouragement for larger utility-scale solar projects was announced in the same year under the "Golden Sun" program, which provided up to 50 percent of project costs, and up to 70 percent of such costs for projects in more remote areas. Provinces also provided local incentives for solar development.[145]

The primary focus for the domestic market of the Chinese government was wind and biofuel, as solar was judged too expensive, but the government was strongly supportive of the growth of locally owned firms in the global solar industry. It provided Chinese firms, such as Yingli Green Energy and Trina, with both low-interest loans and favorable deals for land to buy factories. At the early stages of the growth of the industry, firms extensively recruited Chinese who had graduate degrees from abroad, enabling an unusually fast ramp-up of expertise. Often beginning as suppliers to Western firms, they quickly leveraged their low cost advantage, established their own brands, and grew their international sales.[146]

Unlike wind, there was a distinctly boom and bust dimension to the Chinese solar industry. The Australian-educated Shi Zhengrong founded the solar panel maker Suntech in 2001, supported by local government in the city of Wuxi. By 2005 sales had reached $226 million, primarily from exports. The local government, the China Development Bank, and other Chinese banks helped finance the growth. The company also raised $455 million in an IPO on the New York Stock Exchange. It became the largest manufacturer of PV modules in the world.[147] The problem was that success encouraged new entrants, supported by their own local governments and banks. There was also a surge of new polysilicon factories after 2006 in China as other solar companies sought access to the growing market. Shi had secured polysilicon, an essential ingredient for solar panels, through long-term contracts. When prices fell 95 percent between 2008 and 2013, Suntech was stuck with its original fixed-price contracts, as well as the falling price of solar panels. The highly indebted company went bankrupt in 2013.[148]

There were controversial business practices as well: the Hanergy Group founded by Li Hejun rose and fell between 2011 and 2015 as the world's largest listed solar group. The firm employed thin-film technology, which was less efficient than the crystalline silicon technology employed in most solar panels. It was eventually discovered that revenues were driven almost entirely by inter-group sales and alleged share price manipulation.[149] There were also controversial environmental practices. PV solar manufacturing was inherently a dirty process, but the fast-growing Chinese polysilicon manufacturers had especially poor pollution processes and regularly dumped toxic waste directly on neighboring lands, amongst other foul practices.[150]

In China, then, the power of governments to co-create renewable energy markets along with talented and passionate entrepreneurs and companies was again on display. Equally evident was the susceptibility of the heady cocktail of extensive subsidies and booming markets to lead to disorderly busts and unethical practices. China's solar boom in particular transformed the cost structure of the global industry, bankrupting many previous incumbents in the process. The price fall was so dramatic that the cost of solar energy for the first time began reaching so-called grid parity with fossil fuels, without the need for subsidy. During 2015 two wind turbines were installed every hour in China, and in the world as a whole half a million solar panels were installed every day.[151]

Conclusion

Before 1980, entrepreneurs and inventors had pioneered innovative, green-friendly methods of managing waste and producing wind and solar energy technologies. But with public policies focused on supporting landfills, fossil fuels, and nuclear energy, it was impossible to build a market and to raise the amounts of capital needed to finance innovation to reduce costs. The policy shift among governments after 1980 towards encouraging recycling and growing the wind and solar industries was remarkable. Through a combination of subsidies and tax incentives, it aligned profits with sustainability and enabled businesses in these industries to innovate and, perhaps most importantly, to scale. Firms could begin to access capital markets; in some cases, subsidies and credit functioned as a form of quasi-venture capital. Without such policies, it would surely not be the case that today two-thirds of German waste is recycled, 40 percent of Danish electricity is produced from wind, and Chinese firms have sharply reduced the cost of solar panels.

Although governments worldwide have been galvanized by the crisis of climate change, especially after the Kyoto Protocol in 1997, the striking differences in both recycling rates and the importance of solar and wind in electricity generation among even the developed countries demonstrate how much policies differ between countries. The contrast between Germany and the United States in both industries was noteworthy. There were several broad explanations for these policy differences, from the strength of social movements and the industrial structure of countries, to differences in national political systems. In many key areas, as we have seen, the United States lags behind some of its European counterparts green-wise. The election as President in November 2016 of Donald Trump, who described climate change as a hoax, was indicative of the chasm.[152]

The variations in public policy played out, once more, in the context of continuing debates about the meaning of sustainability. The importation of modern waste management firms into developing countries was seen as a step towards enhancing sustainability, and indeed it resulted in falling carbon emissions, but poor scavengers produced higher rates of recycling, and their small incomes were vital for the social sustainability of their communities. Wind and solar energy addressed global warming, but wind turbines killed birds and PV solar energy involved a polluting manufacturing process and toxic waste.

The Janus-face of public policy was evident. Subsidies, feed-in tariffs, tax breaks, legislation to promote recycling, and other policies had a positive effect on the growth of new technologies, but they were also prone to generate rent-seeking behavior, as repeated corporate scandals in waste management indicated. Even without such behavior, distorted outcomes were frequent. The boom and bust cycles in solar and wind energy were manifestations of the downsides faced by industries dependent on subsidies and tax breaks. As subsidies and other policies enabled and encouraged the scaling of the renewable energy and waste management industries, the advantages of scale began to be matched by some disadvantages of conventional business. The large oil corporations which invested in solar, and the large engineering conglomerates which invested in both wind and solar, offered a portfolio of both sustainable and polluting technologies to the world. They were patient investors in still-evolving technologies, but their renewable energy businesses alleviated only a fraction of the pollution their other businesses created. Perhaps most contradictory of all, the large integrated waste management companies depend on the continuation of a wasteful world. The challenge of making more profit by producing less waste and using less energy remains to be solved.

Notes

1. David Vogel, *The Politics of Precaution* (Princeton: Princeton University Press, 2012), pp.133–7, 226.

2. Ibid., pp.33, 35–6.

3. Lois Marie Gibbs, *Love Canal and the Birth of the Environmental Health Movement* (Washington, DC: Island Press, 2011).

4. Timothy Jacobson, *Waste Management: An American Corporate Success Story* (Washington, DC: Gateway Business Books, 1993), pp.97–8.

5. Louis Blumberg and Robert Gottlieb, *War on Waste* (Washington, DC: Island Press, 1989), pp.39–41, 48–52.

6. Richard N. L. Andrews, "The EPA at 40: An Historical Perspective," *Duke Environmental Law & Policy Forum* 21 (Spring 2011), p.244; Vogel, *Politics*, pp.223–4.

7. <https://www.epa.gov/smm/energy-recovery-combustion-municipal-solid-waste-msw>, accessed July 11, 2016.

8. Blumberg and Gottlieb, *War on Waste*, pp.203–18.

9. Robert A. Bohm, David H. Folz, Thomas C. Kinnaman, and Michael J. Podolsky, "The Costs of Municipal Waste and Recycling Programs," *Resources, Conservation and Recycling* 54 (2010), p.864.

10. Waste Business Journal, *Waste Market Overview & Outlook 2012* (San Diego: Waste Business Journal, 2012).

11. IBIS World, US Industry Reports, <http://clients1.ibisworld.com.ezp-prod1.hul.harvard.edu/reports/us/industry/majorcompanies.aspx?entid=1511#MP348500>, accessed August 13, 2016.

12. Harold Crooks, *Giants of Garbage: The Rise of the Global Waste Industry and the Politics of Pollution Control* (Toronto: James Lorimer, 1993), p.51; Lanny Hickman, *American Alchemy: The History of Solid Waste Management in the United States* (Santa Barbara: Forester Press, 2003), p.90.

13. Crooks, *Giants*, pp.88–102; Waste Management Inc., Final Report by Edward L. Miller, District Attorney for San Diego, March 1992, <http://infohouse.p2ric.org/ref/26/25041.pdf>, accessed June 4, 2015.

14. <http://www.sec.gov/litigation/complaints/complr17435.htm>, accessed June 8, 2015.

15. Barnaby J. Feder, "Waste-Hauling Companies announce $13 Billion Merger," *New York Times*, March 12, 1998.

16. Jenna Russell, "Wheelabrator OK's Settlement of $7.5 Million," *Boston Globe*, May 3, 2011.

17. Crooks, *Giants*, p.37.

18. David Barboza and Laura M. Holson "A Trash Hauler is Buying a Much Bigger Rival, a Type of Deal that Makes Wall Street a Bit Nervous," *Wall Street Journal*, March 9, 1999; Hickman, *American Alchemy*, p.90.

19. Daniel Hoornweg and Perinaz Bhada-Tata, *What a Waste: A Global Review of Solid Waste Management* (Washington, DC: World Bank, 2012), Annex L.

20. Ibid., p.8, Annex J. Municipal waste generation in tonnes per day for Japan was 144,466; Germany 127,816; Britain 97,342; and Turkey 86, 301. This source does not give daily rates for Cambodia.

21. Ibid., pp.29, 32–3.

22. Raymond G. Stokes, Roman Köster, and Stephen C. Sambrook, *The Business of Waste: Great Britain and Germany, 1945 to the Present* (Cambridge: Cambridge University Press, 2014), pp.259–60.

23. Tina Emslander, *Das duale Entsorgungssystem für Verpackungsabfall* (Wiesbaden: Springer Fachmedien, 1995), pp.138–9.

24. Stokes, Köster, and Sambrook, *Business of Waste*, p.281.

25. Peter Mugay, Hermann Niehues, Reinhard Lohmann, and Claus Andreas, *"Verantwortung übernehmen und unternehmerisch handeln": Norbert Rethmann 60 Jahre* (Selm: Rethmann, 1999), pp.62–3, 67–70, 80.

26. Thomas Rummler and Wolfgang Schutt, *Verpackungsverordnung: Praxishandbuch mit Kommentar* (Hamburg: Behr's Verlag, 1991), pp.25–6; Lilo Fischer and Ulrich Petschow, "Municipal Waste Management in Germany," in Nicolas Buclet and Olivier Godard (eds.), *Municipal Waste Management in Europe: A Comparative Study in Building Regimes* (Dordrecht: Kluwer, 2000), pp.23–9; Bette Fishbein, *Germany, Garbage, and the Green Dot: Challenging the Throwaway Society* (New York: INFORM, 1994), pp.21–2.

27. Rummler and Schutt, *Verpackungsverordnung*, pp.26–8.

28. Christian Thywissen, *Die Abfallwirtschaft in der Bundesrepublik Deutschland* (Frankfurt: Peter Lang, 1995), p.128.

29. Gernot Klepper and Peter Michaelis, "Economic Incentives for Packaging Waste Management: The Dual System in Germany," in Alberto Curzio, Luigi Prosperetti, and Roberto Zoboli (eds.), *The Management of Municipal Solid Waste in Europe: Economic, Technological and Environmental Perspectives* (Amsterdam: Elsevier, 1994), pp.175–6; Thywissen, *Abfallwirtschaft*, p.132.

30. Agnes Bünemann, "Duales System Deutschland—Ein Rückblick über die Entwicklung in Deutschland," in Peter Kurth (ed.), *Ressource Abfall: Politische und wirtschaftliche Betrachtungen anlässlich des 50-jährigen Bestehens des BDE* (Neuruppin: TK Verlag, 2011); Fritz Vorholz, "Punkte gegen die Umwelt," *Die Zeit*, January 7, 1994.

31. Thywissen, *Abfallwirtschaft*, p.132; Stokes, Köster, and Sambrook, *Business of Waste*, pp.274–8.

32. Axel Seidel, *Kreislaufwirtschaft im Spannungsfeld zwischen Ökonomie und Ökologie in Deutschland* (Cologne: Wirtschafts- und Sozialgeographisches Institut der Universität zu Köln, 2000), pp.130–65; Annette Fritz, *Die Entsorgungswirtschaft im Spannungsfeld zwischen Abfallpolitik und Kartellrecht* (Frankfurt: Peter Lang, 2001), pp.114ff.

33. Seidel, *Kreislaufwirtschaft*, pp.130, 133; Fritz, *Entsorgungswirtschaft*, pp.122ff.

34. H. Rylander, "Waste Management in Sweden: A National Report," *Waste Management & Research* 3 (1985), pp.81–7.

35. CSI Resource Systems, Inc., "Environmental Legislation and the Regulation of Waste Management in Sweden" (Golden, CO: National Renewable Energy Laboratory, 1995), pp.14–15.

36. Lennart Lundqvist, *Sweden and Ecological Governance* (Manchester: Manchester University Press, 2004), p.70; OECD, *Improving Recycling Markets* (Paris: OECD, 2006), p.121.

37. Stokes, Köster, and Sambrook, *Business of Waste*, pp.255–8, 294; Steve Davies, "Politics and Markets: The Case of UK Municipal Waste Management," *Cardiff University School of Social Sciences Working Paper* No. 95 (November 2007).

38. Stokes, Köster, and Sambrook, *Business of Waste*, pp.283–90.

39. Vogel, *Politics*, p.185.

40. Nathan Kunz, Atalay Atasu, Kieren Mayers, and Luk Van Wassenhove, "Extended Producer Responsibility: Stakeholder Concerns and Future Developments," *INSEAD Social Innovation Centre Report* (2014), p.7.

41. "Facts and Figures on E-Waste and Recycling," <http://www.electronicstakeback.com/wp-content/uploads/Facts_and_Figures_on_EWaste_and_Recycling.pdf>, accessed June 10, 2016; Kunz et al., "Extended Producer Responsibility," p.8.

42. Interview with Mamoru Mitsumoto (Takeei Corporation), Tokyo, May 30, 2010.

43. Mitsubishi Research Institute, "Report on Global Warming Issues 2014: Prospects of Waste Management and Recycling Industry" (March 13, 2015); Japanese Ministry of Environment, March 25, 2013.

44. Japan Ministry of the Environment, "Solid Waste Management and Recycling Technology of Japan: Towards a Sustainable Society" (2011), <https://www.env.go.jp/en/recycle/smcs/attach/swmrt.pdf>, accessed October 23, 2016.

45. Japan Ministry of the Environment, "History and Current State of Waste Management in Japan" (2014), <https://www.env.go.jp/en/recycle/smcs/attach/hcswm.pdf>, accessed June 8, 2016.

46. Interview with Mamoru Mitsumoto. Takeei Corporation had revenues of $250 million in 2015.

47. Interview with Yoshita Koga (Dowa Holdings), Tokyo, May 31, 2010.

48. Interview with Hirokazu Yoshikawa (Dowa Holdings), Tokyo, May 31, 2010.

49. Ibid.

50. For Veolia, see Veolia Environnement, *Veolia Environnement, 1853–2003: 150 ans au service de l'environnement* (Paris: Éditions Cercle d'Art, 2003).

51. "Sound Group's Wen Yibo: 'We Make Our Lives on Technology and Capability,'" Knowledge@Wharton, <http://knowledge.wharton.upenn.edu/article/sound-groups-wen-yibo-we-make-our-lives-on-technology-and-capability>, accessed August 29, 2012; "The House of Wen," <http://www.emersonanalytics.co/downloads/Sound%20Global%20Presentation%20v25.pdf>, accessed June 2, 2016.

52. Judy Li, "Ways Forward from China's Urban Waste Problem," February 1, 2015, <http://www.thenatureofcities.com/2015/02/01/ways-forward-from-chinas-urban-waste-problem>, accessed June 3, 2016.

53. Martin Medina, *The World's Scavengers: Salvaging for Sustainable Consumption and Production* (Lanham, MD: AltaMira Press, 2007); Martin Medina, "Living off Trash in Latin America," *ReVista* (Winter 2015), pp.20–3.

54. <http://www.nyc.gov/html/ia/gprb/downloads/pdf/SaoPaulo_landfills.pdf>, accessed June 2, 2016.

55. "Why Bill Gates Loves These 'Garbage' Stocks," June 30, 2014, <http://www.nasdaq.com/article/why-bill-gates-loves-these-garbage-stocks-cm366259>, accessed July 8, 2015.

56. Based on sources for Figure 8.2.

57. Data from Earth Policy Institute (hereafter EPI), <http://www.earth-policy.org/data_center>, accessed June 15, 2016.

58. Noel Maurer and Richard Vietor, "Note on Wind Energy," Harvard Business School Note 9-714-021 (rev. October 24, 2013).

59. Dustin Mulvaney, "Hazardous Materials Used in Silicon PV Cell Production: A Primer," <http://www.solarindustrymag.com/online/issues/SI1309/FEAT_05_Haz ardous_Materials_Used_In_Silicon_PV_Cell_Production_A_Primer.html>, accessed June 23, 2016; Paul Gipe, *Wind Energy Comes of Age* (New York: John Wiley, 1995), chapters 9 and 10.

60. <http://www.iea.org/publications/freepublications/publication/KeyWorld2014.pdf>, accessed June 2, 2016.

61. Data from EPI; 2015 data from "China to More Than Triple Solar Power Capacity in Five Years," *Bloomberg News*, March 21, 2016.

62. Data from EPI.

63. International Atomic Energy Association, "50 Years of Nuclear Energy," <https:// www.iaea.org/About/Policy/GC/GC48/Documents/gc48inf-4_ftn3.pdf>, accessed June 4, 2016.

64. Jimmy Carter, "Solar Energy Message to the Congress," June 20, 1979, <http:// www.presidency.ucsb.edu/ws/?pid=32503>, accessed July 1, 2016.

65. Travis Bradford, *Solar Revolution: The Economic Transformation of the Global Energy Industry* (Cambridge, MA: MIT Press, 2006), p.98.

66. Janet L. Sawin, "The Role of Government in the Development and Diffusion of Renewable Technologies: Wind Power in the United States, California, Denmark and Germany," Tufts University Ph.D., September 2001, pp.105–6; Alexis Madrigal, *Powering the Dream* (Philadelphia: Da Capo, 2011), pp.238–9.

67. Matt Hopkins, "The Makings of a Champion or, Wind Innovation for Sale: The Wind Industry in the United States 1980-2011," AIR Working Paper #13-08/02, 2012.

68. Robert Righter, *Windfall: Wind Energy in America Today* (Norman: University of Oklahoma Press, 2011), pp.190–6.

69. Ibid., pp.165–6.

70. Peter Asmus, *Reaping the Wind* (Washington, DC: Island Press, 2001), pp.124, 72–6; Geoffrey Jones, "Entrepreneurship, Policy, and the Geography of Wind Energy," in Hartmut Berghoff and Adam Rome (eds.), *Green Capitalism? Business and the Environment in the Twentieth Century* (Philadelphia: University of Pennsylvania Press, 2017), pp.219–20.

71. Asmus, *Reaping the Wind*, p.75; Righter, *Windfall*, pp.196–7.

72. Gipe, *Wind Energy*, pp.33–4.

73. Sawin, "Role," pp.205–8.

74. Ibid., pp.200–20, 205–8, 216.

75. Ibid., p.198.

76. Righter, *Windfall*, p.214; Asmus, *Reaping the Wind*, pp.86–7; Ion Bogdan Vasi, *Winds of Change: The Environmental Movement and the Global Development of the Wind Energy Industry* (Oxford: Oxford University Press, 2011), pp.161–3.

77. Sawin, "Role," p.213.

78. Asmus, *Reaping the Wind*, pp.97–100, 151.

79. Righter, *Windfall*, pp.218–19.

80. Gipe, *Wind Energy*, p.36. Mitsubishi Heavy Industries had entered the California market in 1987 when it sold 660 units at the Techachapi wind farm.

81. Bob Johnstone, *Switching to Solar* (New York: Prometheus Books, 2011), p.81.

82. Righter, *Windfall*, p.216.

83. Michael W. Handsen, Marcus M. Larsen, Torben Pedersen, and Bent Petersen, *Strategies in Emerging Markets: A Case Book on Danish Multinational Corporations in China and India* (Copenhagen: Copenhagen Business School Press, 2010), pp.141–2.

84. Asmus, *Reaping the Wind*, p.174.

85. Malcolm Salter, *Innovation Corrupted: The Origins and Legacy of Enron's Collapse* (Cambridge, MA: Harvard University Press, 2008), pp.235–6.

86. Loren Fox, *Enron: The Rise and Fall* (Hoboken, NJ: John Wiley, 2003), pp.131–2; Hopkins, "Makings of a Champion."

87. John Perlin, *From Space to Earth: The Story of Electricity* (Ann Arbor, MI: Aatec, 1999), p.68, n. 26.

88. "A Shakedown shapes Up in Photovoltaics," *Chemical Week*, February 3, 1982, p.33.

89. John J. Berger, *Charging Ahead: The Business of Renewable Energy and What It Means for America* (New York: Henry Holt, 1997), p.81.

90. Stephen W. Hinch, "Solar Power," *High Technology*, August 1984, p.46. Polaroid, Box M 60.

91. James Bates, "Sale of Arco Unit Casts Shadow on Future of Solar Energy Ventures," *Los Angeles Times*, March 7, 1989.

92. Berger, *Charging Ahead*, pp.80–8; Johnstone, *Switching to Solar*, p.82.

93. Interview with Peter Varadi, September 7, 2011.

94. Peter F. Varadi, *Sun Above the Horizon* (Singapore: Pan Stanford, 2014), pp.249–51.

95. Berger, *Charging Ahead*, p.68.

96. Ibid., p.69.

97. Ibid., p.70.

98. Ibid., pp.68–70.

99. Madrigal, *Powering the Dream*, pp.117–23; Berger, *Charging Ahead*, pp.24–5; Ruthie Blum Leibowitz, "One on One: Reaching for the Sun," *The Jerusalem Post*, June 12, 2008, <http://www.jpost.com/Features/One-on-One-Reaching-for-the-sun>, accessed April 8, 2015.

100. Madrigal, *Powering the Dream*, pp.123–6.

101. Ibid., pp.126–30; Carl J. Weinberg and Robert H. Williams, "Energy from the Sun," *Scientific American* (September 1990), pp.147–55.

102. Leibowitz, "Reaching for the Sun."

103. Madrigal, *Powering the Dream*, pp.132–6.

104. Data from EPI.

105. Bradford, *Solar Revolution*, p.98.

106. "Wondering About Wind," *The Economist*, August 1, 2015; Thomas P. Lyon and Haitao Yin, "Why Do States Adopt Renewable Portfolio Standards? An Empirical Investigation," *Energy Journal* 31, no. 3 (2010).

107. Katie Valentine, "Obama Administration Becomes the Third to Install Solar Panels on White House Grounds," *Climate Progress*, August 15, 2013.

108. Vasi, *Winds of Change*, pp.68–9.

109. Ben Blackwell, *Wind Power: The Struggle for Control of a New Global Industry* (London: Routledge, 2015), pp.14–16.

110. Vasi, *Winds of Change*, pp.70–5.

111. Svend Auken, "Issues and Policy: Answers in the Wind: How Denmark Became a World Pioneer in Wind Power," *Fletcher Forum on World Affairs* 26 (2002), p.149.

112. Peter Karnoe, "When Low-Tech Becomes High-Tech: The Social Construction of Technological Learning Processes in the Danish and the American Wind Turbine Industry," in Peter Karnoe, Peer Hull Krisensen, and Poul Houman Andersen (eds.), *Mobilizing Resources and Generating Competencies* (Copenhagen: Copenhagen Business School Press, 1999).

113. Michael W. Hansen, Marcus M. Larsen, Torben Pedersen, and Bent Petersen, *Strategies in Emerging Markets: A Case Book on Danish Multinational Corporations in China and India* (Copenhagen: Copenhagen Business School Press, 2010), p.141.

114. Vasi, *Winds of Change*, p.55.

115. Volker Lauber and Lutz Mez, "Three Decades of Renewable Electricity Policies in Germany," *Energy and Environment* 15, no. 4 (2004), pp.599–623; Sawin, "Role," pp.289–91; Geoffrey Jones and Loubna Bouamane, "'Power from Sunshine': A Business History of Solar Energy," *Harvard Business School Working Paper*, No. 12-105, May 2012.

116. Johnstone, *Switching to Solar*, pp.170–6.

117. Kerstin Krupp, "Der Bill Gates von Ostfriesland," *Berliner Zeitung*, September 17, 2005.

118. Gipe, *Wind Energy*, pp.56, 219.

119. Ibid., pp.39–40.

120. "Aloys Wobben, Chairman and Managing Director, Enercon," *Wind Directions*, May/June 2004.

121. Sawin, "Role," pp.293–4.

122. Varadi, *Sun*, p.328; Jones and Bouamane, "'Power from Sunshine.'"

123. Johnstone, *Switching to Solar*, pp.197–201.

124. Steve Gelsi, "For First Solar's Michael Ahearn, A Year in the Sun," *Market Watch*, December 6, 2007.

125. Vasi, *Winds of Change*, pp.75–6.

126. Jordi de la Hoz, Oriol Boix, et al., "Promotion of Grid-Connected Photovoltaic Systems in Spain: Performance Analysis of the Period 1998–2008," *Renewable and Sustainable Energy Reviews* 14 (2010), pp.2547–63.

127. IEA, *World Energy Outlook 2001* (Paris: IEA); for Germany, see Table 8.2.

128. Joanna I. Lewis, "A Comparison of Wind Power Industry Development Strategies in Spain, India and China," Center for Resource Solutions, July 17, 2007.

129. <http://www.abengoa.com/web/en/compania/nuestra_historia>, accessed June 19, 2016.

130. Martin Chick, *Electricity and Energy Policy in Britain, France and the United States since 1945* (Cheltenham: Edward Elgar, 2007), pp.7–11, 29.

131. Interview with Philippe Vignal, WPD, April 8, 2011.

132. Helen Pidd, "Germany to Shut All Nuclear Reactors," *The Guardian*, May 30, 2011.

133. Usha Haley and Douglas Schuler, "Government Policy and Firm Strategy in the Solar Photovoltaic Industry," *California Management Review* 54, no. 1 (Fall 2011), p.20; Glenn Meyers, "Abengoa Granted Bankruptcy Protection in USA," CleanTechnica.com, May 4 2016, <https://cleantechnica.com/2016/05/04/abengoa-granted-bankruptcy-protection-usa/>; "Siemens and Gamesa to merge wind businesses," *Financial Times*, June 17, 2016.

134. Andrew Curry, "Can You Have Too Much Solar Energy?" <http://www.slate.com/articles/health_and_science/alternative_energy/2013/03/solar_power_in_germany_how_a_cloudy_country_became_the_world_leader_in_solar.2.html>, accessed August 3, 2016.

135. In 2011 many US solar firms went bankrupt, including Solyndra, which had received over $528 million in federal green energy loan guarantees. "The Solyndra Scandal: The FBI Raids a Beneficiary of Federal Loan Guarantees," *Wall Street Journal*, September 9, 2011.

136. Ed Crooks, "Swanson's Law Provides Green Ray of Sunshine," *Financial Times*, January 19, 2016; Matt Hopkins and William Lazonick, "Soaking Up the Sun and Blowing in the Wind: Clean Tech Needs Patient Capital," *AIR Working Paper* 13-08/01.

137. Richard J. Campbell, "China and the United States: A Comparison of Green Energy Programs and Policies," *Congressional Research Service Report* 77-5700, April 30, 2014.

138. Wen-Qiang Liu, Lin Gan, and Xi-Liang Zhang, "Cost-Competitive Incentives for Wind Energy Development in China: Institutional Dynamics and Policy Changes," *Energy Policy* 30, no. 9 (2002), pp.753–65.

139. Elizabeth C. Economy, *The River Runs Black: The Environmental Challenge to China's Future* (Ithaca: Cornell University Press, 2004), p.18; H. Yu, "Global Environment Regime and Climate Policy Coordination in China," *Journal of Chinese Political Science* 9, no. 2 (2004), pp.63–77.

140. Ben Backwell, *Wind Power: The Struggle for Control of a New Global Industry* (New York: Routledge, 2015), p.40.

141. Yingqi Liu and Ari Kokko, "Wind Power in China: Policy and Development Challenges," *Energy Policy* 38 (2010), pp.5520–9.

142. Mark L. Clifford, *The Greening of Asia* (New York: Columbia University Press, 2015), pp.48–51; Lewis, "Comparison."

143. Backwell, *Wind*, pp.44–51.

144. Clifford, *Greening of Asia*, pp.54–9.

145. Campbell, "China and the United States."

146. Gabrielle Meersohn and Michael W. Hansen, "The Rise of Chinese Challenger Firms in the Global Solar Industry," in Rolf Wüstenhagen and Robert Wuebker (eds.), *Handbook of Research on Energy Entrepreneurship* (Northampton, MA: Edward Elgar, 2011), p.107; Christian Binz, "Low-Carbon Leapfrogging and Globalization: How China Developed Its Solar PV Industry," paper given at Energy Policy Seminar Series, Harvard Kennedy School, Spring 2015.

147. Clifford, *Greening of Asia*, pp.17–21.

148. Ibid., pp.22–8.

149. Obert Kwong, Miles Johnson, and Cynthia O'Murchu, "Hanergy Unit Plunges 47% in Just 24 Minutes," *Financial Times*, May 21, 2015.

150. Yingling Liu, "The Dirty Side of a 'Green' Industry," <http://www.worldwatch.org/node/5650>, accessed June 25, 2016.

151. International Energy Agency, "IEA raises its five-year renewable growth forecast as 2015 marks record year," <https://www.iea.org/newsroom/news/2016/october/iea-raises-its-five-year-renewable-growth-forecast-as-2015-marks-record-year.html>, accessed October 26, 2016.

152. Erik Mack, "Most of you don't agree with Donald Trump that climate change is a hoax," *Forbes*, November 23, 2016.

9

Corporate Environmentalism and the Boundaries of Sustainability

Beginning in the 1980s, the world of green business became much bigger—and a lot more diversified. Some pioneering, values-driven green entrepreneurs grew their businesses to a scale that resembled conventional big businesses. Meanwhile, large conventional businesses assumed the mantle of sustainability. Indeed, in this era of "new corporate environmentalism," as one study termed it, these large businesses asserted a leading role in solving the world's environmental challenges.[1]

The sudden apparent mainstreaming of sustainability was remarkable compared to the century before 1980. In 2016 the annual rankings of the world's most sustainable companies by the magazine *Corporate Knights*, a sustainability-focused media and research company based in Canada, were headed by BMW, the German luxury car manufacturer; Dassault Systems, the French software company; Outotec, the Finnish construction company; the Commonwealth Bank of Australia, a commercial bank; and Adidas, the German apparel and sportswear company.[2] By the 2000s chief executives of the world's largest firms had donned the garb of visionary prophets, once worn by the likes of Jerome Rodale. In 2014 Peter Brabeck, the chairman of the Swiss consumer goods corporation Nestlé, made newspaper headlines when he proclaimed that although climate change was a major issue, water scarcity was even more critical. "Humankind is running out of water at an alarming pace," Brabeck warned. "We're going to run out of water long before we run out of oil."[3] In the same year a survey by a public opinion research consultancy identified Nestlé's competitor, the Anglo-Dutch Unilever whose vast business spanned consumer products from detergents and soaps to margarine and ice cream, as the most sustainable company on the planet, exceeding by a long margin firms such as Natura.[4]

The greening of large corporations occurred across industries. Chinese state-owned firms and Western electronics conglomerates came to dominate wind and solar energy. GE's acquisition of Enron's wind business in 2002, for the price of $358 million, made it at a stroke one of the world's largest wind energy business.[5] In the following year GE launched its Ecomagination program, which bundled wind energy with its nuclear power technology and fossil fuel businesses together "to build innovative solutions for today's environmental challenges while driving economic growth."[6] Ecomagination fitted into GE's careful tax planning, which enabled the giant corporation to pay no federal taxes in the United States.[7] The German electrical conglomerate Siemens entered wind energy on a large scale in 2004 by buying Bonus in Denmark and, not long afterward, German-based Winergy, the world's largest turbine gearbox manufacturer. In 2016 Siemens's merger with Gamesa's wind business (the fifth-largest in the world) further increased its position as one of the largest turbine manufacturers.[8]

It was not only capital-intensive industries where big businesses became sustainability champions. In 2008 Starbucks, the coffee retail chain, launched the Shared Planet program "to do business in ways that are good for people and the planet."[9] In the same year the giant retailer Walmart announced its Sustainability Initiative, based on the belief, a subsequent study observed, that sustainability can be "good for the business, good for competitiveness, good for the bottom line."[10] In 2010 Unilever, led by a new chief executive named Paul Polman, launched the Sustainability Living Plan designed to double the size of the business within a decade, but to halve the firm's environmental impact.[11]

The optimistic interpretation of the blossoming of corporate environmentalism was that conventional business, like governments and consumers, had recognized the rising scale of environmental damage inflicted since the Industrial Revolution, and had begun to change course in response. The proposals for green capitalism, offered by John Elkington, Paul Hawken, and others in the 1980s and 1990 and discussed in Chapter 5, have borne fruit. Big business, by definition, has a much greater capacity than smaller green entrepreneurs to invest in the technological innovation—always fraught with high failure rates—needed to repair environmental degradation and lighten the environmental footprint of their activities. Some management scholars have emphasized a synergy between large corporations and green entrepreneurial firms. "Emerging Davids," as management scholars Kai Hockerts and Rolf

Wüstenhagen have described entrepreneurial firms, were more radical in their pursuit of sustainability-related opportunities but typically lacked the capabilities to reach a mass market. "Greening Goliaths," as they termed large corporations, might be less ambitious in their environmental and social goals, but they possessed a greater capacity to make things happen.[12]

Pessimists, on the other hand, saw a lack of genuinely green ambition by the Goliaths. A study by Peter Dauvergne and Jane Lister, entitled *Eco-Business*, interpreted the adoption by large corporations of sustainability strategies primarily as a competitive strategy to gain efficiencies, control supply chains, and enhance the legitimacy of brands. Environmental gains, if any, were seen as primarily incremental.[13] The author and activist Naomi Klein's book on the role of capitalism and climate change, entitled *This Time It Is Different*, concluded that unregulated capitalism could not in itself significantly ameliorate climate change because the imperative of seeking profits would always limit too greatly corporations' commitments to sustainability. "It will have to be legislated," Klein concluded, "using the kinds of tough regulations, higher taxes, and steeper royalty rates these sectors have resisted all along."[14]

While the scale of big firms held out promise to those who believed in technological breakthroughs—the potential could be seen in the radical reduction of the cost of PV cells as large Chinese firms invested in the technology—others returned to the arguments made by E. F. Schumacher that scale as such was the problem, and not the solution, for sustainability. This argument lay at the heart of the bioregional movement associated with Peter Berg, whose disillusionment with the United Nations Stockholm Conference in 1972 led him to espouse the cause of breaking down the world into separate biotic provinces or bioregions to achieve sustainable living.[15] The mandate of avoiding scaling was also taken up by the Slow Food Movement, established by the Italian culinary expert Carlo Petrini in 1989. The philosophy of Slow Food included the belief that "good, clean and fair food" should be grown and bought locally.[16] Faith in the local as the path forward for sustainability was the central belief of the Business Alliance for Local Living Economies, co-founded in 2000 by the Philadelphia restaurant entrepreneur Judy Wicks. She aspired not to see the greening of large global corporations but, rather, the creation of "a decentralized global network of sustainable local economies comprised of independent, locally owned businesses that support their local communities and ecosystems."[17]

Whether it is termed "new corporate environmentalism" or "eco-business," the sudden apparent embrace of sustainability by big business represented a fundamental break from the past, but one whose meaning remains contested. This chapter examines how this happened by exploring the interaction between big business and green entrepreneurial firms. The critical question for the possibility of green business as a model is whether, and how far, profits and sustainability can become truly aligned.

The greening of corporations

Although the greening of big business galloped forward at a striking pace from the 1980s onward, it built on earlier foundations of both reactive and proactive corporate environmentalism. Among the former, firms in heavy industries such as chemicals and petroleum as early as the 1960s found themselves facing criticism about the pollution they caused. As criticism translated into regulation, firms both in the United States and Europe responded with embryonic environmental strategies. Typically, as managers on both sides of the Atlantic disliked the extra costs of responding to regulation, these strategies were initially focused on compliance.[18]

German chemical companies were among the first large Western corporations which embraced more proactive environmental strategies during the 1970s. This reflected the broader emergence of environmental issues in German society and government, but more specifically, it was driven by the location of the head offices of leading firms Bayer and Henkel in the state of North Rhine-Westphalia near the Rhine River. Senior management was directly exposed to criticism by local activists and regional politicians about polluted water and bad odors, posing a threat to reputations developed over more than a century. They came to the conclusion that investing in technologies and products which were more eco-friendly could provide an opportunity to create value rather than simply impose costs on their firms, and that self-identifying as green had commercial as well as reputational benefits.[19]

These German companies were not the only pioneers of corporate environmentalism. Beginning in the 1970s Swedish automobile company Volvo began to invest in reducing industrial pollutants and toxic materials, starting with the development of safe alternatives to the solvent-based paints used on vehicles. This was motivated by growing citizen activism in the country, the holding of the UN Conference on the Environment in Stockholm, and the appointment of a new chief executive, Pehr Gyllenhammar, who expressed strong environmentalist views.[20] The engineer recruited in 1974 to develop safer paints had developed environmental concerns having seen the impact of acid rain on the Swedish countryside, which was particularly acute as the country's soil was low in limestone which could have better absorbed it.[21]

The much more explicit, and public, greening of big business which began from the 1980s was in a different league compared to the past. There is no one answer to explain why this happened. Its causes are several and overlapping. There are at least six interrelated, simultaneous developments that can help us make sense of this sweeping change.

The first development was the redefining of environmental issues under the category of sustainability by the Brundtland Commission in 1987. The joining of social issues and economic growth in the concept of sustainability made it more compatible with large corporations, not least in apparently sanctioning practices which might not be environmentally positive but could be seen as helping society by providing employment, for example. Subsequently, the emergence of climate change as a global crisis raised sustainability to a commitment like a loyalty oath that all were expected to uphold, including CEOs of major corporations.

Second, the work of providing arguments, definitions, certifications, and metrics was done by leaders of green thought, including entrepreneurs themselves. This made the concept of sustainability more readily adaptable by business than if it had been solely the work of radical activists outside the business world. The concept of the triple bottom line, for example, resonated with the chief executives of leading global firms. The oil company Shell sought advice from its pioneer, John Elkington, and used the triple bottom line concept in its annual report for 1999.[22] The growth of green certification and the Global Reporting Initiative provided metrics which enabled big business to demonstrate publicly that it was becoming sustainable. Business school academics took up sustainability too. Michael Porter, a strategy professor at the Harvard Business School, became an influential voice from the mid-1990s asserting that sustainability and profitability were fully compatible.[23] Business and sustainability courses spread in the top business schools.[24]

Individual authors and their books sometimes converted business leaders. Paul Hawken's *The Ecology of Commerce*, to give one example, had a transformational impact on Ray Anderson, the founder of a large US commercial carpet manufacturer called Interface, who at the age of 60 became a sudden convert to environmentalism after reading it. As he later recalled in his own book, Anderson was at first horrified to see himself, and other business leaders, "indicted as a plunderer, a destroyer of the earth." He was energized by Hawken's view that business was also "the only institution large enough, wealthy enough, and pervasive and powerful enough to lead humankind out of the mess we were making." He set about a campaign to reduce the environmental impact of his own firm and industry and became a vocal prophet of the view that making profits and saving the planet were not contradictory.[25]

A third factor in the greening of conventional corporations was the advent of the green consumer. As the green consumer segment expanded far beyond initial clusters from the 1980s to embrace a wide range of consumers, it emerged as an attractive market to many conventional firms. These green consumers wanted to buy organic food, install solar panels on their roofs, recycle their waste, buy homes marked green, and stay in eco-resorts, although the premium they were willing to pay to do these things was not clear.

As the green consumer came of age, large corporations perceived the possibilities of gaining value from green reputations—or at least deflecting unwanted criticisms of adverse environmental impacts.[26] The greening of corporate identities became an important source of work for the public relations industry. By 1995 US corporations were estimated to spend $1 billion per year on public relations guidance from a cluster of agencies which specialized in providing advice to firms interested in building green credibility. With each successive Earth Day, more and more corporations went on a "feeding frenzy" to attach their brands to the occasion.[27]

Policies beyond building corporate images were shaped, in part, by how green consumers really were. For example, during the late 1980s it emerged that toxic and carcinogenic substances called dioxins were formed in the manufacture of bleached pulp, which was used in many consumer products from coffee filters to toilet paper. The Swedish paper and pulp industry developed a chlorine-free pulp. In 1992 the Swedish retailer IKEA, one of the largest producers of catalogues in the world, switched to the new technology, but US firms like Starbucks and McDonald's declined to do so on the grounds that demand was too weak to justify the costs.[28]

By the 2000s, however, conventional firms even in the United States were entering markets once considered exotic. A noteworthy case was organic food, once the preserve of radical idealists, which became progressively main-streamed. In the United States, conventional retailers such as Kroger, the largest supermarket chain in the United States, entered the organic market in the 2000s and eventually became a large participant in it. By 2010 conventional retailers surpassed the specialty natural foods stores such as Whole Foods Market: they were responsible for 54 percent of organic food sales, while natural retailers brought in 39 percent of total organic food sales.[29] In 2014 Walmart introduced its first organic food with a claim to sell it as the same price as non-organic.[30]

Fourth, sustainability had additional attractions beyond appealing to consumers. In some industries, future profits depend on taking stock of sustainability. As the reality of climate change became undeniable, its potential negative impacts stimulated corporate environmentalism. The reinsurance industry, dominated by a handful of large firms led by Swiss Re and Munich Re, were among the first to consider the effects of global warming as a long-term threat to the industry, because they were directly exposed to underwriting climate-related risks. Ever since Greenpeace published a pioneering report in 1993 on climate change and the insurance industry, the reinsurance industry and NGOs have collaborated to spread awareness of the problem.[31] The industry presented policy papers at the First Conference of the Parties to the Framework Convention on Climate Change in Berlin in 1995 and became an early advocate of both reducing carbon emissions and taking steps to adapt to the effects of global warming. Because reinsurance is one of the few industries whose business models reach out many decades ahead, it became acutely aware of the potential damage of rising sea levels and shifts in rain and temperature patterns.[32]

A fifth factor in the spread of sustainability concerns among big business was government policies. Governments have increasingly mandated more environmental policies and provided incentives in selected industries to invest in improving sustainability. Whether it was feed-in tariffs for wind and solar energy, government adoption of LEED and other standards for some of their buildings, tourism ministries' promotion of eco-tourism, or government sponsorship of organic certification, public policies worked to reduce financial barriers of investing in sustainability and, sometimes, to make doing so very profitable.

Finally, the growth in the number and impact of NGOs encouraged the greening of conventional capitalism, both through their ability to shame firms by publicly exposing poor environmental practices, but also by providing an institutional opportunity to enhance reputations through partnerships. NGOs concerned with the natural environment were not a post-1980 invention, as some of the earliest, such as the Sierra Club, dated back to the first environmental wave. The era of Earthrise and the first Earth Day saw a new generation, including Friends of the Earth and Greenpeace. After 1980 there was a proliferation of environmental NGOs. At the Earth Summit in Rio de Janeiro in June 1992, there were over 20,000 participants from 9,000 NGOs working in 171 countries; over 1,000 meetings were held between NGO representatives in a forum parallel to official intergovernmental discussions.[33] By 2000 the United Nations estimated that there were about 35,000 large established NGOs, spanning a wide range of both social and environmental concerns.[34]

A range of collaborative relations developed between big business and some NGOs which ranged from donating money and time, to using NGOs for product certification, to jointly managed environmental alliances involving such matters as product development or supply chain management.[35] An early example of such a partnership was forged between the fast food chain McDonald's and the Environmental Defense Fund to improve McDonald's waste-generation management. This arose after sustained criticism of McDonald's for its use of styrofoam packaging and the non-degradable waste it generated. EDF proposed cooperation, which led in 1990 to a program for reducing waste and a new commitment to recycling.[36] EDF became especially supportive of corporate environmentalism and during the 1990s was prominent in promoting corporate partnerships and market-based solutions to environmental challenges.[37] Partnerships between NGOs and multinationals became prominent in industries which sourced raw materials in agriculture and forestry. One example was the alliance between Unilever and the World Wildlife Fund (WWF) in creating the Marine Stewardship Council in 1996.[38]

A recurring pattern emerged where a corporation which was under criticism from NGOs for poor environmental practices, would then turn to NGOs to work on improvements. This was the case with Starbucks, which experienced critical campaigns from the mid-1990s concerning its supply chain policies, especially the wages and living conditions of its suppliers in Central America. In 1997 the Washington, DC-based NGO Conservation International approached Starbucks to support a project it had started in Chiapas,

Mexico, to encourage conservation practices by promoting a shift to shade-grown coffee, better for soil protection and wildlife, among other ecological benefits, among small producers. The NGO believed that two things would happen if Starbucks agreed to buy this kind of coffee: small producers would have ample market incentive to convert; and Starbucks would secure a stable long-term supply of higher-quality coffee while helping to preserve the bio-diversity of the region. Initially, Starbucks provided a grant. It created a new retail brand for the product from the region in 1999.[39]

In 2004 Conservation International, Starbucks, and USAID formed a for-mal Conservation Alliance, with Starbucks committing to provide $1.5 million and USAID $1.2 million over three years. Starbucks developed a set of sustainable coffee guidelines which were progressively modified to suit small producers. In 2004 Starbucks and Conservation International created the Coffee and Farmer Equity Practices (CAFÉ), a third-party verified program for farmers to ensure certain human rights and environmental standards are met. By 2015, 99 percent of the coffee Starbucks bought was certified by either CAFE Practices or Fairtrade. As often with certification schemes, the results were mixed. There was evidence that CAFÉ Practices improved wages and curbed canopy loss, as almost no participating farm converted forest to coffee production. However, the standards only encouraged rather than mandated shade production, and prohibited only dangerous pesticides rather than man-dating organic.[40] Critics noted that NGOs had strong organizational interests in positive outcomes from partnerships with prominent brands, which helped the NGOs raise money and build membership.[41]

A controversy between Greenpeace and Shell over how to sink the obsolete Brent Spar oil storage platform in the North Sea in 1995 became a classic example of how an NGO could delegitimize a global company, The sight of activists scaling Shell's platform, followed by mass consumer boycotts of Shell stations in Europe, defeated the company, whatever the scientific evidence in the case.[42] Yet often environmental NGOs focused more on influencing and criticizing govern-ments rather than attacking big business.[43] NGOs which focused on human rights and other social rather than ecological issues, such as the anti-sweatshop campaigns against the American sportswear company Nike focused on its factories in Asia, appeared the most vocal critics of conventional large firms.[44]

The outcomes of corporate environmentalism were as multi-faceted as the drivers of the trend. It has never been easy to disaggregate rhetoric and reality in corporate strategies, not least because many uncertainties in scientific knowledge sometimes render judgments about optimum environmental impact difficult.[45] However, at the highest level of generalization, there was some positive impact arising from the world's largest firms seeking to use energy and water more efficiently, reduce waste, invest large sums in solar and wind energy technologies, model and warn about climate change, and work with NGOs to introduce more environmentally friendly practices in growing coffee and other commodities.

Pioneering green entrepreneurs sometimes saw the irony of the greening of big business, but also welcomed it. As some conventional retailers in the United States experimented with selling organic food products, for example, Paul Keene of Walnut Acres wrote about how "large multinational food companies, having first unmercifully ridiculed the truth-seekers' eccentricity, began ever so cautiously to reverse themselves... Unable to hold back the wave of the future, they decided to ride it in," Keene observed in 1988. Although he declined to supply them natural foods—or let his company be acquired—he judged that "the world is better for their change in direction. Walnut Acres could not feed the whole planet, and half a loaf is better than none."[46]

Individual corporate sustainability reports documented often impressive environmental gains. The Starbucks 2014 Global Responsibility report, for example, documented that 500 stores were now LEED-certified, 47 percent of its stores in the United States and Canada had front-of-store recycling, 59 percent of its global energy use was renewable, and its water consumption had decreased by 23 percent since 2008.[47] If large firms had been the active agent of the harm done to the natural environment since the nineteenth century, they needed to be active agents in reducing this damage and healing the Earth.

Yet the limitations of corporate environmentalism were also apparent. The broadening of the definition of sustainability which enabled corporations to adopt the concept also resulted in a semi-devaluation of it. Sustainability rankings provided corporations with tools to address investors and others, but within carefully defined borders and typically employing such broad criteria that some very unlikely corporations could appear to be champions of sustainability. In the Corporate Knights rankings of the world's most sustainable companies, for example, four criteria were energy, carbon, water, and waste, but eight others included percentage of tax paid, pension fund status, and leadership diversity.[48]

While the concept of sustainability was broadened sufficiently in these decades to allow a luxury car manufacturer to be identified in a leading ranking as the world's most sustainable company, the concepts of both profit and costs were not equally broadened. In fact, if anything, there was a narrowing of those concepts. This was because the rise of corporate environmentalism coincided with the spread from the 1980s of the idea that the primary purpose of boards was to maximize shareholder value rather than serve a wider range of stakeholders.[49] By the new century the pressure on boards from analysts and institutional shareholders to provide good quarterly returns was acute. In the United States, the SEC had mandated that US companies submit semi-annual reports in 1955, and quarterly reports in 1970. From the 1980s as shareholder value became the norm as corporations' raison d'être, stock price and quarterly earnings came under intense scrutiny from investment analysts and 24-hour business news channels.[50] This need to report gains constantly presented a major constraint on publicly quoted firms to pursue long-term strategies. In 2011 the head of the management consultancy McKinsey described the "tyranny of short-termism," and the need to shift from what it termed "quarterly capitalism" to "long-term capitalism."[51]

Quarterly capitalism provided no incentive to make deep investments in environmental sustainability, which might take years to make a positive impact on a corporation's bottom line, although it did encourage incremental changes to cut costs and enhance corporate images which could be expected to improve quarterly earnings, or at least not subdue them. It did incentivize growth in corporate revenues, however. This model of capitalism did not mean that individual chief executives did not have strong views about the need for sustainability, but few corporate strategies reflected CEOs' personal commitments, which, in any case, were vulnerable to leadership changes.[52]

At Unilever, Paul Polman launched the Sustainability Living Plan and suspended quarterly earnings reports in 2009, a move which led to a fall in its share price of 6 percent on the day it was announced.[53] It was not until 2014 when the Financial Conduct Authority, the British regulator, removed the requirement for listed firms to issue management interim statements that a few other large British public companies followed.[54] In the United States quarterly statements remained mandated by law.

It seemed hard to combine truly radical environmental policies and a public listing. The Body Shop's Anita Roddick later criticized her own decision to undertake an IPO in 1984, even though the funds raised enabled her to expand quickly. She observed that it meant that control was handed over to "financial intermediaries who were contemptuous of what we were trying to do."[55]

A number of prominent green entrepreneurs kept their businesses out of the capital markets explicitly for this reason. This was the case with the high-profile Patagonia outdoor apparel brand, created by Yvon Chouinard in 1973. This California-based business grew through a series of clothing innovations, including the use of bright colors and the concept of wearing base-, mid-, and outer-layers, and global expansion. While the company grew rapidly, with sales reaching $100 million in 1990 and $750 million in 2015, it also progressively adopted green policies. In 1986 the company created the policy of annually donating 10 percent of profits to environmentally focused organizations; that standard was later raised to 1 percent of sales. Over the following two decades Patagonia started printing catalogues on recycled paper, developed recycled polyester, and abandoned anti-odor chemicals out of concerns to reduce environmental impact. By the 2000s it was asking consumers concerned about the environment not to buy its jackets, and launched repair services to extend the life of its products, while also volunteering to recycle used Patagonia clothing on its customers' behalf. Patagonia also pioneered, and shared, standards and methods for incorporating environmental externalities into traditional accounting statements.[56]

The Chouinards retained full ownership of the company, despite being approached "almost weekly" by buyers who wanted to take it public. "Being a publicly held corporation," Yvon Chouinard wrote in 2005, "would put shackles on how we operate, restrict what we do with our profits, and put us on a growth/suicide track. Our intent is to remain a closely held private company, so we can continue to focus on our bottom line, doing good."[57]

It was these "shackles" which constrained the meaning of corporate environmentalism. While Paul Hawken's Ecology of Commerce had called for business to take a leading role in combating environmental degradation, it did so in the context of a call for major structural reforms, including green taxes and an end to large corporations' ability to lobby governments to shape policies.[58] Instead of discussions about effective waste management, Hawken wanted corporations to "re-imagine themselves as cyclical corporations" which produced no waste.[59] Corporate environmentalism did not engage in such re-imagining. The very companies that were doing their best to save water and recycle were the drivers of the global consumerism which created many of the environmental problems in the first place. Within the confines of quarterly capitalism, there was no other way to generate the revenues needed for chief executives to keep their jobs.

Both optimists and pessimists could find support for their positions from the spread of corporate environmentalism. Despite the influence of quarterly capitalism, big businesses did begin to shift towards a more environmentally stance from the 1980s. They acted because there were profits that could now be made from being green, from consumers, from governments, and through increased efficiency, and because there were reputational costs from being seen as polluters and not green. However, there was also a great deal of hyperbole and what Hawken called "meaningless eco-speak."[60] Corporations remained the principal drivers of environmental damage through their pursuit of growth via increased consumption, and the realities of quarterly capitalism meant that the ability of well-intentioned executives to reduce the damage their corporations caused was limited.

Acquiring green brands in food and beauty

Corporate environmentalism met green entrepreneurship head on when large corporations began acquiring pioneer firms. This had first happened during the 1970s when start-ups in solar and wind energy were acquired by oil companies and others. From the 1990s large corporations in food and beauty began buying brands associated with environmental and social responsibility. These acquisitions testified to the perceived strength of the green consumer segment and to the inability of big business to convince such consumers that their own brands had legitimacy in this regard. The trend did raise new questions concerning the boundaries of sustainability, as large corporations emerged as coordinators of portfolios of brands, some green, some socially responsible, and some simply regular.

Table 9.1 documents the more prominent acquisitions between 1994 and 2016 in the food and drink and beauty industries.

For the most part, these acquisitions involved pioneering US green brands being bought by large US and European consumer products companies. The main outlier was the assembly of the Hain Celestial group of natural food and

Table 9.1 Major acquisitions of natural and socially responsible food and beauty brands, 1993–2016

Date	Acquired	Acquirer	Price ($ million)	Price ($ million 2016)
1993	Hain Pure Food	Irwin Simon	na	na
1997	Aveda	Estée Lauder	300	449
1998	Earth's Best	Heinz	30	44
1998	Arrowhead Mills	Hain	80	118
2000	Celestial Seasonings	Hain	387	539
2000	Ben & Jerry's	Unilever	334	474
2001	Odwalla	Coca-Cola	181	245
2001	Lima N.V.	Hain	20	27
2001–3	Stonyfield Farm	Danone	125 (80%)	167
2002	White Wave	Dean's Foods	189	252
2003	Jurlique	Consolidated Press Holdings	26	34
2003	Walnut Acres	Hain Celestial	na	na
2003	Horizon Organic	Dean Foods	273	356
2005	Green & Black's	Cadbury Schweppes (now Mondelez International)	33	41
2006	The Body Shop	L'Oréal	1,147	1,367
2006	Sanoflore	L'Oréal	na	na
2006	Dagoba	Hershey	17	20
2006	Tom of Maine's	Colgate Palmolive	100	119
2006	Naked Juice	Pepsico	na	na
2007	Burt's Bees	Clorox	925	1,072
2008	Melvita	L'Occitane	na	na
2008–11	Honest Tea	Coca-Cola	43 (2008)	48
2010	Bare Escentuals	Shiseido	1,743	1,921
2012	Jurlique	Pola	279	292
2012	BluePrint	Hain Celestial	25	26
2013	Ella's Kitchen	Hain Celestial	na	na
2014	Earthbound Farm	WhiteWave	600	609
2014	Annie's	General Mills	816	828
2015	Belvedere	Hain Celestial	na	na
2015	Empire Kosher	Hain Celestial	58	58
2015	REN Skincare	Unilever	na	na
2015	Applegate Farms	Hormer Foods	775	785
2016	WhiteWave	Danone	12,500	12,500

Source: Thomson SDC Platinum.

personal care brands by the Nova Scotia-born Irwin Simon. By 2014 this venture had revenues of over $2 billion, three-fifths of which were made in the United States and a further 30 percent in Britain, making it the world's largest natural products company.

Simon was a former marketer in consumer products companies who began an entrepreneurial career by purchasing a maker of kosher food in 1993 after losing his job with the weight-loss company Slim Fast in New York. The company quadrupled its size by adding Hain Pure Food, a long-established natural foods and cooking oils business, and went public. Simon began purchasing small niche natural foods brands and managing them more professionally. "People thought I was crazy," he recalled. "They thought I had to be a tree hugger, or someone on some type of cause, because natural, organic or granola-crunchy meant you had to be weird. A lot of people didn't accept me as part of the industry, but I had a vision."[61]

Simon's vision was to make profits out of his prediction that the market for healthy food was set to grow rapidly. Now renamed, Hain acquired Arrowhead Mills in 1999 and Celestial Seasonings in 2000. Renamed Hain Celestial, Simon's company went on to acquire dozens of small companies, mainly in the United States, but also in Europe and Canada, including the British baby food brand Ella's Kitchen and Belvedere, which included the Live Clean brand which had over 200 products, sold primarily in Canada.[62] The focus was on well-managed brands, not organic values. "I've bought a lot of companies from so-called natural, organic tree-huggers," Simon observed in 2007. "They were poorly run, and I've taken them to a whole other level."[63] The business was profitable, even though margins were lower than those of conventional foods companies; it grew to become the largest supplier to Whole Foods Market, and for some years the biggest shareholder was Carl Icahn.[64]

Other strategic acquisitions by large corporations resulted in many iconic green brands finding ostensibly unlikely owners. Coca-Cola and Pepsico, whose core businesses were carbonated sugary soft drinks and potato chips, acquired healthy drink brands like Odwalla, Naked Juice, and Honest Tea. The last, founded in Maryland in 1998, had launched the world's first organic bottled tea.[65] The Clorox Corporation, which acquired Burt's Bees, had as its core product a bleach which was regarded by many environmentalists as harmful to the environment. Hormer Foods, which bought Applegate Farms, a supplier of natural and organic meat which strictly avoided antibiotics, was the manufacturer of multiple processed foods, including Spam, a canned precooked meat. "Hormel Foods may not seem to be a likely partner to do business with," Applegate's founder noted in a statement after the acquisition was announced.[66]

The sale of these iconic green brands to large conventional firms sometimes brought scorn on their founders for hypocrisy. These founders, many of whom had high profiles as environmental activists, were oftentimes cast as "selling out" in return for a large amount of money, although often their companies had already gone public or had multiple investors. When Gary Hirshberg sold most of the equity of Stonyfield Farm to the French food company Danone in 2001, for example, the firm had 297 shareholders, including dairy farmers, family and friends, employees, angel investors, and one venture capitalist.[67]

The most common response of entrepreneurial founders to criticisms about selling out was that they could carry on the mission of sustainability better still in a large conventional firm—or even convert that firm to the cause. In the language of Hockets and Wüstenhagen, it was frequently asserted that the absorption of an Emerging David could help propel a Greening Goliath along the journey to sustainability. "Many people warned me: 'Don't sell out to the cosmetic giant. They will destroy your mission,'" Horst Rechelbacher recalled being told when he sold Aveda to Estée Lauder. "But I felt just the opposite. I felt that the sustainable and socially responsible business practices and products that Aveda embodied, that were its ethical and practical foundation, could help to shift the direction of Estée Lauder, and if Estée Lauder could change its direction, it would in turn affect corporate America."[68]

The importance of scaling was frequently emphasized by founders in their justification for "selling out," as well as their careful choice of acquirers. These arguments were made by the co-founders of the successful organic chocolate brand Green & Black's to justify its sale to the then-leading British chocolate company Cadbury Schweppes. Sams, a pioneer organic retailer in Britain discussed in Chapter 3, had co-founded the brand with his wife Josephine Fairley in 1991.[69] It was successful but experienced constant cash-flow problems, leading to the sale of most of the equity to a serial entrepreneur called William Kendall at the end of the decade. Fairley wrote that she would have been horrified if the business had been sold to Cadbury's competitor Nestlé after she had "long supported the Nestlé baby milk boycott...as a protest against the promotion in the Third World of costly formula milk for babies."[70] Sams also remained the non-executive president of the brand after the acquisition. "The net effect for Green & Black's is that we have gone from dealing with 200 to 10,000 cocoa farmers," Sams told a conference in 2010, "and so you see more and more farmers converting to organic."[71] Seth Goldman made the same point about the sale of Honest Tea to Coca-Cola. He noted that the subsequent growth had enabled the company to increase purchases of organic ingredients from 800,000 pounds to 6.7 million between 2007 and 2015, while a sharp fall in the cost of buying bottles had funded the firm to move to entirely buying Fair Trade sugar.[72]

Accusations of personal hypocrisy against founder-entrepreneurs were often belied by the fact that most went on to engage in other green ventures. A decade after he sold Aveda, Rechelbacher formed a new company, Intelligent Nutrients, which innovated in certified organic beauty products. Until his death in 2014 he signed all his correspondence, "Yours in service for a green, healthy and non-violent planet."[73] Roxanne Quimby, co-founder of Burt's Bees, who reportedly earned $300 million on the sale to Clorox, bought tens of thousands of acres of Maine forest land for conservation.[74]

Yet few outcomes from these acquisitions were truly glorious. The best case was represented by Stonyfield Farm. After most of the equity of Stonyfield Farm was sold to Danone, Gary Hirshberg remained chief executive until 2012, after which he served as chairman. Wanting to build an organic yogurt business, Danone, which was the world's largest yoghurt manufacturer, gave Stonyfield the autonomy to grow and accepted the lower margins which came from sourcing only organic milk. There was a scaling of the organic yogurt brand without a noticeable dilution of its principles.[75] By 2012 sales had reached $360 million, the brand had been taken to Europe, and a lot of sustainability initiatives had been launched from farming to packing.[76]

A more typical outcome was the incremental modification of products and practices to make them align more closely with the practices of the large corporations and to assist scaling of the brands. This process can be seen in the case of the ice cream company Ben & Jerry's, founded by Ben Cohen and Jerry Greenfield in Vermont in 1978. Their ice cream was not an organic product—indeed the high saturated fat content made it anything but a health product—but the founders developed strong views on the role of business as an agent of social change: they were among the first signatories of CERES and became prominent campaigners against the use of hormones to enhance milk production.[77] The firm had gone public in 1984, against the better judgment of the founders, and in the late 1990s a new chief executive resolved to sell to a growing number of corporate bidders. In 2000, Unilever acquired Ben & Jerry's. The shock to the socially progressive business community was enormous. It was indeed a primary reason why Judy Wicks, who was close friends with Cohen, resolved to found the Business Alliance for Local Living Economies. "How could it be that such a cutting-edge company," she remembered thinking, "would become a cog in the wheel of a huge global conglomerate."[78]

The sale gave Cohen $41 million and Greenfield $9.5 million, but the key negotiations had concerned preserving the company's social mission. Unilever agreed to create an independent board with legal authority to protect the social mission and product quality, in perpetuity, and to pay employees a living wage.[79] Few other acquired companies secured such a formal legal arrangement, and it proved useful.

After the acquisition a process began to secure increased efficiency at Ben & Jerry's. The co-founders soon left the independent board after disagreeing with Unilever's choice of chief executive, although they remained employed by Unilever with long-term contracts with few duties and no obligation to endorse products. There was a decrease in product quality as butterfat content was reduced and other changes made to the product. The affiliate was put under the control of the company's North American ice cream business, which included all of the company's other ice cream brands. In 2008 the independent board pushed back on Unilever regarding the sale agreements by preparing a law suit. Two years later the two parties reached an agreement which affirmed the affiliate's continued autonomy to maintain its values concerning social responsibility.[80]

The evidence that pioneer green entrepreneurs were able to act as evangelists within larger corporations is not strong, however. Rudolf Balz, the founder of the organic beauty brand Sanoflore, which was acquired by L'Oréal alongside The Body Shop, was skeptical of the ability of such large corporations to learn from firms like his own. "The problem is that for a company that already has a base of clients, to move to bio product, is a huge financial risk," he noted. "You have to invest money in marketing to explain to your clients: 'no, we didn't use to sell you crap before but why don't you try our new line of bio-products?'"[81] The Body Shop itself languished under its new ownership, with sales in 2015 less than 4 percent of L'Oréal and the lowest margins in the business.[82]

In some cases, relationships between acquired and acquirer deteriorated over time. The acquisition of Cadbury by Kraft was followed by a deteriorating relationship with the Green & Black's founders. Sams remained non-executive president of the brand, but there was a great deal of turbulence as Kraft in turn broke itself up, and Green & Black's became one of the many brands of the newly created Mondelez. A decade after the sale William Kendall spoke publicly of his regrets over selling Green & Black's to Cadbury, noting both that the subsequent push to grow the brand rapidly did enormous damage, especially in the United States, and that its edgy campaigning, such as questioning the value of the Fairtrade mark, was immediately closed down, as it was considered "dangerous territory."[83]

In other cases, dilution of brands occurred. Deans Food, and WhiteWave which was spun out of it in 2012, was subject to frequent criticism. After the purchase of the original WhiteWave in 2002, the Silk organic soy brand, which had been exclusively organic, quickly converted to conventional ingredients, with only 6 percent of the brand being organic by 2014. In 2013 Horizon Organic also abandoned its exclusive organic status to start selling "classic" versions.[84] WhiteWave, whose sales had reached $4 billion, was acquired for $12.5 billion by Danone three years later, in a move which reflected the consolidation of the organic food market in the hands of large conventional firms.[85]

The acquisition of green brands by large companies in the food and beauty industries was striking testimony to the perceived new importance of the green consumer. Like corporate acquisitions in general, some were more successful than others, but often they had the result of growing brands which had been niche-oriented, and making them far more widely available. The best outcomes happened when acquired firms were ring-fenced and allowed to keep their standards and values within the larger organization. However, there was no strong evidence that the acquisitions played a transformational role in greening the firms that acquired them. Rather, green brands became more conventional, sometimes through modified content and processes but more directly by pursuing growth. They existed as one point of view within corporations which sought to encompass as many viewpoints as possible to maximize their market. The Organic Consumer Association held a list of "traitor brands," many of which are listed in Table 9.1, who were involved in campaigns to secure mandatory labeling in the United States of foods containing GMOs, but whose parents were active opponents of such labeling.[86]

Greenwashing

There is a widespread view that greenwashing, defined in a recent study as "communication that misleads people into forming overly positive beliefs about an organization's environmental practices or products," has increased exponentially in recent years.[87] This is probably an ahistorical assumption, although as the term is as porous as sustainability itself, accurate mapping the history of greenwashing is challenging.

It can be confidently asserted that the phenomenon goes back to the 1960s, as previously there were no commercial benefits for a business to make environmental claims. During the late 1960s the former advertising executive and social critic Jerry Mander described the efforts of some large American corporations to falsely portray themselves in environmental language as "eco-pornography."[88] The phenomenon found a more attractive name in the mid-1980s when a New York environmental activist named Jay Westerveld picked up a card in a hotel room in Samoa, where he was studying tooth-billed pigeons, and read about helping to save the world's resources by not having the towels washed. The card was decorated with the three green arrows that made up the recycling symbol. Westerveld perceived the "save the towel" movement to be more about saving the hotel money than saving the planet. In 1986 he published an essay that coined the phrase "greenwashing."[89] The term "greenwashing" spread to other languages. It was often used in preference to local versions, which included "Grünfärberei" (coloring it green) in Germany, "grönmålning" (green painting) in Sweden, or "engaño verde" and "mercadeo verde" in parts of Latin America.

The popularity of the term clearly indicated consumers' recognition that the phenomenon was real, but what it really meant was more difficult to determine. The academic literature on greenwashing focused on the selective disclosure of information about environmental impacts in annual reports and corporate sustainability reports. This literature has pointed to a wide spectrum of practices among large firms, but with little consensus on why firms differed in these practices. A body of theory in sociology suggested that an organization's visibility affected compliance with institutional pressures in environmental reporting. There was evidence that greater visibility made organizations more concerned with their legitimacy and anxious to avoid appearing to greenwash, although other research has suggested that the more powerful an organization was, the more it could afford to resist pressures from external stakeholders.[90]

In any case, the focus on selective disclosure captures only part of the greenwashing issue, which includes misleading claims about the eco-friendly nature of particular products or services, empty green claims, misleading labels and visual imagery, or indeed the reimagining of whole companies as green businesses.[91] Large corporations are complex organizations which can make both sustainability improvements and greenwash at the same time. Unilever, for example, began developing environmental policies as early as the 1960s in response to consumer criticism and health scares about food additives, wasteful packaging, and factory effluent. By the following decade these policies were increasingly proactive, if done in a very low-profile way as befit a decentralized corporation which generally preferred to be known for its hundreds of individual brands rather than as the single conglomerate Unilever.[92] However, the firm followed the general trend in consumer products companies of inserting word "natural" into descriptions of consumer brands. During the 1970s it marketed, to give one of many examples, a successful shampoo brand called Timotei, which was packed in a white bottle with green text and cap and a small oval green-and-white flower and grass design marketed as "naturally mild" and advertised by models standing in fields.[93]

Overall the word "natural" proliferated in both the personal care and food industries, helped by the fact that no regulatory agency defined what a natural product was. The meaningless term natural was an ideal vehicle for corporate greenwashing, as it made no explicit claims. Gary Hirshberg disdainfully referred to the use of natural in the food industry as "the barn on the package."[94]

By the 2000s whole corporations were being rebranded. The environmental strategy of the British-based oil company BP provides one much-discussed example. Rebranded as "Beyond Petroleum," and lauded as a pioneer of emissions trading, the company was placed Number 1 on Fortune and AccountAbility's annual rankings of the world's most responsible companies in 2007.[95] Three years later the gap between visionary rhetoric and reality was painfully exposed by an explosion on the Deepwater Horizon oil rig in the

Gulf of Mexico which caused massive environmental pollution. BP was revealed as a company which had prioritized cost-cutting over safety and environmental impact. Subsequently the corporation also exited entirely from its four-decades-old solar energy businesses and sharply reduced its wind energy business, although it retained wind farms in the United States.[96]

BP was not the first or last case where corporate champions of sustainability in oil and other industries came to public grief. Philipp Watts, Shell's chief executive after 2001, became a high-profile campaigner for sustainability and chairman of the World Business Council for Sustainable Development. In 2002 he co-authored a book with Stephan Schmidheiny on corporate sustainability called *Walking the Talk*.[97] Two years later Watts was obliged to resign after allegations emerged that he knew that the company was overstating its oil reserves.[98] There were many such examples.[99] Accusations of hypocrisy could be leveled at virtually any corporation claiming to be sustainable, as there were so many uncertainties about what sustainable really meant, as well as how it was interpreted over time. Managers engaged in Socially Responsible Investing lived with the problem all the time. "It's a constantly evolving moving target on what we think is good," Stephanie Leighton of Trillium Asset Management observed in 2013. "One person's Ben & Jerry's is another person's high-fat food."[100]

Greenwashing was also a dynamic phenomenon which assumed new forms. There was some evidence that increased scrutiny, whether from social networking or other forces, might work against more blatant and purposeful forms of greenwashing, but other forms were evident and probably increasing. The term "symbolic corporate environmentalism" was used to describe situations where managers did not explicitly pursue strategies to mislead but in which greenwashing still occurred. For example, the commissioning of a LEED-certified head office might by association build the image of a company as green, even if the company avoided making explicit claims.[101]

Definitional difficulties made it impossible to really quantify the extent of greenwashing in the corporate world, but it was evidently a widespread and diffuse phenomenon. The adoption and endorsement of environmental language was pervasive among large corporations, though with much variation in the size of the gap between rhetoric and reality. An upside might be that when firms like BP emphasized the importance of going "Beyond Petroleum," they helped to continue to raise awareness of environmental challenges. However, greenwashing had costs. It helped undermine consumer confidence in the very idea of sustainability by encouraging widespread confusion and, often, cynicism. It made efforts to create markets and to educate consumers and policymakers harder. Meanwhile, pioneering green entrepreneurs faced the new and formidable challenge of having their cases heard in a world where every company claims to be sustainable.

Conclusion

The expansion of corporate environmentalism from the 1980s onward represented a remarkable turn of events. Since the nineteenth century green entrepreneurs had sought to offer an alternative to conventional capitalism and to respond to its negative environmental impact—and for much of that time span had very little progress to show for their efforts. Suddenly, green entrepreneurs and big business appeared to be traveling along the same path, and it seemed to be a promising one. Large global corporations had the technological and financial resources to drive technological innovation. They had the ability to develop new processes to save water and electricity. Governments listened to them, as did many consumers. There were alternative visions available, of bioregional and local economies, which in theory seemed to lead to radically improved sustainability outcomes, but there was no plausible way in sight for today's world to move towards them.

The key problem was that the growth of corporate environmentalism coincided with the advent of quarterly capitalism. While the owners of Alnatura or Patagonia were prepared to accept lower returns in exchange for greater sustainability, the chief executives of large listed companies faced huge pressures to meet quarterly returns, and their personal compensation was related to financial and not environmental performance. This meant that, even if they were persuaded of the urgency of the problem, they could only move sharply towards more sustainable strategies involving significant trade-offs with short-term profitability as fast as consumers which bought their products, and the financial institutions which held most of their shares, would permit. These "shackles," as Chouinard described them, were significant. Few consumers appeared willing to pay a great deal more for a green product or service, although they might pay a little more for organic milk for their children. Despite the efforts of pioneering SRI and impact investors, the financial system remained thoroughly conventional in orientation, and bound by rules concerning fiduciary obligations.

The result was a system that worked incrementally towards becoming more environmentally efficient, which was itself a huge turnaround from the past, but not likely or even able to take truly radical measures like suggesting consumers buy less of their brands and use less of their services. Yet, absent unknown technological breakthroughs, only by consuming less—certainly in the affluent West—was much progress likely to be made on sustainability.

The gap between corporate rhetoric and reality presented almost as big a challenge as had the past neglect of environmental challenges. It was not simply that much more needed to be done more quickly. Green as the new normal reduced the issue of sustainability to being one strategy among many, conceived as useful in marketing, and valuable for cost-cutting. The understanding of what needed to be done to achieve sustainability, which was so prominent in the thoughts of many green pioneers, was lost as consumers were led to believe that they were participating in saving the planet by eating organic carrots, staying in eco-lodges, and getting their houses LEED-certified. Certification, environmental reporting, and outright greenwashing conspired to make the boundaries of the concept of sustainability so wide that any corporation could claim to be engaged in it. In contrast, there had been no such broadening of the concept of profits or investor returns, either to reward environmental gains or to penalize environmental damage.

While entrepreneurial firms lacked the reach of Greening Goliaths, they also had the ability to conceptualize radical new paths, while their authenticity gave them the possibility to influence one individual at a time to make different choices in their lifestyles. Yet sustainability reduced to one component inside a global corporation coexisting with environmentally damaging activities offered little hope for radical change. Rhetoric too often drowned out urgency.

Notes

1. Linda C. Forbes and John M. Jermier, "The New Corporate Environmentalism and the Ecology of Commerce," *Organization & Environment* 23, no. 4 (2010), pp.465–81.

2. Kathryn Dill, "The World's Most Sustainable Companies 2016," *Forbes*, January 22, 2016.

3. Pilita Clark, "Water Shortages More Pressing than Climate Change, Warns Nestlé Chair," *Financial Times*, July 15, 2014.

4. "Unilever: In Search of the Good Business," *The Economist*, August 9, 2014.

5. Christopher Mumma, "Firm Tells Bankruptcy Judge It Overpaid for Manufacturing Assets It Brought in May," *Los Angeles Times*, November 15, 2002.

6. <http://www.ge.com/about-us/ecomagination>, accessed August 10, 2016.

7. David Kocieniewski, "G.E.'s Strategies Let It Avoid Taxes Altogether," *New York Times*, March 24, 2011.

8. Joshua S. Hill, "Goldwind Edges out Vestas as World's Leading Wind Turbine Supplier," May 19, 2016, <http://cleantechnica.com/2016/05/19/goldwind-edges-vestas-worlds-leading-wind-turbine-supplier>, accessed June 2, 2016.

9. <http://www.starbucks.com/responsibility/learn-more/starbucks-shared-planet>, accessed June 8, 2016.

10. Edward Humes, *Force of Nature: The Unlikely Story of Wal-Mart's Green Revolution* (New York: Harper Business, 2011), p.9.

11. Christopher A. Bartlett, "Unilever's New Global Strategy: Competing through Sustainability," Harvard Business School Case No. 9-916-414 (rev. August 24, 2016).

12. Kai Hockerts and Rolf Wüstenhagen, "Greening Goliaths versus Emerging Davids—Theorizing about the Role of Incumbents and New Entrants in Sustainable Entrepreneurship," *Journal of Business Venturing* 25 (2010), pp.481–92.

13. Peter Dauvergne and Jane Lister, *Eco-Business: A Big Brand Takeover of Sustainability* (Cambridge, MA: MIT Press, 2013), chapter 1.

14. Naomi Klein, *This Changes Everything: Capitalism vs. the Climate* (New York: Simon & Schuster, 2014), p.254.

15. Peter Berg, *Envisaging Sustainability* (San Francisco: Subculture Books, 2009).

16. Stephen Schneider, "Good, Clean, Fair: The Rhetoric of the Slow Food Movement," *College English* 70, no. 4 (2008), pp.384–402; Slow Food, *Welcome to Our World* (2008).

17. Judy Wicks, *Good Morning, Beautiful Business* (White River Junction, VT: Chelsea Green Publishing, 2013), p.210.

18. Andrew J. Hoffman, *From Heresy to Dogma: An Institutional History of Corporate Environmentalism* (Stanford, CA: Stanford Business Books, 2001); Daniel Boullet, *Entreprises et Environnement en France de 1960 à 1990: Les Chemins d'une Prise de Conscience* (Geneva: Droz, 2006).

19. Geoffrey Jones and Christina Lubinski, "Making 'Green Giants': Environment Sustainability in the German Chemical Industry, 1950s–1980s," *Business History* 56 (2014), pp.623–49.

20. Sandra Rothenberg and James Maxwell, "Volvo: A Case in the Implementation of Proactive Environmental Management" (unpublished paper, November 1993).

21. Interview with Inge Horkeby (Volvo), Göteborg, February 16, 2010; Charles J. Hanley, "Acid Rain: Swedes Lead World in Fight against Pollution Threat," *The Courier*, May 27, 1983.

22. Keetie Sluyterman, *Keeping Competitive in Turbulent Markets, 1973–2007: A History of Royal Dutch Shell* (Oxford: Oxford University Press, 2007), pp.358–9.

23. Michael E. Porter and Claas van der Linde, "Toward a New Conception of the Environment–Competitiveness Relationship," *Journal of Economic Perspectives* 9, no. 4 (1995), pp.97–118.

24. John R. Ehrenfield, "Beyond the Brave New World: Business for Sustainability," in Pratima Bansal and Andrew J. Hoffman (eds.), *The Oxford Handbook of Business and the Natural Environment* (Oxford: Oxford University Press, 2012).

25. Ray C. Anderson, *Confessions of a Radical Industrialist* (New York: St. Martin's Press, 2009), pp.5, 14; Emily Langer, "Ray Anderson, 'Greenest CEO in America,' Dies at 77," *Washington Post*, August 10, 2011.

26. Gerald Markowitz and David Rosner, *Deceit and Denial: The Deadly Politics of Industrial Pollution* (Berkeley: University of California Press, 2002), pp.210–11.

27. Sharon Beder, *Global Spin: The Corporate Assault on Environmentalism* (Totnes: Green Books, 1997), chapter 8.

28. Ann-Kristin Bergquist and Kristina Söderholm, "Transition to Greener Pulp: Regulation, Industry Responses and Path Dependency," *Business History* 57, no. 6 (2015), p.875.

29. Dana Hunsinger Benbow, "Natural, Organic Items Grab Bigger Share in Supermarkets," July 7, 2012, <http://usatoday30.usatoday.com/money/industries/food/story/2012-07-07/natural-organic-groceries/56085280/1>.

30. Andrew Martin, "Wal-Mart Promises Organic Food for Everyone," *Bloomberg*, November 6, 2014.

31. Jeremy Leggett, *Climate Change and the Insurance Industry: Solidarity among the Risk Community?* (Greenpeace, 1993), <http://www.greenpeace.org/international/en/publications/reports/leggett-insurance-climate>, accessed July 2, 2016.

32. Niels Viggo Hauter and Geoffrey Jones, "Risk and Reinsurance," in Hauter and Jones (eds.), *Managing Risk in Reinsurance: From City Fires to Global Warming* (Oxford: Oxford University Press, 2016), pp.7–8, 44–5; Roman Lechner, Niels Viggo Haueter, and Lawrence Kenny, "Continuity and Change in Reinsurance," in Hauter and Jones (eds.), *Managing Risk*, pp.293–4.

33. Carrie A. Meyer, "Opportunism and NGOs: Entrepreneurship and Green North–South Transfers," *World Development* 23, no. 8 (1995), pp.1277–89.

34. David Lewis, "Nongovernmental Organizations, Definition and History," in *International Encyclopedia of Civil Society* (New York: Springer, 2010), pp.1056–62.

35. Esben Rahbek Gjerdrum Pedersen and Janni Thusgaard Pedersen, "Introduction: The Rise of Business–NGO Partnerships," *Journal of Corporate Citizenship* 50 (2013), pp.6–19; Dennis Rondinelli and Ted London, "How Corporations and Environmental Groups Cooperate: Assessing Cross-Sector Alliances and Collaborations," *Academy of Management Executive* 17, no. 1 (2003), pp.61–76.

36. Edwin R. Stafford and Cathy L. Hartman, "Green Alliances: Strategic Relations between Business and Environmental Groups," *Business Horizons* 39, no. 2 (1996), pp.54–7.

37. <https://www.edf.org/about/our-history>, accessed July 24, 2015.

38. Jem Bendell (ed.), *Terms for Endearment: Business, NGOs, and Sustainable Development* (Sheffield, UK: Greenleaf, 2000), chapters 8 and 10.

39. Paola Perez-Aleman and Marion Sandilands, "Building Value at the Top and the Bottom of the Global Supply Chain: MNC–NGO Partnerships," *California Management Review* 51, no. 1, pp.30–3.

40. Margaret Badore, "Starbucks Says It Now Serves '99 Percent Ethically Sourced Coffee.' So What Does That Mean?" *Treehugger*, April 9, 2015, <http://www.treehugger.com/corporate-responsibility/starbucks-says-it-now-serves-99-per cent-ethically-sourced-coffee-so-what-does-mean.html>, accessed April 11, 2016.

41. John Maxwell, "An Economic Perspective on NGO Strategies and Objectives," in Thomas P. Lyon (ed.), *Good Cop, Bad Cop: Environmental NGOs and Their Strategies toward Business* (Washington, DC: RFF Press, 2010); Christine MacDonald, *Green, Inc.: An Environmental Insider Reveals How a Good Cause Has Gone Bad* (Guilford, CT: Lyons Press, 2008); Ans Kolk, "Partnerships as Panacea for Addressing Global Problems?" in M. May Seitanidi and Andrew Crane (eds.), *Social Partnerships and Responsible Business: A Handbook* (London: Routledge, 2014).

42. Ragnar Löfstedt and Ortwin Renn, "The Brent Spar Controversy: An Example of Risk Communication Gone Wrong," *Risk Analysis* 17, no. 2 (1997), pp.131–6; David Vogel, *The Market for Virtue* (Washington, DC: Brookings Institution Press, 2005), pp.112–14; Frank Zelko, *Make it a Green Peace!: The Rise of Countercultural Environmentalism* (New York: Oxford University Press, 2013), pp.320–1; Sluyterman, *Keeping Competitive*, pp.335–9.

43. Donald Gibson, *Environmentalism: Ideology and Power* (Huntington, NY: Nova Science, 2002), p.65.

44. Ann Harrison and Jason Scorse, "Multinationals and Anti-Sweatshop Activism," *American Economic Review* 100, no. 1 (2010), p.249.

45. Keetie Sluyterman, "Royal Dutch Shell: Company Strategies for Dealing with Environmental Issues," *Business History Review* 84, no. 2 (2010); Ann-Kristen Bergquist and Kristina Söderholm, "Green Innovation Systems in Swedish Industry, 1960–1989," *Business History Review* 85, no. 4 (2011).

46. Paul Keene, *Fear Not to Sow* (Chester, CT: Globe Peqot Press, 1988), p.61.

47. <https://news.starbucks.com/uploads/documents/Starbucks_GR_Report_-_2014.pdf>, accessed June 11, 2016.

48. Chris MacDonald, "Corporate Knights Gets Sustainability Wrong: How and Why Words Matter," *Canadian Business*, January 23, 2013, <http://www.can adianbusiness.com/companies-and-industries/corporate-knights-gets-sustainability-wrong>, accessed June 28, 2016.

49. Geoffrey Jones, "Debating the Responsibility of Capitalism in Historical and Global Perspective," *Harvard Business School Working Paper* 14-004 (2013).

50. David Benoit, "Time to End Quarterly Reports, Law Firm Says," *Wall Street Journal*, August 19, 2015.

51. Dominic Barton, "Capitalism for the Long Term," *Harvard Business Review* (March 2011).

52. Vogel, *Market for Virtue*, pp.135–6.

53. Jo Confino, "Unilever's Paul Polman: Challenging the Corporate Status Quo," *Guardian*, April 24, 2012.

54. Claer Barrett and David Oakley, "National Grid Pulls Plug on Quarterly Reporting," *Financial Times*, January 27, 2015.

55. <http://www.anitaroddick.com/readmore.php?sid=547>, accessed June 4, 2016.

56. Forest Reinhardt, Ramon Casadesus-Masanell, and Hyun Jin Kim, "Patagonia," Harvard Business School Case No. 9-711-020 (rev. October 10, 2010); Yvon Chouinard, Jib Ellison, and Rick Ridgeway, "The Sustainable Economy," *Harvard Business Review* (October 2011); Geoffrey Jones and Ben Gettinger, "Alternative Paths to Green Entrepreneurship: The Environmental Legacies of The North Face's Doug Tompkins and Patagonia's Yvon Chouinard," *Harvard Business School Working Paper* 17-034 (2016).

57. Yvon Chouinard, *Let My People Go Surfing* (New York: Penguin, 2005), p.164.

58. Forbes and Jermier, "New Corporate Environmentalism."

59. Paul Hawken, *The Ecology of Commerce* (New York: HarperCollins, 1993), p.54.

60. Ibid., p.128.

61. Gordon Pitts, "Hain Celestial's Irwin Simon: An Insatiable Appetite for Organic Foods," *The Globe and Mail*, July 26, 2013.

62. There is a full list of acquisitions in David E Bell, Jose B. Alvarez, James Weber, and Mary Shelman, "The Hain Celestial Group," Harvard Business School Case No. 9-516-007 (December 22, 2015), Exhibit 13.

63. "Competition Evolves in Natural Foods: Hain Celestial Fends Off Challenges from Mainstream Foes," May 7, 2007, <http://www.soyatech.com/print_news.php?id=2591>, accessed July 7, 2016.

64. Clare O'Connor, "Juiced Up: Inside $3.5 Billion Organic Giant Hain Celestial, Whole Foods' Biggest Supplier," *Forbes*, July 24, 2013.

65. Seth Goldman and Barry Nalebuff, *Mission in a Bottle* (New York: Crown Business, 2013).

66. Statement from Stephen McDonnell, Founder, Applegate, <http://applegate. com/statement-from-stephen-mcdonnell-founder-applegate>, accessed August 15, 2016.

67. Nancy F. Koehn, Nora N. Khan, and Elizabeth W. Legris, "Gary Hirshberg and Stonyfield Farm," Harvard Business School Case No. 9- 312-122 (rev. October 10, 2012).

68. Horst M. Rechelbacher, *Minding Your Business: Profits that Restore the Planet* (San Rafael, CA: EarthAware, 2008), p.125.

69. Craig Sams and Josephine Fairley, *The Story of Green & Black's* (London: Random House, 2009).

70. Ibid., p.212.

71. Natural Products News, April 19, 2010, <http://www.naturalproductsonline.co. uk/dont-punish-successful-pioneers-do-nurture-small-brands>, accessed July 4, 2016.

72. Jay Moye, "Honest and Beyond: Seth Goldman on His Evolving Role at Honest Tea, New Challenge with Beyond Meat," November 4, 2015, <http:// www.coca-colacompany.com/stories/business/2015/seth-goldman-s-evolving-role-at-honest-tea–new-challenge-with-b>, accessed January 2, 2016.

73. Horst M. Rechelbacher, Obituary, February 23, 2014, <http://www.startribune. com/obituaries/detail/14016588/?fullname=horst-m-rechelbacher>, accessed November 8, 2016.

74. David Sharp, "Burt's Bees Icon Says Affair Led to Ouster," *Boston Globe*, June 5, 2014; Michael Charles Tobias, "Maine vs Thoreau: The Roxanne Quimby Question?" *Forbes*, October 3, 2011.

75. Gary Hirshberg, *Stirring It Up: How to Make Money and Save the World* (New York: Hyperion, 2008), p.119.

76. Koehn, Khan, and Legris, "Gary Hirshberg."

77. Brad Edmondson, *Ice Cream Social: The Struggle for the Soul of Ben & Jerry's* (San Francisco: Berrett-Koehler, 2008), pp.78–9; Ben Cohen and Jerry Greenfield, *Ben & Jerry's Double-Dip* (New York: Simon & Shuster, 1997).

78. Wicks, *Good Morning*, p.203.

79. Edmonson, *Ice Cream*, chapters 9 and 10.

80. Ibid., chapters 12 and 13.

81. Telephone interview with Rodolph Balz, April 13, 2011.

82. Andrew Roberts, "Body Shop Heads Back to the Body Shop to Repair Battered Margins," *Bloomberg*, April 7, 2016.

83. Rebecca Burn-Callander, "'I Wish I'd Never Sold Green & Blacks to Cadbury,'" *The Telegraph*, October 24, 2015.

84. Cornucopia Institute, "Leading Organic Brand, Horizon, Blasted for Betraying Organics," February 13, 2014, <https://www.cornucopia.org/2014/02/leading-organic-brand-horizon-blasted-betraying-organics/>.

85. The Cornucopia Institute, "Danone's Acquisition of WhiteWave Foods Could Harm Ethical Dairy Farmers and Consumers," August 18, 2016, <https://www.cornucopia.org/2016/08/danones-acquisition-of-whitewave-foods-could-harm-ethical-dairy-farmers-and-consumers>, accessed October 23, 2016.

86. Organic Consumers Association, "Boycott the Organic and 'Natural' Traitor Brands Whose Parent Companies Oppose Your Right to Know," <https://www.organicconsumers.org/old_articles/bytes/ob343.htm>, accessed June 27, 2016.

87. Thomas P. Lyon and A. Wren Montgomery, "The Means and End of Greenwash," *Organization & Environment* 28, no. 2 (2015), p.223.

88. Joshua Kaliner, *The Corporate Planet: Ecology and Politics in the Age of Globalization* (San Francisco: Sierra Club Books, 1997), p.170.

89. Jim Motavalli, "A History of Greenwashing: How Dirty Towels Impacted the Green Movement," February 12, 2011, <http://www.aol.com/article/2011/02/12/the-history-of-greenwashing-how-dirty-towels-impacted-the-green/19628686>, accessed July 4, 2016.

90. Pratima Bansal and Kendall Roth, "Why Companies Go Green: A Model of Ecological Responsiveness," *Academy of Management Journal* 43, no. 4 (2000), pp.717–36; Ilya Okhmatovskiy and Robert J. David, "Setting Your Own Standards: Internal Corporate Governance Codes as a Response to Institutional Pressure," *Organization Science* 23, no. 1 (2012), pp.155–76.

91. Lyon and Montgomery, "Means and End," pp.236–8.

92. Geoffrey Jones, *Renewing Unilever: Transformation and Tradition* (Oxford: Oxford University Press, 2005), pp.339–47.

93. Ibid., p.122.

94. Beth Kowitt, "The War on Big Food," *Fortune* 171, no. 7 (June 1, 2015).

95. David G. Victor and Joshua C. House, "BP's Emissions Trading System," *Energy Policy* 34 (2006), pp.2100–12; Vogel, *Market for Virtue*, pp.123–5.

96. Sylvia Pfeifer and Pilita Clark, "BP to Exit Solar Business after 40 Years," *Financial Times*, December 20, 2011; James Montgomery, "BP Selling US Wind Unit, Pares Renewable Energy Interests to Fuels," *Renewable Energy World*, April 3, 2013.

97. C. O. Holliday, S. Schmidheiny, and Philipp Watts, *Walking the Talk: The Business Case for Sustainable Development* (Sheffield, UK: Greenleaf, 2002).

98. Watts subsequently studied theology and became a minister of the Church of England. Michael Owens, "Former Shell Boss Turned Reverend to Begin New Church Post," *Maidenhead Advertiser*, February 8, 2013.

99. For the case of Richard Branson and the Virgin Group, see Klein, *This Changes Everything*, pp.238–48.

100. Interview with Stephanie Leighton (Trillium), Boston, MA, December 3, 2013.

101. Frances Bowen, *After Greenwashing: Symbolic Corporate Environmentalism and Society* (Cambridge: Cambridge University Press, 2014).

10

Conclusion

Green entrepreneurship has a long history stretching back to the nineteenth century. This book has tried to recover its stories, even though they have not figured prominently in business history. This neglect arose primarily because the first generations of green entrepreneurs were, for much of the period covered, marginal figures, often seen as eccentric or outlandish by their contemporaries. Yet their voices and arguments remain prescient today, and their experiences provide compelling insights on whether, and how, profits and sustainability are compatible.

Part of the reason why these pioneering figures have seldom been noticed is that both the nature of perceived environmental challenges, and the language in which they are expressed, have changed markedly over time. Academics first talked of green entrepreneurs in the 1990s, but this does not mean that such figures did not exist earlier, even a century earlier. The changing temporal context in which entrepreneurs operated is essential to understanding both the industries they chose to invest in, and to judging their performance, even though, as we have seen, there were some striking similarities over time.

The era between the middle of the nineteenth century and the late 1920s focused on conservation and Romantic nationalism, and was primarily led by the social elites of Europe and the United States. It was driven by the shock of seeing the negative impact of industrialization on the natural environment, and especially the countryside and wildlife such as birds. The conservation movement led to the first national parks being created and the first NGOs formed to protect nature. The conservation of nature threatened by industrialization was the key concern of these decades. Manufacturing industry, and the capitalists who owned it, were seen, rightly, as the primary drivers of environmental degradation.

The pioneer green entrepreneurs were, then, an unusual and small set of people who believed that business could help sustainability rather decimate it. The focus of attention at this time was the health of humanity, both physical and spiritual. American and British figures such as Sylvester Graham, John Harvey Kellogg, and John Henry Cook warned of the risks of applying chemistry to agriculture and of processing foods, and they sought to offer healthier alternatives. Their German counterparts, such as Carl Mann and Benedict Lust, built small retail stores to sell healthy food and preached the benefits of natural healing. Lust was a particularly interesting figure, transferring both German naturopathic ideas and Indian Ayurveda concepts to the United States, even as he was harassed for his eccentric ideas, including nudism.

Lust's perceived eccentricities were, however, modest compared to those of Rudolf Steiner, who from an early age talked to dead people, and whose ideas are best described as unorthodox. Steiner, however, can also be seen as offering a profoundly radical vision of a need for healing to embrace in a holistic fashion all of the dimensions of human society. His vision of an economic-spiritual enterprise offered a model for a firm that would seek to make profits, but as a means to an end rather than a purpose in itself. It was because Steiner's esoteric views were combined with practical solutions that he served as a source of inspiration for green entrepreneurs going forward. This was despite the fact that it remained wholly unclear how many of the practical solutions Steiner offered, including the "preparations" and cosmic influences employed in biodynamic agriculture, worked, if they worked at all.

This era also saw others turn to business to develop practical solutions to the emerging problem of how to make societies without access to electricity sustainable. Poul la Cour and Frank Shuman stand out for their understanding of the importance of access to electricity, and their perception that wind and sun could provide a viable source of energy other than fossil fuels. La Cour pursued his vision in rural Denmark but left a legacy which created a trajectory leading, over many decades, to the modern wind energy industry. Shuman traveled over three continents to find the money and the locations to pursue his dream of building a viable solar energy industry. He shared with the conservation movement of the time the insight that natural resources such as fossil fuels were a finite resource, but he moved to the next level in his determination to find a practical alternative as an energy source.

Between the 1930s and the 1960s environmental concerns were generally subdued. The Great Depression and World War II were all-consuming and immediate events which left little space to debate the problems of the natural environment. Subsequently, there was exuberant optimism as economic recovery, facilitated by cheap fossil fuels, led to rising per capita incomes, alongside accumulating piles of garbage in the cities of the West and Japan. There was also a race for leadership between the West and the Communist world, leading among other things to huge investment in nuclear technology and the space program. There was great confidence in the possibility of science and technology to solve the world's environmental problems, and compelling reasons to invest in it for the survival of rival political systems.

Within this context, a handful of green entrepreneurs stood out for their continued highlighting of the need for sustainability. Their stance was all the more remarkable as so few listened, or bought the goods and services on offer. Jerome Rodale stands out as an emblematic figure, less through the commercial success of his businesses than for his insight into the importance of making the case to consumers, farmers, and others that there were real problems with the natural environment which needed attention. While Rodale's most concrete impact was helping to forge an identity for the tiny organic food movement in the United States, his publications were noteworthy for articulating the view that it was the nature of consumer society itself which was driving many environmental challenges. Architects, too, stood at the forefront of reimagining man's relationship with the natural environment. The American architects Frank Lloyd Wright and Buckminster Fuller were prime examples, as was Hassan Fathy, a true visionary in both his demonstration that traditional architecture held valuable lessons for more sustainable practices, and his identification of the cultural erosion and social inequalities caused by Western-style modernization.

The third era between the 1960s and the 1980s saw a re-igniting of environmental concerns as authors such as Rachel Carson and the iconic image of Earthrise re-awoke awareness of the fragility of the planet. In an era of intensified social movements, environmental concerns spread to much wider sections of society than previously, resulting on occasion in mass demonstrations, as seen at the first Earth Day in 1970. Environmental agencies were established in the United States and Europe, new environmental NGOs were founded, and the first United Nations conference on the environment was held in Stockholm. Unrelated to these developments, the oil price rises of the early 1970s abruptly ended the era of cheap oil and made Western policy-makers open, for the first time, to at least exploring the potential of solar and wind energy.

This era saw no sudden breakthrough for green businesses. Some influential environmental thinkers of the era thought that replacing free markets and capitalism entirely was the key to sustainability, not values-driven, for-profit entrepreneurial start-ups. Most others pinned their hopes on much more government regulation over polluting industries. There were interesting, and sometimes visionary, figures, but their businesses remained wholly on the margins of their industries. This was as true for Ian McHarg and Sim Van der Ryn in architecture, as it was of Michio Kushi and Craig Sims in organic food. It was only at the end of the 1970s that some entrepreneurs, such as Horst Rechelbacher and Anita Roddick in natural beauty, began to scale their businesses. They were all, in different ways, part of the counter-cultural movement of the era, as were the Danish wind energy entrepreneurs of the 1970s, such as Erik Grove-Nielsen, who were angered by the dangers of nuclear power.

Not all of the emblematic entrepreneurs of these decades, however, were countercultural or social protestors. In photovoltaic solar energy, Elliot Berman sensed a potential transformational social impact, while Joseph Lindmeyer and Peter Varadi saw a profitable market outside the space program. Wilhelm Barkhoff, the banker, came from earlier anthroposophical and Christian traditions. Lars-Eric Lindblad took an older tradition of nature-based tourism to a new level by showing how well-managed and educational nature tourism could contribute to the sustaining of unique natural environments such as Antarctica and the Galapagos Islands.

The contemporary era of green capitalism beginning in the 1980s saw a mainstreaming of environmental concerns, energized especially by the growing evidence of man-made and global environmental damage, especially damage to the planet's ozone layer and, later, climate change. This was an era of major international conferences and international agreements. The Montreal Protocol in 1987 secured agreement to ban the chlorofluorocarbons which were damaging the ozone layer, with great apparent success. Attempts to reduce carbon emissions, beginning with the Kyoto Protocol in 1997, proved far less successful. This was partly because this was also a period of great structural change in the global economy as emerging economies experienced fast economic growth and urbanization. Growth resulted in falling poverty rates, especially in China, but also sharply rising carbon emissions, while the growth of mega-cities in Asia and Latin America resulted in highly polluted air and water pollution and shortages. Pope Francis's encyclical *Laudato Si* in 2015 highlighted both the scale of the environmental problems faced by the Earth, of which climate change was the most immediate, and the minimal progress made in addressing them.

The prospects for green entrepreneurship were transformed in this period. Governments moved from being major obstacles for green business to creating at least some opportunities and incentives, albeit with huge differences in policies between countries, and even states within individual countries. Beginning with California in the first half of the 1980s, there were periods of heavy, if rarely sustained, public support for renewable energy through feed-in tariffs, tax breaks, and other means. This government support enabled wind and solar energy to break away from the margins. In a handful of countries renewable energy became very significant, with Denmark getting two-fifths of its electricity from wind. Governments supported certification in organic agriculture, recycling, greener buildings, and much else. An equally significant change was the emergence of green consumers, especially in the United States and Western Europe, willing to buy green products and services. As a result, green products moved from tiny niches to significant niches. In a handful of European countries, organic food sales reached 7 percent of total food sales. Global natural beauty sales were $30 billion, or 6 percent of the world market.

This was the era when the idea that for-profit businesses could meaningfully contribute to environmental sustainability took hold as part and parcel of the rebirth of liberal ideology after half a century of regulation and restriction of unfettered capitalism. John Elkington, Paul Hawken, and others were important figures in making the case that green entrepreneurship was viable and not just a fantasy—it deserved wider societal legitimacy. Profits and sustainability were now more broadly accepted as compatible, if an appropriate business model was adopted. Government subsidies and mandated feed-in tariffs offered new opportunities for renewable energy entrepreneurs such as Stanley Charren and Russell Wolfe, Arnold Goldman, Reiner Lemoine, and Aloys Wobben, even if some of their businesses were subsequently crushed by the vagaries of public policies. It was now possible, as John Mackey of Whole

Foods Market showed, to scale businesses through access to capital markets, although this was largely confined to atypically successful businesses. William Vidal, David Gottfried, Megan Epler Wood, and others built institutions and certification programs to support sustainable activities, while other entrepreneurs such as Joan Bavaria, Bob Massie, and Allen White developed metrics to measure environmental impact.

There were noteworthy changes in the composition of entrepreneurship in these decades also. Most of the history of green entrepreneurship previously had been a story of men living in the United States or Western Europe; this now changed. Female entrepreneurs became more evident, especially in services. These included Joan Bavaria, Tessa Tennant, and Mizue Tsukushi in social investing; Susan Maxman and Gail Lindsey in architecture; and Christine Ervin in LEED building rating.

The biggest shift of all was the sudden advent of corporate environmentalism, as large corporations embraced products and technologies they had previously ridiculed. They acquired leading green brands in the process. Luxury car makers topped rankings of the world's most sustainable companies. Sustainability measures spread across corporate reports. Yet although the ozone layer was healing, global warming continued, a global water crisis intensified, and the Anthropocene Age was well underway.

Motivations

In terms of intent, there were two distinct types of entrepreneurs who became involved in green businesses: green entrepreneurs and conventional entrepreneurs. This distinction does not imply a value judgment, still less a judgment on outcomes. Nor does it imply that either category was homogeneous. In fact, both the green and conventional entrepreneurs were quite varied in their characteristics and motivations.

Both personal and institutional explanations shaped the green entrepreneurs who developed many of the industries discussed in this book. Among the former, personal life events were important factors in their motivation. Health concerns, often experienced very personally by being ill or seeing family ill, were very important as a motivation, especially for the entrepreneurs in organic food. John Harvey Kellogg was a doctor. Benedict Lust contracted tuberculosis on his first visit to the United States. Rudolf Steiner did his foundational work with Dr. Ita Wegman on the treatment of illness by natural methods. Jerome Rodale was very sick as a child, while Mo Siegel's mother died when he was two. The young Ian McHarg's illness at Harvard and his difficult recovery in the 1950s revealed to him the power of nature to heal. It was not only entrepreneurs for whom sickness seems to have been a formative influence. Rachel Carson emphasized the impact of DDT on human health, and she was terminally ill with cancer as she wrote *Silent Spring*.

Early encounters with nature proved important, too. John Elkington recalled the formative influence of a nighttime encounter with baby eels. Joan Bavaria grew up in rural Massachusetts, loved nature and animals, and was an avid gardener. Elper Wood's walk along the Appalachian Trail motivated her interest in nature.

In a significant number of cases, religion provided an important influence in the motivation of green entrepreneurs. Religious belief was important in generating both a sense of responsibility for the planet and encouraging engagement in ventures which were not likely to yield enormous profits in the short run. The long list of Christians, of many denominations, among the entrepreneurs included John Harvey Kellogg, Wilhelm Barkhoff, Thomas Harttung, Claus Hipp, Hans Müller, and Mizue Tsukushi. There were also Muslims such as Ibrahim Abouleish, Jews such as Arnold Goldman, and Buddhists such as Kazuo Inamori. A number of other esoteric philosophies, as in the case of Mo Siegel and his *Urantia* book, were influential in individual cases.

More broadly anthroposophy became a surprisingly resilient inspiration for green entrepreneurship. This was most evident in organic agriculture and food retailing, and natural medicine, where biodynamic concepts exercised a worldwide influence. Followers supplied data to help Rachel Carson write *Silent Spring*, made deserts bloom in Egypt, delivered food baskets to households in Copenhagen, and much more. However, the impact of Steiner was uniquely broad, inspiring over the decades architects, bankers, and educators. Biodynamists pioneered the idea of certification and its rigorous auditing. They founded a distinct set of firms, among them Sekem, Triodis, and Weleda, which proved durable manifestations of alternative means of conducting business.

A distinct subset of green entrepreneurs were engineers, or even tinkerers, who believed in the potential of technical innovation either to achieve goals they had set for religious or social reasons, or simply because they were fascinated or obsessed by machines. They were prominent among the early wind and solar entrepreneurs, such as Paul la Cour and Frank Shuman onwards. Their later incarnations included Elliot Berman and Ishaq Shahryar, who perceived solar energy as a way to tackle poverty in the developing world. Recycling and composting were another category where figures such as Raoul Heinrich and Annie Francé, Kurt Gerson, Kai Petersen, and Arthur Schurig, were among those infuriated by waste and who sought to capture greater value from it through machines.

Both geographical and temporal context also mattered in shaping entrepreneurial consciousness. Although the importance of individual agency has been emphasized here, this does not mean that entrepreneurs should be seen as lone heroes acting in a vacuum. They perceived opportunities within distinct institutional and geographical contexts.

Environmental commitments and green entrepreneurship arose from concerns about the impact of industrialization on the health of people and the planet. It was not surprising, as a result, that until recently green entrepreneurship was concentrated in the industrialized regions of northwest Europe and the United States. It was here that the environmental problems caused by early urbanization and pollution first arose, and where chemical fertilizers were employed to feed urban populations. This was where consumers lived who had sufficient income to be able to think beyond how to survive the next day. Germany and the United States appear particularly well-represented in the history of green entrepreneurship told in this book, but this may be primarily because it was slightly easier to grow businesses in those countries. Certainly we have seen significant entrepreneurial stories from elsewhere, including Britain, Denmark, and France in Europe, and Egypt and Japan beyond the West. From the 1980s onward, values-driven green entrepreneurs arose far more widely around the world than in the past, as the environmental costs of economic growth and prosperity became evident, as they had earlier in the West. They included entrepreneurs in beauty in Brazil, eco-tourism in Costa Rica, ecological architecture in Malaysia, and renewable energy in China.

Chronology mattered also as a formative influence on green entrepreneurship. The 1930s and the years following the end of World War II were not an auspicious moment for green businesses. They remained wholly at the margins of societies. The countercultural and social movements seen in the 1960s were a different matter. Many new businesses emerged out of these settings, even if the businesses initially remained small. However, the relationship between engagement in social movements and green business was not always straightforward. A number of the influential figures in the emergence of Costa Rican eco-tourism, for example, had countercultural and environmentalist backgrounds in California. Insofar as the pioneering Danish wind start-ups of the 1970s were influenced by social movements in Denmark, it was in California that they achieved scale.

The intention of the conventional entrepreneurs who were preeminent in early natural tourism, as well as waste collection and disposal, was more straightforward than that of the green entrepreneurs in that making profits and reducing environmental impact were broadly aligned. This was the case for the owners and managers of railroad companies and hotels who opened up the western United States for nature tourism in the nineteenth century, although the desire for profitability did not rule out some explicit conservation motives. Indeed, it is evident that individuals sometimes traveled along a spectrum from conventional to greener. This was true of foreign hunters in East Africa, such as Frederick Selous and Edward North Buxton, who transitioned from killing animals to photographing them.

The growth of corporate environmentalism after 1980 greatly expanded the role of conventional firms in sustainability far beyond waste and tourism. Large global corporations issued sustainability reports. Chief executives assumed the mantle of visionary. The context had again changed with the rise in the priority of environmental concerns in societies and their governments, resulting in both the growth in the number of green consumers and the advent of government policies to support greener businesses as well as to regulate bad practices. NGOs now both scrutinized large corporations and sought alliances with them. The broadening of the concept of sustainability beginning with the Brundtland Commission in 1987 was important in shaping this new context, as it made it more plausible that large corporations could be seen as environmentally friendly. The growth of certification and other schemes provided metrics which enabled corporations to demonstrate their environmental credentials ... it was now profitable to be seen as sustainable.

Creating markets

From the middle of the nineteenth century, green entrepreneurs created new markets, products, and categories. They were in some respects well prepared for this difficult task, as they imagined a different world than the one currently existing. The major problem was that in every industry there were established conventional incumbents which almost always delivered existing products and services at lower prices. Market creation involved explaining to consumers, clients, and sometimes policy-makers, why they should pay more for products and services which already existed.

Making this case involved, at least from one perspective, imagining the meaning of sustainability. This reflected in part the evolving understanding of what the primary environmental challenges were, and what sustainability ought to include. The threat to human health from pollution, waste, and the application of chemistry to agriculture were initial concerns, which was why so much formative thought was related to healthy diet and organic agriculture. Another major challenge was to societies without access to the electricity generated by fossil fuels. Both of these issues resonate to the present day, but they were joined by others, like the risks of applying products with dangerous ingredients to our bodies, and the separation of the built environment from the natural environment. From the 1960s the threat to biodiversity and tropical rainforests, acid rain, and the depletion of the ozone layer became matters of public attention. Then, from the 1990s, human-induced climate change caused by carbon emissions rose to occupy center stage.

Each generation of green entrepreneurs faced a changing canvass of the nature of the environmental challenges faced by the world. However, there were other dimensions of defining sustainability beyond temporal shifts in understanding the nature of environmental challenges. Products acquired associations and claims which enhanced, or otherwise, their identities and attractiveness as being sustainable. Organic food became associated with personal health benefits, even though these were more asserted than proved, and later with wider environmental sustainability, even though establishing the positive impact of organic agriculture on climate change remains a work in progress. Early attempts at selling cosmetics made entirely from plants gained little traction, until Anita Roddick and others extended the concept of natural beauty to issues such as banning animal testing, promoting gender equality, and support for environmentalist NGOs.

In other cases, the imagining of products as sustainable involved stressing the positives and ignoring the negatives. While wind and solar energy were renewable and produced no carbon emissions, the industrial processes used to make windmills and solar panels left carbon footprints, as did disposing of the equipment eventually. Eco-tourism thus stresses not only careful respect for and preservation of the natural environment, but how it can contribute positively to the incomes of impoverished, indigenous, societies. This argument has proved sufficiently appealing to attract a large client base, partly because it relieved guilty feelings of affluent Western tourists engaging in lavish spending in poor countries. These considerable positives did not take into account the carbon emissions from tourists flying to faraway sites and traveling through congested cities and roads to see them. This imagining, or social construction, of sustainability became more explicit during the era of green capitalism after 1980. Certification often involved compromises and trade-offs between different parties to secure wide acceptance. There were more races to the bottom than races to the top.

Green entrepreneurs needed to sell not only their products, as do all entrepreneurs, but also their ideas. As a result, businesses faced the cost of educating consumers above and beyond the costs involved in a conventional business. The shops of the small retailers who struggled to sell organic foods were full of leaflets and ideologically convinced staff anxious to tell consumers why buying organic mattered. Natural beauty brands often opted for opening their own shops, or direct selling, because they wanted to talk to consumers about why their products differed from conventional brands. The education of clients was central to the businesses of the eco-tourism pioneers. In many cases, and over the longer term, educating consumers and securing legitimacy involved extensive institutional entrepreneurship, embracing such activities as the creation of trade associations and the development of standards and certifications.

There was a similar educational effort required with banks and investors who were not inclined to support ventures which were unlikely to make profits in the immediate term. This obstacle only began to recede in the 1980s, when a few successful green ventures were able to raise money on the capital markets, but it remained difficult, as funding unconventional and sometimes ideologically driven start-ups was never easy. It was for this reason, as well as to respond to the desires of environmentally concerned retail investors, that the first green banks and investment funds were launched. The insight of Joan Bavaria, Tessa Tennant, Tammy Newmark, and their peers that capital could be used to support sustainability rather than erode it was profound, though it was a vision which did not prove easy to execute.

The challenges faced by green entrepreneurs in creating new markets, products, and categories meant that they often succeeded first in small geographical areas. The importance of such clustering was in some respects paradoxical, both because environmental challenges were planet-scale problems, and because many entrepreneurs were motivated by global ideologies, whether religious, biodynamic, or other. Nevertheless, these clusters provided initial customers, staff, and knowledge spillovers, as well as a positive reputation which gave credibility to businesses located there. Clusters of small firms reduced transaction, information, and other costs because of proximity advantages and higher trust levels.

The origins of such clusters were often serendipitous and sometimes the result of a handful of successful pioneering figures. The existence (or otherwise) of mountains and rainforests, wind, and agricultural land seems a necessary, but not sufficient, explanation for the origins of much clustering, but geography cannot be discounted as an influence. Clustering in green businesses was quite often related to the presence of aesthetically striking natural beauty, such as that of California and Colorado in the United States, or impressive biodiversity, as in Costa Rica, which attracted foreign environmental enthusiasts including some entrepreneurial types, as well as providing them with an accessible initial market. In the early stages of cluster formation, an openness to attracting people from elsewhere, and a tolerance for alternative lifestyles, were important preconditions for such first-order geographical effects to become significant.

Politics mattered, too. The wind energy cluster in California in the 1980s was the result of the policies of the state government; Costa Rica benefited from more political stability than its Central American neighbors. Although many surrounding countries enjoyed similarly striking biodiversity, the region was also characterized by extended periods of political turbulence, military dictatorships, macroeconomic instability, and extreme income inequality, none of which were attractive features to entrepreneurial start-ups or foreign tourists.

Conversely, some institutional contexts made building businesses extremely tough. New Zealand's organic food businesses fought against a widespread public belief that the country was already "clean and green." Entrepreneurs were left with the task of challenging their own country's self-image. Industrial structures varied greatly also. Danish wind energy entrepreneurs in the 1970s, for example, operated in an economy with few energy-intensive industries. It was plausible to imagine that wind energy might eventually be able to supply the energy needs of such a society. Their potential counterparts in Sweden needed to make the case that wind energy could be a realistic supplier of the country's energy-intensive iron, steel, copper, aluminum, and paper and pulp industries. These industries require both a lot of energy and, more importantly, a continuous supply of energy, even when the wind is not blowing.

The creation of markets sometimes also involved engaging governments. Historically, and across the board, including recycling and wind and solar energy, entrepreneurs innovated technologies and products before government support, and sometimes in direct opposition to governments. In waste management, public authorities prioritized public health over recycling and reducing environmental impact. In energy, government favoritism and subsidies for fossil fuels, and later nuclear energy, presented the single greatest obstacle to entrepreneurs trying to develop solar and wind technologies, as they faced an impossible competitive situation.

Yet across industries public policy support was also often the key to breaking out of the niche and the marginal from the 1980s. As governments were prone to make wrong-headed decisions, as in the case of trying to build giant windmills, the best outcomes were when policies were co-created between business and government, as in the case of Germany's Dual System of waste collection and the development of Costa Rica's eco-tourism industry. Government support for organic food standards became an important dimension of the growth of the industry in the late twentieth century. This only came about through intensive lobbying by the industry and was preceded by decades of voluntary standards. Corporate lobbying on policy formation was, of course, hardly a panacea for outcomes beneficial to the environment. Lobbying by vested corporate interests was among the most serious obstacles green businesses faced, and continue to face.

It was in solar and wind power that supportive government policies were most essential to achieving a breakthrough. Van der Ryn and Jerome Cashman's persuasion of Governor Jerry Brown to implement PURPA in 1978 and to provide other supportive public policies in California was the turning point for the wind industry, and was hugely important for solar as well. Of course, these policies did not in and of themselves create those industries: the technological foundations had been laid earlier, including by many small-scale engineers in Denmark and the United States. Nor did they solve the many difficult challenges of building wind farms and pushing down the cost of solar panels. Nevertheless, these policies facilitated a unique scaling of renewable energy. Subsequently, the solar roof programs in first Germany and then Japan were really important in the scaling of the solar industry.

It was equally obvious in renewable energy, as in other categories, that businesses that depended on government support were vulnerable. The spectacular boom-and-bust cycles in solar and wind energy were manifestations of the downsides faced by industries dependent on subsidies and tax breaks. The destructive impact of changing and unpredictable government policies offers many examples: the decimation of the wind industry after the end of California's wind boom; the chronic under-performance of US-owned wind companies caught in the trap of making investments in time to catch the latest public subsidy; the decimation of much of the European and American solar industries at the end of the 2000s. Public policies also remained chronically lop-sided, with limited attempts, for example, made to price environmental externalities into fossil fuels and plastics.

Outcomes

History shows that profits and sustainability have been hard to reconcile. This is still the case. It has rarely paid to be very green. This was because the modern industrial society that developed from the Industrial Revolution was so efficient. It drove fast economic growth, at least in Europe and North America. A huge population surge was successfully clothed and fed. These successes rested on the environmental costs being ignored, including in the calculation of corporate profits. The pioneering green entrepreneurs who attempted to address adverse environmental outcomes thus found themselves charging more for their products and services than their conventional counterparts. Saving the planet was just too expensive, absent the incorporation of the costs of not saving the planet into accounting systems.

It was, therefore, not surprising that many of the businesses considered here were neither long-lasting nor greatly profitable. Quite a number of ventures went bankrupt. Commercial failure, however, was not a proxy for an overall failure of impact. The green entrepreneurs and firms covered in this book imagined worlds that did not exist and made multiple innovations designed to make them realities. They developed organic food products and farming methods, early solar and wind energy technologies, eco-lodges and sustainable finance, and much else. These categories required lengthy incremental innovations and improvements which took decades, and equally lengthy periods to convince consumers and governments to take them seriously. The ideologies which inspired many green entrepreneurs, like anthroposophy, exercised an impressively global reach. Significant institutional entrepreneurship was important, too. Certification schemes made new categories legitimate. The development of metrics started the process of measuring environmental impact. Institutions such as sustainability indexes have become established features of the global business environment.

Nor should the positive impact of some conventional businesses be ignored. The US national park system was the co-creation of railroad companies pursuing a tourist market, beginning with Jay Cooke and his manager A. B. Nettleton's significant role in the creation of Yellowstone National Park. The Container Corporation of America was a huge proponent of recycling and was responsible for the sponsorship and dissemination of today's global recycling symbol. Nineteenth-century scavengers in Europe and the United States, and their descendants in much of the developing world today, were hardly green entrepreneurs, but they achieved, and continue to achieve, high rates of recycling, albeit living miserable and impoverished lives.

These positive contributions do not take away from the point made earlier that sustainable business was in part a social or imagined construct, with the "real" impact on the natural environment sometimes debatable and typically partial. Part of the problem was that individual categories addressed only one element of environmental challenges. Recycling was an environmentally positive solution to the disposal of waste, for example, but it did not address the underlying creation of waste through consumption. In fact, the commercial viability of the recycling industry depended on the generation of waste, rather than reducing or eliminating it. As the use of wind and solar expanded in national energy systems, the continuing inability to store power sometimes led electricity systems to depend more on coal and other dirty energy sources to guarantee reliable supplies. Natural cosmetics enabled consumers to avoid putting potentially hazardous ingredients on their faces, but were a part of an industry which invested heavily in persuading consumers to spend money on products that were primarily for adornment. LEED certification encouraged more sustainable buildings, but still allowed a house built in an unsustainable location to be certified as green.

The apparent success and much higher profile of green business since the 1980s also raised a new set of issues. Many of these centered around the issue of scaling. The scaling of sustainable architecture was a positive development as buildings and cities were such drivers of environmental degradation. The reduction of the cost of solar panels caused by scaling was an equally positive development, even if the process involved huge industrial dislocation as Chinese production ramped up. Yet while the expansion of organic agriculture and retailing enabled many more consumers to eat food grown without chemicals or laced with additives, it came to involve the transportation of organic food over great distances. As they scaled, organic foods, windmills, ecological architecture, and other products and services, whose origins were embedded in a wider set of sustainability values, tended to be stripped of the ideologies which had put their consumption in a much broader context of sustainability challenges faced by humanity and the Earth.

Corporate environmentalism raised such complexities acutely. Given that large conventional firms had been drivers of environmental degradation in the past, corporate environmentalism and resultant strategies to reduce carbon footprints and other negative impacts were a positive development. Yet as large conventional corporations became central actors in industries from renewable energy to organic agriculture, environmental rhetoric became one convenient means of securing both tax breaks and legitimacy. Even with the best of intentions, chief executives, under the pressures of quarterly capitalism, were mostly incentivized to pursue incremental strategies which reduced environmental impact, while continuing to engage in core businesses activities which adversely impacted the planet. The all-embracing adoption of the language of sustainability diminished the distinctiveness, and the urgency, of the concept and the message. In a world where almost every business enterprise claimed to be helping the environment, individual consumers were left confused, or even bored, by the whole concept. And future green entrepreneurs pursuing radical ideas and technologies needed to struggle harder to make their voices heard.

Yet such considerations should not distract from recognizing the most important historical contribution of the green entrepreneurs in this book, which was their role in asserting that there were major problems with the natural environment which needed addressing. They were often far ahead of their societies and governments in identifying environmental challenges and trying to find solutions. People like Jerome Rodale and Hassan Fathy persisted in making the case for sustainability during the middle decades of the twentieth century when societies as a whole lost interest in the challenges faced by the natural environment. They offered productive alternatives to wrong-headed public policies, such as building giant windmills during the 1970s and 1980s. Importantly, the many small businesses made an impact on an individual level, by making the case to individual people why organic food, or wind energy, or more sustainable architecture, mattered to themselves, and to the planet. Making customers, who were also citizens more broadly, more aware of the importance of environmental issues was perhaps the only long-term route to making the world more sustainable, because it marked a needed change in societal values, lifestyles, and voting priorities. By a willingness to be "crazy" and to think outside of traditional boxes, green entrepreneurs opened up new ways of thinking about sustainability. Yesterday's crazies turn out to be the historical origins of the sustainable world of the future.

Bibliography

Primary sources

This book draws on a number of archival collections. The Baker Library at the Harvard Business School was used extensively for quantitative data and qualitative information on all the industries examined in the book. The Polaroid Corporate Archives in the Baker Library Historical Collections were also consulted. The Peter S. Thacher Environment Collection, 1960–96, Environmental Science and Public Policy Archives, Harvard College, was consulted extensively. In Germany, extensive materials on the history of the waste industry were found at the Sammlung Erhard Collection, held in the Federal Environment Ministry, in Dessau, and the City Sanitation and Waste Management Collection (Sammlung aus Städtereinigung und Entsorgung gGmbH, SASE) in Iserlohn.

Collections of oral histories proved invaluable. There are important interviews on the American environmental movement in the Sierra Club Oral History Series, Regional Oral History Office, Bancroft Library, UC Berkeley Library. For organic farming in the United States, the Cultivating a Movement: An Oral History Series on Sustainable Agriculture and Organic Farming on California's Central Coast collection held at the University of California at Santa Cruz Library was used extensively. For the Costa Rica eco-tourism industry, extensive use was made of the Royal G. Jackson Papers, Series II.1, Oregon State University Special Collections, Corvallis, Oregon. Also valuable were the interviews and other materials in the Creating Emerging Markets Project (CEM), Baker Library Historical Collections, Harvard Business School.

Interviews were conducted between 2010 and 2016 with practitioners by the author, Loubna Bouamane, Zhengyang Koh, and Andrew Spadafora. Many are cited in the text, while others provided essential background for the book. Dates and locations of cited interviews are given in the endnotes. My thanks to José Abascal, Ibrahim Abouleish, Oswaldo Acevedo, Anna Aloma, Claude Aubert, Rodolphe Balz, Roger Barnett, Tamara Budowski, Peter Busby, Efrain Chacón, Marino Chacón, Chris Clark, Jim Damalas, Pat Davidson, Paul Ellis, Jack Ewing, Hirofumi Fezuka, Jonathan Frey, Patrick Frick, Myra Goodman, John Hansen, Thomas Harrtung, Claus Hipp, Inge Horkeby, Hideaki Horie, Kazuo Inamori, Ross Jackson, Paul Jacobs, Noel Josephson, Mariko Kawaguchi, Michael Kaye, Jim Kebbell, Yoshita Koga, Karsten Korting, Defne

Koryürek, Juliet Lamont, Phil LaRocco, Stephanie Leighton, Jimmy Lim, Richard Marietta, Jan Martenson, Yuji Matsunami, Sam McKay, Mamoru Mitsumoto, Enrique Jose Molina, Yukihiro Mora, Noel Morrin, Chris Morrison, Satoshi Nagata, James Niven, Matthew Patsky, Lars Pehrson, Robert Quinn, Malcolm Rands, Bary Roberts, Wayne Robertson, Thomas Roland, Cheryl Smith, Gus Smith, Dave Spalter, Thomas Steiner, Ayhan Sümerli, Kohei Takashima, Yasushi Tamura, Tessa Tennant, Charlie Thomas, Mizue Tsukushi, Can Turhan, Gustavo Urrea, Sim Van der Ryn, Peter Varadi, Philippe Vignal, Jim Walker, Pam Waring, Tony Watkins, Tony Weekes, Rodnie Whitlock, Megan Epler Wood, Marion Woods, Alan Yates, and Hirokazu Yoshikawa.

Secondary sources

Abouleish, Ibrahim, *SEKEM: A Sustainable Community in the Egyptian Desert* (Edinburgh: Floris Books, 2005).

Asmus, Peter, *Reaping the Wind: How Mechanical Wizards, Visionaries, and Profiteers Helped Shape Our Energy Future* (Washington, DC: Island Press, 2001).

Backwell, Ben, *Wind Power: The Struggle for Control of a New Global Industry* (New York: Routledge, 2015).

Bansal, Pratima and Andrew J. Hoffman (eds.), *The Oxford Handbook of Business and the Natural Environment* (Oxford: Oxford University Press, 2012).

Baumgartner, Judith, *Ernährungsreform: Antwort auf Industrialisierung und Ernährungswandel* (Frankfurt: Peter Lang, 1992).

Beeman, Randal S. and James A. Pritchard, *A Green and Permanent Land: Ecology and Agriculture in the Twentieth Century* (Lawrence: University of Kansas Press, 2001).

Berger, John J., *Charging Ahead: The Business of Renewable Energy and What It Means for America* (New York: Henry Holt, 1997).

Berghoff, Hartmut and Adam Rome (eds.), *Green Capitalism? Business and the Environment in the Twentieth Century* (Philadelphia: University of Pennsylvania Press, 2017).

Bergquist, Ann-Kristin and Kristina Söderholm, "Green Innovation Systems in Swedish Industry, 1960–1989," *Business History Review* 85, no. 4 (2011), pp.677–98.

Bergquist, Ann-Kristin and Kristina Söderholm, "Sustainable Energy Transition: The Case of the Swedish Pulp and Paper Industry 1973–1990," *Energy Efficiency* 9, no. 5 (2016), pp.1179–92.

Bergquist, Ann-Kristen and Kristina Söderholm, "Transition to Greener Pulp: Regulation, Industry Responses and Path Dependency," *Business History* 57, no. 6 (2015), pp.862–84.

Boullet, Daniel, *Entreprises et Environnement en France de 1960 à 1990: Les Chemins d'une Prise de Conscience* (Geneva: Droz, 2006).

Bradford, Travis, *Solar Revolution: The Economic Transformation of the Global Energy Industry* (Cambridge, MA: MIT Press, 2006).

Brüggemeier, Franz-Josef, Mark Cioc, and Thomas Zeller (eds.), *How Green Were the Nazis?* (Athens: Ohio University Press, 2005).

Carson, Rachel, *Silent Spring* (Boston: Houghton Mifflin, 1962).

Conford, Philip, *The Development of the Organic Network* (Edinburgh: Floris Books, 2011).

Conford, Philip, *The Origins of the Organic Movement* (Edinburgh: Floris Books, 2001).

Cronin, William, *Nature's Metropolis: Chicago and the Great West* (New York: W. W. Norton, 1991).

Crooks, Harold, *Giants of Garbage: The Rise of the Global Waste Industry and the Politics of Pollution Control* (Toronto: James Lorimer, 1993).

Dalton, Russell J., *The Green Rainbow: Environmental Groups in Western Europe* (New Haven: Yale University Press, 1994).

Dauvergne, Peter and Jane Lister, *Eco-Business: A Big Brand Takeover of Sustainability* (Cambridge, MA: MIT Press, 2013).

Ditt, Karl and Jane Rafferty, "Nature Conservation in England and Germany 1900–70: Forerunner of Environmental Protection," *Contemporary European History* 5, no. 1 (1996), pp.1–28.

Dobrow, Joe, *Natural Prophets* (New York: Rodale, 2014).

Dohmen, Caspar, *Good Bank: Das Modell der GLS Bank* (Freiburg: Orange Press, 2011).

Elkington, John, *Cannibals with Forks: The Triple Bottom Line of 21st Century Business* (Oxford: Capstone Publishing, 1997).

Elkington, John with Tom Burke, *The Green Capitalists* (London: Victor Gollancz, 1987).

Elkington, John and Julia Hailes, *The Green Consumer Guide: From Shampoo to Champagne, High-Street Shopping for a Better Environment* (London: Victor Gollancz, 1988).

Evans, Sterling, *The Green Republic: A Conservation History of Costa Rica* (Austin: University of Texas Press, 1999).

Fathy, Hassan, *Architecture for the Poor* (Chicago: University of Chicago Press, 1973).

Fritzen, Florentine, *Gesünder leben: die Lebensreformbewegung im 20. Jahrhundert* (Stuttgart: Steiner, 2006).

Frohn, Hans-Werner and Friedemann Schmoll, *Natur und Staat: staatlicher Naturschutz in Deutschland, 1906–2006* (Bonn-Bad Godesberg: Bundesamt für Naturschutz, 2006).

Fromartz, Samuel, *Organic, Inc.: Natural Foods and How They Grew* (New York: Harcourt, 2006).

Garud, Raghu and Peter Karnøe, "Bricolage Versus Breakthrough: Distributed and Embedded Agency in Technology Entrepreneurship," *Research Policy* 32 (2003), pp.277–300.

Gipe, Paul, *Wind Energy Comes of Age* (New York: John Wiley, 1995).

Gottfried, David, *Greed to Green: The Transformation of an Industry and a Life* (Berkeley: Worldbuild Publishing, 2004).

Gould, Kira and Lance Hosey, *Women in Green: Voices of Sustainable Design* (Bainbridge Island, WA: Ecotone, 2007).

Guha, Ramachandra, *Environmentalism: A Global History* (New York: Longman, 2000).

Guthman, Julie, *Agrarian Dreams: The Paradox of Organic Farming in California* (Berkeley: University of California Press, 2004).

Hawken, Paul, *The Ecology of Commerce* (New York: HarperCollins, 1993).

Hawken, Paul, Amory Lovins, and L. Hunter Lovins, *Natural Capitalism: Creating the Next Industrial Revolution* (Boston: Little, Brown and Company, 1999).

Hickman, Lanny, *American Alchemy: The History of Solid Waste Management in the United States* (Santa Barbara: Forester Press, 2003).

Hipp, Claus, *Das Hipp Prinzip: Wie wir können, was wir wollen* (Freiburg: Herder, 2012).

Hockerts, Kai and Rolf Wüstenhagen, "Greening Goliaths Versus Emerging Davids—Theorizing about the Role of Incumbents and New Entrants in Sustainable Entrepreneurship," *Journal of Business Venturing* 25, no. 5 (2010), pp.481–92.

Hoffman, Andrew J., *From Heresy to Dogma: An Institutional History of Corporate Environmentalism* (Stanford, CA: Stanford Business Books, 2001).

Honey, Martha, *Ecotourism and Sustainable Development*, 2nd edn. (Washington, DC: Island Press, 2008).

Hussey, Stephen and Paul Thompson (eds.), *Environmental Consciousness* (New Brunswick: Transaction Publishers, 2004).

Isaak, Robert, "Globalization and Green Entrepreneurship," *Greener Management International* 18 (1997), pp.80–90.

Jacobson, Timothy C., *Waste Management: An American Corporate Success Story* (Washington, DC: Gateway Business Books, 1993).

Johnstone, Bob, *Switching to Solar: What We Can Learn from Germany's Success in Harnessing Clean Energy* (Amherst, NY: Prometheus, 2010).

Jones, Geoffrey, *Beauty Imagined: A History of the Global Beauty Industry* (Oxford: Oxford University Press, 2010).

Jones, Geoffrey, "Entrepreneurship, Policy, and the Geography of Wind Energy," in Hartmut Berghoff and Adam Rome (eds.), *Green Capitalism? Business and the Environment in the Twentieth Century* (Philadelphia: University of Pennsylvania Press, 2017), pp.206–30.

Jones, Geoffrey, *Renewing Unilever: Transformation and Tradition* (Oxford: Oxford University Press, 2005).

Jones, Geoffrey and Christina Lubinski, "Making 'Green Giants': Environment Sustainability in the German Chemical Industry, 1950s–1980s," *Business History* 56, no. 4 (2014), pp.623–49.

Jones, Geoffrey and Simon Mowatt, "National Image as a Competitive Disadvantage: The Case of the New Zealand Organic Food Industry," *Business History* 58, no. 8 (2016), pp.1262–88.

Klein, Naomi, *This Changes Everything: Capitalism vs. the Climate* (New York: Simon & Schuster, 2014).

Koepf, Herbert H. and Bodo von Plato, *Die biologisch-dynamische Wirtschaftsweise im 20. Jahrhundert: Die Entwicklungsgeschichte der biologisch-dynamischen Landwirtschaft* (Dornach: Verlag am Goetheanum, 2001).

Lachman, Gary, *Rudolf Steiner: An Introduction to His Life and Work* (New York: Penguin, 2007).

Lee, Brandon H., "The Infrastructure of Collective Action and Policy Content Diffusion in the Organic Food Industry," *Academy of Management Journal* 52, no. 6 (2009), pp.1247–69.

Lockeretz, William (ed.), *Organic Farming: An International History* (Wallingford: CAB International, 2007).

Lovins, Amory B., *Soft Energy Paths* (New York: Ballinger, 1977).

McHarg, Ian L., *Design with Nature* (New York: American Museum of Natural History, 1969).

Mackey, John and Rajendra Sisodia, *Conscious Capitalism: Liberating the Heroic Spirit of Business* (Boston: Harvard Business School Press, 2013).

McNeil, John R., *Something New Under the Sun: An Environmental History of the Twentieth-Century World* (New York: W. W. Norton, 2000).

Madrigal, Alexis, *Powering the Dream. The History and Promise of Green Technology* (Cambridge, MA: Da Capo, 2011).

Marquis, Christopher, Michael W. Toffel, and Yanhua Zhou, "Scrutiny, Norms, and Selective Disclosure: A Global Study of Greenwashing," *Organization Science* 27, no. 2 (March–April 2016), pp.483–504.

Medina, Martin, *The World's Scavengers: Salvaging for Sustainable Consumption and Production* (Lanham, MD: AltaMira, 2007).

Melosi, Martin, *Garbage in the Cities: Refuse, Reform, and the Environment*, rev. edn. (Pittsburgh: University of Pittsburgh Press, 2005).

Pfister, Christian, "The '1950s Syndrome' and the Transition from a Slow-Going to a Rapid Loss of Global Sustainability," in Frank Uekötter (ed.), *The Turning Points of Environmental History* (Pittsburgh: University of Pittsburgh Press, 2010), pp.90–118.

Plato, Bodo von (ed.), *Anthroposophie im 20. Jahrhundert: Ein Kulturimpuls in biografischen Porträts* (Dornach: Verlag am Goetheanum, 2003).

Righter, Robert W., *Wind Energy in America: A History* (Norman: University of Oklahoma Press, 1996).

Righter, Robert W., *Windfall: Wind Energy in America Today* (Norman: University of Oklahoma Press, 2011).

Rodale, Jerome I., *Our Poisoned Earth and Sky* (Emmaus, PA: Rodale Books, 1964).

Rome, Adam, *The Genius of Earth Day* (New York: Hill & Wang, 2013).

Rosen, Christine Meisner, "Businessmen against Pollution in Late Nineteenth-Century Chicago," *Business History Review* 69, no. 3 (1995), pp.351–97.

Schaper, Michael (ed.), *Making Ecopreneurs: Developing Sustainable Entrepreneurship* (Aldershot: Ashgate, 2005).

Selg, Peter, *Dr. Oskar Schmiedel, 1887–1959: Der erste anthroposophische Pharmazeut und Weleda-Direktor. Eine Dokumentation* (Arlesheim: Ita Wegman Institut, 2010).

Selg, Peter, *Rudof Steiner: Life and Work*, vol. 1 (Great Barrington, MA: Steiner Books, 2014).

Sine, Wesley D. and Brandon H. Lee, "Tilting at Windmills? The Environmental Movement and the Emergence of the U.S. Wind Energy Sector," *Administrative Science Quarterly* 54 (2009), pp.123–55.

Sluyterman, Keetie, "Royal Dutch Shell: Company Strategies for Dealing with Environmental Issues," *Business History Review* 84, no. 2 (2010), pp.203–26.

Steele, James, *Ecological Architecture: A Critical History* (London: Thames & Hudson, 2005).

Stokes, Raymond G., Roman Köster, and Stephen C. Sambrook, *The Business of Waste: Great Britain and Germany, 1945 to the Present* (Cambridge: Cambridge University Press, 2013).

Strasser, Susan, *Waste and Want: A Social History of Trash* (New York: Metropolitan, 1999).

Tucker, Richard P., *Insatiable Appetite: The United States and the Ecological Degradation of the Tropical World* (Berkeley: University of California Press, 2000).

Uekötter, Frank, *The Age of Smoke* (Pittsburgh: University of Pittsburgh Press, 2009).

Uekötter, Frank, *The Green and the Brown: A History of Conservation in Nazi Germany* (Cambridge: Cambridge University Press, 2006).

Uekötter, Frank, *The Greenest Nation? A New History of German Environmentalism* (Cambridge, MA: MIT Press, 2014).

United Nations, *Report of the World Commission on Environment and Development: Our Common Future* (New York: United Nations 1987).

Van der Ryn, Sim, *Design for Life: The Architecture of Sim Van der Ryn* (Salt Lake City: Gibbs Smith, 2005).

Varadi, Peter F., *Sun Above the Horizon: Meteoric Rise of the Solar Industry* (Singapore: Pan Stanford, 2014).

Vasi, Ion Bogdan, *Winds of Change: The Environmental Movement and the Global Development of the Wind Energy Industry* (Oxford: Oxford University Press, 2011).

Vogel, David, *The Market for Virtue* (Washington, DC: Brookings Institution Press, 2005).

Vogel, David, *The Politics of Precaution* (Princeton: Princeton University Press, 2012).

Vogt, Gunter, *Entstehung und Entwicklung des ökologischen Landbaus im deutschsprachigen Raum* (Bad Dürkheim: Stiftung Ökologie & Landbau, 2000).

Ward, Barbara and René Dubos, *Only One Earth: The Care and Maintenance of a Small Planet* (New York: W. W. Norton, 1972).

Weart, Spencer R., *The Discovery of Global Warming* (Cambridge, MA: Harvard University Press, 2008).

Werner, Uwe, *Anthroposophen in der Zeit des Nazionalsozialismus, 1933–1945* (Munich: Oldenbourg, 1999).

Werner, Uwe, *Das Unternehmen Weleda, 1921–1945: Entstehung und Pionierzeit eines menschengemässen und nachhaltig ökologischen Unternehmens* (Berlin: BWV, 2014).

Williams, Neville, *Chasing the Sun* (Gabriola Island, BC: New Society Publishers, 2005).

Windmüller, Sonja, *Die Kehrseite der Dinge: Müll, Abfall, Wegwerfen als kulturwissenschaftliches Problem* (Münster: LIT, 2004).

Zimring, Carl A., *Cash for Your Trash: Scrap Recycling in America* (New Brunswick, NJ: Rutgers University Press, 2005).

Index